Lecture Notes in Computer Science

Lecture Notes in Artificial Intelligence   13890

Founding Editor

Jörg Siekmann

Series Editors

Randy Goebel, *University of Alberta, Edmonton, Canada*
Wolfgang Wahlster, *DFKI, Berlin, Germany*
Zhi-Hua Zhou, *Nanjing University, Nanjing, China*

The series Lecture Notes in Artificial Intelligence (LNAI) was established in 1988 as a topical subseries of LNCS devoted to artificial intelligence.

The series publishes state-of-the-art research results at a high level. As with the LNCS mother series, the mission of the series is to serve the international R & D community by providing an invaluable service, mainly focused on the publication of conference and workshop proceedings and postproceedings.

Vicenç Torra · Yasuo Narukawa
Editors

Modeling Decisions for Artificial Intelligence

20th International Conference, MDAI 2023
Umeå, Sweden, June 19–22, 2023
Proceedings

Springer

Editors
Vicenç Torra (iD)
Umeå University
Umeå, Sweden

Yasuo Narukawa (iD)
Tamagawa University
Tokyo, Japan

ISSN 0302-9743   ISSN 1611-3349 (electronic)
Lecture Notes in Artificial Intelligence
ISBN 978-3-031-33497-9   ISBN 978-3-031-33498-6 (eBook)
https://doi.org/10.1007/978-3-031-33498-6

LNCS Sublibrary: SL7 – Artificial Intelligence

This Springer imprint is published by the registered company Springer Nature Switzerland AG
The registered company address is: Gewerbestrasse 11, 6330 Cham, Switzerland

Preface

This volume contains papers presented at the 20th International Conference on Modeling Decisions for Artificial Intelligence (MDAI 2023), celebrated at Umeå, Sweden, June 19th–22th, 2023.

This conference followed MDAI 2004 (Barcelona), MDAI 2005 (Tsukuba), MDAI 2006 (Tarragona), MDAI 2007 (Kitakyushu), MDAI 2008 (Sabadell), MDAI 2009 (Awaji Island), MDAI 2010 (Perpinyà), MDAI 2011 (Changsha), MDAI 2012 (Girona), MDAI 2013 (Barcelona), MDAI 2014 (Tokyo), MDAI 2015 (Skövde), MDAI 2016 (Sant Julià de Lòria), MDAI 2017 (Kitakyushu), MDAI 2018 (Mallorca), MDAI 2019 (Milano), MDAI 2020, MDAI 2021 (Umeå), and MDAI 2022 (Sant Cugat).

The aim of MDAI is to provide a forum for researchers to discuss different facets of decision processes in a broad sense. This includes model building and all kinds of mathematical tools for data aggregation, information fusion, and decision-making; tools to help make decisions related to data science problems (including, e.g., statistical and machine learning algorithms as well as data visualization tools); and algorithms for data privacy and transparency-aware methods so that data processing procedures and the decisions made from them are fair, transparent, and avoid unnecessary disclosure of sensitive information.

The MDAI 2023 conference included tracks on the topics of (a) data science, (b) machine learning, (c) data privacy, (d) aggregation functions, (e) human decision-making, and (f) graphs and (social) networks.

The organizers received 28 papers, 17 of which are published in this volume. Each submission received at least three Single-blind reviews from the Program Committee and a few external reviewers. We would like to express our gratitude to them for their work.

The conference celebrates this year the 50th anniversary of graded logic, introduced by Jozo Dujmović in a paper in 1973. In this paper, he also introduced the concept of andness, a key concept to define adjustable aggregators with a variable conjunction degree. These MDAI 2023 proceedings include a paper by Jozo Dujmović, which has also been approved by the program committee, on logic aggregators and their implementation. The paper presents the necessary properties of these aggregators and compares major implementations (including means and the weighted power mean, t-norms and conorms, OWA, and fuzzy integrals).

The conference was supported by Umeå University, the European Society for Fuzzy Logic and Technology (EUSFLAT), the Catalan Association for Artificial Intelligence (ACIA), the Japan Society for Fuzzy Theory and Intelligent Informatics (SOFT), and the UNESCO Chair in Data Privacy.

April 2023

Vicenç Torra
Yasuo Narukawa

Organization

General Chair

Vicenç Torra   Umeå University, Sweden

Program Chairs

Vicenç Torra   Umeå University, Sweden
Yasuo Narukawa   Tamagawa University, Japan

Advisory Board

Didier Dubois   Institut de Recherche en Informatique de
                                   Toulouse, CNRS, France
Jozo Dujmović   San Francisco State University, USA
Lluis Godo   IIIA-CSIC, Spain
Janusz Kacprzyk   Systems Research Institute, Polish Academy of
                                   Sciences, Poland
Cengiz Kahraman   Istanbul Technical University, Turkey
Sadaaki Miyamoto   University of Tsukuba, Japan
Pierangela Samarati   Università degli Studi di Milano, Italy
Sandra Sandri   Instituto Nacional de Pesquisas Espaciais, Brazil
Michio Sugeno   Tokyo Institute of Technology, Japan
Ronald R. Yager   Iona University, USA

Program Committee

Kayode S. Adewole   Umeå University, Sweden
Laya Aliahmadipour   Shahid Bahonar University, Iran
Cláudia Antunes   Universidade de Lisboa, Portugal
Eva Armengol   IIIA-CSIC, Spain
Edurne Barrenechea   Universidad Pública de Navarra, Spain
Gloria Bordogna   Consiglio Nazionale delle Ricerche, Italy
Humberto Bustince   Universidad Pública de Navarra, Spain
Alina Campan   North Kentucky University, USA

Francisco Chiclana	De Montfort University, UK
Susana Díaz	Universidad de Oviedo, Spain
Josep Domingo-Ferrer	Universitat Rovira i Virgili, Spain
Yasunori Endo	University of Tsukuba, Japan
Vladimir Estivill-Castro	Griffith University, Australia
Zoe Falomir	Universitat Jaume I, Spain
Javier Fernandez	Universidad Pública de Navarra, Spain
Katsushige Fujimoto	Fukushima University, Japan
Joaquin Garcia-Alfaro	Institut Mines-Télècom and Institut Polytechnique de Paris, France
Michel Grabisch	Université Paris I Panthéon-Sorbonne, France
Yukihiro Hamasuna	Kindai University, Japan
Tove Helldin	University of Skövde, Sweden
Enrique Herrera-Viedma	Universidad de Granada, Spain
Aoi Honda	Kyushu Institute of Technology, Japan
Van-Nam Huynh	JAIST, Japan
Masahiro Inuiguchi	Osaka University, Japan
Simon James	Deakin University, Australia
Aránzazu Jurío	Universidad Pública de Navarra, Spain
Yuchi Kanzawa	Shibaura Institute of Technology, Japan
Ali Karaşan	Yildiz Technical University, Turkey
Hiroaki Kikuchi	Meiji University, Japan
Petr Krajča	Palacky University Olomouc, Czech Republic
Marie-Jeanne Lesot	Université Pierre et Marie Curie (Paris VI), France
Giovanni Livraga	Università degli Studi di Milano, Italy
Jun Long	National University of Defense Technology, China
Beatriz López	University of Girona, Spain
Jean-Luc Marichal	University of Luxembourg, Luxembourg
Radko Mesiar	Slovak University of Technology, Slovakia
Andrea Mesiarová-Zemánková	Slovak Academy of Sciences, Slovakia
Anna Monreale	University of Pisa, Italy
Pranab K. Muhuri	South Asian University, India
Toshiaki Murofushi	Tokyo Institute of Technology, Japan
Guillermo Navarro-Arribas	Universitat Autònoma de Barcelona, Spain
Shekhar Negi	Umeå University, Sweden
Jordi Nin	Esade Universitat Ramon Llull, Spain
Miguel Núñez del Prado Cortez	Universidad de Ingeniería & Tecnologia, Peru
Anna Oganyan	National Institute of Statistical Sciences (NISS), USA
Gabriella Pasi	Università di Milano-Bicocca, Italy
Oriol Pujol	University of Barcelona, Spain

Maria Riveiro	Jönköping University, Sweden
Julian Salas	Universitat Oberta de Catalunya, Spain
Robyn Schimmer	Umeå University, Sweden
H. Joe Steinhauer	University of Skövde, Sweden
László Szilágyi	Sapientia-Hungarian Science University of Transylvania, Hungary
Aida Valls	Universitat Rovira i Virgili, Spain
Paolo Viappiani	Université Paris Dauphine, France
Zeshui Xu	Southeast University, China

Local Organizing Committee Chair

Vicenç Torra	Umeå University, Sweden

Additional Referee

Sergio Martinez Lluis	Najeeb Moharram Salim Jebreel, Rami Haffar

Supporting Institutions

Umeå University
The European Society for Fuzzy Logic and Technology (EUSFLAT)
The Catalan Association for Artificial Intelligence (ACIA)
The Japan Society for Fuzzy Theory and Intelligent Informatics (SOFT)
The UNESCO Chair in Data Privacy

Invited Talks

Partially Observing Graphs - When Can We Infer Underlying Community Structure?

Fiona Skerman

Uppsala University, Sweden

Abstract. Suppose edges in an underlying graph G appear independently with some probability in our observed graph G' - or alternately that we can query uniformly random edges. We describe how high a sampling probability we need to infer the modularity of the underlying graph.

Modularity is a function on graphs which is ubiquitous in algorithms for community detection. For a given graph G, each partition of the vertices has a modularity score, with higher values indicating that the partition better captures community structure in G. The (max) modularity $q*(G)$ of the graph G is defined to be the maximum over all vertex partitions of the modularity score, and satisfies $0 \geq q*(G) \geq 1$.

It was noted when analysing ecological networks that under-sampled networks tended to over-estimate modularity - we indicate how the asymmetry of our results gives some theoretical backing for this phenomenon - but questions remain. In the seminar I will spend time on intuition for the behaviour of modularity, how it can be approximated, links to other graph parameters and to present some open problems.

Joint work with Colin McDiarmid.

AI for the Public Good - Reflections on Ethics, Decision Making and Work

Robyn Schimmer

Department of Psychology, Umeå University, Sweden

Abstract. We are seeing increasing interest in AI in all parts of society, including the public sector. Although there are still few examples of AI applications being implemented in the public sector, there is no doubt that it will be, and that we are facing a radical change in how work is organized. In the Swedish context, AI is mentioned as a potentially beneficial technology in governmental policies. Also, networks have been set up connecting actors in the public sector with the aim of strengthening knowledge of AI and exchanging experiences. Given these ambitions to implement, paired with the rapid technical development we will probably see a fast increase in AI-enhanced work processes in the public sector. The disruptive potential of AI is however also raising many questions, especially about how it might affect workplaces and people using these systems. It is therefore important to discuss various ethical implications in order to foresee and react to the transformational power of AI, to make us aware of possible outcomes, and also to decide if they are wanted or not.

In this presentation, we will look into the status of AI in the public sector, with an emphasis on the Swedish context. The main focus will be on ethics, in a broad sense, and to reflect on how AI will impact the way we do work, make decisions, and how work is organized. Issues such as trust and accountability will be discussed, especially in relation to AI-based decision-making. Implications for workers and citizens will also be brought up, highlighting both potential advantages as well as challenges. At the end of the presentation, we will also attempt to sketch out a number of principles that could act as guidance in AI for the public good.

Imprecise Probability in Formal Argumentation

Juan Carlos Nieves

Department of Computing Science, Umeå University, Sweden

Abstract. Formal argumentation has been revealed as a powerful conceptual tool for exploring the theoretical foundations of reasoning and interaction in autonomous systems and multiagent systems. Formal Argumentation usually is modeled by considering argument graphs that are composed of a set of arguments and a binary relation encoding attacks between arguments. Some recent approaches of formal argumentation assign uncertainty values to the elements of the argument graphs to represent the degree of belief in arguments or attacks. Some of these works assign the uncertainty values to the arguments, others to the attacks, and others to both arguments and attacks. These works use precise probability approaches to model the uncertainty values. However, precise probability approaches have some limitations to quantify epistemic uncertainty, for example, to represent group disagreeing opinions. These can be better represented by means of imprecise probabilities, which can use lower and upper bounds instead of exact values to model the uncertainty values. During this talk, we will present some recent results on how to model the degree of belief in arguments with imprecise probability values by means of credal sets. We will show how to use credal networks theory for modeling causality relations between arguments. Some applications of imprecise probability in Formal Argumentation will be also discussed.

Contents

Plenary Talk

Logic Aggregators and Their Implementations 3
  Jozo Dujmović and Vicenç Torra

Decision Making and Uncertainty

Multi-target Decision Making Under Conditions of Severe Uncertainty 45
  Christoph Jansen, Georg Schollmeyer, and Thomas Augustin

Constructive Set Function and Extraction of a k-dimensional Element 58
  Ryoji Fukuda, Aoi Honda, and Yoshiaki Okazaki

Coherent Upper Conditional Previsions Defined by Fractal Outer Measures
to Represent the Unconscious Activity of Human Brain 70
  Serena Doria and Bilel Selmi

Discrete Chain-Based Choquet-Like Operators 83
  Michał Boczek, Ondrej Hutník, and Miriam Kleinová

On a New Generalization of Decomposition Integrals 96
  Adam Šeliga

Bipolar OWA Operators with Continuous Input Function 106
  Martin Kalina

Machine Learning and Data Science

Cost-constrained Group Feature Selection Using Information Theory 121
  Tomasz Klonecki, Paweł Teisseyre, and Jaesung Lee

Conformal Prediction for Accuracy Guarantees in Classification
with Reject Option 133
  Ulf Johansson, Tuwe Löfström, Cecilia Sönströd, and Helena Löfström

Adapting the Gini's Index for Solving Predictive Tasks 146
  Eva Armengol

Bayesian Logistic Model for Positive and Unlabeled Data 157
  Małgorzata Łazęcka

A Goal-Oriented Specification Language for Reinforcement Learning 169
  Simon Schwan, Verena Klös, and Sabine Glesner

Improved Spectral Norm Regularization for Neural Networks 181
  Anton Johansson, Niklas Engsner, Claes Strannegård, and Petter Mostad

Preprocessing Matters: Automated Pipeline Selection for Fair Classification ... 202
  Vladimiro González-Zelaya, Julián Salas, Dennis Prangle,
  and Paolo Missier

Predicting Next Whereabouts Using Deep Learning 214
  Ana-Paula Galarreta, Hugo Alatrista-Salas, and Miguel Nunez-del-Prado

A Generalization of Fuzzy c-Means with Variables Controlling Cluster Size ... 226
  Yuchi Kanzawa

Data Privacy

Local Differential Privacy Protocol for Making Key–Value Data Robust
Against Poisoning Attacks 241
  Hikaru Horigome, Hiroaki Kikuchi, and Chia-Mu Yu

Differentially Private Graph Publishing Through Noise-Graph Addition 253
  Julián Salas, Vladimiro González-Zelaya, Vicenç Torra,
  and David Megías

Author Index 265

Plenary Talk

Logic Aggregators and Their Implementations

Jozo Dujmović[1]([✉]) and Vicenç Torra[2]

[1] Department of Computer Science, San Francisco State University, San Francisco, CA, USA
jozo@sfsu.edu
[2] Department of Computer Sciences, Umeå University, Umeå, Sweden
vtorra@ieee.org

Abstract. In this paper we present necessary properties of logic aggregators and compare their major implementations. If decision making includes the identification of a set of alternatives followed by the evaluation of alternatives and selection of the best alternative, then evaluation must be based on graded logic aggregation. The resulting analytic framework is a graded logic which is a seamless generalization of Boolean logic, based on analytic models of graded simultaneity (various forms of conjunction), graded substitutability (various forms of disjunction) and complementing (negation). These basic logic operations can be implemented in various ways, including means, t-norms/conorms, OWA, and fuzzy integrals. Such mathematical models must be applicable in all regions of the unit hypercube $[0,1]^n$. In order to be applicable in various areas of decision making, the logic aggregators must be consistent with observable patterns of human reasoning, supporting both formal logic and semantic aspects of human reasoning. That creates a comprehensive set of logic requirements that logic aggregators must satisfy. Various popular aggregators satisfy these requirements to the extent investigated in this paper. The results of our investigation clearly show the limits of applicability of the analyzed aggregators in the area of decision making.

1 Introduction

In mathematical literature [1–3] aggregators are defined as functions $A : I^n \to I$, $I = [0,1]$ that satisfy nondecreasing monotonicity in all arguments and idempotency in extreme points: $A(0,\ldots,0) = 0$ and $A(1,\ldots,1) = 1$. The arguments are anonymous real numbers, i.e. they are not restricted by any particular semantic identity. This minimally restrictive definition creates a huge family of aggregation functions which includes many functions that are not observable in human reasoning. Unsurprisingly, the applicability of aggregators in decision support systems depends on their concordance with observable properties of human reasoning. For example, aggregators that have discontinuities and/or oscillatory properties of first derivatives are not observable in human evaluation logic and not used in intuitive decision making [4].

In this paper we are interested in graded logic aggregators, i.e., aggregators that aggregate degrees of truth. Such aggregators are present in most decision problems. We assume that decision making commonly consists of three steps: (1) identification of stakeholder/decision maker which has goals and interests, (2) identification of one or more alternatives that make possible or contribute to the achievement of stakeholder's

V. Torra and Y. Narukawa (Eds.): MDAI 2023, LNAI 13890, pp. 3–42, 2023.
https://doi.org/10.1007/978-3-031-33498-6_1

goals, and (3) evaluation of alternatives and selection of the most suitable alternative. Stakeholders can be organizations or individuals. Alternatives can be arbitrary objects, candidates, or courses of action. We assume that selection of the best alternative is not a pairwise comparison problem because the number of alternatives can be one (selecting or rejecting a single candidate), and obviously, that is not a pairwise comparison problem. In the case of a single candidate, we have the evaluation problem of computing an overall degree of suitability of the evaluated candidate [5, 6], based on goals and requirements of specific stakeholder/decision maker.

To provide consistency with the case of a single candidate, the evaluation and comparison of two or more candidates must also be based on individual evaluation of each candidate. The LSP evaluation process [4] is based on *suitability attributes* $(a_1, \ldots, a_n) \in \mathbb{R}^n$, defined as those attributes of evaluated objects that affect their suitability for a specific stakeholder (decision maker). Suitability attributes $a_1, \ldots, a_n$ are individually evaluated using attribute criteria $g_i : \mathbb{R} \to I$, $i = 1, \ldots, n$ that reflect stakeholder's needs. The resulting attribute suitability degrees $(x_1, \ldots, x_n) = (g_1(a_1), \ldots, g_n(a_n)) \in I^n$ are interpreted as degrees of truth of attribute value statements (assertions that the suitability attributes completely satisfy stakeholder's requirements). The attribute suitability degrees are then aggregated to generate the overall suitability degree $X = A(x_1, \ldots, x_n) \in I$. The overall suitability X is interpreted either as a degree of truth of the statement that the evaluated object completely satisfies all stakeholder's requirements, or (alternatively and equivalently) as the degree of fuzzy membership in a fuzzy set of objects that completely satisfy stakeholder's goals and requirements [7–9]. Thus, $A(x_1, \ldots, x_n)$ is a logic function, i.e., a compound *logic aggregator* of arguments that have clearly defined semantic identity. Obviously, degrees of truth (or, in the evaluation context, suitability degrees) are *not* anonymous real numbers. Degrees of truth are always generated and interpreted by a stakeholder/decision maker and derived from clearly defined value statements which they represent. By definition, each value statement is an assertion that a specific stakeholder's requirement is fully satisfied. Such statements are regularly only partially true. Consequently, degrees of truth are graded logic variables that have semantic identity derived from the meaning, role, interpretation, and importance of value statements for specific decision maker. The aggregation of individual degrees of truth is necessary to compute the overall suitability of evaluated object/alternative. The overall suitability is interpreted as the degree of truth of the value statement claiming that the evaluated object/alternative completely satisfies all requirements of stakeholder/decision maker. The aggregation of degrees of truth is performed using a *graded propositional calculus* which belongs to the area of *graded logic* (GL). Consequently, GL is a soft computing mathematical infrastructure necessary for building aggregation models for decision making [4, 21, 40, 41].

Logic aggregation of degrees of truth has conditions and restrictions not encountered when aggregating anonymous real numbers. Aggregation of suitability degrees is a logic process and the role of graded logic is to provide logic aggregators supporting various properties observable in human evaluation reasoning. Our main goal is to identify, analyze and compare various mathematical models of logic aggregators.

This paper is organized as follows. In Sect. 2 we introduce and geometrically characterize a set of border logic aggregators. The semantic aspects of logic aggregation are presented in Sect. 3. In Sect. 4 we present a detailed classification of GL functions. The requirements that logic aggregators must satisfy are presented in Sect. 5. In Sect. 6 we propose benchmark problems for comparison of logic aggregators. Sections 7, 8, 9, and 10 present four characteristic implementations of logic aggregators (GCD/ADIA, OWA, fuzzy integrals, t-norms, and various means). Section 11 presents the evaluation and comparison of all implementations of logic aggregators. The conclusions of this study are summarized in Sects. 12 and 13.

2 Geometric Characterization of Logic Aggregators and the Set of Border Aggregators

Let us aggregate n degrees of truth $X = (x_1, \ldots, x_n)$, $n > 1$, $x_i \in I$, $i = 1, \ldots, n$. A *general logic aggregator* $A : I^n \to I$ is defined as a continuous function that is nondecreasing in all components of X and satisfies the boundary conditions: $A(\mathbf{0}) = 0$, $A(\mathbf{1}) = 1$. In many evaluation problems [4, 10] it is useful to define *basic logic aggregators* using additional restrictive conditions $X > \mathbf{0} \Rightarrow A(X) > 0$, and $X < \mathbf{1} \Rightarrow A(X) < 1$. The condition $X > \mathbf{0} \Rightarrow A(X) > 0$ is called the sensitivity to positive truth: if all input arguments of the aggregator are to some extent true the result of aggregation cannot be false. Similarly, the condition $X < \mathbf{1} \Rightarrow A(X) < 1$ is called the sensitivity to incomplete truth: if none of input arguments is completely true, then the result of aggregation cannot be completely true. These two conditions are dual, and hold in all cases where basic logic aggregators can be modeled using means.

All logic aggregators are models of simultaneity (various forms of conjunction) and substitutability (various forms of disjunction), and GL is a seamless soft computing generalization of classical Boolean logic [4]. Similarly to Boolean logic, in GL all compound logic aggregators can be created as superposition of conjunctive aggregators, disjunctive aggregators, and negation (regularly modeled as a complement $x \mapsto 1 - x$). Consequently, in this paper we will focus on modeling conjunctive and disjunctive aggregators.

To geometrically characterize conjunctive or disjunctive logic aggregators $A(X)$, we assume that all arguments have the same degree of importance. The overall properties of such aggregators can be geometrically characterized using the volume under their surface inside the unit hypercube I^n: $V = \int_{I^n} A(X) dx_1 \ldots dx_n$. Since the volume of I^n is 1, it follows that $0 \le V \le 1$. This volume is used to define the continuously adjustable conjunction degree, or the *global andness* α, and its complement, the continuously adjustable disjunction degree, or the *global orness* ω, as follows [11]:

$$\alpha = \frac{n - (n+1)V}{n - 1}, \qquad \omega = \frac{(n+1)V - 1}{n - 1}, \qquad \alpha + \omega = 1. \tag{1}$$

The global andness α denotes the degree of simultaneity, and the global orness ω denotes the degree of substitutability of a logic aggregator $A(X)$. As we will see later, this definition is adjusted so that the minimum function (conjunction) has andness $\alpha = 1$ and the maximum function (disjunction) has orness $\omega = 1$. Andness and orness depend on the volume V under the surface of aggregator and can be called the *volume-based andness/orness*. For any given andness/orness we can compute the corresponding volume under the surface of aggregator: $V = [n - (n-1)\alpha]/(n+1) = [(n-1)\omega + 1]/(n+1)$. Thus, the volume, andness, and orness can be interpreted as global geometric properties of conjunctive and disjunctive aggregators.

In the range $0 \le V \le 1$, there are regions inside I^n where all aggregators have the same general logic properties (idempotency, annihilator support, simultaneity, and substitutability, described in Sect. 4 and Fig. 1); in such regions we use the adjustable andness/orness for additional fine tuning of logic properties. In the points of transition from region to region we have *border aggregators*. The following is a short description of all important border aggregators.

Drastic Conjunction ($V = 0$) and Drastic Disjunction ($V = 1$). The minimum possible orness corresponds to the minimum volume $V = 0$, and from (1) it follows $\omega_{min} = -1/(n-1)$. The minimum volume denotes the maximum andness $\alpha_{max} = n/(n-1)$. So, the minimum orness corresponds to the maximum andness and vice versa. The maximum orness for the maximum volume $V = 1$ is $\omega_{max} = n/(n-1)$, and it corresponds to the minimum andness $\alpha_{min} = -1/(n-1)$. Since $\alpha_{min} \le \alpha \le \alpha_{max}$ and $\omega_{min} \le \omega \le \omega_{max}$, the range of andness and orness is $[-1/(n-1), n/(n-1)]$. The largest range is obtained in the case of two variables: $-1 \le \alpha \le 2$ and $-1 \le \omega \le 2$. As the number of variables increases, the ranges of andness and orness reduce, approaching $0 \le \alpha \le 1$ and $0 \le \omega \le 1$.

The next obvious question is to identify logic functions that correspond to minimum volume $V = 0$ and the maximum volume $V = 1$. In [4], these two functions are identified as the drastic conjunction $\hat{C}(X) = \lfloor x_1 \cdots x_n \rfloor$ and the drastic disjunction $\hat{D}(X) = \overline{\lfloor \overline{x_1} \cdots \overline{x_n} \rfloor} = 1 - \lfloor (1 - x_1) \cdots (1 - x_n) \rfloor$. In other words, $\hat{C}(X) = 1$ if and only if $x_1 = \cdots = x_n = 1$, and $\hat{D}(X) = 0$ if and only if $x_1 = \cdots = x_n = 0$. The drastic conjunction and the drastic disjunction are two dual functions: $\hat{D}(X) = 1 - \hat{C}(1 - X)$, and $\hat{C}(X) = 1 - \hat{D}(1 - X)$. The drastic conjunction specifies the ultimate conjunctive requirement: we accept only candidates that perfectly (fully) satisfy *all* requirements; everybody else is rejected. The meaning of drastic disjunction is the ultimate disjunctive requirement: we reject only candidates that completely fail to satisfy *all* requirements; everybody else is accepted. According to the definition of (basic and general) logic aggregators, neither $\hat{C}(X)$ nor $\hat{D}(X)$ are basic logic aggregators because they are insensitive to positive and incomplete truth. However, the product-power functions $C_h(X) = \Pi_{i=1}^n x_i^p$, $p \ge 1$ and $D_h(X) = 1 - \Pi_{i=1}^n (1 - x_i)^p$ are basic logic aggregators and they can be used to approximate the drastic functions:

$$\hat{C}(X) = \lfloor x_1 \cdots x_n \rfloor = \lim_{p \to +\infty} \Pi_{i=1}^n x_i^p;$$

$$\hat{D}(X) = \overline{\lfloor \overline{x_1} \cdots \overline{x_n} \rfloor} = 1 - \lim_{p \to +\infty} \Pi_{i=1}^n (1 - x_i)^p.$$

Therefore, the drastic conjunction and the drastic disjunction are two extreme logic functions, flanking an infinite number of logic aggregators that are located between them. In human logic reasoning it is observable that all variables and parameters are graded and continuously adjustable. This also holds for andness and orness; consequently, there must be a continuous transition from the drastic conjunction to the drastic disjunction. This transition is either andness-directed (or andness-parameterized) or, what is equivalent, orness-directed (or orness-parameterized). In human logic reasoning, andness and orness are the inputs and not the outputs. In the mental process of creating evaluation criteria each stakeholder/decision maker specifies the desired degree of simultaneity or substitutability of suitability attributes, and then rewards alternatives that can provide desired simultaneity or substitutability and penalizes alternatives that cannot satisfy these logic requirements; this is called andness/orness-directedness. The same must be done when creating mathematical models of evaluation criteria and the methods for achieving andness-directedness and orness-directedness can be found in [39–44]. Therefore, all aggregators of degrees of truth or fuzzy membership must provide the full spectrum of logic properties in the range from the drastic conjunction to the drastic disjunction. Some aggregators can provide and some cannot provide these properties, and our goal is to investigate the most popular aggregators from this point of view.

Full Conjunction ($V = 1/(n + 1)$) and Full Disjunction ($V = n/(n + 1)$). The drastic conjunction and the drastic disjunction are much stronger operations (i.e. more conjunctive or more disjunctive) than the classical aggregators of full conjunction $C_{con}(X) = min(x_1, \ldots, x_n)$ and full disjunction $D_{dis}(X) = max(x_1, \ldots, x_n)$. According to [12],

$$V_{con} = \int_{I^n} min(x_1, \ldots, x_n)dx_1 \ldots dx_n = 1/(n+1) \Rightarrow \alpha_{con} = 1, \quad \omega_{con} = 0 \ ;$$

$$V_{dis} = \int_{I^n} max(x_1, \ldots, x_n)dx_1 \ldots dx_n = n/(n+1) \Rightarrow \alpha_{con} = 0, \quad \omega_{con} = 1.$$

Full conjunction and disjunction are extreme idempotent aggregators bordering an infinite number of *idempotent aggregators* located between them and implemented as means. Indeed, if $min(x_1, \ldots, x_n) \leq A(x_1, \ldots, x_n) \leq max(x_1, \ldots, x_n)$, then for $x_1 = \cdots = x_n = x$ we have $A(x, \ldots, x) = x$. In other words, $A(X)$ is a mean and it is idempotent. The definition of global andness/orness (1) is selected so that for any number of variables the range of andness and orness of idempotent aggregators is $0 \leq \alpha \leq 1$ and $0 \leq \omega \leq 1$.

It is useful to note that idempotent aggregators are usually modeled using means, and among means the most useful is the weighted power mean $y = \left(\sum_{i=1}^{n} W_i x_i^r\right)^{1/r}$, $W_i > 0, i = 1, \ldots, n, -\infty \leq r \leq +\infty$, because its special cases are the most important arithmetic, geometric, and harmonic means. Obviously, the idempotency condition $x = \left(\sum_{i=1}^{n} W_i x^r\right)^{1/r}$ is equivalent to the request that weights must be normalized: $\sum_{i=1}^{n} W_i = 1$.

Logic Neutrality ($V = 1/2$). The central point in the spectrum of conjunctive and disjunctive aggregators is characterized by $\alpha = \omega$ and from this condition and (1) it follows $\alpha = \omega = V = 1/2$. The arithmetic mean $A_{ari}(X) = (x_1 + \cdots + x_n)/n$ is the aggregator that satisfies this condition. The central location inside the unit hypercube corresponds to the arithmetic mean which cuts the unit hypercube in two equal halves: $V_{ari} = 1/2$. Thus, $\alpha_{ari} = \omega_{ari} = 1/2$. The arithmetic mean is the only idempotent logic aggregator with this property (it is linear, continuous, and commutative – all inputs have the same importance). The arithmetic mean is the border between conjunctive and disjunctive aggregators: it is the central point of the universe of conjunctive and disjunctive aggregators and therefore it has the important role of the centroid of all logic aggregators.

Threshold Partial Conjunction ($V = V_\theta$) with Default Andness $\alpha_\theta = 3/4$. The fundamental property of conjunctive aggregators is the selective support for annihilator 0, and the fundamental property of disjunctive aggregators is the selective support for annihilator 1. If aggregators support the annihilators, they are called *hard* and if they do not support annihilators, they are called *soft*. Both hard and soft aggregators are permanently present and clearly visible in human reasoning [4]. Thus, they are necessary in analytic models of aggregators and designers of logic aggregators must decide about the ranges of andness reserved for hard and soft aggregators. The threshold andness $1/2 < \alpha_\theta < 1$ is defined as the smallest andness of hard conjunctive aggregators, and if $\alpha \geq \alpha_\theta$ the corresponding aggregator is hard. Soft conjunctive aggregators are in the range $1/2 < \alpha < \alpha_\theta$. The selected threshold andness determines the conjunctive threshold volume $V_\theta = [n - (n-1)\alpha_\theta]/(n+1)$.

The region of aggregators between the arithmetic mean and the full conjunction is the area of idempotent simultaneity (or partial conjunction). Generally, the threshold andness can be selected anywhere inside the range $]1/2, 1[$. The central point in that range is characterized by andness $\alpha_\theta = \alpha_{uni} = 3/4$. This point is important because it creates the uniform distribution of the soft/low partial conjunction ($1/2 < \alpha < 3/4$) which does not support the annihilator 0, and the hard/high partial conjunction ($3/4 \leq \alpha < 1$) which supports the annihilator 0. From $[n - (n+1)V_{uni}]/(n-1) = 3/4$ it follows $V_{uni} = (1/4)(n+3)/(n+1) = (V_{ari} + V_{con})/2$.

If designers of aggregators have reasons why the region of hard aggregators should be greater than or less than the region of soft aggregators, then α_θ can take any value inside $]1/2, 1[$. If such reasons cannot be provided, then it is reasonable to use the default value $\alpha_\theta = \alpha_{uni}$, offering equal opportunities for hard and soft aggregators. In this case the threshold simultaneity can be called *medium idempotent simultaneity*.

The graded logic supports duality: any conjunctive aggregator $C(X)$ has a dual disjunctive aggregator $D(X) = 1 - C(1 - X)$, and vice versa $C(X) = 1 - D(1 - X)$. For example, in the case of unweighted harmonic mean, we have $C(X) = 2x_1x_2/(x_1 + x_2)$ and its dual is $D(X) = 1 - 2(1 - x_1)(1 - x_2)/(2 - x_1 - x_2)$; the annihilator of $C(X)$ is 0, and the annihilator of $D(X)$ is 1. Both the harmonic mean and its disjunctive dual are the hard aggregators. The threshold orness $1/2 < \omega_\theta < 1$ is defined as the smallest orness of hard disjunctive aggregators. If $\omega \geq \omega_\theta$ the corresponding disjunctive aggregator is hard and supports the annihilator 1, and for $1/2 < \omega < \omega_\theta$ the corresponding partial disjunction is soft and the annihilator 1 is not supported. To preserve the duality of conjunctive and disjunctive aggregators, we always assume that $\omega_\theta = \alpha_\theta$, and most frequently $\omega_\theta = \alpha_\theta = 3/4$.

Medium Hyperconjunction ($V = 1/2^n$). An important hyperconjunctive aggregator located approximately halfway between the full conjunction and the drastic conjunction is the product t-norm $C_t(X) = x_1 \cdots x_n$. Following are the andness and orness of

$C_t(X)$:

$$V_t = \int_{I^n} x_1 \cdots x_n dx_1 \ldots dx_n = 1/2^n \quad \Rightarrow \quad \alpha_t = \frac{n-(n+1)/2^n}{n-1} > 1,$$

$$\omega_t = \frac{(n+1)/2^n - 1}{n-1} < 0, \ 1 < \alpha_t < n/(n-1), \qquad -1/(n-1) < \omega_t < 0. \tag{2}$$

A hyperconjunctive aggregator located halfway between the full conjunction and the drastic conjunction should have the andness $\alpha_h = [1 + n/(n-1)]/2 = (2n-1)/(2n-2)$. From $\alpha_t = \alpha_h$ it follows $n = 3$ (of course, if $n \neq 3$ then $\alpha_t \neq \alpha_h$). So, in the case of three variables the product t-norm is volume-wise located exactly in the middle between the full conjunction and the drastic conjunction, justifying the status of the product t-norm as "the medium hyperconjunction." That is a strategic position, suitable for interpolative implementations of hyperconjunctive aggregators, and for interpreting aggregators between the full conjunction and the product t-norm as "low hyperconjunction," and aggregators between the product t-norm and the drastic conjunction as "high hyperconjunction." In addition, the product t-norm is also the model of probability of n independent events, indicating the equivalence of logic and probabilistic interpretations of the same aggregator.

3 Semantic Identity and Noncommutativity

All degrees of truth have semantic identity, expressed as the role, meaning, importance, and relation to goals and interests of specific stakeholder/decision maker [13]. Since the arguments of aggregators are semantically differentiated degrees of truth and not anonymous real numbers, the fixed commutativity of aggregators is *not* a desired GL property. In a special case, all inputs can be equally important, and the notation of aggregator $A(X)$ assumes that $x_1, \ldots, x_n$ have exactly the same role and importance. Equal importance can be a provable property, or an acceptable simplification, or (most frequently) an unacceptable oversimplification. In a general case, equal importance is not acceptable, because the degrees of truth $x_1, \ldots, x_n$ have different importance for a decision maker. The degrees of importance are quantified using "importance weights" $w_1, \ldots, w_n$. In such cases, the aggregation process is based on graded concepts of suitability and importance, and it combines formal logic and semantic components. The corresponding aggregators are denoted $A(X; W)$ where $W = (w_1, \ldots, w_n)$. Depending on the type of aggregator, the weights are usually normalized. Three most frequent normalization techniques are $w_1 + \cdots + w_n = 1$ (sum-normalized weights) or $max(w_1, \ldots, w_n) = 1$ (max-normalized weights [20]) or $w_1 + \cdots + w_n = n$ (count-normalized weights). An analysis of their applicability can be found in [4].

We assume that weights denote the degrees of relative importance of inputs. Consequently, the weights must be positive: $0 < w_i < 1$, $i = 1, \ldots, n$. Indeed, $w_i = 0$ would denote a completely insignificant input, and such inputs are justifiably omitted. Similarly, in the case of sum-normalized weights $w_i = 1$ yields $n = 1$ what is not possible in aggregation.

Noncommutativity of aggregators based on weights is the prerequisite for modeling the semantic identity of degrees of truth that are arguments of all logic aggregators. Therefore, all logic aggregators must be weighted, and those aggregators that are not weighted cannot be directly used in GL. However, in the case of idempotent aggregators, all commutative aggregators can be transformed to weighted aggregators using the method of binary aggregation trees, but that method increases algorithmic and computational complexity [4, 14].

Both importance and andness/orness affect the human percept of the overall importance of logic arguments. At high levels of andness (or orness) the impact of each argument becomes very strong, enhancing (and equalizing) the human percept of the overall importance of each individual argument. For example, for $\alpha \geq 1$ all arguments are mandatory and requested to be sufficiently satisfied, equalizing their individual degrees of importance that are now much less exposed than at the lower levels of andness. According to [4], that phenomenon can be used for accepting the full conjunction as a strictly commutative aggregator and extending such reasoning to all hyperconjunctive (and hyperdisjunctive) aggregators. The phenomenon of *equalization of weights at high andness/orness* can be frequently used as the justification for commutativity of hyperconjunctive aggregators.

In some special cases, however, we can find examples of noncommutative hyperconjunction. E.g., a candidate for a position of computational biologist might be evaluated using the product t-norm $Q = CB, \quad C \in I, \ B \in I$, where C and B denote separately evaluated candidate's competence in the areas of computing and biology, respectively. The product can have a probabilistic interpretation, assuming that the quality of candidate Q is decided as a probability that the candidate can solve computational biology problems where computational and biological components are equally present. It is obvious that many problems require unequal presence of computational and biologic component, and in such cases the right criterion would be both highly conjunctive and weighted: $Q = C^\gamma B^{2-\gamma}, \ 0 < \gamma < 2$.

The concept of weighted hyperconjunction and the concept of equalization of weights at high andness can be properly justified and do not exclude each other. The cases where at high andness the weights should have a low impact seem to be considerably more frequent than the cases where the weights must be different and have significant impact.

4   Classification of Graded Logic Functions and Andness-Directedness of Logic Aggregators

The selection of logic properties of an aggregator by specifying its desired andness is called *andness-directedness*. Since andness/orness specifies a desired degree of simultaneity or substitutability, it follows that andness/orness represents the most important *input* in the process of creating a logic aggregator. Most logic aggregators are not naturally andness-directed, but they have adjustable parameters that affect andness/orness. Andness-directedness is realized by computing aggregator parameters as functions of the desired andness.

Our concept of logic aggregation is based on logic, and it is different from the concept of aggregation used in mathematical literature. For example, in [3], the drastic conjunction is identified as the "smallest conjunctive aggregation function" and denoted $A_\perp(X)$, while $min(X)$ is identified as the "greatest conjunctive aggregation function." The reason for this difference is that in mathematical literature conjunctive functions are not related to andness, are not developed as models of human reasoning, and contrary to GL, aggregation structures are not interpreted as models of logic propositional calculus. In graded logic, conjunctive functions are functions that have andness greater than orness, and functions that have andness greater than 1 are called hyperconjunction (and similarly, for andness less than 0, hyperdisjunction). According to definition (1), we interpret andness and orness as overall geometric properties related to the volume under the surface of aggregator inside the unit hypercube.

Basic graded logic functions can be *conjunctive*, *disjunctive*, or *neutral*. Conjunctive functions have andness greater than orness ($\alpha > \omega$). Similarly, disjunctive functions have orness greater than andness ($\alpha < \omega$), and neutral is only the arithmetic mean where $\alpha = \omega = 1/2$. Between the drastic conjunction and the drastic disjunction, we have andness-directed logic aggregators that are special cases of a fundamental logic function called *graded conjunction/disjunction* (GCD) [4, 15]. GCD has the status of a logic aggregator, and it can be idempotent or nonidempotent, as well as *hard* (supporting annihilators) or *soft* (not supporting annihilators). The annihilator of hard conjunctive aggregators is 0, and the annihilator of hard disjunctive aggregators is 1.

The whole range of conjunctive aggregators is presented in Fig. 1. The range of idempotent aggregators extends from the logic neutrality to the full conjunction. Between the full conjunction and the drastic conjunction, we have a range of nonidempotent aggregators. The group of five border aggregators, presented in Sect. 2, creates four aggregation segments between them. Each segment includes an infinite number of andness-directed aggregators that have the same fundamental properties (idempotency and annihilators) but differ in andness.

Based on De Morgan duality, the range of disjunctive aggregators is a mirror image of the range of conjunctive aggregators. Therefore, the problem of creating all graded logic functions from drastic disjunction to drastic conjunction consists of two steps: (1) creating nine border aggregators (drastic conjunction, medium hyperconjunction, full conjunction, threshold partial conjunction, logic neutrality, threshold partial disjunction, full disjunction, medium hyperdisjunction, and drastic disjunction), and (2) creating eight aggregation segments between the border aggregators (high hyperconjunction, low hyperconjunction, hard partial conjunction, soft partial conjunction, soft partial disjunction, hard partial disjunction, low hyperdisjunction, and high hyperdisjunction).

Idempotent aggregators have the property $A(\underline{X}; W) = x$, $\underline{X} = (x, \ldots, x)$, $x \in I$. If $0 < x < 1$ then the nonidempotent conjunctive aggregators satisfy $A(\underline{X}; W) < x$, and nonidempotent disjunctive aggregators satisfy $A(\underline{X}; W) > x$. Hard conjunctive aggregators (either idempotent or nonidempotent) satisfy $\forall i \in \{1, \ldots, n\}$, $x_i = 0 \Rightarrow A(X; W) = 0$. Similarly, all hard disjunctive aggregators satisfy $\forall i \in \{1, \ldots, n\}$, $x_i = 1 \Rightarrow A(X; W) = 1$. Soft conjunctive aggregators have the property $\forall i \in \{1, \ldots, n\}$, $\forall j \neq i$, $x_i > 0$, $x_j = 0 \Rightarrow A(X; W) > 0$. Similarly, for soft disjunctive aggregators we have $\forall i \in \{1, \ldots, n\}$, $\forall j \neq i$, $x_i < 1$, $x_j = 1 \Rightarrow A(X; W) < 1$.

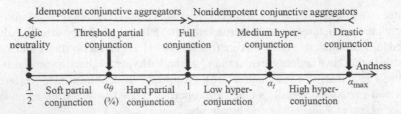

Fig. 1. The range of conjunctive aggregators: border aggregators and aggregation segments.

Table 1. Classification of andness-directed graded logic functions and aggregators.

		Logic function/aggregator	I	T	A	Global andness (α)	
G R A D E D L O G I C F U N C T I O N S	**C O N J U N C T I V E**	Drastic conjunction	N	H	0	$\alpha = \alpha_{max} = n/(n-1)$	**B A S I C G L A G G R E G A T O R S**
		High hyperconjunction	N	H	0	$\alpha_t < \alpha < \alpha_{max}$	
		Medium hyperconjunction	N	H	0	$\alpha = \alpha_t = (n2^n - n - 1)/(n-1)2^n$	
		Low hyperconjunction	N	H	0	$1 < \alpha < \alpha_t$	
		Full conjunction	Y	H	0	$\alpha = 1$	
		Hard partial conjunction	Y	H	0	$\alpha_\theta \leq \alpha < 1$; $\frac{1}{2} < \alpha_\theta < 1$	
		Soft partial conjunction	Y	S	-	$\frac{1}{2} < \alpha < \alpha_\theta$	
		Neutrality	Y	S	-	$\alpha = \frac{1}{2}$	
	D I S J U N C T I V E	Soft partial disjunction	Y	S	-	$1 - \alpha_\theta < \alpha < \frac{1}{2}$	
		Hard partial disjunction	Y	H	1	$0 < \alpha \leq 1 - \alpha_\theta$	
		Full disjunction	Y	H	1	$\alpha = 0$	
		Low hyperdisjunction	N	H	1	$1 - \alpha_t < \alpha < 0$	
		Medium hyperdisjunction	N	H	1	$\alpha = 1 - \alpha_t$	
		High hyperdisjunction	N	H	1	$\alpha_{min} < \alpha < 1 - \alpha_t$	
		Drastic disjunction	N	H	1	$\alpha = \alpha_{min} = -1/(n-1)$	
Columns: **I**=idempotent, **Y/N**=yes/no; **T**=type, **H/S**=hard/soft; **A**=annihilator							

A detailed classification of GCD aggregators, based on combinations conjunctive/ disjunctive, idempotent/nonidempotent, and hard/soft aggregators is presented in Table 1. The presented classification reflects the *graded logic conjecture* [4] that specifies that all graded logic functions can be created using *ten necessary and sufficient fundamental types of logic operations*: the "magnificent seven" idempotent functions (the full conjunction, hard partial conjunction, soft partial conjunction, neutrality, soft partial disjunction, hard partial disjunction and the full disjunction), two nonidempotent functions (hyperconjunction and hyperdisjunction), and standard negation. It is important to note that this set of fundamental logic functions is observable and provably present in intuitive human reasoning. Therefore, all aggregation functions can be evaluated from the standpoint of their ability to model the necessary ten types of basic logic operations. Decision support systems cannot be incompatible with observable human reasoning and the basic level of compatibility is the support for aggregators that can realize andness-directed continuous transition from drastic conjunction to drastic disjunction.

All disjunctive aggregators can be realized as De Morgan duals of conjunctive aggregators: $D(X; W) = 1 - C(1 - X; W)$; so, it is sufficient to analyze only the conjunctive aggregators. Seven functions in Table 1 have the fixed andness, and eight aggregators have a range of andness: users first select the type of function and then adjust the desired degree of andness. The adjustability of andness in the whole range $[\alpha_{min}, \alpha_{max}]$ is the necessary property of all functions that aspire to play the role of logic aggregators.

One of the most important properties of logic aggregators is the nonincreasing monotonicity in andness (or the nondecreasing monotonicity in orness). Indeed, by increasing the conjunction degree we increase the severity of requirements for simultaneous satisfaction of several inputs and therefore the results of aggregation must decrease when the andness increases. The only exception is the case of idempotency, for those aggregators that are based on means. In all other cases logic aggregators must be strictly decreasing in andness and strictly increasing in orness. These properties must be supported by all implementations of andness-directed (or orness-directed) logic aggregators.

5 Specification of Requirements for Logic Aggregators

In all applications of logic aggregators, decision makers first specify requirements that a desired aggregator must satisfy, and then search for a mathematical model that has the required properties. Most aggregation structures are based on superposition of two fundamental types of aggregators: GCD and partial absorption. The partial absorption can be conjunctive (mandatory/optional) or disjunctive (sufficient/optional) and its parameters are computed using a desired penalty/reward pair as inputs [4]. All partial absorption aggregators are constructed using the superposition of hard and soft GCD aggregators. Consequently, in this study we have reasons to omit an explicit investigation of the partial absorption aggregators.

In the case of fundamental GCD aggregator, the specification of requirements consists of providing justified answers to the following questions:

Step 1. *Idempotent or nonidempotent?* Idempotent aggregators are implemented as means and can be either hard or soft. Nonidempotent aggregators are always hard and (according to Table 1) can be a hyperconjunction or a hyperdisjunction. In cases where all inputs are equal x, $(0 < x < 1)$ and the expected aggregated value is less than x, the aggregator is a hyperconjunction.

Step 2. *Simultaneity or substitutability?* Basic logic aggregator (GCD) can be a model of simultaneity (various forms of conjunction) or substitutability (various forms of disjunction). De Morgan duality, which is valid in graded logic, permits the study of only one of these two options; let us arbitrarily select simultaneity (conjunction). In a special case, an aggregator can be neutral, i.e., providing equal support for simultaneity and substitutability. Such an aggregator is the (weighted) arithmetic mean, which must be supported by all models of logic aggregators.

Step 3. *Hard or soft?* Generally, in GL annihilators can be either indispensable, or unacceptable. If all inputs are mandatory (any zero input causes zero output) the corresponding conjunctive GCD aggregator must be hard. If that is not the case, the aggregator must be soft. All idempotent GCD aggregators must provide hard/soft adjustability (nonidempotent aggregators are always hard).

Step 4. *What is the desired strength of simultaneity/substitutability?* All decision makers always know the desired degree of conjunction (andness) or disjunction (orness) that reflects their goals and requirements. Since the andness must be continuously adjustable, that is the reason why we need andness-directed aggregators that provide a continuous transition from drastic conjunction to drastic disjunction. The requested andness is the most important input for the design of GCD aggregators.

Step 5. *What are the degrees of importance?* Strict commutativity is *not* a desired property of logic aggregators. Generally, we assume that noncommutativity is a necessary property of all aggregators: only in special cases all inputs can be equally important. Therefore, strictly commutative aggregators deserve separate attention only in unlikely cases where they have some unique and particularly attractive properties, and in such cases, we can use the binary tree method [4, 14] to provide the desired noncommutativity. Generally, we assume that all inputs of all aggregators have different degrees of importance and consequently all logic aggregators must be weighted. We assume that decision makers explicitly specify (or use a method to compute [46]) the necessary *importance weights*. Thus, logic aggregators must provide a way to implement the desired values of importance weights.

Based on known semantic identity of inputs, in real life applications of conjunctive (or disjunctive) GCD aggregators, the presented five steps are reduced to only three fundamental questions that can be given in arbitrary order: (1) specification of the desired conjunction degree (the strength of simultaneity or substitutability expressed as andness), (2) specification of the relative importance of inputs, expressed as importance weights, and (3) specification of the use of annihilators (any GCD aggregator must be either hard or soft). Therefore, any method for creating logic aggregators can be evaluated from the standpoint of its ability to create aggregators with desired andness, desired importance of inputs, and desired use of annihilators.

6   Benchmark Problems for Logic Aggregators

Evaluation of methods for design of logic aggregators can include benchmark problems, selected as typical representatives of logic aggregation that frequently occur in evaluation criteria. Let us consider a realistic case where we have $n = 4$ inputs $x_1 = 0.8$, $x_2 = 0.4$, $x_3 = 1$, $x_4 = 0.6$ with increasing importance weights $w_1 = 0.1$, $w_2 = 0.2$, $w_3 = 0.3$, $w_4 = 0.4$. For inputs with these levels of importance we must create three benchmark aggregators with the following properties:

S benchmark: A soft partial conjunction with andness $\alpha = 0.625$ (no annihilators).

H benchmark: A hard partial conjunction with andness $\alpha = 0.875$ (annihilator 0).

C benchmark: A hyperconjunctive aggregator with andness $\alpha = 1.25$ (annihilator 0).

These benchmark problems are realistic examples of aggregator requirement specifications. Each method for creating logic aggregators can be evaluated from the standpoint of the capability to solve problems S, H, and C. The S benchmark is a popular
and frequently used weak partial conjunction, and the H benchmark is equally popular
and frequently used strong partial conjunction. The C benchmark is a hyperconjunctive
aggregator close to medium hyperconjunction.

All logic aggregators that support the selectability of weights, annihilators, and andness are not equally suitable. In addition to these mandatory requirements, they must
also be analytically and computationally simple. The expected computational complexity of logic aggregators with n arguments is $O(n)$. Benchmark problems are useful as
tools for evaluation and comparison of computational complexity of competitive logic
aggregators.

7 Implementation of Logic Aggregators Using GCD and Andness-Directed Interpolative Aggregation

The andness-directed interpolative method for implementing GCD consists of implementing the border aggregators shown in Fig. 1 and then using interpolative aggregators
in the range of andness between them. This method can be used to implement all logic
GCD aggregators shown in Table 1. Taking into account that simplicity is the fundamental requirement for all aggregators, we use the weighted power mean (WPM)
$y = (w_1 x_1^r + \cdots + w_1 x_1^r)^{1/r}$, $-\infty \leq r \leq +\infty$, $w_1 + \cdots + w_1 = 1$ as the main component for building idempotent logic aggregators. The desired andness of this aggregator
is easily adjusted by selecting the appropriate value of exponent r, and the degrees of
importance of attributes are selected using the normalized positive weights.

7.1 Andness-Directed Interpolative Aggregation (ADIA)

ADIA is the interpolative method derived from the mean andness theorem [13]. Suppose
that we have two aggregators, $A_1(X; W, \alpha_1)$ and $A_2(X; W, \alpha_2)$, $\alpha_1 < \alpha_2$, and we need
the aggregator $A(X; W, \alpha)$ for the range of andness $\alpha \in [\alpha_1, \alpha_2]$. So, $\alpha = (1 - q)\alpha_1 +
q\alpha_2$, $0 \leq q \leq 1$, and the volume under this aggregator is $V = [n - \alpha(n - 1)]/(n + 1)$.
From $\alpha - \alpha_1 = q(\alpha_2 - \alpha_1)$ we have parameters $q = (\alpha - \alpha_1)/(\alpha_2 - \alpha_1)$ and $1 - q =
(\alpha_2 - \alpha)/(\alpha_2 - \alpha_1)$. The interpolative aggregators in the andness range $[\alpha_1, \alpha_2]$ can be
derived from the fact that the volume V can be obtained using a linear interpolation
between volumes of boundary aggregators as follows [13]:

$$V_1 = \int_{I^n} A_1(X; \underline{W}, \alpha_1) dx_1 \ldots dx_n, \quad V_2 = \int_{I^n} A_2(X; \underline{W}, \alpha_2) dx_1 \ldots dx_n,$$

$$\underline{W} = (1/n, \ldots, 1/n)$$

$$\alpha = (1 - q)\alpha_1 + q\alpha_2 = (1 - q)\frac{n - (n + 1)V_1}{n - 1} + q\frac{n - (n + 1)V_2}{n - 1}$$

$$= \frac{n - (n + 1)[(1 - q)V_1 + qV_2]}{n - 1} = \frac{n - (n + 1)V}{n - 1}.$$

Therefore,

$$V = (1-q)V_1 + qV_2 = \int_{I^n} A(X; \underline{W}, \alpha) dx_1 \ldots dx_n$$
$$= \int_{I^n} \big[(1-q)A_1(X; \underline{W}, \alpha_1) + qA_2(X; \underline{W}, \alpha_2) \big] dx_1 \ldots dx_n.$$

The linear interpolation of volumes can be achieved if the resulting interpolative aggregators for $W = \underline{W}$ have the following form:

$$A(X; \underline{W}, \alpha) = (1-q)A_1(X; \underline{W}, \alpha_1) + qA_2(X; \underline{W}, \alpha_2)$$
$$= \frac{(\alpha_2 - \alpha)A_1(X; \underline{W}, \alpha_1) + (\alpha - \alpha_1)A_2(X; \underline{W}, \alpha_2)}{\alpha_2 - \alpha_1}, \quad \alpha \in [\alpha_1, \alpha_2].$$

As a summary, in a general case of weighted border aggregators $A_1(X; W, \alpha_1)$ and $A_2(X; W, \alpha_2)$, the weighted andness-directed interpolative aggregators, for arbitrary weights W, are the following:

$$A(X; W, \alpha) = \frac{(\alpha_2 - \alpha)A_1(X; W, \alpha_1) + (\alpha - \alpha_1)A_2(X; W, \alpha_2)}{\alpha_2 - \alpha_1}. \tag{3}$$

7.2 Five Conjunctive Border Aggregators

Conjunctive border aggregators (Fig. 1) include neutrality, threshold partial conjunction, full conjunction, medium hyperconjunction, and drastic conjunction. Disjunctive border aggregators are simply obtained as De Morgan duals of conjunctive border aggregators.

Neutrality. This aggregator is the traditional weighted arithmetic mean obtained from WPM for $r = 1$:

$$A_{ari}(X; W, {}^1/_2) = w_1 x_1 + \cdots + w_n x_n, \quad 0 < w_i < 1, \quad i = 1, \ldots, n,$$
$$w_1 + \cdots + w_n = 1, \quad n > 1.$$

Threshold Partial Conjunction. This aggregator is a hard partial conjunction with the threshold andness $\alpha = \alpha_\theta$ and the default value $\alpha_\theta = {}^3/_4$. It is implemented as the following WPM:

$$A_{tpc}(X; W, \alpha_\theta) = \left(\sum_{i=1}^{n} W_i x_i^{r_{wpm}(\alpha_\theta, n)} \right)^{1/r_{wpm}(\alpha_\theta, n)}.$$

The WPM exponent depends on the desired andness α. However, the function $\alpha \mapsto r_{wpm}(\alpha, n)$ is known only numerically, either as a table, or as the following approximation:

$$r_{wpm}(\alpha, n) = \frac{0.25 + a_n(1/2 - \alpha) + b_n(1/2 - \alpha)^2 + c_n(1/2 - \alpha)^3 + d_n(1/2 - \alpha)^4}{\alpha(1-\alpha)}.$$

The $r_{wpm}(\alpha, n)$ tables and the numerical values of parameters a_n, b_n, c_n, d_n depend on the number of variables n and can be found in [4]. If $\alpha_\theta = 3/4$ and $n = 4$ then $R = r_{wpm}(3/4, 4) = -0.7205$. We assume that α_θ is selected so that $r_{wpm}(\alpha_\theta, n) \leq 0$ and consequently $A_{hpc}(X; W, \alpha_\theta)$ is a hard conjunctive aggregator.

Full Conjunction. This is the only commutative idempotent aggregator:

$$A_{con}(X; \underline{W}, 1) = min(x_1, \ldots, x_n) = x_1 \wedge \cdots \wedge x_n.$$

It satisfies commutativity, monotonicity, associativity, neutral element, and the annihilator 0. The full conjunction is the end of the range of idempotent aggregators and the beginning of the range of t-norms. The commutativity of full conjunction can be logically explained as the consequence of high andness: since all inputs are indispensable, in the case of zero input each of them has equal power to affect the output. To avoid the problems of weight domination [4, 20], the full conjunction should *not* be weighted in logic aggregation and evaluation models.

Medium Hyperconjunction. The product t-norm seems to be the best candidate for the medium hyperconjunction. This aggregator that has the fixed andness $\alpha = \alpha_t$:

$$A_{mhc}(X; \underline{W}, \alpha_t) = \prod_{i=1}^{n} x_i$$

Again, an interesting question is whether the hyperconjunction should be weighted or not weighted. If we adopt the view that high andness implies commutativity, then the use of the product t-norm is fully justified. The product is also the probability of simultaneous occurrence of independent events. So, if we want to make decisions based on the likelihood of simultaneous satisfaction of multiple independent criteria, then the product is an appropriate model. However, if all attributes are provably not equally important, then it is right to use a weighted medium hyperconjunction:

$$A_{mhc}(X; W, \alpha_t) = \prod_{i=1}^{n} x_i^{p_i}, \quad p_1 + \cdots + p_n = nw_1 + \cdots + nw_n = n.$$

Drastic Conjunction. This ultimate form of conjunction, $A_{drc}(X) = \lfloor x_1 \cdots x_n \rfloor$, is a general logic aggregator; it is important as the highest andness border of all conjunctive aggregators.

7.3 Four Families of Conjunctive Interpolative Aggregators

According to Fig. 1, there are four families (andness regions) of conjunctive ADIA aggregators: the soft and hard partial conjunction, followed by the low and high hyperconjunction. Since we know the sequence of five conjunctive border aggregation functions, all families of conjunctive interpolative aggregators can be based on the same interpolative model (3).

Soft Partial Conjunction. This family of ADIA aggregators is sometimes called "nice-to-have," as opposed to the hard partial conjunction family which can be called "must-have." This aggregator is necessary in all cases where the inputs $x_1, \ldots, x_n$ are desirable, but none of them is mandatory. So, the soft partial conjunction tolerates the situation where some of desired inputs are false (absent, or not satisfied). The andness α is selected from the interval $1/2 < \alpha < \alpha_\theta$, where most frequently $\alpha_\theta = 3/4$. The value of andness depends on the degree of penalty we want to have in cases where the inputs $x_1, ..., x_n$ are not simultaneously satisfied.

The soft partial conjunction ADIA aggregators are interpolated between the weighted arithmetic mean and the threshold partial conjunction, using (3) as follows:

$$A_{spc}(X; W, \alpha) = \frac{(\alpha_\theta - \alpha)A_{ari}(X; W, 1/2) + (\alpha - 1/2)A_{tpc}(X; W, \alpha_\theta)}{\alpha_\theta - 1/2},$$

$$1/2 < \alpha < \alpha_\theta. \tag{4}$$

If $\alpha_\theta = 3/4$, then the range of soft partial conjunction is the same as the range of hard partial conjunction, and the corresponding GCD is called the uniform GCD or UGCD.

Hard Partial Conjunction. This is a "must-have" family of andness-directed aggregators where we need simultaneous satisfaction of all inputs $x_1, \ldots, x_n$ without any exception. If any input true value is 0 then $A_{hpc}(X; W, \alpha) = 0$. Therefore, the hard partial conjunctions are models of mandatory requirements The hard partial conjunctions are among the most frequently used models in evaluation criteria used in decision support systems. The simplest andness-directed analytic model of hard partial conjunction is directly the WPM:

$$A_{hpc}(X; W, \alpha) = \left(\sum_{i=1}^{n} W_i x_i^{r_{wpm}(\alpha,n)}\right)^{\frac{1}{r_{wpm}(\alpha,n)}}, \quad \alpha_\theta \leq \alpha < 1, \ n > 1. \tag{5}$$

The weighted geometric mean and the weighted harmonic mean are the most popular special cases of this aggregator. If $\alpha = 1$ then $r_{wpm}(1, n) = -\infty$ and we get the full conjunction.

Low Hyperconjunction. This family of ADIA aggregators is interpolated between the full conjunction and the medium hyperconjunction, using (3) as follows:

$$A_{lhc}(X; W, \alpha) = \frac{(\alpha_t - \alpha)A_{con}(X; \underline{W}, 1) + (\alpha - 1)A_{mhc}(X; W, \alpha_t)}{\alpha_t - 1}, \quad 1 < \alpha < \alpha_t$$

Because of interpolation, this aggregator inherits some properties of the full conjunction, including the generally undesirable discontinuity of the first derivative. Since $A_{mhc}(X; W, \alpha_t)$ can be weighted or not weighted, $A_{lhc}(X; W, \alpha)$ can also be weighted or not weighted.

High Hyperconjunction. The product t-norm is a suitable base for building the family of commutative highest andness aggregators, using an adjustable exponent p, as follows:

$$A_{hhc}(X; \alpha) = \left(\prod_{i=1}^{n} x_i\right)^p, \quad 1 < p < +\infty, \quad \alpha_t < \alpha < \alpha_{max};$$

$$A_{hhc}(X; \alpha_{max}) = \left\lfloor \prod_{i=1}^{n} x_i \right\rfloor.$$

The volume-based andness and the exponent p as a function of andness are the following:

$$V = \int_{I^n} x_1^p \cdots x_n^p dx_1 \ldots dx_n = 1/(p+1)^n \Rightarrow \alpha = \frac{n - (n+1)/(p+1)^n}{n-1},$$

$$p = \left[\frac{n+1}{n - (n-1)\alpha} \right]^{1/n} - 1. \tag{6}$$

Thus, the weighted version of the andness-directed high hyperconjunction is based on exponential weights, as follows:

$$A_{hhc}(X; W, \alpha) = \left(\prod_{i=1}^{n} x_i^{p_i} \right)^{\{(n+1)/[n-(n-1)\alpha]\}^{1/n}-1},$$

$$p_1 + \cdots + p_n = n, \quad p_i = nw_i, \quad i = 1, \ldots, n, \quad \alpha_t < \alpha < \alpha_{max}. \tag{7}$$

Both the hard partial conjunction and the high hyperconjunction aggregators can be defined using the interpolative form (3). However, the presented models (5) and (7) offer simpler implementations of andness-directed aggregation.

7.4 Solutions of Benchmark Problems

If the S benchmark is realized in the context of UGCD, then $\alpha_\theta = 3/4$ and the corresponding soft partial conjunction aggregators based on (4) are the following:

$$A_{spc}(X; W, \alpha) = (3 - 4\alpha)(0.1x_1 + 0.2x_2 + 0.3x_3 + 0.4x_4)$$

$$+ (4\alpha - 2)(0.1x_1^{-0.7205} + 0.2x_2^{-0.7205} + 0.3x_3^{-0.7205}$$

$$+ 0.4x_4^{-0.7205})^{-1/0.7205}, \quad 1/2 < \alpha < 3/4.$$

So, the desired S benchmark aggregator can be obtained from the above formula as $A_{spc}(X; W, 0.625) = 0.669$. However, there is also a simpler solution. The desired aggregator can be obtained directly from WPM. According to andness tables for WPM [4], the andness of 0.625 is obtained for exponent 0.1561 and the desired aggregator is the following:

$$A_{spc}(X; W, 0.625) = \left(0.1x_1^{0.1561} + 0.2x_2^{0.1561} + 0.3x_3^{0.1561} + 0.4x_4^{0.1561} \right)^{1/0.1561}$$

$$= 0.669.$$

If the H benchmark is realized in the context of UGCD, then $\alpha = 0.875 > \alpha_\theta = 3/4$ and the hard partial conjunction aggregators can be modeled directly as WPM, using (5) as follows:

$$A_{hpc}(X; W, \alpha) = \left(0.1x_1^{r_{wpm}(\alpha,4)} + 0.2x_2^{r_{wpm}(\alpha,4)} + 0.3x_3^{r_{wpm}(\alpha,4)} \right.$$

$$\left. + 0.4x_4^{r_{wpm}(\alpha,4)} \right)^{\frac{1}{r_{wpm}(\alpha,4)}}, \quad 3/4 \leq \alpha < 1.$$

$$A_{hpc}(X; W, 0.875) = \left(0.1x_1^{-2.8233} + 0.2x_2^{-2.8233} + 0.3x_3^{-2.8233}\right.$$

$$\left. +0.4x_4^{-2.8233}\right)^{-\frac{1}{2.8233}} = 0.572.$$

In the case of C *benchmark*, according to (2), for $n = 4$ we have $\alpha_t = 59/48 = 1.2292$. Since $a = 1.25 > \alpha_t$ we are slightly inside the high hyperconjunction area. In the case of commutative hyperconjunction, according to (6), we have $p = \sqrt[4]{20} - 1 = 1.1147$ and therefore,

$$A_{hhc}(X; 1.25) = (x_1 x_2 x_3 x_4)^{1.1147} = 0.159.$$

In the case of weighted hyperconjunction, from (7) we have

$$A_{hhc}(X; W, 1.25) = \left(x_1^{0.4} x_2^{0.8} x_3^{1.2} x_4^{1.6}\right)^{1.1147} = 0.161.$$

ADIA can be compared with other methods for creating weighted logic aggregators, as summarized in Table 5.

7.5   Implementation of Hyperconjunction Using Andness-Directed t-norms

Any t-norm T is a hyperconjunctive function located between the minimum function and the drastic intersection ($T_{dr}(a, 1) = a$, $T_{dr}(1, b) = b$, and in all other cases $T_{dr}(a, b) = 0$, yielding $\alpha = n/(n-1)$). Therefore, for $n = 2$, the andness of T satisfies $1 \leq \alpha \leq 2$. For parameterized families of t-norms, the parameter permits the function to range between the drastic intersection and the minimum. An example is Yager's family of t-norms [48]:

$$T_Y(a, b; w) = 1 - min\left(1, \left[(1-a)^w + (1-b)^w\right]^{\frac{1}{w}}\right), \quad 0 \leq w \leq +\infty.$$

The parameter w permits $T_Y(a, b; w)$ to range between the drastic intersection and the minimum: when w converges to 0, Yager's t-norm converges to the drastic intersection; when $w = 1$, we have $T_Y(a, b; 1) = max(0, a + b - 1)$; and when w converges to $+\infty$, then T_Y tends to $min(a, b)$.

Other examples of families of t-norms, including those introduced by Dombi's [49] and by Schweizer and Sklar [50], can be found in [51]. As another example, one of the families by Schweizer and Sklar is the following:

$$T_{SS}(a, b; p) = e^{-\left(|\ln a|^p + |\ln b|^p\right)^{\frac{1}{p}}}, \quad p > 0.$$

When p converges to zero, T_{SS} converges to the drastic intersection; when $p = 1$, it converges to ab; and when p converges to $+\infty$, it converges to $min(a, b)$.

We can implement the andness-directed hyperconjunction using these parameterized t-norms. For each parameter value in the range $[0, +\infty]$, we can compute the corresponding andness, and vice versa, for each desired value of andness in the hyperconjunction range, we can compute the corresponding value of the t-norm parameter. For example, for a t-norm with two arguments and a desired andness $\alpha = 1.5$, the corresponding Yager's norm is obtained for $w = 1$ (the volume under $max(0, a + b - 1)$ is $1/6$, and $\alpha = 2 - 3V = 1.5$).

We can construct andness-directed t-norm for each family of this type. This is reported in [44]. The paper also reports the maximum difference between pairs of t-norms of the above-mentioned families (Yager, Dombi and Schweizer and Sklar). For any andness level, this maximum difference is at most 0.09, and for most pairs and a given andness, the difference is well below 0.05. $T_{SS}(a, b; p)$ seems a quite average t-norm in the sense that the maximum difference with other t-norms is small.

8 Implementations of Logic Aggregators Using OWA Family of Aggregators

OWA is a popular family of idempotent aggregators that cover the range of andness from full conjunction to full disjunction. The initial operator $OWA(X; \alpha)$ defined by Yager in 1988 [16] is a commutative aggregator. It is similar to the weighted arithmetic mean, but it uses *logic weights* to express *andness* and not *importance weights* to express the *relative importance* of inputs. OWA assigns weights to input arguments after ordering them in decreasing order. The motivation for using logic weights is to emphasize the impact of low values (in the case of conjunctive polarization) or high values (in the case of disjunctive polarization). Let $\sigma(i)$ correspond to the index of the ith largest element. Then, for the "andness weight" vector $v = (v_1, \ldots, v_n)$ with $0 \le v_i \le 1$ and normalization $v_1 + \cdots + v_n = 1$, we have

$$OWA(X; \alpha) = v_1 x_{\sigma(1)} + \ldots + v_n x_{\sigma(n)}, \quad x_{\sigma(1)} \ge \cdots \ge x_{\sigma(n)},$$
$$x_{\sigma(1)} = max(X) = disjunction, \quad x_{\sigma(n)} = min(X) = conjunction,$$
$$\alpha = 1 - \omega = 1 - \left[(n-1)v_1 + (n-2)v_2 + \cdots + v_{n-1}\right]/(n-1). \tag{8}$$

It is important to note that definitions of andness (1) and (8) are equivalent. For example, for $n = 4$, $v_1 = 0.1$, $v_2 = 0.2$, $v_3 = 0.3$, $v_4 = 0.4$ and $A(X) = 0.1x_{\sigma(1)} + 0.2x_{\sigma(2)} + 0.3x_{\sigma(3)} + 0.4x_{\sigma(4)}$ the resulting andness is

$$\alpha = 1 - \left(v_1 + \frac{2v_2}{3} + \frac{v_3}{3}\right) = \frac{2}{3} = \frac{1}{3}\left(4 - 5\int_0^1 dx_1 \int_0^1 dx_2 \int_0^1 dx_3 \int_0^1 A(X)dx_4\right).$$

Therefore, $A(X)$ has andness close to the geometric mean $\left(\alpha_{geo}\big|_{n=4} = 0.65\right)$, but the geometric mean is hard, and $A(X)$ is soft. The idea of OWA aggregator is clearly visible for $n = 2$, where

$$\omega = v_1 = 1 - \alpha \Rightarrow OWA(X; \alpha) = v_1 \, max(x_1, x_2) + (1 - v_1) \, min(x_1, x_2)$$
$$= \omega \, max(x_1, x_2) + \alpha \, min(x_1, x_2).$$

The neutrality is achieved for the OWA aggregator when $v_1 = \cdots = v_n = 1/n$. In this case the andness is $\alpha = 1 - [(n-1) + (n-2) + \cdots + 1]/n(n-1) = 1 -$

$[n(n-1)/2]/n(n-1) = 1/2$. The full disjunction is obtained for weights $v_1 = 1$, $v_2 = \cdots = v_n = 0, \alpha = 0$ and the full conjunction for weights $v_1 = \cdots = v_{n-1} = 0$, $v_n = 1$, $\alpha = 1$.

From the standpoint of GL, the initial version of OWA had the following drawbacks:

(1) No importance weights: the weights are used to adjust andness and cannot be used as parameters that directly describe the desired relative importance of arguments.
(2) No simple andness-directedness: OWA andness is not an input and the computation of n weights from the desired value of andness/orness is not straightforward and simple [17, 23].
(3) OWA uncertainty property: for $n > 2$ a desired degree of simultaneity does not produce a unique aggregated value (a given andness $\alpha \in]0, 1[$ in (8) corresponds to an infinite number of distributions of weights and each of them can generate a different value $OWA(X; \alpha)$).
(4) No annihilators: using the arithmetic mean, the original OWA becomes a strictly soft aggregator without capability to support annihilators.

All the above drawbacks can be mitigated or eliminated as shown in subsequent sections. Consequently, the modern OWA is a family of aggregators that provide most features necessary for applicability in GL.

The OWA family of aggregators also includes the iterative OWA (ItOWA) initially proposed in [45] and numerically transformed into andness-directed aggregator in [42]. The idea of ItOWA aggregation is to iteratively apply the elementary bivariate additive form $y = c(x_1 \wedge x_2) + d(x_1 \vee x_2)$ to various pairs of arguments, so that in each iteration the dispersion of the set of n arguments reduces, and after several iterations converges to the resulting aggregated value. In this process the given conjunction degree c and the disjunction degree $d = 1 - c$ penetrate into the aggregation process and characterize its logic properties. ItOWA can also be weighted and expanded to support soft/hard aggregators.

8.1 WOWA: OWA with Importance Weights

The Weighted OWA (WOWA), as it was proposed in [22], was defined with the objective of introducing importance weights into OWA. In this case there are two vectors of weights: $\mathbf{w}$ are the importance weights (w_i is the degree of importance of the ith input $x_i, i = 1, \ldots, n$ and users specify normalized weights $w_1 + \cdots + w_n = 1$), and $\mathbf{v}$ are the logic weights as in the ordinary OWA operator (v_i is the weight of the ith input in the decreasingly sorted list of inputs (8)). The definition, which makes the WOWA a non-commutative version of the OWA, is as follows:

$$WOWA(X; v, w) = \sum_{i=1}^{n} p_i x_{\sigma(i)},$$

$$p_i = \begin{cases} \hat{v}\left(w_{\sigma(1)}\right), & i = 1 \\ \hat{v}\left(\sum_{j=1}^{i} w_{\sigma(j)}\right) - \hat{v}\left(\sum_{j=1}^{i-1} w_{\sigma(j)}\right), & 1 < i \le n. \end{cases} \qquad (9)$$

A nondecreasing function $\hat{v}$ interpolates the points $\{(0, 0)\} \cup \{\left(i/n, \sum_{j=1}^{i} v_j\right)\}_{i=1,\ldots,n}$. In the special case of the arithmetic mean we have

$v_1 = \cdots = v_n = 1/n$ and consequently the points $\{(0, 0)\} \cup \{(i/n, \ i/n)\}_{i=1,\ldots,n}$ are interpolated by the line $\hat{v}(x) = x$. In all cases, $\hat{v}(1) = 1$.

Since WOWA is a mean, it satisfies both $\sum_{i=1}^{n} p_i = 1$ and $\sum_{j=1}^{n} w_{\sigma(j)} = 1$. If we insert $i = n$ in (9) we have $p_n = \hat{v}(1) - \hat{v}\left(\sum_{j=1}^{n-1} w_{\sigma(j)}\right) = 1 - \sum_{i=1}^{n-1} p_i$ and $\hat{v}\left(\sum_{j=1}^{n-1} w_{\sigma(j)}\right) = \sum_{i=1}^{n-1} p_i$. Therefore, the WOWA (9) can be written as follows:

$$WOWA(X; v, w) = \sum_{i=1}^{n} p_i x_{\sigma(i)}; \quad p_i = \hat{v}\left(\sum_{j=1}^{i} w_{\sigma(j)}\right) - \sum_{j=1}^{i-1} p_j, \quad 1 < i \le n.$$

It is useful to note that the computation of parameters of the aggregator occurs dynamically at the run time, and not statically at the criterion design time.

The function $\hat{v} : [0, 1] \to [0, 1]$ can be interpreted as a fuzzy quantifier. The domain $[0,1]$ corresponds to the fraction of arguments that satisfy a property, and $\hat{v}(c)$ is the degree of truth that the property specified by the quantifier is satisfied for all $x \le c$. For example, the quantifier *for all* is defined as 1 for all $x > 0$, the quantifier *more than 50%* as 1 for all $x > 0.5$, and the quantifier *there exists* is defined as 1 only when $x = 1$. Then, $\hat{v}(x) = x^2$ is a fuzzy quantifier of *a few*, while $\hat{v}(x) = \sqrt{x}$ can be seen as a fuzzy quantifier of *almost all*.

Based on the interpretation of fuzzy quantifier we can consider two equivalent definitions of OWA with importance.

- $WOWA(X; v, w)$: WOWA based on logical weights v and importance weights w, as defined in (9).
- $WOWA(X; \hat{v}, w)$: WOWA based on a fuzzy quantifier $\hat{v}$ and importance weights w. This approach was proposed by Yager [30, 31] and Torra [22]. The fuzzy quantifier $\hat{v} : [0, 1] \to [0, 1]$ is such that $\hat{v}(0) = 0$, $\hat{v}(1) = 1$ and increasing. We will use this approach as it has advantages later for andness-directedness.

The selected approach is used as follows. If the importance of the input at the ith position (i.e., $x_{\sigma(i)}$) is w, then its weight is $p_i = \hat{v}(s_{\sigma(i-1)} + w) - \hat{v}(s_{\sigma(i-1)})$, where $s_{\sigma(i-1)}$ denotes the sum of importance weights of its predecessors in the decreasingly sorted list of importance weights. Of course, the largest input has no predecessors and, in that case, $p_1 = \hat{v}(w)$. For example, in the case of our benchmarks, the decreasingly sorted inputs are $1, 0.8, 0.6, 0.4$, and their corresponding importance weights are $0.3, 0.1, 0.4, 0.2$. The 3rd largest input has importance $w = 0.4$, and the accumulated importance of its predecessors is $s_2 = 0.3 + 0.1 = 0.4$. So, the weight of the 3rd largest input is $p_3 = \hat{v}(0.4 + 0.4) - \hat{v}(0.4)$. Using the quantifier $\hat{v}(x) = x^2$ the resulting weight is $p_3 = 0.8^2 - 0.4^2 = 0.48$.

It is easy to see that WOWA generalizes the weighted arithmetic mean when $v_i = 1/n$ or when $\hat{v}(x) = x$ (as in this case $p_i = w_{\sigma(i)}$), and generalizes the OWA when $w_i = 1/n$ (as $p_i = v_i$).

8.2 Distribution of OWA Weights

Definition (8) gives the andness of OWA for a weighting vector v. The determination of OWA weighting vector given the andness is not straightforward. Except for andness/orness equal to 0 and 1, for $n > 2$ there are infinite weighting vectors with the same andness. One of them is assigning weights to the largest and smallest elements, $v_1 = 1 - \alpha$, $v_n = \alpha$, and zero to all others: $v_2 = \ldots = v_{n-1} = 0$. By definition, in this case the andness is $1 - \frac{(n-1)(1-\alpha)+0+\ldots+0}{n-1} = \alpha$, and the resulting OWA is a linear combination of minimum and maximum while all other arguments are ignored.

For given andness and given values of input arguments, the infinite number of logic weighting vectors yields an infinite number of aggregated degrees of truth. In order to realize a deterministic mapping $[0, 1]^n \to [0, 1]$, the OWA approach to aggregation needs a restrictive condition that for each desired andness selects a single logic weight distribution. MEOWA, introduced in [36], consists of selecting the logic weighting vector with weights as much dispersed as possible, in order to give all inputs equal opportunities to affect the output. MEOWA is defined in terms of an optimization problem (see [29] and [23]). In the case of OWA/WOWA definitions based on fuzzy quantifiers (instead of on logic weights) we face the same problem, as multiple quantifiers yield the same andness. Note that the same difficulties and approach apply to WOWA as importance weights are not relevant when computing global andness.

In order to make the problem tractable, we constrain $WOWA(X; \hat{v}, w)$ to use a selected family of quantifiers so that there is a unique quantifier for a given andness. To support a spectrum of properties, we use the family of functions $Q_a(x) = x^a$. If $a \to 0$ then the quantifier Q_a tends to the quantifier *for all*, WOWA becomes the maximum, and andness is 0. If $a = 1$ we have $Q_a(x) = x$, WOWA is the weighted mean and andness is 0.5. If $a \to +\infty$ then Q_a tends to the quantifier *there exists*, WOWA becomes the minimum, and andness is one. Details on these properties are presented in [7]. In [39] we provide an analysis of andness using alternative families of quantifiers. We can see that different families provide quite similar results for a given andness.

8.3 Annihilators for OWA: GOWA and OWG

Neither OWA nor WOWA allow for annihilators. In contrast, the geometric OWA or ordered weighted geometric mean (OWG [17, 28]) has zero as annihilator, and it is derived as a special case of the Generalized OWA aggregator (GOWA) [17]:

$$GOWA(X; r, v) = \left(\sum_{i=1}^{n} v_i x_{\sigma(i)}^r \right)^{1/r}, \quad -\infty \le r \le \infty, \quad \sum_{i=1}^{n} v_i = 1. \quad (10)$$

GOWA is a very general aggregator, because for weights equal to $1/n$ GOWA becomes the power mean $(x_1^r/n + \cdots + x_n^r/n)^{1/r}$ providing the possibility of continuous transition from the full conjunction to the full disjunction. For example, when $r \to +\infty$ the GOWA becomes the maximum (the full disjunction) and when $r \to -\infty$ the GOWA becomes the minimum (the full conjunction). When $r \to 0$ the GOWA (10) becomes the following geometric OWA or ordered weighted geometric mean (OWG):

$$OWG(X; v, w) = \prod_{i=1}^{n} x_{\sigma(i)}^{v_i}, \quad \sum_{i=1}^{n} v_i = 1.$$

The geometric OWA has the annihilator zero in the same way as the geometric mean. In addition, GOWA supports the annihilator 0 for any value $r \leq 0$.

It is easy to generalize $GOWA(X; v)$ and $OWG(X; v)$ to incorporate importance weights. This can be done in the same way as we did with the WOWA. So, again, we have two options: using either the logical weights v, or a fuzzy quantifier $\hat{v} : [0, 1] \to [0, 1]$. We introduce the second approach and expand the GOWA as follows:

$$GWOWA\left(X; r, \hat{v},\ w\right) = \left(\sum_{i=1}^{n} p_i x_{\sigma(i)}^r\right)^{1/r}, \quad -\infty \leq r \leq \infty,$$

where $p_i = \hat{v}\left(\sum_{j=1}^{i} w_{\sigma(j)}\right) - \hat{v}\left(\sum_{j=1}^{i-1} w_{\sigma(j)}\right)$. Any fuzzy quantifier can be used here, but we will restrict our analysis to $\hat{v}(x) = Q_a(x) = x^a$.

8.4 Andness-Directed OWA with Annihilators

There are no closed forms for the volume-based global andness and orness of OWG or GOWA. The same applies to GWOWA as its andness does not depend on the importance weights. In [17], Yager introduced the indicator $\omega_{GOWA} = \left(\sum_{i=1}^{n} v_i((n - i)/(n - 1))^r\right)^{1/r}$, called "the attitudinal character of aggregator" and similar to orness. However, for $r \neq 1, \omega_{GOWA} \neq \omega$, and the global andness must be computed numerically using Eq. (1). This is the approach we use here.

For an OWA-like aggregator that supports uniform distribution of soft and hard properties we need the annihilator 0 for $\alpha \geq 0.75$ and no annihilators for $0.25 < \alpha < 0.75$. For $\alpha < 0.5$ we use De Morgan's duality to provide the annihilator 1 for $\alpha \leq 0.25$. For $\alpha = 0.5$ our approach reduces to WOWA with $\hat{v}(x) = x$, and the application of De Morgan's rule is valid because autoduality $1 - WOWA\left(X; \hat{v}, w\right) = WOWA\left(1 - X; \hat{v}, w\right)$, and continuity at $\alpha = 0.5$.

Our approach is to use GWOWA with a family of fuzzy quantifiers that depend on r. In the case of four inputs, we will use the following family of quantifiers:

$$\hat{v}_r(x) = x^{e^{\frac{1-r}{2.6}}}, \quad -\infty \leq r \leq \infty.$$

This family of functions and the constant 2.6 are selected to provide a convenient form of mapping between the parameter r and the desired GWOWA andness, shown in Table 2. First, GWOWA with this quantifier only depends on the parameter r, the importance weights w and the input data X: $GWOWA\left(X; r, \hat{v}_r, w\right)$. Next, the fuzzy quantifiers are defined so that for $r \to -\infty$ GWOWA becomes the minimum (that is, $\hat{v}_{-\infty}(x) = x^a$ with $a \to \infty$). For $r \to 0$ the GWOWA becomes a geometric-like OWA with $\hat{v}_0(x) = x^{1.469}$ and andness equal to 0.75 (so that for values of α smaller than 0.75 GWOWA has zero as annihilator). For $r = 1$ GWOWA is equivalent to WOWA (because $\hat{v}_1(x) = x$), and for $r \to +\infty$ GWOWA becomes the maximum ($\hat{v}_{+\infty}(x) = x^a$ with $a \to 0$).

Table 2. Andness for $GWOWA(X; r, \hat{v}_r, w)$ for different values of the parameter r.

Parameter r for $GWOWA(X; r, \hat{v}_r, w)$	Andness of $GWOWA(X; r, \hat{v}_r, w)$
−8.00	0.999
−1.00	0.894
−0.80	0.876
−0.70	0.865
0.00	0.751
0.50	0.627
0.55	0.614
1.00	0.500

We need to point out that for each number of inputs we need to define a slightly different family of fuzzy quantifiers so that for $r = 0$ andness is 0.75.

Now we can numerically compute the global andness for each r. The andness is by definition computed for equal importance weights. Its range is [0,1] because we can represent both maximum and minimum, and there is a smooth transition between them. In fact, andness is monotonic with respect to the parameter r. Table 2 shows the andness for different values of r (this table is a summary of a working table with much higher precision). Then, we can use interpolation and the information in this table, to find r for desired andness degree. For example, if we require an andness equal to 0.625, we need to use $r = 0.508$. In this way we can compute any andness-directed GWOWA (see Sect. 8.6).

In [39] we discuss a similar approach for other quantifiers. In addition, we show how to find the GOWA and quantifier for a given andness α and a given α_θ. Therefore, it is possible to use threshold andness different from $\alpha_\theta = 0.75$.

8.5 The OWA Family for GCD

With the OWA family we can implement most GCD requirements (see also [42, 43]). We consider the different conjunctive functions discussed in Sect. 4 and summarized in Table 1. Recall that disjunctive operators can be defined by duality. Neutrality can be implemented with OWA and equal weights, and, thus, corresponds to $GWOWA(X; r, \hat{v}_r, w)$ with $r = 1$. Soft partial conjunction can be modeled with OWA for any andness level smaller than 0.75. $GWOWA(X; r, \hat{v}_r, w)$ for any $r > 1$ becomes a soft partial disjunction. Hard partial conjunction can be implemented with OWG, for any andness level. Hard partial disjunction is created as a dual of hard partial conjunction. GOWA functions for any $r \leq 0$ have annihilators zero. Full conjunction can be achieved by OWA, OWG, and GOWA when we assign weights to the lowest element and the operators are equal to the minimum. For the full disjunction we select the highest of sorted arguments. Neither low hyperconjunction, medium hyperconjunction nor high hyperconjunction can be modeled by OWA, OWG or GOWA, because these functions are defined as idempotent means.

8.6 Solutions of Benchmark Problems

Benchmark S. We use GWOWA with andness $\alpha = 0.625$ and importance weights $w_1 = 0.1$, $w_2 = 0.2$, $w_3 = 0.3$ and $w_4 = 0.4$. A numerical approximation based on Table 2, for andness of 0.625 yields $r = 0.508$. Therefore, we use GWOWA with the following fuzzy quantifier:

$$\hat{v}_r(x) = x^{e^{(1-r)/2.6}} = x^t, \quad t = 1.208526.$$

Actual weights can be computed only after the variables x_1, x_2, x_3, x_4 are known, because the weights depend on the ordering of inputs. These weights are computed as follows:

$$p_i = \left(\sum_{j=1}^{i} w_{\sigma(j)} \right)^t - \left(\sum_{j=1}^{i-1} w_{\sigma(j)} \right)^t$$

$$= \left(\sum_{j=1}^{i} w_{\sigma(j)} \right)^t - \sum_{j=1}^{i-1} p_j, \quad i = 1, \ldots, n.$$

So, we need to decreasingly sort the input values (i.e., 1, 0.8, 0.6, 0.4) and arrange accordingly the importance (i.e., 0.3, 0.1, 0.4, 0.2). Then, we compute the following weights:

$p_1 = (0.3)^t = 0.234$
$p_2 = (0.3 + 0.1)^t - (0.3)^t = (0.3 + 0.1)^t - p_1 = 0.097$
$p_3 = (0.3 + 0.1 + 0.4)^t - (0.3 + 0.1)^t = (0.3 + 0.1 + 0.4)^t - p_2 - p_1 = 0.433$
$p_4 = (0.3 + 0.1 + 0.4 + 0.2)^t - (0.3 + 0.1 + 0.4)^t = 1 - p_3 - p_2 - p_1 = 0.236.$

Assuming $r = 0.508$, we can now compute the aggregated degree of truth:

$$GWOWA(X; r, \hat{v}_r, w) = \left(\sum_{i=1}^{n} p_i x_{\sigma(i)}^r \right)^{1/r}$$

$$= \left(0.234 \cdot 1^r + 0.097 \cdot 0.8^r + 0.433 \cdot 0.6^r + 0.236 \cdot 0.4^r \right)^{1/r} = 0.649.$$

Benchmark H. In this case, in addition to the importance weights $w_1 = 0.1$, $w_2 = 0.2$, $w_3 = 0.3$ and $w_4 = 0.4$ and andness $\alpha = 0.875$, we have the requirement to support the annihilator zero. As GWOWA with $\alpha > 0.75$ results in an operator with annihilator zero, the process is the same as for Benchmark S. Using a numerical approximation based on Table 2, it follows that andness of 0.875 corresponds to $r = -0.795$. Therefore, we use GWOWA with the following fuzzy quantifier:

$$\hat{v}_r(x) = x^{e^{(1-r)/2.6}} = x^t, \quad t = 1.994.$$

Using the same procedure as in the case of the S benchmark we have the following results:

$$p_1 = 0.091, \quad p_2 = 0.070, \quad p_3 = 0.480, \quad p_4 = 0.359$$

$$GWOWA(X; r, \hat{v}_r, w) = (0.091 \cdot 1^{-0.795} + 0.070 \cdot 0.8^{-0.795} + \\ + 0.480 \cdot 0.6^{-0.795} + 0.359 \cdot 0.4^{-0.795})^{-1/0.795} = 0.537.$$

Benchmark C. This problem cannot be solved neither with the OWA nor with GOWA.

9 Implementations of Logic Aggregators Using Fuzzy Integrals

Fuzzy integrals (FI, see [7]) can be interpreted as aggregators. If an aggregator has n inputs, then there are 2^n subsets of inputs. FIs offer the possibility to separately define specific aggregation properties for each subset of inputs. That can describe specific interactions between inputs in a way that is more general than the cases of aggregation based on OWA or WPM aggregators where we assume independence of arguments. Of course, the price of generality is very high, because adding a single argument doubles the complexity (in terms of the number of required parameters) and effort in using fuzzy integrals.

Choquet and Sugeno integrals [35, 37] are the two most used FIs. They generalize the weighted mean, OWA, WOWA and both weighted minimum and maximum. Constraining the parameters of the integrals in appropriate ways, the FIs reduce to some of well-known aggregation operators (e.g. the weighted means). In this way, we can implement all kind of weighted means, and, particularly, to provide a way to represent importance weights.

If our requirements for logic aggregators are about the use of annihilators, importance weights and a given andness degree, the use of operators from the OWA family and the WPM-based aggregators as described in the two previous section seems sufficient, as they already provide these capabilities. In this case, the advantage of using the FI armamentarium is unclear.

In the literature, FIs are regularly exemplified using aggregators with small number of interdependent inputs. Most professional evaluation problems have aggregators with independent inputs, large number of aggregators and aggregators with more than 3 inputs, where the use of FIs frequently becomes rather difficult and unjustified. In addition, there are open questions related to using FIs in aggregation structures. First, there is a possibility that some FI aggregators with more than 2 inputs can be approximated with simple logic aggregation structures that use 2 or more GCD aggregators. Second, there is a possibility that some of interdependencies of inputs can be modeled using nonstationary WPM aggregators [4] where weights and andness are appropriate functions of input arguments. Therefore, we see the comparison of FIs and nonstationary GCD aggregators as a topic for future research.

FIs can be built to generalize the members of the OWA family. Consequently, it is justifiable to consider that FIs provide the capability to solve benchmark problems that is equivalent to the capabilities of the OWA family.

10 Implementations of Logic Aggregators Using Means

Idempotent logic aggregators are based on means. Of course, the number of candidate means is very large, and a natural question is how to select the most appropriate mean.

The criterion for comparison and selection of means is based on the following five basic requirements that the candidate means must satisfy:

- Support for aggregation of any number of arguments ($n \geq 2$)
- Nondecreasing monotonicity in all arguments (i.e. the analyzed mean is an aggregator)
- Continuous parameterized transition from conjunction to disjunction using a single parameter (andness-directedness)
- Support for hard and soft aggregation (selectability of annihilators)
- Support for importance-weighted aggregation (noncommutativity)

Weighted power means naturally support all the above requirements. Regarding other means, if they are aggregators, they can be analyzed from the standpoint of their comparison with WPM, or with interpolative aggregators based on WPM (GCD/ADIA). More precisely, for each idempotent aggregator we can ask a critical question "what is the characteristic property and distinctive difference between the analyzed mean and the WPM?" The basic analysis can be reduced to the case of two variables and equal weights. Indeed, all unweighted bivariate means can be transformed to weighted idempotent means of n variables using the method of binary aggregation trees [4, 14]. If a specific mean has no advantages with respect to WPM in the simplest case of two variables, there is no reason to believe that the situation will be more favorable in the case of more than two variables.

The analysis and comparison of means can be exemplified using the case of Bonferroni means [19] that attracted attention of many researchers [18, 32–34]. In the case of two variables let us consider the following Bonferroni mean:

$$B_2^{p,q}(x, y) = \left(0.5x^p y^q + 0.5x^q y^p\right)^{\frac{1}{p+q}}, \quad p \geq 0, \quad q \geq 0, \quad p + q > 0.$$

If $p = q = r > 0$ then $B_2^{r,r}(x, y) = (x^r y^r)^{1/2r} = \sqrt{xy}$, i.e. $B_2^{r,r}$ reduces to the geometric mean. If $p = 0$, $q = r > 0$, then $B_2^{0,r}(x, y) = (0.5x^r + 0.5y^r)^{1/r}$ and again $B_2^{0,r}$ reduces to the power mean aggregator. So, let us see a Bonferroni mean that has some properties different from power means, e.g. $p = 0.5$, $q = 1.5$. Now we have

$$B_2^{0.5,1.5}(x, y) = \left(0.5x^{0.5}y^{1.5} + 0.5x^{1.5}y^{0.5p}\right)^{1/2} = \left((0.5y + 0.5x)\sqrt{xy}\right)^{1/2}.$$

This Bonferroni mean is again a combination of power means (the geometric mean of the arithmetic and geometric means). So, let us now compare $B_2^{0.5,1.5}$ with the original power mean $M^{[\alpha]}(x, y) = (0.5x^{r(\alpha)} + 0.5x^{r(\alpha)})^{1/r(\alpha)}$, $0 \leq \alpha \leq 1$. To analyze the differences between the Bonferroni mean and the power mean let us define the following mean and maximum differences between an arbitrary mean $F(x, y)$ and the adjusted power mean $M^{[\alpha_{opt}]}(x, y)$ which is the closest approximation of $F(x, y)$:

$$D_{ave} = \min_{0 \leq \alpha \leq 1} \frac{1}{(n+1)^2} \sum_{i=0}^{n} \sum_{j=0}^{n} \left| F\left(\frac{i}{n}, \frac{j}{n}\right) - M^{[\alpha]}\left(\frac{i}{n}, \frac{j}{n}\right) \right|$$

$$= \frac{1}{(n+1)^2} \sum_{i=0}^{n} \sum_{j=0}^{n} \left| F\left(\frac{i}{n}, \frac{j}{n}\right) - M^{[\alpha_{opt}^{ave}]}\left(\frac{i}{n}, \frac{j}{n}\right) \right|$$

$$D_{max} = \min_{0 \leq \alpha \leq 1} \max_{i,j} \left| F\left(\frac{i}{n}, \frac{j}{n}\right) - M^{[\alpha]}\left(\frac{i}{n}, \frac{j}{n}\right) \right| = \max_{i,j} \left| F\left(\frac{i}{n}, \frac{j}{n}\right) - M^{[\alpha_{opt}^{max}]}\left(\frac{i}{n}, \frac{j}{n}\right) \right|.$$

So, α_{opt}^{ave} and α_{opt}^{max} are the values of andness that correspond to the power means that are closest (most similar) to the analyzed mean $F(x, y)$. In the unit hypercube, the values of D_{ave} and D_{max} must be less than 1. If they are significantly less than 1, that indicates that the analyzed mean $F(x, y)$ is very similar to the power mean. In the case of $B_2^{p,q}(x, y)$, if $p = 0.5$, $q = 1.5$, then for $\alpha_{opt}^{ave} = 0.5937$ we have the smallest average difference $D_{ave} = 0.004$, and for $\alpha_{opt}^{max} = 0.6296$ we have the smallest maximum difference $D_{max} = 0.0529$. Obviously, from the practical applicability standpoint, in many cases these differences are negligible. For bigger values of p and q the differences are slightly bigger: e.g., in the case $p = 1$, $q = 3$, for $\alpha_{opt}^{ave} = 0.5457$ we have the smallest average difference $D_{ave} = 0.011$ and for $\alpha_{opt}^{max} = 0.6202$ we have the smallest maximum difference $D_{max} = 0.0928$. These results indicate that for the analyzed cases of Bonferroni mean there is always a power mean that can be adjusted to behave in a very similar way. So, we cannot offer an answer to the critical question "what is a distinctive advantage of the Bonferroni mean with respect to the power mean for applications in GL?".

Generalized logarithmic mean (GLM) is one of rare means that provide andness-directedness based on adjustment of the parameter r, as follows:

$$GLM(x, y) = \begin{cases} \min(x, y), & r = -\infty & \text{(conjunction)} \\ (x - y)/(\log x - \log y), & r = -1 & \text{(logarithmic)} \\ \left(\frac{y^{r+1} - x^{r+1}}{(r+1)(y-x)}\right)^{1/r}, & r \notin \{-\infty, -1, 0, +\infty\} & \text{(general)} \\ e^{-1}(x^x/y^y)^{1/(x-y)}, & r = 0 & \text{(identric)} \\ \max(x, y), & r = +\infty & \text{(disjunction)} \end{cases}$$

In addition to Bonferroni mean, in Table 3 we present the results of the same analysis of differences between the power mean for the following characteristic cases of means/aggregators: OWA, OWG, GOWA, exponential mean, Heronian mean, generalized logarithmic mean, centroidal mean, and the counter-harmonic mean (in the range of exponents where the counter-harmonic mean is monotonically nondecreasing). Generally, the resulting values of D_{ave} and D_{max} are small. The average difference between the analyzed aggregators and the power mean are typically less than 2%, and the maximum differences are frequently less than 5%. The reasons for the small differences are the following: (1) all analyzed functions and the power mean are idempotent and the differences along the line $z = x = y$ are zero, (2) the power mean can be hard or soft and therefore the differences along the coordinate axes ($x = 0$ and $y = 0$) are either zero or small, and (3) both the power means and the analyzed functions are monotonically nondecreasing (i.e. aggregators) and this property enhances the similarity. Small differences prove the expressive power of WPM and ADIA to adapt to variety of aggregation forms provided by a spectrum of popular means/aggregators.

Table 3. Differences between selected means and the weighted power mean.

Analyzed mean of two variables				Closest power mean			
Name	$F(x, y)$	Parameters	Andness	α_{opt}^{ave}	D_{ave}	α_{opt}^{max}	D_{max}
OWA	$a\,min(x, y) + (1 - a)max(x, y)$	$a = 0.125$	0.125 S	0.136	0.016	0.146	0.0412
OWA	$a\,min(x, y) + (1 - a)max(x, y)$	$a = 0.25$	0.250 S	0.2748	0.020	0.292	0.0505
OWG	$min(x, y)^a max(x, y)^{(1-a)}$	$a = 0.6$	0.750 H	0.7358	0.0117	0.722	0.0290
GOWA	$\left(0.5\,min(x, y)^r + 0.5\,max(x, y)^r\right)^{1/r}$	$r = -1$	0.773 H	0.773	0	0.773	0
GOWA	$\left(0.5\,min(x, y)^r + 0.5\,max(x, y)^r\right)^{1/r}$	$r = 3.93$	0.250 S	0.250	0	0.250	0
GLM	$\left(\left(y^{r+1} - x^{r+1}\right)/(r + 1)(y - x)\right)^{1/r}$	$r = -4.525$	0.750 H	0.7517	0.002	0.742	0.0100
Log	$(x - y)/(log\,x - log\,y)$	$r = -1$	0.614 H	0.614	0.0014	0.633	0.0410
GLM	$\left(\left(y^{r+1} - x^{r+1}\right)/(r + 1)(y - x)\right)^{1/r}$	$r = -0.95$	0.611 S	0.611	0.0011	0.625	0.0297
Identric	$e^{-1}(x^x/y^y)^{1/(x-y)}$	$r = 0$	0.553 S	0.554	0.0003	0.551	0.0035
GLM	$\left(\left(y^{r+1} - x^{r+1}\right)/(r + 1)(y - x)\right)^{1/r}$	$r = 12.9$	0.250 S	0.253	0.005	0.260	0.0144
C-harm	$(x^r + y^r)/\left(x^{r-1} + y^{r-1}\right),\ 0 \le r \le 1$	$r = 0.7$	0.607 H	0.606	0.0027	0.633	0.0412
Expo	$r^{-1}log(0.5\,exp(rx) + 0.5\,exp(ry))$	$r = -1$	0.561 S	0.557	0.0067	0.549	0.0331
Expo	$r^{-1}log(0.5\,exp(rx) + 0.5\,exp(ry))$	$r = 1$	0.439 S	0.438	0.0050	0.444	0.0240
Heron	$(x + \sqrt{xy} + y)/3$	n/a	0.555 S	0.5555	0.0004	0.559	0.0051
Centroid	$2\left(x^2 + xy + y^2\right)/3(x + y)$	n/a	0.409 S	0.409	0	0.408	0.0016
Bonferroni	$\left(0.5x^p y^q + 0.5x^q y^p\right)^{1/(p+q)}$	$p = 0.5$ $q = 1.5$	0.595 H	0.5937	0.0040	0.630	0.0529

Note: S = soft aggregator (no annihilator), H = hard aggregator (conjunctive annihilator 0)

Table 4. Basic properties of selected important means.

Aggregator	Number of arguments	Nondecreasing monotonicity	Andness directedness	Hard	Soft	Importance weights
OWA	n	Yes	Yes	No	Yes	No
OWG	n	Yes	No	Yes	No	No
GOWA	n	Yes	Yes	Yes	Yes	No
ItOWA	n	Yes	Yes	Yes	Yes	Yes
GLM	2	Yes	Yes	Yes	Yes	No
Expo	n	Yes	Yes	No	Yes	Yes
WPM	n	Yes	Yes	Yes	Yes	Yes

Considering that imprecision and uncertainty in human reasoning easily cause variations of degrees of truth that are of the order of 10% or more, it follows that differences between an adjusted WPM and various other aggregators based on means are less than the imprecision of arguments generated by decision makers [43]. The comparison of basic properties of selected important means is shown in Table 4. Therefore, we have a reason to believe that GCD/ADIA provides simplicity and flexibility that are sufficient for modeling logic aggregators in GL and to create decision models based on interpretable and explainable criterion functions [38].

11   Evaluation and Comparison of Logic Aggregators

Whenever there are alternative ways to solve a problem, it is natural to ask for evaluation and comparison of alternatives. In the case of logic aggregators and their implementations, the evaluation process can be based on the following main suitability attributes (a more detailed analysis can be found in [40, 41]):

- Consistency with human reasoning
- Functionality and generality
- Readability and usability (simplicity of use)
- Performance and computational complexity

Consistency with human reasoning is the fundamental requirement for all logic aggregation structures. Indeed, logic aggregators are defined and developed with explicit and justifiable intention to model human mental activities in the area of decision making. In humancentric graded logic, all aggregators are based on GCD and serve as functional components of a soft computing propositional calculus. Properties such as nondecreasing monotonicity, noncommutativity, sensitivity to positive and incomplete truth, absence of discontinuities in aggregation functions and their derivatives, semantic interpretation of arguments and importance weights, parameterized continuous transition from drastic conjunction to drastic disjunction, adjustability of simultaneity and substitutability, andness-directedness, selectability of annihilators, nonincreasing monotonicity in andness, etc. are all derived from observation of human reasoning [4]. These properties also support interpretability and explainability of evaluation results [39].

Consistency with human reasoning is an important area that requires delicate experiments with human subjects [47]. Among the earliest research results, the minimum function (conjunction) and the product (hyperconjunctive t-norm) were analyzed from the standpoint of correct fitting of an empirically defined conjunctive aggregator [24]. Insufficient success in those experiments indicated that means could be useful conjunctive aggregators, and was the motivation for creating a compensative Gamma aggregator that implements a continuous transition between conjunctive and disjunctive aggregation: $X = (\Pi_{i=1}^n x_i)^{1-\gamma}(1 - \Pi_{i=1}^n(1 - x_i))^\gamma$ [25]. The parameter γ plays the role similar to the disjunction degree (orness). This aggregator is nonidempotent and strictly hard, but provided a sufficiently good fit of selected experimental data. It was subsequently successfully investigated in [26] and expanded with an additive disjunctive form $X = (1 - \gamma)(\Pi_{i=1}^n x_i) + \gamma(1 - \Pi_{i=1}^n(1 - x_i))$. A similar experimental analysis was provided in [27]. A comparison of Gamma aggregator and GCD can be found in [4], and it shows that GCD fits the Gamma aggregator experimental data slightly better than the Gamma aggregator itself, while fully supporting the humancentric concepts of GL, which is not the case with the Gamma aggregator. This result indicates the consistency of idempotent GCD with human reasoning, as well as a need for empirical investigation of the suitability of ADIA in the area of hyperconjunction and hyperdisjunction.

Table 5. Comparison of methods for realization of logic aggregators.

Logic function	GCD / ADIA	OWA	OWG	WOWA	ItOWA	FI	Means
Drastic conjunction	Yes	No	No	No	No	No	No
High hyper-conjunction	Yes:W	No	No	No	No	No	No
Medium hyper-conjunction	Yes:W	No	No	No	No	No	No
Low hyper-conjunction	Yes: W	No	No	No	No	No	No
Full conjunction	Yes	Yes	Yes	Yes	Yes	Yes	Yes
Hard partial conjunction	Yes: W	No	Yes	No: G	No: G	No: G	Y/N
Soft partial conjunction	Yes: W	Yes	No	Yes: W	Yes: W	Yes: W	Y/N
Neutrality	Yes: W	Yes	No	Yes: W	Yes: W	Yes: W	Yes
Soft partial disjunction	Yes: W	Yes	No	Yes: W	Yes: W	Yes: W	Y/N
Hard partial disjunction	Yes: W	No	No	No: G	No: G	No: G	Y/N
Full disjunction	Yes	Yes	No	Yes	Yes	Yes	Yes
Low hyper-disjunction	Yes: W	No	No	No	No	No	No
Medium hyper-disjunction	Yes: W	No	No	No	No	No	No
High hyper-disjunction	Yes: W	No	No	No	No	No	No
Drastic disjunction	Yes	No	No	No	No	No	No

Notes: W denotes the availability of importance weights. Y/N denotes variations between various types of weighted, unweighted, parameterized and non-parameterized means. G denotes that the logic function can only be supported using the variants of OWA, WOWA, ItOWA and FI based on product (OWG, GOWA, and similar operators).

Functionality and generality are the primary criteria for evaluation of suitability of logic aggregators. The comparison of functionality can be organized as shown in Table 5. While some of the selected aggregators do not satisfy the whole GL functionality range, they are certainly applicable in the area of their primary definition. For example, in the area of soft aggregation OWA and WOWA can be equally applicable as ADIA. In addition, while most of aggregators shown in Table 5 are not originally defined in the areas of hyperconjunction and hyperdisjunction they can be extended in these areas using the same interpolative expansion that is used for GCD/ADIA.

Table 6. Idempotent aggregator selection query.

Q1	Is the aggregator symmetric or asymmetric?		
A1	Symmetric (GCD)	Asymmetric (partial absorption, PA)	
Q2	Is the GCD conjunctive or disjunctive?	Is the PA conjunctive or disjunctive?	
Q3	Is the aggregator hard or soft?	Conjunctive	Disjunctive
Q4	Select the desired andness	Select the desired mean penalty	
Q5	Select the desired importance weights	Select the desired mean reward	

Readability and usability are two related properties that affect the simplicity of use of aggregators. Unsurprisingly, from the standpoint of decision engineering practice, the simplicity of use is an extremely important criterion for the evaluation of logic aggregators. It is clearly visible in professional evaluation projects. Complex evaluation criteria, e.g. those based on the LSP method [4], are developed aggregator by aggregator, and the number of aggregators can be large. The idempotent aggregators are selected according to the selection query summarized in Table 6, and the andness of GCD is selected according to a verbalized process discussed below.

The design of an aggregator consists of using $(Q_1, ..., Q_5)$ to derive the corresponding analytical form of the aggregator, $A(x_1, ..., x_n)$. This process can be symbolically denoted as $(Q_1, Q_2, Q_3, Q_4, Q_5) \Rightarrow A(x_1, ..., x_n)$. The readability of aggregators is defined as the possibility to easily perform the opposite transformation, $A(x_1, ..., x_n) \Rightarrow (Q_1, Q_2, Q_3, Q_4, Q_5)$, i.e. to quickly read the vital parameters of an aggregator from its analytic form. Consequently, the concept of usability can be based on bidirectional relation $A(x_1, ..., x_n) \Leftrightarrow (Q_1, Q_2, Q_3, Q_4, Q_5)$: usability of logic aggregators is high if the effort necessary to go in both directions of the bidirectional relation is low.

The first question is the selection between GCD and partial absorption (PA, models of mandatory/optional, and sufficient/optional requirements). If the desired aggregator is the symmetric GCD then the next question is to select conjunctive, disjunctive, or neutral variant of GCD. The third question, hard or soft, is very easy to answer: in the case of conjunctive GCD, the stakeholder decides whether the absence of one of inputs can be tolerated (soft aggregator, "nice-to-have") or cannot be tolerated (hard aggregator, "must-have"). If the selected option is hard, then it is necessary to select the conjunction degree or andness. The andness is the most natural input because it reflects the desired strength of hard simultaneity. This easiest way to select the andness is to use a verbalized scale like the scale shown in Table 7 where for each of hard and soft, conjunctive and disjunctive segments, we have three simple levels: low, medium, and high. The last step is to directly specify importance weights. Because of independence of relative importance and andness, the weights can be selected before or after the selection of andness.

Table 7. Selection of andness in the case of UGCD15.

	Conjunctive GCD						Neu-tral GCD	Disjunctive GCD						
	Hard conjunction			Soft conjunction				Soft disjunction			Hard disjunction			
min	High	Med	Low	High	Med	Low	GCD	Low	Med	High	Low	Med	High	max
C	HC+	HC	HC-	SC+	SC	SC-	A	SD-	SD	SD+	HD-	HD	HD+	D
1	0.93	0.86	0.79	0.71	0.64	0.57	0.5	0.43	0.36	0.29	0.21	0.14	0.07	0
Andness with step 1/14														

The presented procedure is simple, natural, and fully consistent with human logic reasoning. The question is how this intuitive procedure translates to creating aggregators with GCD/ADIA, OWA, OWG, WOWA, means, and FI. For example, let the number of inputs be $n = 3$. The decision maker thinks that the first input is more important than the second input, which is more important than the third input. If the first input is equally important as the remaining two inputs together, the appropriate importance weights might be 0.5, 0.3, and 0.2. Suppose now that the decision maker feels that the aggregator must be a hard partial conjunction, and its level is medium, yielding (from Table 7) the andness of 0.86. Therefore, the simple procedure [Q1 → Q2 → Q3 → Q4 → Q5] = [GCD → conjunctive → hard → medium → w] creates the desired input parameters $\alpha = 0.86$, $w_1 = 0.5$, $w_2 = 0.3$, $w_3 = 0.2$. From this specification of desired parameters, we now have to create the aggregator.

An important aspect of readability and simplicity of aggregators is related to the difference between two forms of aggregators: *stationary* and *nonstationary*. The stationary form is the definitional form with constant parameters that is obtained when the desired andness, annihilators, and importance weights are selected, and it is independent of the values of input arguments. The nonstationary form is the form where parameters are functions of input arguments. For example, all versions of OWA aggregators cannot aggregate arguments unless the arguments are sorted. Parameters of the aggregator (e.g. logic weights) must be separately computed for each specific set of arguments. So, all OWA aggregators don't have the stationary form. Obviously, nonstationary aggregators are less readable and more computationally demanding than stationary aggregators.

In the case of GCD/ADIA we use $r = r_{wpm}(0.86, 3) = -2.62$ and the resulting stationary aggregator is $y = (0.5x_1^{-2.62} + 0.3x_2^{-2.62} + 0.2x_3^{-2.62})^{-1/2.62}$. This aggregator is readable, and it uses fixed parameters independent of input values. In the case of other aggregators, the production of this functionality would be much more complex.

For $GWOWA(X; r, \hat{v}_r, w)$, we follow the approach in Sect. 8 and use $\hat{v}_r(x) = x^a$ for $a = (e^{-r+1})^{1/2.91} = 1.792$ and $r = -0.697$. The expression of the quantifier is computed from the fact that we have three inputs and we want an andness equal to 0.86. Then, we have to compute weights in the $y = (p_1 x_1^{-0.697} + p_2 x_2^{-0.697} + p_3 x_3^{-0.697})^{-1/0.697}$. Note that this aggregator does not have constant parameters: the weights p_1, p_2, p_3 depend on the values of input arguments. Consequently, the readability of the aggregator is rather low.

If we try to use other means, only GLM offers continuous and parameterized transition from conjunction to disjunction. Unfortunately, GLM supports only two variables and is not weighted. We would have to use a binary tree of such aggregators to transform it to a corresponding logarithmic aggregator with three inputs and equal weights. For that aggregator we would need to numerically compute the andness for a sequence of values of exponent r, i.e. to create the function $\alpha = f_{log}(r, n)$. Then it would be necessary to numerically create the inverse function $r = r_{log}(\alpha, n)$. From this function we could compute $r_3 = r_{log}(0.86, 3)$. The next step would be to use r_3 and once again create the binary tree of unweighted logarithmic aggregators $[(y^{r_3+1} - x^{r_3+1})/(r_3 + 1)(y - x)]^{1/r_3}$ and adjust it to create the final aggregator with desired weights 0.5, 0.3, and 0.2.

What would be the result obtained at the end of this painful acrobatics? Most likely, the result would be an aggregator that is very similar to the WPM aggregator that can be obtained in no time. In addition, we would not be able to explain what the distinctive properties of the resulting logarithmic aggregator are, and to justify the reasons of using it instead of WPM.

Comparable situations regarding the similarity with WPM would be encountered with other investigated aggregators in the families of OWA and fuzzy integrals. In the latter case, only when information about more complex relationships between attributes (e.g., explicit interactions between attributes) is available the use of fuzzy integrals would be appropriate, but at the cost of an increased number of parameters (i.e., 2^n parameters).

Performance and computational complexity are two related aspects, where performance reflects the consumption of computing resources and computational complexity reflects the algorithmic complexity which affects both the performance and the necessary human effort in building logic aggregators and GL aggregation structures. In the case of aggregation structures that have N input arguments the largest number of individual logic aggregators (for the case of binary aggregation tree) is N-1. In the case of professional evaluation criteria the value of N is between a few dozen and a few hundred.

Differences in performance and computational complexity are visible in the previous example of three inputs, desired andness equal to 0.86, and importance weights 0.5, 0.3, 0.2 where the stationary GCD aggregator needs only the computation of WPM. For the same problem, the computation of GWOWA consists of six steps (1) sorting of arguments, (2) selection of the fuzzy quantifier, (3) computation of Table 2 (performed only once, at the definition time), (4) computation of exponent r, (5) computation of weights p_1, p_2, p_3, and (6) computation of WPM. Therefore, the first five steps are the GWOWA overhead, which is significant both as a human effort and as consumption of computing resources.

12   Aggregation as a Graded Propositional Calculus

The history of graded logic and logic aggregation, from its first components (andness-directed transition from conjunction to disjunction introduced in 1973) to its current status, is the history of an effort to interpret aggregation as a soft computing propositional calculus (for historical details see [4]). It is rather amazing that the key elements of that interpretation are always in plain view, but almost all research in the aggregation area is either ignoring or denying the logic aspects of aggregation. First, means have been used for centuries, and they are located between the *min* and *max* functions. Of course, *min* is conjunction, and *max* is disjunction, and it is obvious that means can (and should) be interpreted as logic functions. Aggregation should be focused on arguments that have semantic identity (e.g., degrees of truth of precisely defined statements), and not on anonymous real numbers.

Boolean logic is defined in vertices $\{0, 1\}^n$, and once we accept that truth belongs to [0, 1], it is obvious that the soft computing graded logic aggregation must be defined in the whole volume of $[0, 1]^n$ and must be a generalization of Boolean logic. So, the conjunction must become partial conjunction and model adjustable simultaneity, the disjunction must become partial disjunction and model adjustable substitutability, and the Boolean total absorption must become partial absorption and model logic relationship between mandatory/optional and sufficient/optional requirements. Consequently, there must be a path of continuous transition from conjunction to disjunction, and along that path there must be a measure of distance (or difference) between an aggregator and the pure conjunction or the pure disjunction. In other words, we need andness and orness as geometric properties because aggregation happens inside the unit hypercube. There must be andness-directedness, and andness/orness is the *main input* of each GCD aggregator. Both Boolean logic and graded logic must share the same concept of duality (in De Morgan sense). All that was introduced in 1973 but for many authors it stayed invisible for almost half a century. For example, in mathematical aggregation literature, aggregators that are means are still called "averaging functions" with implicit statistical connotation. So, means are denied the status of andness-directed logic aggregators. Aggregators are considered conjunctive (but not characterized by andness) only if they are less than or equal to *min* (and not when *andness* > *orness*). They are considered disjunctive (but not characterized by orness) only if they are greater than or equal to *max* (and not when *orness* > *andness*). Except for *min* and *max,* such conjunctive and disjunctive functions are not idempotent. Annihilators of such aggregators are fixed and not freely selectable. A simple common sense tells us that if *min* is the *logic function conjunction,* then all functions in its neighborhood should naturally be both "conjunctive" and "logic functions." That holds for both those that are for ε below min and those that are for ε above *min.* All such functions have not only the right, but also the obligation to be "conjunctive logic functions," same as *min.* The same reasoning applies for *max.* These natural rights are unjustifiably denied by the theoretical aggregation literature.

In the huge majority of applications, primarily in decision-support systems, aggregators are models of observable human reasoning. Such reasoning always has semantic components and uses noncommutative weighted aggregation. Real life requires aggregators to be defined as noncommutative functions. However, in the aggregation literature that accumulated thousands of references, many respectable aggregators are without any excuse defined as commutative; in addition, as far as we know, the number of papers that tried to empirically investigate relationships between aggregation models and actual recorded human reasoning is around 5 and all of them are related to [26]. Obviously, most authors see aggregation as a theoretical discipline.

Our presentation of the GCD aggregator based on ADIA technique interprets aggregation as a graded propositional logic calculus. It is easy to see that this is the correct approach. Means can be easily interpreted as logic functions. OWA aggregators have logic properties, and each of their updates was logic-inspired. Fuzzy integrals can also be interpreted as generalizations of logic functions, and primarily used in decision-support systems. Indeed, in almost all soft computing applications, aggregation is a graded propositional calculus.

13 Conclusions

In the area of aggregation functions, we regularly face a number of strategic questions. Is aggregation a part of logic? Should all aggregation be defined as a logic aggregation? Is decision making based on logic aggregation? Are existing aggregators sufficiently related to observable properties of human reasoning? What fraction of existing aggregators is applicable in real life problems, and what are distinctive properties of such aggregators? What fraction of existing aggregators is not applicable in real life problems and what are distinctive properties of such aggregators? What fraction of applicable aggregators is the group of logic aggregators used in decision engineering? What fraction of applicable aggregators are aggregators used in areas different from decision engineering? Since fuzzy membership can be interpreted as a degree of truth, what is the role of logic aggregation in fuzzy logic? What are differences between logic aggregators and other types of aggregators? What are methods for systematic evaluation and comparison of aggregators? In what direction should the current aggregator research move? Are the above questions legitimate questions, and is there any legitimate interest in providing answers to these questions?

We strongly believe that the presented questions are not only legitimate, but also fundamental and crucial for the whole area of aggregation. The goal of this study is to contribute to the search for answers to the above questions, and both implicit and explicit answers are included in our presentation.

Logic aggregators are practical models of observable human reasoning [46, 47], and consequently they belong to logic that is graded and defined as a strict generalization of classic Boolean logic. All aggregators that are related to human reasoning must be capable to model ten fundamental graded logic functions: (1) hyperconjunction, (2) conjunction, (3) hard partial conjunction, (4) soft partial conjunction, (5) logic neutrality, (6) soft partial disjunction, (7) hard partial disjunction, (8) disjunction, (9) hyperdisjunction, and (10) negation. These functions are observable and provably present in human reasoning; the graded logic conjecture [4] claims that they are both necessary and sufficient. Except for negation, all of them are special cases of the GCD aggregator which is a model of simultaneity and substitutability in graded logic. GCD and negation are observable in human intuitive reasoning, and necessary and sufficient to form a graded propositional calculus.

To be certified as a basic logic aggregator, an aggregator must satisfy a spectrum of conditions [40, 41]. Ten core conditions include the following: (1) two or more input logic arguments that are degrees of truth and have clearly defined semantic identity, (2) the capability to cover the complete range of andness, making continuous transition from drastic conjunction to drastic disjunction, (3) nondecreasing monotonicity in all arguments, and nonincreasing monotonicity in andness, (4) andness-directedness in the full range from drastic conjunction to drastic disjunction, and parameter-directedness for penalty and reward in the case of partial absorption aggregators, (5) importance weighting of inputs, (6) selectivity of conjunctive and disjunctive annihilators (0 and 1), (7) adjustability of threshold andness/orness, (8) sensitivity to positive and incomplete truth, (9) absence of discontinuities and oscillatory properties, and (10) simplicity, readability, performance, and the suitability for building compound aggregators. The requirement (10) specifies the efficient applicability as a justifiable fundamental property of logic aggregators: if aggregators are developed to model human reasoning, they must be easily applicable, because their only purpose is to help real people in solving real decision problems.

GCD aggregator based on andness-directed interpolative aggregation (GCD/ADIA) is developed with explicit goal to serve as a basic logic aggregator and consequently it fully satisfies all requirements of basic logic aggregators. It exploits natural properties of WPM and uses techniques of interpolation and regression to combine and integrate the areas of means and t-norms, unifying logic and probabilistic reasoning.

Unsurprisingly (or unfortunately), many aggregators are not developed as basic logic aggregators. That is expected, because the aggregation theory is *not* explicitly related either to humans or to logic, and many aggregators are rightfully developed as mathematical objects, without any interest in applicability. The only requirements of such aggregators are nondecreasing monotonicity in all arguments and idempotency in extreme points $(0,...,0)$ and $(1,...,1)$. The ultimate permissiveness of these conditions creates a huge family of aggregation functions. Some of these functions are either basic logic aggregators, or functions similar to them (e.g., the Gamma aggregators [25, 26]).

The family of graded logic functions and similar aggregators, investigated in Sects. 7–10, includes GCD (introduced in 1973), various OWA aggregators (introduced in 1988), Gamma aggregators (introduced in 1979), aggregators based on fuzzy integrals (introduced in 1974), and various means (introduced more than 2000 years ago). Except for GCD, these aggregators were not introduced with intention to create a complete system of logic functions with necessary human-centric logic properties, such as andness-directedness, andness-monotonicity, the selectability of annihilators, adjustability of threshold andness/orness, and explicit support for semantic identity of arguments expressed through noncommutativity and importance weights. Regardless being logic functions, such aggregators were neither designed nor used as general fundamental components of some kind of graded logic, consistent with a specific logic framework, such as Boolean logic. Except for GCD and Gamma aggregator, they were always introduced as independent mathematical objects and not as the infrastructure for logic modeling of observable human reasoning. E.g., according to Sect. 8, the popular OWA aggregator was introduced as a dot product of logic weights and sorted arguments; the result is a strictly soft and commutative aggregator without explicit andness-directedness. Subsequently, OWA was upgraded multiple times to come closer to necessary logic properties. Andness-directedness was proposed as one of upgrades, and explicitly introduced in the ItOWA (an iterative version of OWA [42]), as well as in parameterized t-norms [44]. The next OWA upgrade was the introduction of importance weights [22] which was not simple since the natural OWA weights were used for other purposes (adjustment of andness). The additive nature of OWA prevents hard aggregation based on annihilators; so, the subsequent upgrade was to make OWG and GOWA as hard aggregators. Each of these upgrades added an increment of algorithmic and computational complexity and eventually made OWA aggregators similar to the WPM. However, in the case of WPM, the importance weights, andness-directedness, and support for annihilators comes automatically without any upgrades, as native properties of the initial WPM aggregator. Regardless the efforts to upgrade logic properties, OWA was never interpreted as the fundamental graded logic function intended to support a graded propositional calculus and suitable to produce compound asymmetric aggregators such as partial absorption and other compound functions needed in a graded logic.

Generalization does not mean simplification. In most cases, each generalization introduces an added layer of logic and computational complexity. For example, all versions of OWA aggregators cannot aggregate arguments unless the arguments are sorted. So, all OWA aggregators don't have the stationary form (the form with constant parameters, independent of arguments): all members of the OWA family are nonstationary aggregators. In contrast, GCD/ADIA and various means are stationary aggregators, simpler than OWA.

Fuzzy integrals can be interpreted as a generalization of OWA and weighted means. Consequently, they contribute an additional layer of logic and computational complexity, including exponential growth of complexity, where adding a single input argument can sometimes double the necessary effort. They are mostly used in cases where the number of inputs is very small and there are specific interacting conditions that subsets of input arguments must satisfy.

Graded logic aggregators are indispensable components of most decision models. They must support ten fundamental types of basic logic functions and satisfy ten core requirements. The main families of logic aggregators, GCD/ADIA, OWA, OWG, GOWA, WOWA, GWOWA, ItOWA, Gamma aggregators, fuzzy integrals, t-norms, and weighted means have similarities and do not exclude each other. Each of these aggregators can be used if we have conditions for which the specific aggregator was developed. Of course, in a general case, aggregators can be compared from the standpoint of consistency with properties of human reasoning, generality, functionality, usability, performance, and complexity. This study shows that, in the areas of logic aggregation and decision engineering, these properties are best satisfied by the GCD/ADIA. Indeed, in most practical aggregation problems, GCD and negation create aggregation structures that efficiently implement expressions of a graded propositional calculus.

References

1. Beliakov, G., Pradera, A., Calvo, T.: Aggregation Functions: A Guide for Practitioners. Springer, New York (2007). https://doi.org/10.1007/978-3-540-73721-6
2. Beliakov, G., Bustince Sola, H., Calvo Sanchez, T.: A Practical Guide to Averaging Functions. Studies in Fuzziness and Soft Computing, vol. 329. Springer, New York (2016). https://doi.org/10.1007/978-3-319-24753-3
3. Grabisch, M., Marichal, J.-L., Mesiar, R., Pap, E.: Aggregation Functions. Cambridge University Press, Cambridge (2009)
4. Dujmović, J.: Soft Computing Evaluation Logic. Wiley and IEEE Press (2018)
5. Miller, J.R., III.: Professional Decision-Making. Praeger, New York (1970)
6. Belton, V., Stewart, T.J.: Multiple Criteria Decision Analysis: An Integrated Approach. Kluwer Academic Publishers, Dordrecht (2002)
7. Torra, V., Narukawa, Y.: Modeling Decisions. Springer, Berlin (2007). https://doi.org/10.1007/978-3-540-68791-7

8. Fodor, J., Roubens, M.: Fuzzy Preference Modelling and Multicriteria Decision Support. Kluwer Academic Publishers, Dordrecht (1994)
9. Zimmermann, H.-J.: Fuzzy Set Theory and Its Applications. Springer, New York (1996). https://doi.org/10.1007/978-94-015-8702-0
10. Dujmović, J.: Graded logic aggregation. In: Torra, V., Narukawa, Y., Aguiló, I., González-Hidalgo, M. (eds.) MDAI 2018. LNCS (LNAI), vol. 11144, pp. 3–12. Springer, Cham (2018). https://doi.org/10.1007/978-3-030-00202-2_1
11. Dujmović, J.: Weighted conjunctive and disjunctive means and their application in system evaluation. J. Univ. Belgrade, EE Dept. Ser. Math. Phys. **483**, 147–158 (1974)
12. Dujmović, J.: Two integrals related to means. J. Univ. Belgrade EE Dept. Ser. Math. Phys. **412–460**, 231–232 (1973)
13. Dujmović, J.: Weighted compensative logic with adjustable threshold andness and orness. IEEE Trans. Fuzzy Syst. **23**(2), 270–290 (2015)
14. Dujmović, J., Beliakov, G.: Idempotent weighted aggregation based on binary aggregation trees. Int. J. Intell. Syst. **32**(1), 31–50 (2017)
15. Dujmović, J., Larsen, H.L.: Generalized conjunction/disjunction. Int. J. Approx. Reason. **46**, 423–446 (2007)
16. Yager, R.R.: On ordered weighted averaging aggregation operators in multi-criteria decision making. IEEE Trans. Syst. Man Cybern. **18**, 183–190 (1988)
17. Yager, R.R.: Generalized OWA aggregation operators. Fuzzy Optim. Decis. Making **3**, 93–107 (2004)
18. Yager, R.R.: On generalized Bonferroni mean operators for multi-criteria aggregation. Int. J. Approx. Reason. **50**, 1279–1286 (2009)
19. Bullen, P.S.: Handbook of Means and Their Inequalities. Kluwer, London (2003 and 2010)
20. Dujmović, J.: Implicative weights as importance quantifiers in evaluation criteria. In: Torra, V., Narukawa, Y., Aguiló, I., González-Hidalgo, M. (eds.) MDAI 2018. LNCS (LNAI), vol. 11144, pp. 193–205. Springer, Cham (2018). https://doi.org/10.1007/978-3-030-00202-2_16
21. Dujmović, J.: Graded logic for decision support systems. Int. J. Intell. Syst. **34**, 2900–2919 (2019)
22. Torra, V.: The weighted OWA operator. Int. J. Intell. Syst. **12**, 153–166 (1997)
23. Liu, X., Chen, L.: On the properties of parametric geometric OWA operator. Int. J. Approx. Reason. **35**, 163–178 (2004)
24. Thole, U., Zimmermann, H.-J., Zysno, P.: On the suitability of minimum and product operators for the intersection of fuzzy sets. Fuzzy Sets Syst. **2**, 167–180 (1979)
25. Zysno, P.: One class of operators for the aggregation of fuzzy sets. In: EURO III Congress, Amsterdam (1979)
26. Zimmermann, H.-J., Zysno, P.: Latent connectives in human decision making. Fuzzy Sets Syst. **4**, 37–51 (1980)
27. Kovalerchuk, B., Taliansky, V.: Comparison of empirical and computed values of fuzzy conjunction. Fuzzy Sets Syst. **46**, 49–53, North-Holland (1992)
28. Ralescu, A.L., Ralescu, D.A.: Extensions of fuzzy aggregation. Fuzzy Sets Syst. **86**, 321–330 (1997)
29. Carbonell, M., Mas, M., Mayor, G.: On a class of monotonic extended OWA operators. In: Proc. IEEE Fuzzy (1997)
30. Yager, R.R.: Quantifier guided aggregation using OWA operators. Int. J. Intell. Syst. **11**, 49–73 (1996)
31. Yager, R.R.: Including importances in OWA aggregations using fuzzy systems modeling. IEEE Trans. Fuzzy Syst. **6**(2), 286–294 (1998)
32. Beliakov, G., James, S., Mordelová, J., Rückschlossová, T., Yager, R.R.: Generalized Bonferroni mean operators in multi-criteria aggregation. Fuzzy Sets Syst. **161**, 2227–2242 (2010)

33. Dutta, B., Figueira, J.R., Das, S.: On the orness of Bonferroni mean and its variants. J. Intell. Syst. 1–31 (2019). https://doi.org/10.1002/int.22124
34. Blanco-Mesa, F., León-Castro, E., Merigó, J.M., Xu, Z.S.: Bonferroni means with induced ordered weighted average operators. Int. J. Intell. Syst. **34**, 3–23 (2019). https://doi.org/10.1002/int.22033
35. Marichal, J.L.: Tolerant or intolerant character of interacting criteria in aggregation by the Choquet integral. Eur. J. Oper. Res. **155**(3), 771–791 (2004)
36. O'Hagan, M.: Fuzzy decision aids. In: Proceedings of 21st Annual Asilomar Conference on Signals, Systems, and Computers, vol. 2, pp. 624–628. IEEE and Maple Press (1987) (published in 1988)
37. Grabisch, M.: The application of fuzzy integrals in multicriteria decision making. Eur. J. Oper. Res. **89**, 445–456 (1996)
38. Dujmović, J.: Interpretability and explainability of LSP evaluation criteria. In: Proceedings of the 2020 IEEE World Congress on Computational Intelligence, 978-1-7281-6932-3/20, paper F-22042, July 2020
39. Torra, V.: Andness directedness for operators of the OWA and WOWA families. Fuzzy Sets Syst. **414**, 28–37 (2021)
40. Dujmović, J., Torra, V.: Properties and comparison of andness-characterized aggregators. Int. J. Intell. Syst. **36**(3), 1366–1385 (2021)
41. Dujmović, J., Torra, V.: Aggregation functions in decision engineering: ten necessary properties and parameter-directedness. In: Kahraman, C., Cebi, S., Cevik Onar, S., Oztaysi, B., Tolga, A.C., Sari, I.U. (eds.) INFUS 2021. LNNS, vol. 307, pp. 173–181. Springer, Cham (2022). https://doi.org/10.1007/978-3-030-85626-7_21
42. Dujmović, J.: Andness-directed iterative OWA aggregators. In: Torra, V., Narukawa, Y. (eds.) MDAI 2021. LNCS (LNAI), vol. 12898, pp. 3–16. Springer, Cham (2021). https://doi.org/10.1007/978-3-030-85529-1_1
43. Dujmović, J.: Numerical comparison of idempotent andness-directed aggregators. In: Torra, V., Narukawa, Y. (eds.) MDAI 2021. LNCS (LNAI), vol. 12898, pp. 67–77. Springer, Cham (2021). https://doi.org/10.1007/978-3-030-85529-1_6
44. Torra, V.: Andness directedness for t-Norms and t-Conorms. Mathematics **10**, 1598 (2022). https://doi.org/10.3390/math10091598
45. Dujmović, J.: Preferential neural networks. In: Antognetti, P., Milutinović, V. (eds.) Chapter 7 in Neural Networks - Concepts, Applications, and Implementations. Prentice-Hall Advanced Reference Series, vol. II, pp. 155–206. Prentice-Hall, Upper Saddle River (1991)
46. Dujmović, J.: Andness and orness as a mean of overall importance. In: Proceedings of the IEEE World Congress on Computational Intelligence, 10–15 June 2012, Brisbane, Australia, pp. 83–88 (2012)
47. Dujmović, J., Tomasevich, D.: Experimental analysis and modeling of human conjunctive logic aggregation. In: 2022 IEEE International Conference on Fuzzy Systems (FUZZ-IEEE), Padua, Italy, pp. 1–8 (2022). https://doi.org/10.1109/FUZZ-IEEE55066.2022.9882665
48. Yager, R.R.: On a general class of fuzzy connectives. Fuzzy Sets Syst. **4**, 235–242 (1980)
49. Dombi, J.A.: A general class of fuzzy operators, the De Morgan class of fuzzy operators and fuzziness measures induced by fuzzy operators. Fuzzy Sets Syst. **8**, 149–163 (1982)
50. Schweizer, B., Sklar, A.: Associative functions and abstract semigroups. Publ. Math. Debr. **10**, 69–81 (1963)
51. Klir, G.J., Yuan, B.: Fuzzy Sets and Fuzzy Logic: Theory and Applications. Prentice Hall, London (1995)

Decision Making and Uncertainty

Multi-target Decision Making Under Conditions of Severe Uncertainty

Christoph Jansen$^{(\boxtimes)}$ (ID), Georg Schollmeyer (ID), and Thomas Augustin (ID)

Department of Statistics, Ludwig-Maximilians-Universität, München, Germany
{christoph.jansen,georg.schollmeyer,thomas.augustin}@stat.uni-muenchen.de

Abstract. The quality of consequences in a decision making problem under (severe) uncertainty must often be compared among different targets (goals, objectives) simultaneously. In addition, the evaluations of a consequence's performance under the various targets often differ in their scale of measurement, classically being either purely ordinal or perfectly cardinal. In this paper, we transfer recent developments from abstract decision theory with incomplete preferential and probabilistic information to this multi-target setting and show how – by exploiting the (potentially) partial cardinal and partial probabilistic information – more informative orders for comparing decisions can be given than the Pareto order. We discuss some interesting properties of the proposed orders between decision options and show how they can be concretely computed by linear optimization. We conclude the paper by demonstrating our framework in an artificial (but quite real-world) example in the context of comparing algorithms under different performance measures.

Keywords: Incomplete preferences · Multi-target decision making · Preference systems · Imprecise probabilities · Stochastic dominance

1 Introduction

The basic model of decision making under uncertainty is as simple as it is expressive: an *agent* is asked to choose between different available *actions* X from a known set of actions $\mathcal{G}$. The challenge is that the *consequence* of choosing an action X is not deterministic, but rather depends on which *state of nature* from a known set S of such states turns out to be the true one. Formally, each action is a mapping $X : S \to A$, where A is the set of all possible consequences. The *decision problem* $\mathcal{G}$ is then simply a subset of the set of all possible actions, i.e., the set $A^S = \{X : S \to A\}$.[1] The agent's goal here is to select an optimal action. This goal is formalized by specifying a *choice function* $ch : 2^{\mathcal{G}} \to 2^{\mathcal{G}}$ satisfying $ch(\mathcal{D}) \subseteq \mathcal{D}$ for all $\mathcal{D} \in 2^{\mathcal{G}}$. The sets $ch(\mathcal{D})$ are called *choice sets* and have a slightly different interpretation depending on the quality of the information used to construct the choice function: The *strong view* interprets $ch(\mathcal{D})$ as the set of

---

[1] For an original source, see [16].

V. Torra and Y. Narukawa (Eds.): MDAI 2023, LNAI 13890, pp. 45–57, 2023.
https://doi.org/10.1007/978-3-031-33498-6_2

46   C. Jansen et al.

optimal actions from $\mathcal{D}$. The *weak view*, on the other hand, interprets $ch(\mathcal{D})$ as the set of actions from $\mathcal{D}$ that *cannot be rejected* based on the information.[2]

To construct choice functions, one mainly uses information from two different sources: The first source I_1 is the information about the *process that generates the states of nature*. The second source I_2 is the information about the *agent's preferences* over the consequence set A. In decision theory, it is classically assumed that I_1 has sufficient structure to be expressed in terms of a *single probability measure* over the states from S (see, e.g., [3]), whereas I_2 is assumed to provide enough information to be characterized by a *cardinally interpretable utility function* (see, e.g., [13]). Under these two structural assumptions, a suitable choice function is quickly found: One selects from each set $\mathcal{D}$ those actions which *maximize* the – then well-defined – *expected utility*. Obviously, the choice sets of the choice function based on expected utility comparison can then also be given the strong interpretation.

However, in many realistic applications it turns out that the classical assumptions are systematically too restrictive and should be replaced by relaxed uncertainty assumptions and preference assumptions in order to meet the requirement of a useful theory for practice. A prominent and much discussed such application is *multi-target decision problems*:[3] By considering multiple targets simultaneously, the consequence set becomes multidimensional and generally only partially ordered, and (in general) there is no hope for a partial ordering to be adequately described by a unique cardinal utility function.

In this paper, we aim to contribute a new perspective to the lively discussion on multi-target decision making under severe uncertainty. To this end, we transfer recent developments from decision theory under weakly structured information – based on both complexly structured preferences and imprecise probabilistic models – to the multi-target situation and show how they can be used in a flexible and information-efficient way to generalize classical concepts of multi-target decision making. This transfer allows us to preserve the appeal of the classical approach while simultaneously utilizing *all* available information in a perfect manner in order to pursue more informative decision theory.

Our paper is organized as follows: In Sect. 2, we first recall the modeling approaches for weakly structured information (Sects. 2.1 and 2.2), then define two types of choice functions in this framework (Sect. 2.3) and, finally, give an algorithm for computing the associated choice sets (Sect. 2.4). In Sect. 3, we introduce our version of multi-target decision problems (Sect. 3.1) and transfer the concepts from before to this setting (Sect. 3.2). In Sect. 4 we illustrate our framework in a (synthetic) application example. Section 5 concludes.

---

[2] For more details on the choice function approach to decision making see, e.g., [2].

[3] See, e.g., [9] for a classic source and [19] for recent work. It seems important to us to emphasize the difference to the (related) theory of multicriteria decision making (see, e.g., [1] for a survey): While – roughly speaking – in multi-criteria decision making the same utility function is evaluated with respect to different criteria, in the multi-target setting different utility functions are evaluated under the same criterion.

2 Decision Making Under Weakly Structured Information

The decisive advantage of a generalized decision theory also capturing relaxations of the assumptions on I_1 and I_2, is that it is also applicable in many situations in which classical decision theory fails. It is *information efficient*, as it manages to include every piece of information, no matter how weakly structured. In the following, we present the most important concepts for formally describing the relaxations of I_1 and I_2 and a corresponding decision criterion.

2.1 Weakly Structured Probabilistic Information

We now turn to the relaxation of I_1, i.e., the information about the process that generates the states of nature. It is classically assumed to be describable by a single probability measure. Often, however, imperfect probabilistic information will be present, rather than perfect, e.g., in the form of constraints on the probabilities of certain events or, more generally, on the expectations of certain random variables. To describe this kind of generalized uncertainty, the theory of *imprecise probabilities* as developed in [11,14,21,22] is perfectly suitable. It should be noted here that the term imprecise probabilities is actually an umbrella term for many different generalized uncertainty theories. We restrict ourselves here to a specific one among them, namely convex finitely generated *credal sets*.

Definition 1. *A finitely-generated credal set on a measurable space $(S, \sigma(S))$ is a set*

$$\mathcal{M} = \left\{ \pi \in \mathcal{P} : \underline{b}_\ell \leq \mathbb{E}_\pi(f_\ell) \leq \overline{b}_\ell \text{ for } \ell = 1, \ldots, r \right\}$$

with $\mathcal{P}$ the set of all probabilities on $(S, \sigma(S))$, $f_1, \ldots, f_r : S \to \mathbb{R}$ bounded and measurable, and $\underline{b}_\ell \leq \overline{b}_\ell$ their lower and upper expectation bounds.

It is useful that such credal sets – at least for finite S – have only finitely many extreme points. If so, we denote the set of these by $\mathcal{E}(\mathcal{M}) = \{\pi^{(1)}, \ldots, \pi^{(K)}\}$.

2.2 Weakly Structured Preferences

The information source I_2 is classically assumed to be structured enough to be described by a cardinally interpretable utility function. Relaxing this assumption, it makes sense – comparable to the situation of relaxing the uncertainty model – to work with the set of all utility functions which are consistent with certain preference restrictions. In order to be able to formalize even very complexly structured restrictions, we use so-called preference systems.[4]

Definition 2. *Let A denote a set of consequences. Let further $R_1 \subseteq A \times A$ be a pre-order[5] on A, and $R_2 \subseteq R_1 \times R_1$ be a pre-order on R_1. The triplet $\mathcal{A} = [A, R_1, R_2]$ is called a **preference system** on A. The preference system $\mathcal{A}' = [A', R_1', R_2']$ is called **subsystem** of $\mathcal{A}$ if $A' \subseteq A$, $R_1' \subseteq R_1$, and $R_2' \subseteq R_2$.*

---

[4] The following Definitions 2, 3, and 4 are (essentially) taken from [8] and [5], to which we also refer for their concrete interpretation. General representation results for the formally related concept of a *difference preorder* can be found in [15].

[5] That is, reflexive and transitive.

We rely on the following rationality criterion for preference systems. Here, for a pre-order $R \subseteq M \times M$, we denote by $P_R \subseteq M \times M$ its *strict part* and by $I_R \subseteq M \times M$ its *indifference part*.

Definition 3. *The preference system* $\mathcal{A} = [A, R_1, R_2]$ *is* **consistent** *if there exists a function* $u : A \to [0, 1]$ *such that for all* $a, b, c, d \in A$ *it holds:*

i) *If* $(a, b) \in R_1$, *then* $u(a) \geq u(b)$, *where equality holds iff* $(a, b) \in I_{R_1}$.
ii) *If* $((a, b), (c, d)) \in R_2$, *then* $u(a) - u(b) \geq u(c) - u(d)$, *where equality holds iff* $((a, b), (c, d)) \in I_{R_2}$.

The set of all such **representations** u *satisfying* i) *and* ii) *is denoted by* $\mathcal{U}_{\mathcal{A}}$.

For our later decision rule, it is necessary to consider the set of all normalized representations that account for utility differences only above some threshold δ.

Definition 4. *Let* $\mathcal{A} = [A, R_1, R_2]$ *be a consistent preference system containing* $a_*, a^* \in A$ *such that* $(a^*, a) \in R_1$ *and* $(a, a_*) \in R_1$ *for all* $a \in A$. *Then*

$$\mathcal{N}_{\mathcal{A}} := \left\{ u \in \mathcal{U}_{\mathcal{A}} : u(a_*) = 0 \ \wedge \ u(a^*) = 1 \right\}$$

is called the **normalized representation set** *of* $\mathcal{A}$. *Further, for a number* $\delta \in [0, 1)$, $\mathcal{N}_{\mathcal{A}}^{\delta}$ *denotes the set of all* $u \in \mathcal{N}_{\mathcal{A}}$ *satisfying*

$$u(a) - u(b) \geq \delta \ \wedge \ u(c) - u(d) - u(e) + u(f) \geq \delta$$

for all $(a, b) \in P_{R_1}$ *and all* $((c, d), (e, f)) \in P_{R_2}$. *Call* $\mathcal{A}$ δ-**consistent** *if* $\mathcal{N}_{\mathcal{A}}^{\delta} \neq \emptyset$.

2.3   A Criterion for Decision Making

Naturally, a generalization of the structural assumptions to the information sources I_1 and I_2 also requires a generalization of the decision theory based on these information sources and the associated choice functions. Much work has been done in the literature on the case where the information source I_1 was replaced by an imprecise probabilistic model,[6] while the information source I_2 was typically left untouched. A recent work on choice functions under generalization of both information sources simultaneously is given by [8]. We focus here on only one choice function, which is a generalization of the one induced by the relation $R_{\forall\forall}$ discussed in [8, p. 123].

Definition 5. *Let* $\mathcal{A} = [A, R_1, R_2]$ *be a* δ-consistent preference system, let $\mathcal{M}$ *be a credal set on* $(S, \sigma(S))$, *and let*

$$\mathcal{F}_{(\mathcal{A}, S)} := \left\{ X \in A^S : u \circ X \text{ is } \sigma(S)\text{-}\mathcal{B}_{\mathbb{R}}([0, 1])\text{-measurable for all } u \in \mathcal{U}_{\mathcal{A}} \right\}.$$

---

[6] See, e.g., [17] for a survey or [4, 14, 21] for original sources. Note that there is also quite an amount of literature on computation for that case, see, e.g., [7, 10, 18, 20].

For $X, Y \in \mathcal{F}_{(\mathcal{A},\mathcal{S})}$, the variable Y is called $(\mathcal{A}, \mathcal{M}, \delta)$-**dominated** by X if

$$\mathbb{E}_{\pi}(u \circ X) \geq \mathbb{E}_{\pi}(u \circ Y)$$

for all $u \in \mathcal{N}_{\mathcal{A}}^{\delta}$ and $\pi \in \mathcal{M}$. Denote the induced relation by $\geq_{(\mathcal{A},\mathcal{M},\delta)}$.

The relation $\geq_{(\mathcal{A},\mathcal{M},\delta)}$ induces two choice functions in a perfectly natural way (see Definition 6). The first allows the strong view and selects those actions that dominate all other actions for any compatible combination of utility and probability in expectation. The second allows only the weak view and selects those actions that are not strictly dominated by any other action.

Definition 6. *Consider the situation of Definition 5 and let $\mathcal{D} \subseteq \mathcal{G} \subseteq \mathcal{F}_{(\mathcal{A},\mathcal{S})}$. Define the following two sets associated with the relation $\geq_{(\mathcal{A},\mathcal{M},\delta)}$:*

i) *The set of $\geq_{(\mathcal{A},\mathcal{M},\delta)}$-maximal acts from $\mathcal{D} \subseteq \mathcal{G}$ is given by*

$$max(\mathcal{D}, \mathcal{A}, \mathcal{M}, \delta) := \Big\{ X \in \mathcal{D} : (X, Y) \in \geq_{(\mathcal{A},\mathcal{M},\delta)} \text{ for all } Y \in \mathcal{D} \Big\}.$$

ii) *The set of $\geq_{(\mathcal{A},\mathcal{M},\delta)}$-undominated acts from $\mathcal{D} \subseteq \mathcal{G}$ is given by*

$$und(\mathcal{D}, \mathcal{A}, \mathcal{M}, \delta) := \Big\{ X \in \mathcal{D} : \nexists Y \in \mathcal{D} \text{ such that } (Y, X) \in P_{\geq_{(\mathcal{A},\mathcal{M},\delta)}} \Big\}.$$

The next proposition establishes a relationship between the choice sets of our two choice functions for different values of the regularization parameter δ.

Proposition 1. *Consider the situation of Definition 5 and let $\mathcal{D} \subseteq \mathcal{G} \subseteq \mathcal{F}_{(\mathcal{A},\mathcal{S})}$. For $0 \leq \delta_1 \leq \delta_2 \leq \delta < 1$ it then holds:*

i) $max(\mathcal{D}, \mathcal{A}, \mathcal{M}, \delta_1) \subseteq max(\mathcal{D}, \mathcal{A}, \mathcal{M}, \delta_2)$
ii) $und(\mathcal{D}, \mathcal{A}, \mathcal{M}, \delta_2) \subseteq und(\mathcal{D}, \mathcal{A}, \mathcal{M}, \delta_1)$

Proof. Both parts of the Proposition straightforwardly follow by observing that the condition $0 \leq \delta_1 \leq \delta_2 \leq \delta < 1$ together with δ-consistency implies the property $\mathcal{N}_{\mathcal{A}}^{\delta_2} \subseteq \mathcal{N}_{\mathcal{A}}^{\delta_1}$ by definition. Specifically, in case i) this property implies that if X dominates all $Y \in \mathcal{D}$ in expectation w.r.t. all pairs $(u, \pi) \in \mathcal{N}_{\mathcal{A}}^{\delta_1} \times \mathcal{M}$, then the same holds true for all pairs $(u, \pi) \in \mathcal{N}_{\mathcal{A}}^{\delta_2} \times \mathcal{M}$. Contrarily, in case ii) the property implies that if there is no $Y \in \mathcal{D}$ which strictly expectation-dominates X for some pair $(u_0, \pi_0) \in \mathcal{N}_{\mathcal{A}}^{\delta_2} \times \mathcal{M}$ and weakly expectation-dominates X for all pairs $(u, \pi) \in \mathcal{N}_{\mathcal{A}}^{\delta_2} \times \mathcal{M}$, then it clearly does not exist such Y if expectation-domination must be satisfied over the larger set of pairs $\mathcal{N}_{\mathcal{A}}^{\delta_1} \times \mathcal{M}$. □

Proposition 1 nicely illustrates the role of δ in the choice functions from Definition 6: by coarsening the granularity at which the utility of consequences is measured, i.e., by increasing δ, clearer choices can be made. Specifically, in the case of maximal actions, the choice sets increase with increasing δ, which means that maximal actions can be found at all (the smaller δ, the more likely the choice sets are empty). In the case of undominated actions, the choice sets decrease with increasing δ and fewer actions cannot be rejected given the information.

2.4   Computation

If the sets A and S are finite, we now show – generalizing existing results as a preparation for the multi-target setting – that checking two actions for $\geq_{(\mathcal{A},\mathcal{M},\delta)}$-dominance can be done by solving a series of linear programs. By repeatedly applying this procedure, the choice sets of the choice functions from Definition 6 can also be computed. An important part is that the property of being a representation of a preference system can be expressed by a set of linear inequalities.

Definition 7. *Let $\mathcal{A} = [A, R_1, R_2]$ be δ-consistent, where $A = \{a_1, \dots, a_n\}$, $S = \{s_1, \dots, s_m\}$, and $a_{k_1}, a_{k_2} \in A$ are such that $(a_{k_1}, a) \in R_1$ and $(a, a_{k_2}) \in R_1$ for all $a \in A$. Denote by $\nabla_{\mathcal{A}}^{\delta}$ the set of all $(v_1, \dots, v_n) \in [0,1]^n$ satisfying the following (in)equalities:*

$\cdot\ v_{k_1} = 1$ *and* $v_{k_2} = 0$,
$\cdot\ v_i = v_j$ *for every pair* $(a_i, a_j) \in I_{R_1}$,
$\cdot\ v_i - v_j \geq \delta$ *for every pair* $(a_i, a_j) \in P_{R_1}$,
$\cdot\ v_k - v_l = v_p - v_q$ *for every pair of pairs* $((a_k, a_l), (a_p, a_q)) \in I_{R_2}$ *and*
$\cdot\ v_k - v_l - v_p + v_q \geq \delta$ *for every pair of pairs* $((a_k, a_l), (a_p, a_q)) \in P_{R_2}$.

Equipped with this, we have the following Theorem regarding the computation.

Theorem 1. *Consider the same situation as described above. For $X_i, X_j \in \mathcal{G}$ and $t \in \{1, \dots, K\}$, define the linear program*

$$\sum_{\ell=1}^{n} v_\ell \cdot [\pi^{(t)}(X_i^{-1}(\{a_\ell\})) - \pi^{(t)}(X_j^{-1}(\{a_\ell\}))] \longrightarrow \min_{(v_1,\dots,v_n) \in \mathbb{R}^n} \quad (1)$$

with constraints $(v_1, \dots, v_n) \in \nabla_{\mathcal{A}}^{\delta}$. Denote by $opt_{ij}(t)$ the optimal value of this programming problem. It then holds:

$$X_i \geq_{(\mathcal{A},\mathcal{M},\delta)} X_j \quad \Leftrightarrow \quad \min\{opt_{ij}(t) : t = 1, \dots, K\} \geq 0.$$

Proof. The proof for the case $\mathcal{M} = \{\pi\}$ is a straightforward generalization of the one of Proposition 3 in [6]. For the case of a general convex and finitely generated credal set $\mathcal{M}$ with extreme points $\mathcal{E}(\mathcal{M}) = \{\pi^{(1)}, \dots, \pi^{(K)}\}$, we first observe that the following holds:

$$X_i \geq_{(\mathcal{A},\mathcal{M},\delta)} X_j \quad \Leftrightarrow \quad \forall t = 1, \dots, K : X_i \geq_{(\mathcal{A},\{\pi^{(t)}\},\delta)} X_j \quad (2)$$

Here, the direction $\Rightarrow$ follows by definition and the direction $\Leftarrow$ is an immediate consequence of the fact that the *concave* function $\pi \mapsto \inf_u \mathbb{E}_\pi(u \circ X_i) - \mathbb{E}_\pi(u \circ X_j)$ must attain its minimum on $\mathcal{E}(\mathcal{M})$. Since we already observed that the Theorem is true for the case $\mathcal{M} = \{\pi\}$ for arbitrary $\pi \in \mathcal{M}$, the right hand side of (2) is equivalent to saying $\forall t = 1, \dots, T : opt_{ij}(t) \geq 0$, which itself is equivalent to saying $\min\{opt_{ij}(t) : t = 1, \dots, K\} \geq 0$. This completes the proof. $\square$

3 Adaptation to Multi-target Decision Making

We now show how the framework for decision making under weakly structured information can be applied to the situation of multi-target decision making.

3.1 Multi-target Decision Making

We now turn to the following situation: We again consider a decision problem $\mathcal{G}$ with actions $X : S \to A$ mapping from a state space S to a consequence space A. More specifically than before, however, we now assume that the agent can evaluate the different consequences $a \in A$ with different scores that reflect their compatibility with different targets. The goal is then to determine actions that provide the most balanced good performance under all targets simultaneously.

Definition 8. *Let $\mathcal{G}$ be a decision problem with A as its consequence set. A **target evaluation** is a function $\phi : A \to [0,1]$.*

For a given target evaluation ϕ, the number $\phi(a)$ is interpreted as a measure for a's performance under the underlying target (higher is better). In what follows, we allow each target to be either of *cardinal* or of *ordinal* scale: While for a cardinal target evaluation we may also compare *extents of target improvement*,[7] an ordinal target evaluation forbids such comparisons and is restricted to only comparing the ranks of consequences induced by it. We now give the definition of a multi-target decision problem and introduce two important associated sets.

Definition 9. *Let $\phi_1, \ldots, \phi_r$ be distinct target evaluations for $\mathcal{G}$. Then:*

 i) $\mathbb{M} = (\mathcal{G}, (\phi_j)_{j=1,\ldots,r})$ *is called **multi-target decision problem (MTDP)**.*
 ii) $X \in \mathcal{G}$ *is **uniformly optimal** if $\phi_j(X(s)) \geq \phi_j(Y(s))$ for every $Y \in \mathcal{G}$, $s \in S$ and $j \in \{1, \ldots, r\}$. Denote the set of all such X by uno($\mathbb{M}$).*
 iii) $X \in \mathcal{G}$ *is **undominated** if there is no $Y \in \mathcal{G}$ such that for all $s \in S$ and $j \in \{1, \ldots, r\}$ it holds $\phi_j(Y(s)) \geq \phi_j(X(s))$ and for some $j_0 \in \{1, \ldots, r\}$ and $s_0 \in S$ it holds $\phi_{j_0}(Y(s_0)) > \phi_{j_0}(X(s_0))$. The set of all such X is denoted by par($\mathbb{M}$) and called the **Pareto front** of the MTDP.*

3.2 Transferring the Concepts

In a MTDP as just described, the goodness of actions must be evaluated in a multidimensional space, namely the $[0,1]^r$, with the additional restriction that not all targets may be interpreted on a cardinal scale of measurement. Instead of restricting oneself here exclusively to the consideration of the Pareto front of the component-wise order, one can use the available information more efficiently by defining beforehand a suitable preference system on $[0,1]^r$, which can also include the information in the cardinal dimensions.

---

[7] In the sense that $\phi(a) - \phi(b) \geq \phi(c) - \phi(d)$ allows us to conclude that the improvement from exchanging b by a is at least as high as the one from exchanging d by c.

To do so, we assume – w.l.o.g. – that the first $0 \leq z \leq r$ target evaluations $\phi_1, \ldots, \phi_z$ are of cardinal scale, while the remaining ones are purely ordinal. Concretely, we then consider subsystems of the consistent preference system[8]

$$\text{pref}([0,1]^r) = [[0,1]^r, R_1^*, R_2^*] \tag{3}$$

where

$$R_1^* = \Big\{(x,y) \in [0,1]^r \times [0,1]^r : x_j \geq y_j \text{ for all } j = 1, \ldots, r\Big\}, \text{ and}$$

$$R_2^* = \left\{ ((x,y),(x',y')) \in R_1^* \times R_1^* : \begin{array}{l} x_j - y_j \geq x_j' - y_j' \text{ for all } j = 1, \ldots, z \quad \wedge \\ x_j \geq x_j' \geq y_j' \geq y_j \text{ for all } j = z+1, \ldots, r \end{array} \right\}.$$

While R_1^* can directly be interpreted as a componentwise dominance decision, the construction of the relation R_2^* deserves a few additional words of explanation: One pair of consequences is preferred to another such pair if it is ensured in the ordinal dimensions that the exchange associated with the first pair is not a deterioration to the exchange associated with the second pair and, in addition, there is component-wise dominance of the differences of the cardinal dimensions.

The introduction of a suitable preference system now allows us to transfer the relation $\geq_{(\mathcal{A},\mathcal{M},\delta)}$ from Definition 5 from general decision problems to multi-target decision problems. Here, if $\mathbb{M} = (\mathcal{G}, (\phi_j)_{j=1,\ldots,r})$ is a MTDP, we denote by sub($\mathbb{M}$) the subsystem of pref($[0,1]^r$) obtained by restricting R_1^* and R_2^* to

$$\phi(\mathcal{G}) := \{\phi \circ Z(s) : Z \in \mathcal{G} \wedge s \in S\} \cup \{\mathbf{0}, \mathbf{1}\}$$

where $\phi \circ Z := (\phi_1 \circ Z, \ldots, \phi_r \circ Z)$ for $Z \in \mathcal{G}$ and $\mathbf{0}, \mathbf{1} \in [0,1]^r$ are the vectors containing only 0 and 1. Further, we define $\mathcal{G}^* := \{\phi \circ Z : Z \in \mathcal{G}\}$.

Definition 10. *Let $\mathbb{M} = (\mathcal{G}, (\phi_j)_{j=1,\ldots,r})$ be a MTDP such that the function $\phi \circ Z \in \mathcal{F}_{(\text{sub}(\mathbb{M}),S)}$ for all $Z \in \mathcal{G}$ and let $\mathcal{M}$ denote a credal set on $(S, \sigma(S))$. For $X, Y \in \mathcal{G}$, say that Y is **δ-dominated** by X, if*

$$\phi \circ X \geq_{(\text{sub}(\mathbb{M}),\mathcal{M},\delta)} \phi \circ Y.$$

The induced binary relation on $\mathcal{G}$ is denoted by $\succsim_\delta$.

It is immediate that $X \in \mathcal{G}$ is maximal resp. undominated w.r.t. $\succsim_\delta$ if and only if $X \in \mathsf{max}(\mathcal{G}^*, \text{sub}(\mathbb{M}), \mathcal{M}, \delta)$ resp. $X \in \mathsf{und}(\mathcal{G}^*, \text{sub}(\mathbb{M}), \mathcal{M}, \delta)$. Given this observation, the following Proposition demonstrates that $\succsim_\delta$ is (in general) more informative than a simple Pareto-analysis.

Proposition 2. *Consider the situation of Definition 10. If S is (at most) countable and $\pi(\{s\}) > 0$ for all $\pi \in \mathcal{M}$ and $s \in S$,[9] the following properties hold:*

i) $\mathsf{max}(\mathcal{G}^*, \text{sub}(\mathbb{M}), \mathcal{M}, \delta) \supseteq \mathsf{uno}(\mathbb{M})$

---

[8] A representation is given by $u : [0,1]^r \to [0,1]$ with $u(x) = \frac{1}{r}\sum_{i=1}^r x_i$ for $x \in [0,1]^r$. Even if pref($[0,1]^r$) is not δ-consistent for $\delta > 0$, its subsystems might very well be.

[9] These conditions are only needed for property ii), whereas i) holds in full generality.

ii) $und(\mathcal{G}^*, \mathrm{sub}(\mathbb{M}), \mathcal{M}, \delta) \subseteq par(\mathbb{M})$

Moreover, there is equality in i) and ii) if the restriction of R_2^* is empty, $\delta = 0$ and $\mathcal{M}$ is the set of all probability measures.

Proof. i) If $X \in \mathrm{uno}(\mathbb{M})$, then for all $Y \in \mathcal{G}$ and $s \in S$ we have component-wise dominance of $\phi \circ X(s)$ over $\phi \circ Y(s)$. Thus, $(\phi \circ X(s), \phi \circ Y(s))$ is in the restriction of R_1^* for all $s \in S$. If we choose $u \in \mathcal{N}_{\mathrm{sub}(\mathbb{M})}^{\delta}$ and $\pi \in \mathcal{M}$ arbitrarily, this implies $\mathbb{E}_\pi(u \circ \phi \circ X) \geq \mathbb{E}_\pi(u \circ \phi \circ Y)$, since u is isotone w.r.t. the restriction of R_1^* and the expectation operator respects isotone transformations.

ii) Let $X \in und(\mathcal{G}, \mathrm{sub}(\mathbb{M}), \mathcal{M}, \delta)$ and assume $X \notin par(\mathbb{M})$. Then, there is $Y \in \mathcal{G}$ s.t. for all $s \in S$ and $j \in \{1, \ldots, r\}$ it holds $\phi_j(Y(s)) \geq \phi_j(X(s))$ and for some for some $j_0 \in \{1, \ldots, r\}$ and $s_0 \in S$ it holds $\phi_{j_0}(Y(s_0)) > \phi_{j_0}(X(s_0))$. This implies $(\phi \circ Y(s), \phi \circ X(s))$ is in the restriction of R_1^* for all $s \in S$ and $(\phi \circ X(s_0), \phi \circ Y(s_0))$ is in the restriction of $P_{R_1^*}$. Choose $\pi \in \mathcal{M}$ and $u \in \mathcal{N}_{\mathrm{sub}(\mathbb{M})}^{\delta}$ arbitrary and define $f := u \circ \phi \circ Y - u \circ \phi \circ X$. Then, we can compute

$$\mathbb{E}_{\pi_0}(u_0 \circ \phi \circ Y) - \mathbb{E}_{\pi_0}(u_0 \circ \phi \circ X) = f(s_0) \cdot \pi(\{s_0\}) + \sum_{s \in S \setminus \{s_0\}} f(s) \cdot \pi(\{s\})$$

$$\geq f(s_0) \cdot \pi(\{s_0\}) > 0$$

Here, $\geq$ follows since $f \geq 0$ and $>$ follows since $f(s_0) > 0$ and $\pi(\{s_0\}) > 0$. This is a contradiction to $X \in und(\mathcal{G}, \mathrm{sub}(\mathbb{M}), \mathcal{M}, \delta)$.   □

We conclude the section with an immediate consequence of Theorem 1, which allows to check for δ-dominance in finite MTDPs.

Corollary 1. *Consider the situation of Definition 10. If $\phi(\mathcal{G})$ is finite, checking if $(X_i, X_j) \in \succsim_\delta$ can be done by the linear program (1) from Theorem 1 with X_i, X_j replaced by $\phi \circ X_i$, $\phi \circ X_j$, A replaced by $\phi(\mathcal{G})$, and $\mathcal{A}$ replaced by $\mathrm{sub}(\mathbb{M})$.*

4 Example: Comparison of Algorithms

To illustrate the framework just discussed, we will now take a (synthetic, but potentially realistic) data example: the comparison of algorithms with respect to several targets simultaneously. We assume that six different algorithms $A_1, \ldots, A_6$ are to be compared with respect to three different targets, more precisely:

ϕ_1 Running Time: Cardinal target evaluating a score for the algorithms running time for a specific situation on a $[0, 1]$-scale (higher is better).

ϕ_2 Performance: Cardinal target measuring the goodness of performance of the algorithm for a specific situation on a $[0, 1]$-scale (higher is better).

ϕ_3 Scenario Specific Explainability: Ordinal target assigning each consequence a purely ordinally interpreted label of explainability in $\{0, 0.1, \ldots, 0.9, 1\}$, where 0 corresponds to "not" and 1 corresponds to "perfect".

Further, suppose that the algorithms are to be compared under five different scenarios collected in $S = \{s_1, s_2, s_3, s_4, s_5\}$ that can potentially affect the different targets and for which we assume we can rank them according to their probability of occurring. This can be formalized by the credal set

$$\mathcal{M} = \left\{ \pi : \pi(\{s_1\}) \geq \pi(\{s_2\}) \geq \pi(\{s_3\}) \geq \pi(\{s_4\}) \geq \pi(\{s_5\}) \right\} \qquad (4)$$

whose extreme points are given by $\mathcal{E}(\mathcal{M}) = \{\pi^{(1)}, \ldots, \pi^{(5)}\}$ induced by the formula $\pi^{(k)}(\{s_j\}) = \frac{1}{k} \cdot \mathbb{1}_{\{s_1, \ldots, s_k\}}(s_j)$, where $j, k \in \{1, \ldots, 5\}$ (see, e.g., [12]).

In this situation, we assume the target evaluations are given as in Table 1, where – as already described – the first two targets are cardinal and the third one is purely ordinal (i.e., in construction (3) we have $z = 2$ and $r = 3$). Applying the (series of) linear program(s) described in Corollary 1 to every pair of algorithms (A_i, A_j) separately then allows us to specify the full order $\succsim_\delta$ for this specific situation. The Hasse diagrams of the partial order for three different values of δ are visualized in Fig. 1.[10] The choice sets of the choice functions with weak interpretation ($\mathsf{par}(\cdot)$ and $\mathsf{und}(\cdot)$) are given in Table 2, the ones of the choice functions with strong interpretation ($\mathsf{uno}(\cdot)$ and $\mathsf{max}(\cdot)$) are given in Table 3.

The results show that, among the weakly interpretable choice functions, $\mathsf{par}(\cdot)$ is the least decisive one, not rejecting a single one of the available algorithms. In contrast, the choice function $\mathsf{und}(\cdot)$ can already exclude half of the available algorithms for a minimum threshold of $\delta = 0$. For increasing threshold values, more and more algorithms can be excluded: While for δ_{med} the algorithms A_1 and A_4 are still possible, for δ_{max} only A_1 is potentially acceptable. Among the choice functions with strong interpretation, only $\mathsf{max}(\cdot)$ under the maximum threshold δ_{max} produces a non-empty choice set: Here A_1 is uniquely chosen.

As a conclusion we can say that it can be worthwhile – at least in our synthetic application – to include available partial knowledge about probabilities and preferences in the decision process: We obtain more informative choice and rejection sets because we can perfectly exploit the available information and do not have to ignore – as under a pure Pareto analysis, for example – available partial knowledge about probabilities and preferences.

---

[10] For choosing the three δ-values, we first computed the maximal value δ_{max} for which the considered preference system is still δ_{max}-consistent. We did this computation by running the linear program from [8, Proposition 1]. Then, we picked the values $\delta_{min} = 0$ and $\delta_{med} = 0.5 \cdot \delta_{max}$ and δ_{max}.

Table 1. Synthetic data for the three different targets.

ϕ_1	s_1	s_2	s_3	s_4	s_5
A_1	0.81	0.86	0.68	0.72	0.56
A_2	0.64	0.82	0.62	0.93	0.68
A_3	0.60	0.66	0.62	0.73	0.58
A_4	0.75	0.66	0.97	0.83	0.64
A_5	0.33	0.30	0.53	0.38	0.44
A_6	0.00	0.21	0.56	0.12	0.72

ϕ_2	s_1	s_2	s_3	s_4	s_5
A_1	0.71	0.88	0.82	0.90	0.91
A_2	0.52	0.67	0.68	0.72	0.88
A_3	0.56	0.45	0.81	0.83	0.47
A_4	0.36	0.12	0.54	0.60	0.17
A_5	0.79	0.30	0.47	0.68	0.46
A_6	0.14	0.58	0.30	0.66	0.29

ϕ_3	s_1	s_2	s_3	s_4	s_5
A_1	0.70	1.00	0.80	0.60	0.90
A_2	0.50	0.80	0.60	0.50	0.80
A_3	0.50	0.40	0.60	0.40	0.70
A_4	0.70	0.40	0.70	0.70	0.30
A_5	0.60	0.20	0.20	0.30	0.30
A_6	0.10	0.20	0.40	0.30	0.20

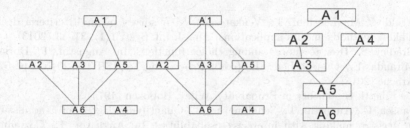

Fig. 1. Hasse diagrams of $\succsim_\delta$ for $\delta = 0$ (left), δ_{med} (middle) and δ_{max} (right).

Table 2. Choice sets of the choice functions with weak interpretation.

par($\mathbb{M}$)	und($\mathcal{G}^*, sub(\mathbb{M}), \mathcal{M}, 0$)	und($\mathcal{G}^*, sub(\mathbb{M}), \mathcal{M}, \delta_{med}$)	und($\mathcal{G}^*, sub(\mathbb{M}), \mathcal{M}, \delta_{max}$)
$\{A_1, \ldots, A_6\}$	$\{A_1, A_2, A_4\}$	$\{A_1, A_4\}$	$\{A_1\}$

Table 3. Choice sets of the choice functions with strong interpretation.

uno($\mathbb{M}$)	max($\mathcal{G}^*, sub(\mathbb{M}), \mathcal{M}, 0$)	max($\mathcal{G}^*, sub(\mathbb{M}), \mathcal{M}, \delta_{med}$)	max($\mathcal{G}^*, sub(\mathbb{M}), \mathcal{M}, \delta_{max}$)
$\emptyset$	$\emptyset$	$\emptyset$	$\{A_1\}$

5 Concluding Remarks

In this paper, we have further developed recent insights from decision theory under weakly structured information and transferred them to multi-target decision making problems. It has been shown that within this formal framework all the available information can be exploited in the best possible way and thus – compared to a classical Pareto analysis – a much more informative decision theory can be pursued. Since this initially theoretical finding has also been confirmed in our synthetic data example, a next natural step for further research is applications of our approach to real data situations. Since for larger applications also very large linear programs arise when checking the proposed dominance criterion, it should also be explored to what extent the constraint sets of the linear programs can still be purged of redundancies (e.g., by explicitly exploiting transitivity) or to what extent the optimal values can be approximated by less complex linear programs.

Acknowledgements. We thank three reviewers for valuable comments. Georg Schollmeyer gratefully acknowledges the support of the LMU Mentoring Program. Thomas Augustin gratefully acknowledges support by the Federal Statistical Office of Germany in the project "Machine Learning in Official Statistics".

References

1. Aruldoss, M., Lakshmi, T., Venkatesan, V.: A survey on multi criteria decision making methods and its applications. Am. J. Inf. Syst. **1**(1), 31–43 (2013)
2. Bradley, S.: How to choose among choice functions. In: Augustin, T., Doria, S., Miranda, E., Quaeghebeur, E. (eds.) Proceedings of ISIPTA 2015, pp. 57–66. Aracne (2015)
3. De Finetti, B.: Theory of Probability. Wiley, Hoboken (1974)
4. Jansen, C., Augustin, T., Schollmeyer, G.: Quantifying degrees of E-admissibility in decision making with imprecise probabilities. In: Augustin, T., Cozman, F., Wheeler, G. (eds.) Reflections on the Foundations of Probability and Statistics: Essays in Honor of Teddy Seidenfeld, Theory and Decision Library A, vol. 54, pp. 319–346. Springer, Cham (2022). https://doi.org/10.1007/978-3-031-15436-2_13
5. Jansen, C., Blocher, H., Augustin, T., Schollmeyer, G.: Information efficient learning of complexly structured preferences: elicitation procedures and their application to decision making under uncertainty. Int. J. Approx. Reason. **144**, 69–91 (2022)
6. Jansen, C., Nalenz, M., Schollmeyer, G., Augustin, T.: Statistical comparisons of classifiers by generalized stochastic dominance (2022). https://arxiv.org/abs/2209.01857
7. Jansen, C., Augustin, T., Schollmeyer, G.: Decision theory meets linear optimization beyond computation. In: Antonucci, A., Cholvy, L., Papini, O. (eds.) ECSQARU 2017. LNCS (LNAI), vol. 10369, pp. 329–339. Springer, Cham (2017). https://doi.org/10.1007/978-3-319-61581-3_30
8. Jansen, C., Schollmeyer, G., Augustin, T.: Concepts for decision making under severe uncertainty with partial ordinal and partial cardinal preferences. Int. J. Approx. Reason. **98**, 112–131 (2018)
9. Keeney, R., Raiffa, H.: Decisions with Multiple Objectives: Preferences and Value Trade-Offs. Cambridge University Press, Cambridge (1993)
10. Kikuti, D., Cozman, F., Shirota Filho, R.: Sequential decision making with partially ordered preferences. Artif. Intell. **175**, 1346–1365 (2011)
11. Kofler, E., Menges, G.: Entscheiden bei unvollständiger information. In: Kofler, E., Menges, G. (eds.) Rationales Entscheiden. LNEMS, vol. 136. Springer, Cham (1976). https://doi.org/10.1007/978-3-662-09669-7_10
12. Kofler, E., Kmietowicz, Z., Pearman, A.: Decision making with linear partial information (L.P.I.). J. Oper. Res. Soc. **35**(12) (1984)
13. Krantz, D., Luce, D., Suppes, P., Tversky, A.: Foundations of Measurement, vol. I: Additive and Polynomial Representations. Academic Press, Cambridge (1971)
14. Levi, I.: On indeterminate probabilities. J. Philos. **71**, 391–418 (1974)
15. Pivato, M.: Multiutility representations for incomplete difference preorders. Math. Soc. Sci. **66**, 196–220 (2013)
16. Savage, L.: The Foundations of Statistics. Wiley, Hoboken (1954)

17. Troffaes, M.: Decision making under uncertainty using imprecise probabilities. Int. J. Approx. Reason. **45**, 17–29 (2007)
18. Troffaes, M., Hable, R.: Computation. In: Augustin, T., Coolen, F., de Cooman, G., Troffaes, M. (eds.) Introduction to Imprecise Probabilities. Wiley, Hoboken (2014)
19. Troffaes, M., Sahlin, U.: Imprecise swing weighting for multi-attribute utility elicitation based on partial preferences. In: Antonucci, A., Corani, G., Couso, I., Destercke, S. (eds.) Proceedings of ISIPTA 2017. Proceedings of Machine Learning Research, vol. 62, pp. 333–345. PMLR (2017)
20. Utkin, L., Augustin, A.: Powerful algorithms for decision making under partial prior information and general ambiguity attitudes. In: Cozman, F., Nau, R., Seidenfeld, T. (eds.) Proceedings of ISIPTA 2005, pp. 349–358. SIPTA (2005)
21. Walley, P.: Statistical Reasoning with Imprecise Probabilities. Chapman and Hall, London (1991)
22. Weichselberger, K.: Elementare Grundbegriffe einer allgemeineren Wahrscheinlichkeitsrechnung I: Intervallwahrscheinlichkeit als umfassendes Konzept, Physica (2001)

Constructive Set Function and Extraction of a k-dimensional Element

Ryoji Fukuda[1]([⊠]), Aoi Honda[2], and Yoshiaki Okazaki[3]

[1] Oita University, 700 Dan-noharu, Oita City, Oita 870-1192, Japan
rfukuda@oita-u.ac.jp
[2] Kyushu Institute of Technology,
680-4 Kawazu, Iizuka City, Fukuoka 820-8502, Japan
aoi@ai.kyutech.ac.jp
[3] Fuzzy Logic Systems Institute,
680-41 Kawazu, Iizuka City, Fukuoka 820-0067, Japan
okazaki@flsi.or.jp

Abstract. We define a constructive non-additive set function as a generalization of a constructively k-additive set function ($k \in \mathbb{N}$). First, we prove that a distortion measure is a constructive set function if the distortion function is analytic.

A signed measure on the extraction space represents a constructive set function. This space is the family of all finite subsets of the original space. In the case where the support of the measure is included in the subfamily whose element's cardinality is not more than k, the corresponding set function is constructively k-additive ($k \in \mathbb{N}$). For a general constructive set function μ, we define the k-dimensional element of μ, which is a set function, by restricting the corresponding measure on the extraction space to the above subfamily. We extract this k-dimensional element by using the generalized Möbius transform under the condition that σ-algebra is countably generated,

Keywords: fuzzy measure · nonadditive measure · k-order additivity · Möbius transform · distorted measure

1 Introduction

k-additivity of a set function on a finite set was introduced by M. Grabisch [1,2]. This reduces some complexities and was used in several situations (see, for example, [3,4]). The Möbius transform of a set function μ is a set function, which gives a one-to-one correspondence between the original set function μ and the transformed set function $\{\tau_B\}_{B \subset X}$. (In this study, we assume that each set function μ satisfies $\mu(\emptyset) = 0$.) A set function μ is k-additive ($k \in \mathbb{N}$) if its Möbius transform $\{\tau_A\}_{A \subset X}$ satisfies $\tau_A = 0$ when the cardinality of A is greater than k.

Next, we consider a measurable space $(X, \mathcal{B})$, where X is not discrete in general, and $\mathcal{B}$ is a σ-algebra over X. The k-additivity of a set function on $(X, \mathcal{B})$ was proposed by R. Mesiar [5]. A signed measure on the product space of the

V. Torra and Y. Narukawa (Eds.): MDAI 2023, LNAI 13890, pp. 58–69, 2023.
https://doi.org/10.1007/978-3-031-33498-6_3

original space represented a generalized k-additive set function. A generalized Möbius transform was defined, and formulaic k-additivity was defined in [7]. We call the former k-additivity constructive k-additivity.

We consider the family of all finite subsets of X whose element's cardinality is not more than k, which we call the extraction space with order k. This space is denoted by $X^{[\leq k]}$, and for each $A \in \mathcal{B}$, $A^{[\leq k]}$ denotes the family of all elements of $X^{[\leq k]}$ which are included in A. The constructive k-additivity was reformulated using $X^{[\leq k]}$, then μ is constructively k-additive if there is a signed (σ-additive) measure $\mu^{[\leq k]}$ on $X^{[\leq k]}$ which satisfies $\mu(A) = \mu^{[\leq k]}(A^{[\leq k]})$ for any $A \in \mathcal{B}$. We call the measure $\mu^{[\leq k]}$ the constructing measure. The measure $\mu^{[\leq k]}$ is uniquely determined in this formulation [8]. On the other hand, for a set function μ on $(X, \mathcal{B})$, the Möbius transform was generalized as a function on the correction of all finite disjoint $\mathcal{B}$-measurable set families $\mathcal{D}$ [8]. μ is formulaic k-additive iff $\tau(\mathbb{D}) = 0$ for any $\mathbb{D} \in \mathcal{D}$ satisfying $|\mathbb{D}| > k$, where $|\mathbb{D}|$ denotes the number of finite sets in $\mathbb{D} \in \mathcal{D}$. A constructively k-additive set function is always formulaic k-additive, and under certain conditions, a formulaic k-additive set function is constructively k-additive [8]. The existence of the constructing measure is an advantage of a constructively k-additive set function, in various arguments. For example, the monotone decreasing convergence theorem for a Pan integral was proved when the corresponding fuzzy measure is constructively k-additive [6].

In this study, we define a constructive set function as a generalized constructively k-additive set function($k \to \infty$). A distorted measure is a set function μ described by $\mu(A) = f(\nu(A))$ using some finite measure ν and a function on $\mathbb{R}^{+}$ vanishing at 0. In Sect. 3, we will prove that a distorted measure is constructive if the distortion function is analytic and satisfies certain additional conditions. Consider the case where f is a polynomial with degree k, then μ is constructively k-additive. In general, a constructively k-additive set function is formulaic k-additive, and in the case where a distorted measure is formulaic k-additive, the distortion function must be a polynomial with degree k if the corresponding finite measure satisfies "strong Darboux property" [7].

The constructing measure $\mu^{[*]}$ concerning a constructive set function μ is defined on $X^{[*]}$, which space is a set of all finite subsets of the original space. Then, logically, we can define the constructively k-additive set function by restricting the constructing measure to $X^{[k]}$, which is the subfamily of $X^{[*]}$ whose element's cardinality is k. We call this restriction the k-dimensional element of a set function. We propose a numerical extraction method for the k-dimensional element using the generalized Möbius transform of a constructive set function.

2   Constructive Set Function

Let $(X, \mathcal{B})$ be a measurable space, X is a set and $\mathcal{B}$ is a σ-algebra over X. We assume that each set function μ defined on $\mathcal{B}$ satisfies $\mu(\emptyset) = 0$. First, we define the space of finite subsets of X.

Definition 1. *Consider the space of all finite subsets of X and denote the space as follows.*

$$X^{[*]} = \left\{ \{x_j\}_{j=1}^n : n \in \mathbb{N}, \ x_j \in X, \ j \leq n \right\},$$

and for each $A \in \mathcal{B}$ we define

$$A^{[*]} = \left\{ \{x_j\}_{j=1}^n : n \in \mathbb{N}, \ x_j \in A, \ j \leq n \right\} \subset X^{[*]}.$$

We call the space $X^{[*]}$ an extraction space.

Let $k \in \mathbb{N}$ be an integer. Then we define the extraction space with order k $X^{[\leq k]}$ and its subsets $A^{[\leq k]}$ ($A \in \mathcal{B}$) as follows.

$$X^{[\leq k]} = \left\{ \{x_j\}_{j=1}^n : n \leq k, \ x_j \in X, \ j \leq n \right\},$$

$$A^{[\leq k]} = \left\{ \{x_j\}_{j=1}^n : n \leq k, \ x_j \in A, \ j \leq n \right\} \subset X^{[\leq k]}.$$

We also define a space $X^{[k]}$. We use this concept to define a k-dimensional element of a set function.

$$X^{[k]} = \left\{ \{x_j\}_{j=1}^k : \ x_j \in X, \ j \leq k \right\}, \quad (n = k).$$

$$A^{[k]} = \left\{ \{x_j\}_{j=1}^k : \ x_j \in A, \ j \leq k \right\} \subset X^{[k]}.$$

Remark that $\{x_j\}_{j=1}^k$ is a set and $x_j \neq x_\ell$ if $j \neq \ell$.

Using the above $X^{[\leq k]}$, constructive k additivity of a set function μ was defined [6] and we define constructive set function by generalizing $k \to \infty$.

Definition 2. *Let $(X, \mathcal{B})$ be a measurable space, we define σ-algebras $\mathcal{B}^{[*]}$ and $\mathcal{B}^{[\leq k]}$ ($k \in \mathbb{N}$) as follows.*

$$\mathcal{B}^{[*]} = \sigma \left\{ A^{[*]} : A \in \mathcal{B} \right\},$$

$$\mathcal{B}^{[\leq k]} = \sigma \left\{ A^{[\leq k]} : A \in \mathcal{B} \right\}.$$

Then a set function μ on $\mathcal{B}$ is constructively k-additive if there exists a signed measure $\mu^{[\leq k]}$ on $(X^{[\leq k]}, \mathcal{B}^{[\leq k]})$ such that

$$\mu(A) = \mu^{[\leq k]}(A^{[\leq k]}). \quad \forall A \in \mathcal{B},$$

and similarly, μ is constructive if there exists a signed measure $\mu^{[*]}$ on $(X^{[*]}, \mathcal{B}^{[*]})$ such that

$$\mu(A) = \mu^{[*]}(A^{[*]}). \quad \forall A \in \mathcal{B}.$$

We call the measure $\mu^{[\leq k]}$ or $\mu^{[*]}$ the constructing measure.

Next, we define a generalized Möbius transform.

Definition 3. *Let $(X, \mathcal{B})$ be a measurable space. We define a family of extraction bases $\mathcal{D}$ on $(X, \mathcal{B})$ as follows.*

$$\mathcal{D} = \{\mathbb{D} = \{D_j\}_{j=1}^n : n \in \mathbb{N}, D_j \in \mathcal{B}, j \leq n, D_j \cap D_k = \emptyset \ (j \neq k).\}$$

The size of each extraction basis $\mathbb{D} \in \mathcal{D}$ is defined by

$$|\mathbb{D}| = |\{D_1, \ldots, D_n\}| = n,$$

and set

$$\cup \mathbb{D} = \bigcup_{j=1}^n D_j.$$

For a set function μ, we define a generalized Möbius transform τ of μ by induction. τ is a function on $\mathcal{D}$.

(a) $\tau(\mathbb{D}) = \tau(\{D_1\}) = \mu(D_1)$ $(|\mathbb{D}| = 1)$.
(b)   *Assume that $\tau(\mathbb{D}')$ are defined for all $\mathbb{D}'$ satisfying $|\mathbb{D}'| < n$ $(n \in \mathbb{N})$. Then, for $\mathbb{D} \in \mathcal{D}$ with $|\mathbb{D}| = n$*

$$\tau(\mathbb{D}) = \mu(\cup \mathbb{D}) - \sum_{\mathbb{D}' \subsetneq \mathbb{D}} \tau(\mathbb{D}').$$

Note that the inclusion $\mathbb{D}' \subsetneq \mathbb{D}$ implies that $\mathbb{D}'$ is a strict subfamily of $\mathbb{D}$ as a family of disjoint measurable sets ($|\mathbb{D}'| < |\mathbb{D}|$).

Fix an element $\mathbb{D}(= \{D_j^{(n)}\}_{j=1}^N) \in \mathcal{D}$, and consider a subfamily $\mathcal{D}_{\mathbb{D}} = \{\mathbb{D}' \subset \mathbb{D}, \mathbb{D}' \in \mathcal{D}\}$. We consider a set function μ, and set $\mu_{\mathbb{D}}$ as follows.

$$\mu_{\mathbb{D}}(\mathbb{D}') = \mu(\cup \mathbb{D}').$$

Let τ be the generalized Möbius transform of μ, $\tau_{\mathbb{D}}$ be its restriction to $\mathcal{D}_{\mathbb{D}}$. Then $\mu_{\mathbb{D}}$ is a set function defined on a finite set, and $\tau_{\mathbb{D}}$ is its classical Möbius transform. Thus, τ provides the classical Möbius transform for each finitely divided subfamily $\mathcal{D}'$. In this point of view, we call an element of $\mathcal{D}$ an extraction basis.

Next, we consider some subsets of the extraction space. This is a critical concept in the proof of the uniqueness of the constructing measure [8].

Definition 4. *Let $\mathbb{D} = \{D_1, \ldots, D_n\}$ be an element of $\mathcal{D}$. Denote*

$$\Gamma(\mathbb{D}) = \{\{x_j\}_{j=1}^m \in X^{[*]} : x_j \in \cup \mathbb{D}, j \leq m, \ D_k \cap \{x_j\}_{j=1}^n \neq \emptyset, \ k \leq n\}$$

We call the set $\Gamma(\mathbb{D})$ the limited extraction concerning the extraction basis $\mathbb{D} \in \mathcal{D}$. This set consists of finite sets U included in $\cup \mathbb{D} = \bigcup_{k=1}^n D_k$, and for each $k \leq n$, $U \cap D_k \neq \emptyset$. Therefore, m(the cardinality of $\{x_j\}_{j=1}^m$) must not be less than $n = |\mathbb{D}|$.

Proposition 1. *Let μ be a constructive set function (or a constructively k-additive set function for some fixed $k \in \mathbb{N}$), $\mu^{[*]}$ (resp. $\mu^{[\leq k]}$) be the corresponding constructing measure, and τ be the corresponding Möbius transform. Then, for any $\mathbb{D} \in \mathcal{D}$, we have*

$$\tau(\mathbb{D}) = \mu^{[*]}(\Gamma(\mathbb{D})) \quad (resp. = \mu^{[\leq k]}(\Gamma(\mathbb{D}))).$$

Let $\mathcal{A}$ be the family of a disjoint finite union of $\Gamma(\mathbb{D})$ ($\mathbb{D} \in \mathcal{D}$). Then, $\mathcal{A}$ is an algebra over $X^{[*]}$ (resp. $X^{[\leq k]}$) and this implies that $\mu^{[*]}$ (resp. $\mu^{[\leq k]}$) is uniquely defined on $(X^{[*]}, \mathcal{B}^{[*]})$ (resp. $(X^{[k]}, \mathcal{B}^{[k]})$).

Proof. For a constructively k-additive set function, the proposition was shown in [8], and we can prove it similarly for a constructive set function.   □

Remark. A set function μ is formulaic k-additive ($k \in \mathbb{N}$) iff $\tau(\mathbb{D}) = 0$ for any $\mathbb{D}$ with $|\mathbb{D}| > k$ [7]. Then, by using Proposition 1, the constructive k-additivity implies the formulaic k-additivity, because $\Gamma(\mathbb{D}) \subset X^{[k]^c}$ if $|\mathbb{D}| > k$.

3   Distortion Measures and Constructive Set Functions

A set function μ on $(X, \mathcal{B})$ is a distorted set function iff there exist a finite non-negative measure ν on $(X, \mathcal{B})$ and a function f on $\mathbb{R}^+$ satisfying $f(0) = 0$, such that $\mu(A) = f(\nu(A))$ for each $A \in \mathcal{B}$. We call the function f a distortion function. Monotonicity of the distortion function is often included in the definition of "distorted measure". In such case, μ is a finite monotone measure. A distorted set function is bounded if the distortion function is continuous.

The following properties are relations between (formulaic and constructive) k-additivities and a distorted measure. These are described in [5,7,8].

Proposition 2. *Let $(X, \mathcal{B})$ be a measurable space, μ be a distorted set function on $(X, \mathcal{B})$, f be the corresponding distortion function, and ν be the corresponding finite σ-additive measure.*

(a)   [5, 7]
  If f is a polynomial of degree k, then μ is formulaic and constructively k-additive.

(b)   [7]
  Assume that, for any $t, s \in \{\nu(A) : A \in \mathcal{B}\}$ ($s < t$) and $A \in \mathcal{B}$ with $\nu(A) = t$, there exists $B \subset A$ such that $\nu(B) = s$ (this property is called "strong Darboux property"). Then, if μ is formulaic k-additive (or constructively k-additive), the degree of f must not be more than k.

As an extension of Proposition 2 (a), we have:

Theorem 1. *Let $(X, \mathcal{B})$ be a measurable space, μ be a distorted set function, f be the corresponding distortion function, and ν be the corresponding finite σ-additive measure. Assume that f is an analytic function described by*

$$f(t) = \sum_{j=1}^{\infty} a_j t^j, \quad a_j \in \mathbb{R},$$

and that

$$\sum_{j=1}^{\infty} |a_j|\, \nu(X)^j < \infty.$$

Then μ is constructive.

Proof. We define a measure values of $\mu^{[\leq k]}$

$$\mu^{[\leq k]}(A^{[\leq k]}) = \sum_{j=1}^{k} a_j \nu(A)^j$$

for any $A \in \mathcal{B}$. This defines the set function $\mu^{[\leq k]}$ on $\mathcal{A}$ because each generalized Möbius transform is determined uniquely by using the above values. Let ν^j be the j-th product measure on X^j, and we restrict this set function on $\mathcal{B}^{[\leq j]} \subset \mathcal{B}^j$. Then, we consider a finite sum of signed measures:

$$\mu^{[\leq k]} = \sum_{j=1}^{k} a_j \nu^j.$$

By the assumption of the theorem, the following limit always exists.

$$\mu^{[*]}(A^{[*]}) = \lim_{k \to \infty} \mu^{[\leq k]}(A^{[\leq k]}).$$

Its finite additivity is clear. Then, we have only to prove, for any set sequence $\{D_m\}_{m \in \mathbb{N}} \subset \mathcal{A}$ satisfying $D_m \searrow$ as $m \to \infty$, $\mu^{[*]}(D_m) \searrow 0$ as $m \to \infty$.

Let $\varepsilon > 0$ be an arbitrarily small positive number. There exists N such that

$$n \geq N \Rightarrow \left| \mu^{[*]}(D) - \mu^{[\leq k]}(D \cap X^{[\leq k]}) \right| < \varepsilon$$

for any $D \in \mathcal{A}$, since the above value can not exceed $\displaystyle\sum_{j=N+1}^{\infty} |a_j|\nu(X)^j$. Using the fact that $\mu^{[\leq k]}$ is a finite measure, we have

$$\lim_{m \to \infty} \mu^{[\leq k]}(D \cap X^{[\leq k]}) = 0.$$

Therefore, we have

$$\limsup_{m \to \infty} \left| \mu^{[\leq k]}(D \cap X^{[\leq k]}) \right| \leq \varepsilon.$$

Using the Carathéodory's extension theorem (see for example [9]) we obtain the claim. $\qquad\square$

4 Extraction of k-dimensional Elements

Let μ be a constructive set function, and $\mu^{[*]}$ be its constructing measure. We define the k-dimensional element μ_k $(k \in \mathbb{N})$ of μ as

$$\mu_k(A) = \mu^{[k]}(A^{[*]}) := \mu^{[*]}(A^{[*]} \cap X^{[k]}).$$

In numerical analyses, only the values of set functions may be available, then we consider some methods to extract a k-dimensional element by using the values of the set function μ.

The following proposition may be elementary. However, we give its proof since this describes some important aspects of our assertions.

Proposition 3. *Let $(X, \mathcal{B})$ be a measurable space, and we assume that $\mathcal{B}$ is countably generated. Then the following (1)–(3) are equivalent.*

(1)   Each one point set $\{x\}$ $(x \in X)$ is measurable.
(2)   For any pair $x, y \in X$ $(x \neq y)$, there exists $A \in \mathcal{B}$ such that $x \in A$ and $y \notin A$.
(3)   There exists a sequence of finite partitions

$$\{\mathbb{D}_n\}_{n\in\mathbb{N}} = \left\{ \{D_j^{(n)}\}_{j=1}^{N(n)} \right\}_{n\in\mathbb{N}}$$

such that
(3-1) $\mathbb{D}_{n+1}$ is a refinement of $\mathbb{D}_n$ for any $n \in \mathbb{N}$.

(3-2) $\mathcal{B} = \sigma \left(\bigcup_{n\in\mathbb{N}} \mathbb{D}_n \right).$

(3-3)   For each pair $x, y \in X$ with $x \neq y$, there exist $n_0 \in \mathbb{N}$ such that, for any $n \geq n_0$, there exist $j, k \leq N(n)$ $(j \neq k)$ satisfying $x \in D_j$, and $y \in D_k$.

Proof. $(1) \Rightarrow (2)$ Set $A = \{x\} \in \mathcal{B}$, then $x \in A$ and $y \notin A$.

$(3) \Rightarrow (1)$ Fix $x \in X$. For each $n \in \mathbb{N}$ there exists $j(n) \leq N(n)$ such that $x \in D_{j(n)}^{(n)}$. Then, using the assumption (3.3), for each $y \neq x$, $y \notin D_{j(n)}^{(n)}$ for large enough $n \in \mathbb{N}$. This implies that

$$\{x\} = \bigcap_{n\in\mathbb{N}} D_{j(n)}^{(n)},$$

And the right-hand side set is measurable.

$(2) \Rightarrow (3)$ Using the assumption that $\mathcal{B}$ is countably generated, there exist a countable set family $\{A_n\}_{n\in\mathbb{N}}$ satisfying $\mathcal{B} = \sigma\left(\{A_n\}_{n\in\mathbb{N}}\right)$. Define $A_n^{(0)} = A$ and $A_n^{(1)} = A^c$, and set a partition Δ_n as follows.

$$\Delta_n = \left\{ \bigcap_{j=1}^{n} A^{i_j} : (i_j)_{j=1}^{n} \in \{0,1\}^n \right\}$$

Several elements in Δ_n may be empty according to the above definition. We may assume that there are no empty sets in Δ_n by removing empty sets. In any case, $\{\Delta_n\}_{n\in\mathbb{N}}$ satisfies (3-1) and (3-2).

Assume that (3-3) is not true, that is, there exists a pair $\{x, y\}$ $(x \neq y)$ satisfying that there exists $A \in \Delta_n$ with $\{x, y\} \subset A$ for any $n \in \mathbb{N}$. Then, we consider a set $\widetilde{X} = X \setminus \{x, y\} \cup \{\alpha\}$, where $\alpha = \{x, y\}$ is defined as a single point.

We replace an element $A \in \Delta_n$ ($n \in \mathbb{N}$) with $\tilde{A} = A \setminus \{x, y\} \cup \{\alpha\}$ if $\{x, y\} \subset A$. By the assumption, we have $\{x, y\} \subset A$ or $\{x, y\} \cap A = \emptyset$. Therefore, $\left\{ \tilde{\Delta}_n \right\}_{n \in \mathbb{N}}$ is a sequence of partition of $\tilde{X}$ satisfying (3.1). Let $\tilde{\mathcal{B}} = \sigma \left(\left\{ \tilde{\Delta}_n \right\}_{n \in \mathbb{N}} \right)$ and set

$$\mathcal{B}' = \left\{ \overline{\tilde{A}} : \tilde{A} \in \tilde{\mathcal{B}}, \overline{\overline{\tilde{A}}} = \tilde{A} \setminus \alpha \cup \{x, y\} \text{ if } \alpha \in \tilde{A}, \text{ otherwise } \overline{\tilde{A}} = \tilde{A}. \right\}$$

Then, $\mathcal{B}'$ is a σ-algebra including $\{\Delta_n\}_{n \in \mathbb{N}}$. This implies $\mathcal{B} \subset \mathcal{B}'$ and that $\{x, y\} \subset A$ or $\{x, y\} \cap A = \emptyset$ for any $A \in \mathcal{B}$. This contradicts the condition of (2). □

We have the following extraction theorem using the above proposition.

Theorem 2. *Let $(X, \mathcal{B})$ be a countably generated measurable space, μ be a constructive set function on $(X, \mathcal{B})$, $\mu^{[\leq *]}$ be the corresponding constructing measure, and $\left\{ \Delta_n = \left\{ D_j^{(n)} \right\}_{j=1}^{N(n)} \right\}_{n \in \mathbb{N}}$ be a sequence of partitions given in Proposition 3. Assume that $\{x\} \in \mathcal{B}$ for any $x \in X$. Then we have*

$$\mu^{[1]}(A^{[*]}) = \mu^{[*]}(A^{[\leq *]} \cap X^{[1]}) = \lim_{n \to \infty} \sum_{j=1}^{N(n)} \mu(D_j^{(n)} \cap A)$$

Proof. Set

$$E_n = \bigcup_{j=1}^{n} (A \cap D_j^{(n)})^{[*]}.$$

Let us consider a sequence of functions $\{f_n\}_{n=1}^{\infty}$ on $X^{[*]}$ defined by

$$f_n(U) = 1_{E_n}(U).$$

Let $U = \{x_\ell\}_{\ell=1}^{L} \in \left(A \cap D_j^{(n)} \right)^{[*]}$ with $|U| > 1$. There exist $N \in \mathbb{N}$ satisfying

$$n \geq N \Rightarrow \{x_1, x_2\} \not\subset D_j^{(n)}, \ j \leq N(n).$$

This implies $U \notin E_n$ for any $n \geq N$. Clearly $\{x\} \in \bigcup_{j \leq N(n)} \left(A \cap D_j^{(n)} \right)^{[*]}$ for any $n \in \mathbb{N}$ if $x \in A$. Thus, we have

$$\lim_{n \to \infty} 1_{E_n}(U) = 1_{A \cap X^{[1]}}(U),$$

for any $U \in X^{[*]}$. On the other hand,

$$\int 1_{E_n}(U) \mu^{[*]}(dU) = \sum_{j=1}^{N(n)} \mu^{[*]}(A \cap D_j^{(n)}) = \sum_{j=1}^{N(n)} \mu(A \cap D_j^{(n)}),$$

and

$$\int 1_{A \cap X^{[\le 1]}}(U) \mu^{[\le *]}(dU) = \mu^{[1]}(A^{[1]}).$$

All functions are bounded since these are the finite sum of characteristic functions concerning the partition. The bounded convergence theorem, therefore, implies

$$\lim_{n \to \infty} \sum_{j=1}^{N(n)} \mu(A \cap D_j^{(n)}) = \mu^{[1]}(A^{[1]}),$$

And this concludes the proof.   □

Example 1. Set $X = [0, 1)$ and let λ be the Lebesgue measure on X. We consider the Borel σ-algebra $\mathcal{B}$ on X. Define $\mu(A) = \lambda(A)^2 + \lambda(A)$ then μ is a distorted measure, and this is constructive (constructively 2-additive).

Consider the following sequence of partitions.

$$\{\Delta_n\} = \left\{ \left\{ \left[\frac{j-1}{2^n}, \frac{j}{2^n} \right) \right\}_{j=1}^{2^n} \right\}.$$

This satisfies the conditions (3-1)–(3-3) in Proposition 3.

Let A be an arbitrary measurable set in $(X, \mathcal{B})$.

$$\sum_{j=1}^{2^n} \mu\left(\left[\frac{j-1}{2^n}, \frac{j}{2^n} \right] \cap A \right)$$

$$= \sum_{j=1}^{2^n} \left(\lambda\left(\left[\frac{j-1}{2^n}, \frac{j}{2^n} \right] \cap A \right) + \lambda\left(\left[\frac{j-1}{2^n}, \frac{j}{2^n} \right] \cap A \right)^2 \right)$$

$$= \lambda(A) + \sum_{j=1}^{2^n} \lambda\left(\left[\frac{j-1}{2^n}, \frac{j}{2^n} \right] \cap A \right)^2.$$

$$0 \le \sum_{j=1}^{2^n} \lambda\left(\left[\frac{j-1}{2^n}, \frac{j}{2^n} \right] \cap A \right)^2$$

$$\le \sum_{j=1}^{2^n} \lambda\left(\left[\frac{j-1}{2^n}, \frac{j}{2^n} \right] \right)^2$$

$$= \sum_{j=1}^{2^n} \frac{1}{(2^n)^2} = \frac{1}{2^n} \to 0, \quad \text{as } n \to \infty.$$

Then, we have

$$\lim_{n \to \infty} \sum_{j=1}^{2^n} \mu\left(\left[\frac{j-1}{2^n}, \frac{j}{2^n} \right] \cap A \right) = \lambda(A)$$

This example describes one important aspect of Theorem 2.

We can also prove the higher dimensional extractions as follows.

Theorem 3. *Assume the same conditions and set the same notations with Theorem 2. Remark that a finite partition $\mathbb{D}$ belongs to $\mathcal{D}$, and $\mathbb{D}' \subset \mathbb{D}$ implies $\mathbb{D}'$ is included in $\mathbb{D}$ as a finite set family. We define, for $\mathbb{D} = \{D_j\}_{j=1}^N \in \mathcal{D}$ and $A \in \mathcal{B}$*

$$A \cap \mathbb{D} = \{A \cap D_j\}_{j=1}^N.$$

Then we have, for any $k \in \mathbb{N}$,

$$\mu^{[k]}(A^{[*]}) = \mu^{[*]}(A^{[\leq *]} \cap X^{[k]}) = \lim_{n \to \infty} \sum_{\mathbb{D} \subset \mathbb{D}_n, |\mathbb{D}| = k} \tau(A \cap \mathbb{D}).$$

Proof. We will give a similar proof with Theorem 2. The critical point is to construct an adequate approximating sequence for $1_{A^{[*]} \cap X^{[k]}}$. We define

$$f_n(U) = \sum_{\mathbb{D} \subset \mathbb{D}_n, |\mathbb{D}| = k} 1_{\Gamma(A \cap \mathbb{D})}(U).$$

First, we prove the pointwise convergence of the above sequence.

Assume that $\mathbb{D} \in \mathcal{D}$ satisfies $|\mathbb{D}| = k$, then $|A \cap \mathbb{D}| = k$, $(A \cap \mathbb{D} = \{A \cap D_1, \ldots, A \cap D_k\})$ if $A \cap \mathbb{D} \neq \emptyset$. Then $|U| < k$ implies $U \notin \Gamma(A \cap \mathbb{D})$ because $U \cap (A \cap D_j) \neq \emptyset$ for any $j \leq k$ if $U \in \Gamma(A \cap \mathbb{D})$. Therefore, $f_n(U) = 0$ for any $n \in \mathbb{N}$.

Let us consider the case $|U| > k$ ($U = \{u_1, \ldots, u_{k'}\}$, $k' > k$). Fix a pair (i, j) $(1 \leq i < j \leq k')$, there exists $N_{i,j} \in \mathbb{N}$ satisfying

$$n \geq N_{i,j}, \ D \in \mathbb{D}_n \Rightarrow \{u_i, u_j\} \not\subset D.$$

This implies that, if $n \geq \max_{1 \leq i < j \leq k'} N_{i,j}$,

$$U \in \mathbb{D} \subset \mathbb{D}_n \Rightarrow |\mathbb{D}| \geq k' > k.$$

and

$$\mathbb{D} \subset \mathbb{D}_n, \ |\mathbb{D}| > k \Rightarrow U \notin \Gamma(A \cap \mathbb{D}).$$

Assume that $|U| = k$ ($U = \{u_1, \ldots, u_k\}$) and $U \cap A^c \neq \emptyset$. By a similar argument to the above, there exists $N \in \mathbb{N}$ such that.

$$n \geq N, D \in \mathbb{D}_n \Rightarrow |\mathbb{D}| \geq k.$$

Then, if $|\mathbb{D}| = k$ ($\mathbb{D} = \{D_1, \ldots, D_k\}$ and $\mathbb{D} \subset \mathbb{D}_n$ ($n \geq N$), there is one-to-one correspondence with the elements of U and the subsets in $\mathbb{D}$. Therefore, sort the elements of U if necessary, we have

$$u_j \in D_j, \quad \text{for each } j = 1, \ldots, k.$$

By the assumption $U \cap A^c \neq \emptyset$, $u_j \notin A \cap D_j$ for some $j \leq k$. Hence, $U \notin \Gamma(A \cap \mathbb{D})$, that is, $f_n(U) = 0$ for any $n \geq N$.

Remark that $\{\Gamma(\mathbb{D}) : \mathbb{D} \subset \mathbb{D}_n, |\mathbb{D}| = k\}$ is a partition of $X^{[k]}$. Then, for each $n \in \mathbb{N}$ and any $U \in A^{[*]} \cap X^{[k]}$, there exist $\mathbb{D} \subset \mathbb{D}_n$ satisfying

$$U \in \Gamma(A \cap \mathbb{D}).$$

That is

$$f_n(U) = 1, \text{ for any } n \in \mathbb{N}.$$

Summing up the above arguments, we have

$$1_{A^{[*]} \cap X^{[k]}}(U) = \lim_{n \to \infty} f_n(U).$$

Using Proposition 1, we have

$$\int_{X^{[*]}} f_n(U) \mu^{[*]}(dU) = \sum_{\mathbb{D} \subset \mathbb{D}_n, \, |\mathbb{D}|=k} \mu(\Gamma(\mathbb{D})) . = \sum_{\mathbb{D} \subset \mathbb{D}_n, \, |\mathbb{D}|=k} \tau(\mathbb{D}).$$

and

$$\int_{X^{[*]}} 1_{A^{[*]} \cap X^{[k]}} d\mu^{[*]} = \mu^{[k]}(A^{[k]}).$$

Then the bounded convergence theorem concludes the proof.   □

5   Conclusion

We defined a constructive set function as an extension of a constructively k-additive set function. A distorted measure is constructive if the distortion function is analytic and satisfies some additional conditions. We introduced the concept of an extraction space, which is the family of all finite subsets of the original space. A signed measure on the extraction space represents a constructive set function. A k-dimensional element of a set function on the extraction space was defined, and we gave some methods to calculate the values of k-dimensional element using generalized Möbius transform. Restriction to k-additive set functions is a valuable method to reduce complexity in numerical analysis. Our theorems will give some checking methods to evaluate the influence of higher dimensional sets.

Some equivalent conditions to be constructive for a distortion measure, to consider the α-dimensional element for a set function for non-integer α, these are future problems.

Acknowledgment. We would like to thank the referees for their careful reading of our manuscript and constructive comments. All of them are invaluable and very useful for the last improvement of our manuscript.

References

1. Grabisch, M.: k-order additive discrete fuzzy measures. In: Proceedings of 6th International Conference on Information Processing and Management of Uncertainty in Knowledge-Based Systems (IPMU), pp. 1345–1350 (1996)
2. Grabisch, M.: k-order additive discrete fuzzy measures and their representation. Fuzzy Sets Syst. **92**, 167–189 (1997)
3. Fujimoto, K., Murofushi, T., Sugeno, M.: k-Additivity and C-decomposability of bi-capacities and its integral. Fuzzy Sets Syst. **158**, 1698–1712 (2007)
4. Miranda, P., Grabisch, M., Gil, P.: Axiomatic structure of k-additive capacities. Math. Soc. Sci. **49**, 153–178 (2005)
5. Mesiar, R.: k-order additivity, and maxitivity. Atti Sem. Mat. Fis. Univ. Modena **51**, 179–189 (2003)
6. Fukuda, R., Honda, A., Okazaki, Y.: Constructive k-additive measure and decreasing convergence theorems. In: Torra, V., Narukawa, Y., Nin, J., Agell, N. (eds.) MDAI 2020. LNCS (LNAI), vol. 12256, pp. 104–116. Springer, Cham (2020). https://doi.org/10.1007/978-3-030-57524-3_9
7. Honda, A., Fukuda, R., Okazaki, Y.: Non-discrete k-order additivity of a set function and distorted measure. Fuzzy Sets Syst. **430**, 36–47 (2022)
8. Fukuda, R., Honda, A., Okazaki, Y.: Suitable L_p spaces for a k-additive set function. Fuzzy Sets Syst. **457**, 25–31 (2023)
9. Neveu, J.: Mathematical Foundations of the Calculus of Probability, Holden-Day Series in Probability and Statistics. Holden-Day, San Francisco (1965)

Coherent Upper Conditional Previsions Defined by Fractal Outer Measures to Represent the Unconscious Activity of Human Brain

Serena Doria[1(✉)] and Bilel Selmi[2]

[1] Department of Engineering and Geology, University G. d'Annunzio, Chieti-Pescara, Italy
serena.doria@unich.it
[2] Analysis, Probability and Fractals Laboratory LR18ES17,
Department of Mathematics, Faculty of Sciences of Monastir, University of Monastir,
5000 Monastir, Tunisia
bilel.selmi@fsm.rnu.tn, bilel.selmi@isetgb.rnu.tn

Abstract. A mathematical model of coherent upper conditional previsions defined by fractal outer measures is proposed to represent the unconscious activity of human brain in AI. By adopting this specific Bayesian approach to human behaviour and reasoning we aim to provide a mathematical representation of fundamental functions of the human brain - usually considered as biased and detrimental to an account of normative rationality - without incurring the usual inconsistencies. In particular, it is proven that the model of the bias of selective attention described in the so-called Invisible Gorilla experiment, is often taken as a typical example of the limitations of human perception.

Keywords: Coherent upper conditional previsions · Fractal measures ·
Unexpected events · Unconscious activity · Selective attention

1 Introduction

Experiments show how human brain is characterized by an unconscious activity of which human beings are not aware and of which they have no decision-making power. In particular, we refer to the selective attention [23], which consists of the ability to select only some of the numerous pieces of information that reach the sense organs when focused on a particular objective. The neglected information is not important to the goal. Unexpected events with respect to the objective are not perceived. Moreover, results described in [24] suggest that cortical functional connectivity networks display fractal character and that this is associated with the level of consciousness in a clinically relevant population, with higher fractal dimensions (i.e. more complex) networks being associated with higher levels of consciousness. In [15] studies indicate that the fractal dimension of functional brain networks is diminished in patients diagnosed with disorders of consciousness arising from severe brain injury. The mathematical model of coherent upper conditional previsions, based on Hausdorff inner and outer measures, [2–6, 8, 9] has been proposed to represent the preference orderings and the equivalences, respectively assigned by the conscious and unconscious thought in human decision making under uncertainty. Complexity of partial information is represented by the Hausdorff dimension of the conditioning event. When the events, that describe the decision problem, are measurable with respect to the s-dimensional Hausdorff outer measure, where s is the Hausdorff dimension of the conditioning event, an optimal decision can be reached. The model is applied and discussed in Linda's Problem and the conjunction fallacy is resolved [7,8]. The model explains mathematically the bias of selective attention [10] described in the so-called Invisible Gorilla experiment [22], which is often taken as a characteristic example of the inescapable limitations of human perception. In a nutshell, once people are concentrated on doing a specific action, they do not notice unexpected events (having 0 probability) occurring in the meantime. Unexpected events are represented in the model as sets with a Hausdorff dimension less than the Hausdorff dimension of the conditioning event, which represents the specific action that people are concentrated on doing. When applying the model, selective attention is no longer a bias since it is able to explain this function of the human brain mathematically and without incoherencies. In this paper, we recall the coherent upper conditional previsions model based on Hausdorff outer measures and introduce new fractal outer measures, such as packing outer measures and φ-Hewitt-Stromberg measures, to define coherent upper conditional previsions and to investigate the mathematical representation of unexpected events. In particular, the new fractal measures, defined in the same metric space, allow describing the participant's reactions to unexpected events in the Invisible Gorilla experiment. The reaction of people who see the Gorilla can be represented by the packing measure which assesses a positive measure of the unexpected event while the reaction of people who did not see the Gorilla is represented by an event with zero Hausdorff measure. In previous papers [10,11] the reaction of people who see the Gorilla in the experiment has been represented in another metric space with a metric which is not bi-Lipschitz with respect the metric of the initial metric space; so the conditional probabilities defined in the two metric spaces are not absolutely continuous and they do not share the same null sets. When information is presented in the form of frequencies; the model works in a different way. The definition of s-dimensional Hausdorff outer measure, for $s > 0$, involves infinite sets. Finite sets have Hausdorff dimension equal to 0 and so coherent upper conditional probabilities, according to Theorem 1, are defined by the 0-dimensional Hausdorff measure, which is the counting measure. So if the model based on Hausdorff outer measures is applied when information is presented in the form of frequencies and the conditioning event is a finite set then a different situation can be represented; the Hausdorff dimension of the conditioning event is 0 and the conditional probability is defined, by the 0-dimensional Hausdorff measure, which is the counting measure. In this case the conditional probability of the intersection between two events is zero if and only if the events are incompatible, i.e. the intersection between the sets which represent the events is the empty set. For a comparison between the model proposed based on fractal measures and other conditioning rules proposed in literature the reader can see Sect. 9 of [11].

2 The Model Based on Hausdorff Outer Measures and the Selective Attention

Let (Ω, d) be a metric space and let **B** be a partition of Ω. A bounded random variable is a function $X : h\Omega \to \mathbb{R} = (-\infty, +\infty)$ such that there exists $M \in \mathbb{R}$ with $X(\omega) \leq M$ $\forall \omega \in \Omega$ and $L(\Omega)$ is the class of all bounded random variables defined on Ω; for every $B \in \mathbf{B}$ denote by $X|B$ the restriction of X to B and by $\sup(X|B)$ the supremum value that X assumes on B. Let $L(B)$ be the class of all bounded random variables $X|B$. Denote by I_A the indicator function of any event $A \in \wp(B)$, i.e. $I_A(\omega) = 1$ if $\omega \in A$ and $I_A(\omega) = 0$ if $\omega \in A^c$.

For every $B \in \mathbf{B}$ coherent upper conditional expectations or previsions $\overline{P}(\cdot|B)$ are functionals defined on $L(B)$ [26].

Definition 1. *Coherent upper conditional previsions are functionals $\overline{P}(\cdot|B)$ defined on $L(B)$, such that the following axioms of coherence hold for every $X|B$ and $Y|B$ in $L(B)$ and every strictly positive constant λ:*

1) $\overline{P}(X|B) \leq \sup(X|B)$;
2) $\overline{P}(\lambda X|B) = \lambda \overline{P}(X|B)$ (positive homogeneity);
3) $\overline{P}(X + Y|B) \leq \overline{P}(X|B) + \overline{P}(Y|B)$ (subadditivity).

Suppose that $\overline{P}(X|B)$ is a coherent upper conditional expectation on $L(B)$. Then its conjugate coherent lower conditional expectation is defined by

$$\underline{P}(X|B) = -\overline{P}(-X|B).$$

Let K be a linear space contained in $L(B)$; if for every X belonging to K we have $P(X|B) = \underline{P}(X|B) = \overline{P}(X|B)$ then $P(X|B)$ is called a coherent linear conditional expectation (de Finetti (1972), de Finetti (1974), Dubins (1975), Regazzini (1985), Regazzini (1987)) and it is a linear, positive and positively homogeneous functional on K (Corollary 2.8.5 Walley (1991)). The unconditional coherent upper expectation $\overline{P} = \overline{P}(\cdot|\Omega)$ is obtained as a particular case when the conditioning event is Ω. Coherent upper conditional probabilities are obtained when only 0–1 valued random variables are considered. From axioms 1)-3) and by the conjugacy property we have that

$$1 \leq \underline{P}(I_B|B) \leq \overline{P}(I_B|B) \leq 1, \text{ so that } \underline{P}(I_B|B) = \overline{P}(I_B|B) = 1.$$

In the model, proposed in [3] and recalled in Theorem 1, coherent upper conditional probability is defined by the Hausdorff measure of order s, or s-dimensional Hausdorff measure, if the conditioning event has a Hausdorff dimension equal to s. Let (Ω, d) be a metric space. The diameter of a non empty set U of Ω is defined as $|U| = sup\{d(x, y) : x, y \in U\}$ and if a subset A of Ω is such that $A \subset \bigcup_i U_i$ and $0 < |U_i| < \delta$ for each i, the class $\{U_i\}$ is called a δ-cover of A. Let s be a non-negative real number. For $\delta > 0$ we define $h_{s,\delta}(A) = \inf \sum_{i=1}^{\infty} |U_i|^s$, where the infimum is over all countable δ-covers $\{U_i\}$. The *Hausdorff s-dimensional outer measure* of A [12, 18] denoted by $h^s(A)$, is defined as

$$h^s(A) = \lim_{\delta \to 0} h_{s,\delta}(A).$$

This limit exists, but may be infinite, since $h_{s,\delta}(A)$ increases as δ decreases. The *Hausdorff dimension* of a set A, $\dim_H(A)$, is defined as the unique value, such that

$$h^s(A) = \infty \text{ if } 0 \le s < \dim_H(A),$$
$$h^s(A) = 0 \text{ if } \dim_H(A) < s < \infty.$$

Theorem 1. *Let (Ω, d) be a metric space and let $\mathbf{B}$ be a partition of Ω. For every $B \in \mathbf{B}$ denote by s the Hausdorff dimension of the conditioning event B and by h^s the Hausdorff s-dimensional outer measure. Let m_B be a 0–1 valued finitely additive, but not countably additive, probability on $\wp(B)$. Thus, for each $B \in \mathbf{B}$, the function defined on $\wp(B)$ by*

$$\overline{P}(A|B) = \begin{cases} \dfrac{h^s(A \cap B)}{h^s(B)} & \text{if } 0 < h^s(B) < +\infty, \\[3mm] m_B & \text{if } h^s(B) \in \{0, +\infty\} \end{cases}$$

is a coherent upper conditional probability.

If $B \in \mathbf{B}$ is a set with positive and finite Hausdorff outer measure in its Hausdorff dimension s the monotone set function μ_B^* defined for every $A \in \wp(B)$ by $\mu_B^*(A) = \frac{h^s(A \cap B)}{h^s(B)}$ is a coherent upper conditional probability, which is submodular, continuous from below and such that its restriction to the σ-field of all μ_B^*-measurable sets is a Borel regular countably additive probability. If the conditioning event B is a fractal set, i.e. a set with non-integer Hausdorff dimension s, then by Theorem 1 we obtain

$$\overline{P}(X|B) = \frac{h^s(A \cap B)}{h^s(B)} \text{ if } 0 < h^s(B) < +\infty.$$

In the following theorem, proven in [3], the coherent upper conditional probability defined in Theorem 1 is· extended to the class of all bounded random variables and, when the conditioning event B has positive and finite Hausdorff outer measure in its Hausdorff dimension, the coherent upper prevision is define by the Choquet integral. The subadditivity of the Choquet integral is assured because it is calculated with respect to Hausdorff outer measures which are submodular.

Theorem 2. *[3] Let (Ω, d) be a metric space and let $\mathbf{B}$ be a partition of Ω. For every $B \in \mathbf{B}$ denote by s the Hausdorff dimension of the conditioning event B and by h^s the Hausdorff s-dimensional outer measure. Let m_B be a 0–1 valued finitely additive, but not countably additive, probability on $\wp(B)$. Then for each $B \in \mathbf{B}$ the functional $\overline{P}(X|B)$ defined on $L(B)$ by*

$$\overline{P}(X|B) = \begin{cases} \dfrac{1}{h^s(B)} \displaystyle\int_B X dh^s & \text{if } 0 < h^s(B) < +\infty, \\[4mm] \displaystyle\int_B X dm_B & \text{if } h^s(B) \in \{0, +\infty\} \end{cases}$$

is a coherent upper conditional prevision.

In the Invisible Gorilla, experiment participants are asked to watch a short video, in which six people-three in white shirts and three in black shirts-pass basketballs around. While they watch, they must keep a silent count of the number of passes made by the people in white shirts. At some point, a gorilla strolls into the middle of the action, faces the camera and thumps its chest, and then leaves, spending nine seconds on screen. Then, study participants are asked, "But did you see the gorilla?" More than half the time, subjects miss the gorilla entirely. It was as though the gorilla was invisible. More than that, even after the participants are told about the gorilla, they're certain they couldn't have missed it. The experiment can be described in terms of coherent upper and lower conditional probabilities defined by Hausdorff's outer and inner measures. Consider the events

E: "You see the Gorilla in the video."
B: "You count the number of passes made by the people in white shirts."

According to the model of the conditional upper conditional probability of Theorem 1 the fact that the event E is unexpected given the event B can be represented by the fact that the Hausdorff dimension of the event E is less than the Hausdorff dimension s of the event B so that

$$\overline{P}(E|B) = \frac{h^s(E \cap B)}{h^s(B)} = 0.$$

The model described in Theorem 1 permits us to represent also the situation where we become aware that we can miss seeing the unexpected when we are concentrating to do something.

Let B_1: "I miss the Gorilla when I watch the video".

This is an unexpected event for us if we do not know the selective attention. When it occurs we become aware of this capacity of the human brain so we update our knowledge. From a mathematical point of view, we can describe the situation in the following way by means of conditional probabilities defined by Hausdorff measures.

Let $\Omega = [0,1]^2$, $B_1 = \{(x,y) \in [0,1]^2 : x = \frac{1}{2}, y \in [0,1]\}$. Then the Hausdorff dimension of Ω is 2 and the Hausdorff dimension of B_1 is 1 so that B_1 is an unexpected event with respect to the 2-dimensional Hausdorff measure h^2, that is

$$P(B_1|\Omega) = \frac{h^2(B_1)}{h^2(\Omega)} = 0.$$

If B_1 occurs, by Theorem 1 we update our knowledge by using the 1-dimensional Hausdorff measure instead of the 2-dimensional Hausdorff measure so that

$$P(B_1|B_1) = \frac{h^1(B_1)}{h^1(B_1)} = 1$$

and for any other event $A \in \wp(\Omega)$

$$P(A|B_1) = \frac{h^1(A \cap B_1)}{h^1(B_1)}.$$

We can observe that, even if B_1 occurs, other unexpected events can be mathematically represented, for instance by finite sets and we can describe the situation that even if we will see the Gorilla in the video next time we will miss other unexpected events when concentrated in doing something.

3 Fractal Measures and Dimensions

In this section, we introduce other fractal outer measures which allow distinguishing among sets of zero dimensions. Moreover when a conditioning event has a Hausdorff measure in its Hausdorff dimension equal to zero then we can analyze if there exists a different fractal measure that assesses positive and finite outer measure to that event.

3.1 Examples and Motivations

This short section discusses more motivations and examples related to these concepts.

- Let $\mathbb{L}$ denote the set of Liouville numbers, i.e.

$$\mathbb{L} = \left\{ x \in \mathbb{R} \backslash \mathbb{Q} \mid \forall\, n \in \mathbb{N}, \exists\, p, q \in \mathbb{N} \text{ with } q > 1 \text{ such that } \left| x - \frac{p}{q} \right| < \frac{1}{q^n} \right\}.$$

It is well known from [16] that the Hausdorff dimension of $\mathbb{L}$ is 0 and $h(\mathbb{L}) = 0$.
- It is well-known that each $x \in (0,1)$ apossesses a unique continued fraction expansion of the form

$$x = \cfrac{1}{a_1(x) + \cfrac{1}{a_2(x) + \cfrac{1}{a_3(x) + \ddots}}},$$

where $a_k(x) \in \mathbb{N} := \{1, 2, 3, \cdots\}$ is the k-th partial quotient of x. This expansion is usually denoted by $x = [a_1(x), a_2(x), a_3(x), \cdots]$. Let $\tau(x)$ be the convergence exponent of the sequence of partial quotients of x which is defined by

$$\tau(x) = \inf \left\{ s \geq 0 : \sum_{n \geq 1} a_n(x)^{-s} < \infty \right\}.$$

Now, for $\alpha \in [0, +\infty]$ we define the following sets

$$X(\alpha) = \left\{ x \in (0,1) : \tau(x) = \alpha \right\},$$

$$X = \left\{ x \in (0,1) : a_n(x) \leq a_{n+1}(x), \ \forall n \geq 1 \right\} \text{ and } E(\alpha) = X(\alpha) \cap X.$$

It follows from [13] that the set $E(\alpha)$ is uncountable for all $\alpha \in (1, +\infty]$ and

$$\dim_H(E(\alpha)) = 0.$$

- In this example, we are concerned with the exponent of convergence of the digit sequence of the Engel series. Let $T : [0, 1) \to [0, 1)$ be the Engel series map defined as follows

$$T(0) := 0 \quad \text{and} \quad T(x) := x \left\lceil \frac{1}{x} \right\rceil - 1, \quad \forall x \in (0, 1),$$

where $\lceil y \rceil$ denotes the least integer not less than y. For $x \in (0, 1)$, if $T^k(x) \neq 0$ for all $k \geq 1$, let

$$d_1(x) := \lceil 1/x \rceil \text{ and } d_{n+1}(x) := d_1(T^n(x)) \text{ for } n \geq 1,$$

which implies that x admits an infinite Engel series expansion of the form

$$x = \frac{1}{d_1(x)} + \frac{1}{d_1(x)d_2(x)} + \cdots + \frac{1}{d_1(x) \cdots d_n(x)} + \cdots$$

If $T^n(x) = 0$ for some n and $T^k(x) \neq 0$ for all $1 \leq k < n$, we can still define $d_1(x), \cdots, d_n(x)$ in the same way, and then x admits a finite Engel series expansion:

$$x = \frac{1}{d_1(x)} + \frac{1}{d_1(x)d_2(x)} + \cdots + \frac{1}{d_1(x) \cdots d_n(x)}.$$

We call $\{d_n(x)\}$ the digit sequence of the Engel series expansion of x. It was shown that $x \in (0, 1)$ is irrational if and only if its Engel series expansion is infinite, and

$$2 \leq d_1(x) \leq \ldots \leq d_{n-1}(x) \leq d_n(x) \leq \ldots,$$

with $d_n(x) \to \infty$ as $n \to \infty$ for any irrational number $x \in (0, 1)$. Let $f(x)$ be the exponent of convergence of the digit sequence of the Engel series expansion of x which is defined as follows

$$f(x) := \inf \left\{ s \geq 0 : \sum_{n \geq 1} d_n(x)^{-s} < +\infty \right\}.$$

We see that $f(x)$ takes values in $[0, \infty]$, $f(x) = 0$ for all rational numbers $x \in (0, 1)$, and $f(e - 2) = 1$. The set $F = \{x \in (0, 1) : f(x) = 0\}$ has full Lebesgue measure and the level set $F(\alpha) = \{x \in (0, 1) : f(x) = \alpha\}$ is uncountable and of Lebesgue measure zero for all $\alpha \in (0, +\infty]$. We have from [21] that $\dim_H(F(\alpha)) = 0$, for all $\alpha \in (0, +\infty]$ and

$$\dim_H \left\{ x \in (0, 1) : \lim_{n \to \infty} \frac{\log d_n(x)}{\log n} = \alpha \right\} = 0 \text{ for all } 0 \leq \alpha < 1.$$

3.2   A General Hausdorff Measure, Packing Measure and Dimensions

While the definitions of the general Hausdorff and packing measures and the general Hausdorff and packing dimensions are well-known [17], we have, nevertheless, decided to briefly recall the definitions below. Let (Ω, d) be a metric space, $E \subseteq \Omega$ and $s \geq 0$. Let also $\varphi : \mathbb{R}_+ \rightarrow \mathbb{R}$ be such that φ is non-decreasing and $\varphi(r) < 0$ for r small enough. Throughout this paper, $B(x, r)$ stands for the open ball

$$B(x, r) = \big\{ y \in \Omega \big|\ \mathrm{d}(x, y) < r \big\}.$$

For $\delta > 0$, we define the φ-Hausdorff measure as follows

$$\mathscr{H}^s_{\varphi, \delta}(E) = \inf \left\{ \sum_i e^{s \varphi(r_i)} \ \bigg|\ E \subseteq \bigcup_i B(x_i, r_i),\ 2r_i < \delta \right\}.$$

This allows defining first the s-dimensional φ-Hausdorff measure $\mathscr{H}^s_\varphi(E)$ of E by

$$\mathscr{H}^s_\varphi(E) = \sup_{\delta > 0} \mathscr{H}^s_{\varphi, \delta}(E).$$

Finally, we define the Hausdorff dimension $\dim^\varphi_H(E)$ by

$$\dim^\varphi_H(E) = \inf \big\{ s \geq 0 \ \big|\ \mathscr{H}^s_\varphi(E) = 0 \big\} = \sup \big\{ s \geq 0 \ \big|\ \mathscr{H}^s_\varphi(E) = +\infty \big\}.$$

Now, we define the φ-packing measure, for $\delta > 0$, by

$$\overline{\mathscr{P}}^s_{\varphi, \delta}(E) = \sup \big\{ e^{s \varphi(r_i)} \big\},$$

where the supremum is taken over all open balls $\big(B_i = B(x_i, r_i) \big)_i$ such that $r_i \leq \delta$ and with $x_i \in E$ and $B_i \cap B_j = \emptyset$ for all $i \neq j$. The s-dimensional φ-packing pre-measure $\overline{\mathscr{P}}^s_\varphi(E)$ of E is now given by

$$\overline{\mathscr{P}}^s_\varphi(E) = \inf_{\delta > 0} \overline{\mathscr{P}}^s_{\varphi, \delta}(E).$$

This makes us able to define the s-dimensional φ-packing measure $\mathscr{P}^s_\varphi(E)$ of E as

$$\mathscr{P}^s_\varphi(E) = \inf \left\{ \sum_i \overline{\mathscr{P}}^s_\varphi(E_i) \ \bigg|\ E \subseteq \bigcup_i E_i \right\},$$

and we define the packing dimension $\dim^\varphi_P(E)$ by

$$\dim^\varphi_P(E) = \inf \big\{ s \geq 0 \ \big|\ \mathscr{P}^s_\varphi(E) = 0 \big\} = \sup \big\{ s \geq 0 \ \big|\ \mathscr{P}^s_\varphi(E) = +\infty \big\}.$$

It follows from the above definitions that

$$\mathscr{H}^s_\varphi(E) \leq \mathscr{P}^s_\varphi(E) \quad \text{and} \quad \dim^\varphi_H(E) \leq \dim^\varphi_P(E).$$

The reader is referred to as Peyrière's classical text [17] for an excellent and systematic discussion of the generalized Hausdorff and packing measures and dimensions. Remark that the log function $\varphi(r) = \log(r)$, we come back to the classical definitions of the Hausdorff and packing measures and dimensions in their original forms (see [12]).

3.3 General Hewitt-Stromberg Measures and Dimensions

We give the definitions of the φ-Hewitt-Stromberg measures to make it easier for the reader to compare and contrast the Hausdorff and packing measures with the less well-known Hewitt-Stromberg measures and to provide a motivation for the φ-Hewitt-Stromberg measures which are therefore extensions of the classical Hewitt-Stromberg measures in [14]. The less known Hewitt-Stromberg measures play an important part in this paper and make it easier for the reader to compare and contrast the definitions of the φ-Hewitt-Stromberg measures and the definitions of the Hausdorff and packing measures it is useful to recall the definitions of the latter measures. Let Ω be a metric space and E be a bounded subset of Ω. For $s \geq 0$, we define the φ-Hewitt-Stromberg pre-measures as follows,

$$\mathscr{L}_\varphi^s(E) = \liminf_{r \to 0} N_r(E)\, e^{s\varphi(r)} \quad \text{and} \quad \overline{\mathscr{U}}_\varphi^s(E) = \sup_{F \subseteq E} \mathscr{L}_\varphi^s(F),$$

and

$$\overline{\mathscr{V}}_\varphi^s(E) = \limsup_{r \to 0} M_r(E)\, e^{s\varphi(r)},$$

where the covering number $N_r(E)$ of E and the packing number $M_r(E)$ of E are given by

$$N_r(E) = \inf \left\{ \sharp\{I\} \,\middle|\, \left(B(x_i, r)\right)_{i \in I} \text{ is a family of open balls with} \right.$$
$$\left. x_i \in E \text{ and } E \subseteq \bigcup_i B(x_i, r) \right\}$$

and

$$M_r(E) = \sup \left\{ \sharp\{I\} \,\middle|\, \left(B_i = B(x_i, r)\right)_{i \in I} \text{ is a family of open balls with} \right.$$
$$\left. x_i \in E \text{ and } B_i \cap B_j = \emptyset \text{ for } i \neq j \right\}.$$

The lower and upper s-dimensional φ-Hewitt-Stromberg measures are now defined, which are denoted respectively by $\mathscr{U}_\varphi^s(E)$ and $\mathscr{V}_\varphi^s(E)$, as follows

$$\mathscr{U}_\varphi^s(E) = \inf \left\{ \sum_i \overline{\mathscr{U}}_\varphi^s(E_i) \,\middle|\, E \subseteq \bigcup_i E_i \right\}$$

and

$$\mathscr{V}_\varphi^s(E) = \inf \left\{ \sum_i \overline{\mathscr{V}}_\varphi^s(E_i) \,\middle|\, E \subseteq \bigcup_i E_i \right\}.$$

We have some basic inequalities satisfied by the φ-Hewitt-Stromberg, the φ-Hausdorff and the φ-packing measure

$$\mathscr{H}_\varphi^s(E) \leq \mathscr{U}_\varphi^s(E) \leq \xi \mathscr{V}_\varphi^s(E) \leq \xi \mathscr{P}_\varphi^s(E),$$

where ξ is the constant that appears in Besicovitch's covering theorem (see [12]). It follows from [18] that the functions $\mathscr{H}_\varphi^s, \mathscr{U}_\varphi^s$ and $\mathscr{P}_\varphi^s$ are outer metric measures on Ω and thus measures on the family of Borel subsets of Ω but the function $\mathscr{V}_\varphi^s$ is not a Borel metric outer measure. Now, we define the lower and upper φ-Hewitt-Stromberg dimension $\underline{\dim}_{MB}^\varphi(E)$ and $\overline{\dim}_{MB}^\varphi(E)$ as follows

$$\underline{\dim}_{MB}^\varphi(E) = \inf\left\{s \geq 0 \mid \mathscr{U}_\varphi^s(E) = 0\right\} = \sup\left\{s \geq 0 \mid \mathscr{U}_\varphi^s(E) = +\infty\right\}$$

and

$$\overline{\dim}_{MB}^\varphi(E) = \inf\left\{s \geq 0 \mid \mathscr{V}_\varphi^s(E) = 0\right\} = \sup\left\{s \geq 0 \mid \mathscr{V}_\varphi^s(E) = +\infty\right\}.$$

These dimensions satisfy the following inequalities,

$$\dim_H^\varphi(E) \leq \underline{\dim}_{MB}^\varphi(E) \leq \overline{\dim}_{MB}^\varphi(E) \leq \dim_P^\varphi(E).$$

It is clear that by taking the log function $\varphi(r) = \log(r)$, we come back to the classical definitions of the Hewitt-Stromberg measures and dimensions in their original forms in [1, 14, 19, 20]. When the conditioning event has Hausdorff outer measure equal to zero in its Hausdorff dimension, instead of defining coherent conditional prevision as the Choquet integral with respect to a 0–1-valued finitely, but not countably, additive probability we can consider a different fractal measure according to the following theorem.

Theorem 3. *Let (Ω, d) be a metric space and let $\boldsymbol{B}$ be a partition of Ω. For $s \geq 0$ let $(\nu^s, \dim) \in \left\{(\mathscr{H}_\varphi^s, \dim_H^\varphi), (\mathscr{U}_\varphi^s, \underline{\dim}_{MB}^\varphi), (\mathscr{V}_\varphi^s, \overline{\dim}_{MB}^\varphi), (\mathscr{P}_\varphi^s, \dim_P^\varphi)\right\}$. For every $B \in \boldsymbol{B}$ denote by s the dimension $\dim$ of the conditioning event B and by ν^s the s-dimensional outer measure.*

1. *Let m_B be a 0–1 valued finitely additive, but not countably additive, probability on $\wp(B)$. Then for each $B \in \boldsymbol{B}$ the functional $\overline{P}(X|B)$ defined on $L(B)$ by*

$$\overline{P}(X|B) = \begin{cases} \dfrac{1}{\nu^s(B)} \displaystyle\int_B X \, d\nu^s & \text{if } 0 < \nu^s(B) < +\infty, \\[2em] \displaystyle\int_B X \, dm_B & \text{if } \nu^s(B) \in \{0, +\infty\} \end{cases}$$

   is a coherent upper conditional prevision.

2. *Let m_B be a 0–1 valued finitely additive, but not countably additive, probability on $\wp(B)$. Thus, for each $B \in \boldsymbol{B}$, the function defined on $\wp(B)$ by*

$$\overline{P}(A|B) = \begin{cases} \dfrac{\nu^s(A \cap B)}{\nu^s(B)} & \text{if } 0 < \nu^s(B) < +\infty, \\[2em] m_B & \text{if } \nu^s(B) \in \{0, +\infty\} \end{cases}$$

   is a coherent upper conditional probability.

4 Mathematical Representation of Unexpected Events

As shown in the previous sections a fundamental tool to mathematically represent the unconscious activity of the human brain is the notion of null sets, which represent unexpected events. The notion of null sets, i.e. sets with zero probability, is involved in the concept of the support of a probability measure, which is the closure of the set of events with a positive measure. A normalized regular Borel measure on a completely compact Hausdorff space can have empty support ([25, Example 4.33]); moreover, the support may not exist if the topological space is not second countable.

Definition 2. *A topological space $\mathcal{T}$ is second-countable if there exists some countable collection $\mathcal{U} = \{U_i\}_{i=1}^{\infty}$ of open subsets of $\mathcal{T}$ such that any open subset of $\mathcal{T}$ can be written as a union of elements of some subfamily of $\mathcal{U}$.*

A separable metric space, i.e. a space which has a countable dense subset, is second countable. In general topological space or in metric space the support of a measure may not exist. The advantage to define coherent upper conditional probability in a metric space by fractal outer measures is that if the metric space is separable the support always exists and if the metric space is not separable then the Hausdorff outer measure of any sets is infinity.

5 Conclusions

Coherent upper conditional previsions are defined with respect to different fractal outer measures, which do not share the same null sets. So the given models can be used to describe the different unconscious reactions to stimuli as it occurs in the experiments about selective attention and to represent different reactions of people to unexpected events.

Acknowledgments. The authors would like to thank the referees for their valuable comments and suggestions that led to the improvement of the manuscript. The first author is partially supported by INdAM-GNAMPA Project CUP E53C22001930001. The second author is supported by Analysis, Probability & Fractals Laboratory (No: LR18ES17).

References

1. Attia, N., Selmi, B.: A multifractal formalism for Hewitt-Stromberg measures. J. Geom. Anal. **31**, 825–862 (2021)
2. Doria, S.: Probabilistic independence with respect to upper and lower conditional probabilities assigned by Hausdorff outer and inner measures. Int. J. Approx. Reason. **46**, 617–635 (2007)
3. Doria, S.: Characterization of a coherent upper conditional prevision as the Choquet integral with respect to its associated Hausdorff outer measure. Ann. Oper. Res. **195**, 33–48 (2012)
4. Doria, S.: Symmetric coherent upper conditional prevision by the Choquet integral with respect to Hausdorff outer measure. Ann. Oper. Res. **229**, 377–396 (2014)

5. Doria, S.: On the disintegration property of a coherent upper conditional prevision by the Choquet integral with respect to its associated Hausdorff outer measure. Ann. Oper. Res. **216**, 253–269 (2017)

6. Doria, S.: Preference orderings represented by coherent upper and lower previsions. Theor. Decis. **87**, 233–259 (2019)

7. Doria, S., Cenci, A.: Modeling decisions in AI: re-thinking Linda in terms of coherent lower and upper conditional previsions. In: Torra, V., Narukawa, Y., Nin, J., Agell, N. (eds.) MDAI 2020. LNCS (LNAI), vol. 12256, pp. 41–52. Springer, Cham (2020). https://doi.org/10.1007/978-3-030-57524-3_4

8. Doria, S.: Coherent lower and upper conditional previsions defined by Hausdorff inner and outer measures to represent the role of conscious and unconscious thought in human decision making. Ann. Math. Artif. Intell. **89**, 947–964 (2021)

9. Doria, S.: Disintegration property for coherent upper conditional previsions defined by Hausdorff outer measures for bounded and unbounded random variables. Int. J. Gen. Syst. **50**, 262–280 (2021)

10. Doria, S.: Coherent upper conditional previsions with respect to outer Hausdorff measures and the mathematical representation of the selective attention. In: Ciucci, D., et al. (eds.) IPMU 2022. CCIS, vol. 1602, pp. 667–680. Springer, Cham (2022). https://doi.org/10.1007/978-3-031-08974-9_53

11. Doria, S.: Coherent conditional previsions with respect to inner and outer Hausdorff measures to represent conscious and unconscious human brain activity. Int. J. Approx. Reason. (2023). https://doi.org/10.1016/j.ijar.2023.02.011

12. Falconer, K.J.: Fractal Geometry: Mathematical Foundations and Applications. Wiley, Chichester (1990)

13. Fang, L., Ma, J., Song, K., Wu, M.: Multifractal analysis of the convergence exponent in continued fractions. Acta Mathematica Scientia **41**(6), 1896–1910 (2021). https://doi.org/10.1007/s10473-021-0607-1

14. Hewitt, E., Stromberg, K.: Real and Abstract Analysis. A Modern Treatment of the Theory of Functions of a Real Variable. Springer, New York (1965). https://doi.org/10.1007/978-3-662-29794-0

15. Luppi, A.I., et al.: Preserved fractal character of structural brain networks is associated with covert consciousness after severe brain injury. NeuroImage: Clin. **30**, 102682 (2021)

16. Oxtoby, J.: Measure and Category. Springer, New York (1980). https://doi.org/10.1007/978-1-4684-9339-9

17. Peyrière, J.: A vectorial multifractal formalism. Proc. Sympos. **72**, 217–230 (2004)

18. Rogers, C.A.: Hausdorff Measures. Cambridge University Press, Cambridge (1970)

19. Selmi, B.: A review on multifractal analysis of Hewitt-Stromberg measures. J. Geom. Anal. **32**, Article Number 12, 1–44 (2022)

20. Selmi, B.: Average Hewitt-Stromberg and box dimensions of typical compact metric spaces. Quaest. Math. (2022). https://doi.org/10.2989/16073606.2022.2033338

21. Shang, L., Wu, M.: On the exponent of convergence of the digit sequence of Engel series. J. Math. Anal. Appl. **504**, 125368 (2021)

22. Simons, D.J., Chabris, C.F.: Gorillas in our midst: sustained in attentional blindness for dynamic events. Perception **28**, 1059–1074 (1999)

23. Stevens, C., Bavelier, D.: The role of selective attention on academic foundations: a cognitive neuroscience perspective. Dev. Cogn. Neurosci. **2**(Suppl 1), S30–S48 (2012). https://doi.org/10.1016/j.dcn.2011.11.001

24. Varley, T.F., et al.: Fractal dimension of cortical functional connectivity networks and severity of disorders of consciousness. PLoS ONE **15**, e0223812 (2020)

25. Wise, G., Hall, E.: Counterexamples in Probability and Real Analysis. Oxford University Press, Oxford (1993)
26. Walley, P.: Statistical Reasoning with Imprecise Probabilities. Chapman and Hall, London (1991)

Discrete Chain-Based Choquet-Like Operators

Michał Boczek[1]([✉])[ID], Ondrej Hutník[2][ID], and Miriam Kleinová[2][ID]

[1] Institute of Mathematics, Lodz University of Technology, al. Politechniki 8,
93-590 Lodz, Poland
michal.boczek.1@p.lodz.pl
[2] Institute of Mathematics, Faculty of Science, Pavol Jozef Šafárik University
in Košice, Jesenná 5, 040 01 Košice, Slovakia
ondrej.hutnik@upjs.sk, miriam.kleinova@student.upjs.sk

Abstract. Using the setting of chains in the power set of subsets of a finite set, we propose new discrete Choquet-like operators. Our approach is based on aggregating values of a considered vector on consecutive sets of the chain and monotone measures of the sets. By means of appropriate binary operations, we define two types of operators and exemplify them. Several basic properties and the comparison with known classes of operators are given.

Keywords: Choquet-like operator · chain integral · IOWA · nonadditive integral · monotone measure · conditional aggregation operator

1 Introduction

The Choquet and the Sugeno integrals are two of the most well-known integrals with respect to monotone measure. There are several approaches in order to unify both integrals in a single framework. In 1991, Murofushi and Sugeno [9] proposed the fuzzy t-conorm integral which is based on the definition of a t-conorm system for integration that generalizes the pairs of operations: the product and sum (used in the Choquet integral) and the minimum and maximum (used in the Sugeno integral). The twofold integral [10] is an alternative generalization building the new integral in terms of operators generalizing both (· and min) and (+ and max) as well as considering two monotone measures (the one used in the Sugeno integral and the one in the Choquet integral). An axiomatic approach to integration called a universal integral is given in [8] where the universality of this approach consists in the possibility to define it on arbitrary measurable spaces. Recently, in [3] authors introduced a Choquet-Sugeno-like operator which is based on concepts of dependence relation between conditional

This work was supported by the Slovak Research and Development Agency under the contract No. APVV-21-0468 and VEGA 1/0657/22.

sets and conditional aggregation operators introduced in [2]. Conditions under which the Choquet-Sugeno-like operator coincides with some Choquet-like integrals defined on finite spaces and appeared recently in the literature are studied in [3,4].

The aim of this paper is to propose new types of operators based on chains. Starting from the generalized Choquet-Sugeno-like operator, we introduce two types of chain-based Choquet-like operators and relate them with the chain integrals and the IOWA operators.

2 Preliminaries

We employ the following notation throughout the paper: $\Sigma_n = 2^{[n]}$ is the power set of subsets of $X = [n] = \{1, \ldots, n\}$ with $n \in \mathbb{N} = \{1, 2, \ldots\}$ and $\Sigma_n^0 = \Sigma_n \setminus \{\varnothing\}$. A *monotone measure* on Σ_n is a nondecreasing set function $\mu \colon \Sigma_n \to [0, \infty)$, i.e., $\mu(B) \leqslant \mu(C)$ whenever $B \subset C$ for $B, C \in \Sigma_n$ with $\mu(\varnothing) = 0$, and $\mu([n]) > 0$, where "$\subset$" means the proper inclusion. We denote the class of all monotone measures on Σ_n by $\mathbf{M}_n$. Moreover, a *capacity* is a normalized monotone measure on Σ_n (i.e., $\mu([n]) = 1$). The weakest capacity μ_* and the strongest capacity μ^* are given by, respectively,

$$\mu_*(E) = \begin{cases} 1, & E = X, \\ 0, & \text{otherwise,} \end{cases} \qquad \mu^*(E) = \begin{cases} 0, & E = \varnothing, \\ 1, & \text{otherwise.} \end{cases}$$

By $\mathbf{F}_n$ we denote the set of all nonnegative functions on $[n]$, i.e., n-dimensional vectors $\mathbf{x} = (x_1, \ldots, x_n)$ with nonnegative entries x_i for $i \in [n]$. For any $K \subseteq [n]$, we let $\mathbb{1}_K \colon [n] \to \{0, 1\}$ denote the characteristic vector of K, that is the n-tuple whose ith coordinate is 1 if $i \in K$, and 0 otherwise. Also we often write $\mathbf{0}$ and $\mathbf{1}$ instead of $\mathbb{1}_\varnothing$ and $\mathbb{1}_{[n]}$, respectively. Finally, for any $\mathbf{x} \in \mathbf{F}_n$ and $E \subseteq [n]$, the vector $\mathbf{x} \cdot \mathbb{1}_E = (y_1, \ldots, y_n)$ is an n-tuple with $y_i = x_i$ if $i \in E$ and $y_i = 0$ otherwise. If $c \in [0, \infty)$, then the ith coordinate of $c \cdot \mathbb{1}_E$ is equal to c whenever $i \in E$ and 0, otherwise. Hereafter $(a)_+ = \max\{a, 0\}$.

Let us fix $E \in \Sigma_n^0$. The operator $\mathsf{A}(\cdot|E) \colon \mathbf{F}_n \to [0, \infty)$ satisfying

$(C1)$ $\mathsf{A}(\mathbf{x}|E) \leqslant \mathsf{A}(\mathbf{y}|E)$ for any $\mathbf{x}, \mathbf{y} \in \mathbf{F}_n$ such that $x_i \leqslant y_i$ for all $i \in E$;
$(C2)$ $\mathsf{A}(\mathbb{1}_{E^c}|E) = 0$

is called a *conditional aggregation operator* (CAO, for short) w.r.t. $E \in \Sigma_n^0$. The set E is called a conditional set. In order to consider arbitrary sets, we denote by $\mathscr{A} = \{\mathsf{A}(\cdot|E) \colon E \in \Sigma_n\}$ a *family of conditional aggregation operators* (FCA, for short). Note that for $E = \varnothing$ we usually have to make some conventions depending on the context. However, in this paper we need not consider the emptyset, see the reasoning after Definition 2, but for the sake of consistency with [2,3] we use the same setting, i.e., $\mathsf{A}(\cdot|\varnothing) = 0$.

Example 1. We will frequently use the following families of CAOs with superscript notation:

- $\mathscr{A}^{\text{sum}} = \{A^{\text{sum}}(\cdot|E) \colon E \in \Sigma_n\}$ with $A^{\text{sum}}(\mathbf{x}|E) = \sum_{i \in E} x_i$ for $E \in \Sigma_n^0$;
- $\mathscr{A}^{\text{prod}} = \{A^{\text{prod}}(\cdot|E) \colon E \in \Sigma_n\}$ with $A^{\text{prod}}(\mathbf{x}|E) = \prod_{i \in E} x_i$ for $E \in \Sigma_n^0$;
- $\mathscr{A}^{\text{AM}} = \{A^{\text{AM}}(\cdot|E) \colon E \in \Sigma_n\}$ with $A^{\text{AM}}(\mathbf{x}|E)$ being the arithmetic mean of $\mathbf{x}$ whose indices belong to $E \in \Sigma_n^0$;
- $\mathscr{A}^{\text{min}} = \{A^{\text{min}}(\cdot|E) \colon E \in \Sigma_n\}$ with $A^{\text{min}}(\mathbf{x}|E) = \min_{i \in E} x_i$ for $E \in \Sigma_n^0$;
- $\mathscr{A}^{\text{max}} = \{A^{\text{max}}(\cdot|E) \colon E \in \Sigma_n\}$ with $A^{\text{max}}(\mathbf{x}|E) = \max_{i \in E} x_i$ for $E \in \Sigma_n^0$.

For more examples and properties of CAOs we refer to [2]. Each FCA in Example 1 consists of *the same* CAOs w.r.t. any set $E \in \Sigma_n^0$. In general, the CAOs in family can differ on sets from Σ_n^0. For instance, if $X = [3]$, then the FCA $\mathscr{A} = \{A(\cdot|E) \colon E \in \Sigma_n\}$ can take the form

$$\mathscr{A} = \begin{cases} A^{\text{Su}_\nu}(\cdot|E) & \text{if } |E| = 1; \\ A^{\text{Ch}_\nu}(\cdot|E) & \text{if } |E| = 2; \\ A^{\text{sum}}(\cdot|E) & \text{if } |E| = 3; \end{cases} \tag{1}$$

where $\nu \in \mathbf{M}_n$, $A^{\text{Ch}_\nu}(\cdot|E) = \text{Ch}(\mathbf{x} \cdot \mathbb{1}_E, \nu)$ and $A^{\text{Su}_\nu}(\cdot|E) = \text{Su}(\mathbf{x} \cdot \mathbb{1}_E, \nu)$ are the Choquet and the Sugeno integrals of $\mathbf{x}$ restricted to E, see [5]. Such family is dealt with in Example 3.

Finally, we highlight several properties of CAOs. We say that a CAO $A(\cdot|E)$ is:

(i) *homogeneous of degree* θ if $A(\lambda^\theta \mathbf{x}|E) = \lambda^\theta A(\mathbf{x}|E)$ for any $\lambda > 0$ and any $\mathbf{x} \in \mathbf{F}_n$;
(ii) *idempotent* if $A(\lambda \cdot \mathbf{1}|E) = \lambda$ for any $\lambda \geq 0$.

A FCA $\mathscr{A} = \{A(\cdot|E) \colon E \in \Sigma_n\}$ is said to have a property P if for any $E \in \Sigma_n^0$, the operator $A(\cdot|E) \in \mathscr{A}$ has the property P.

In various parts of the paper we use some properties of a binary operation $\otimes \colon [0, \infty)^2 \to [0, \infty)$ summarised below:

(nD1) $\otimes$ is *nondecreasing in the first coordinate* if $x \otimes z \leqslant y \otimes z$ for any x, y, z such that $x \leqslant y$;
(H1) $\otimes$ is *homogeneous in the first coordinate* if $(\alpha \cdot x) \otimes y = \alpha \cdot (x \otimes y)$ for any x, y, α;
(H2) $\otimes$ is *homogeneous in the second coordinate* if $x \otimes (\beta \cdot y) = \beta \cdot (x \otimes y)$ for any x, y, β;
(RD) $\otimes$ *is right distributive over* $+$ if $(x + y) \otimes z = (x \otimes z) + (y \otimes z)$ for any x, y, z;
(LD) $\otimes$ *is left distributive over* $+$ if $x \otimes (y + z) = (x \otimes y) + (x \otimes z)$ for any x, y, z;
(RN) 1 is the *right neutral element* of $\otimes$ if $x \otimes 1 = x$ for any x;
(LN) 1 is the *left neutral element* of $\otimes$ if $1 \otimes x = x$ for any x;
(RA) 0 is the *right annihilator* of $\otimes$ if $x \otimes 0 = 0$ for any x;
(LA) 0 is the *left annihilator* of $\otimes$ if $0 \otimes x = 0$ for any x.

Remark 1. In the literature there is another concept related to the operator depending on the set, the so-called interaction operator introduced in [6]. A discussion on the relation between CAOs and interaction operators is presented in [3, Section 4.5].

3 Discrete Chain-Based Choquet-Sugeno-Like Operators

In [3], the authors introduced a wide class of Choquet-Sugeno-like operators. These operators are based on families of CAOs and a relation among the conditional sets which are chosen from a *collection* $\mathcal{D} \subseteq \Sigma_n^0$. A nonempty family $\mathcal{H}$ of collections is called a *decomposition system*, and for a fixed $\mathcal{D} \in \mathcal{H}$, $\mathcal{R} \subseteq (\mathcal{D} \cup \{\varnothing\})^4$ is said to be a *quaternary relation on* $\mathcal{D} \cup \{\varnothing\}$. Although the quaternary relation $\mathcal{R}$ depends on a collection $\mathcal{D}$, we will not indicate this dependence explicitly in the notation. For sets $C_1, D_1, C_2, D_2 \in \mathcal{D} \cup \{\varnothing\}$ being in a quaternary relation $\mathcal{R}$ we write $(C_1, D_1, C_2, D_2) \in \mathcal{R}$. The general definition (rewritten in the context of a discrete basic set $X = [n]$) reads as follows, see [3, Definition 6.1]. The set of all set functions $\widehat{\mu}\colon \Sigma_n \to (-\infty, \infty)$ with $\widehat{\mu}(\varnothing) = 0$ is denoted by $\widehat{\mathbf{M}}_n$.

Definition 1. *Let $\mathcal{H}$ be a decomposition system and $\mathcal{R}$ be a binary relation on $\mathcal{D} \cup \{\varnothing\}$ for $\mathcal{D} \in \mathcal{H}$. For* $L\colon [0,\infty]^3 \times (-\infty, \infty] \to (-\infty, \infty)$, *the generalized Choquet-Sugeno-like operator of* $\mathbf{x} \in \mathbf{F}_n$ *w.r.t.* $\mu \in \mathbf{M}_n$ *and* $\widehat{\mu} \in \widehat{\mathbf{M}}_n$ *is the operator*

$$g\mathrm{CS}^{\mathrm{L}}_{\mathcal{H}, \mathscr{A}, \widehat{\mathscr{A}}}(\mathbf{x}, \mu, \widehat{\mu}) = \sup_{\mathcal{D} \in \mathcal{H}} \sum_{(C_1, D_1, C_2, D_2) \in \mathcal{R}} \mathrm{L}\big(\mathsf{A}(\mathbf{x}|C_1), \widehat{\mathsf{A}}(\mathbf{x}|D_1), \mu(C_2), \widehat{\mu}(D_2)\big),$$

where $\mathscr{A} = \{\mathsf{A}(\cdot|E)\colon E \in \Sigma_n\}$ *and* $\widehat{\mathscr{A}} = \{\widehat{\mathsf{A}}(\cdot|E)\colon E \in \Sigma_n\}$ *are families of CAOs.*

3.1 ChainC-operator of Type 1

Put $\mathcal{H} = \{\Sigma_n^0\}$, $\mathscr{A} = \widehat{\mathscr{A}}$ and, $\mu = \widehat{\mu}$ in Definition 1. In this setup, we introduce a new operator based on chains in Σ_n. Recall that a *chain* in Σ_n is a collection $\mathcal{C} = \{C_0, C_1, \ldots, C_m\}$ of sets $C_i \in \Sigma_n$ for $i = 0, 1, \ldots, m$ with $m \geqslant 1$ such that $\varnothing = C_0 \subset C_1 \subset \cdots \subset C_m$. Denote the set of all chains in Σ_n by $\mathbf{Chain}(\Sigma_n)$. Now, taking the quaternary relation $\mathcal{R} = \{(C_i \setminus C_{i-1}, X, C_i, C_{i-1})\colon i \in [m]\}$ on Σ_n, and the function $\mathrm{L}(x, y, z, w) = x \otimes (z - w)_+$ with $\otimes\colon [0, \infty)^2 \to [0, \infty)$ being a binary operation, the generalized Choquet-Sugeno-like operator reduces to the following operator.

Definition 2. *Let* $(\mu, \mathbf{x}) \in \mathbf{M}_n \times \mathbf{F}_n$. *The chain-based Choquet-like operator of type 1 (shortly, (1)ChainC-operator) w.r.t. a chain* $\mathcal{C} = \{C_0, C_1, \ldots, C_m\}$ *in* Σ_n, *a FCA* $\mathscr{A}$ *and a binary operation* $\otimes\colon [0, \infty)^2 \to [0, \infty)$ *is defined by*

$$(1)\mathrm{CC}^{\otimes}_{\mathcal{C}, \mathscr{A}}(\mathbf{x}, \mu) = \sum_{i=1}^{m} \mathsf{A}(\mathbf{x}|C_i \setminus C_{i-1}) \otimes \Delta_{\mu}(C_i),$$

where $\Delta_{\mu}(C_i) = \mu(C_i) - \mu(C_{i-1})$.

In other words, the (1)ChainC-operator runs through the consecutive sets of the chain $\mathcal{C}$ and aggregates the increment of monotone measure μ on these sets with the aggregated value of $\mathbf{x}$ on their nonempty difference. More precisely, in the kth step, the value $\mathsf{A}(\mathbf{x}|C_k \setminus C_{k-1})$ represents the aggregation of $\mathbf{x}$ on the elements of the nonempty difference $C_k \setminus C_{k-1}$ only. Note that $C_k \setminus C_{k-1} \neq \varnothing$, therefore we need not consider the value of A on the emptyset (compare with the approach in [3]).

For the trivial chain $\mathcal{C} = \{\varnothing, X\}$, we have $(1)\mathrm{CC}_{\mathcal{C},\mathscr{A}}^{\otimes}(\mathbf{x},\mu) = \mathsf{A}(\mathbf{x}|X) \otimes \mu(X)$. So, for a capacity μ and an operation $\otimes$ satisfying (RN), we always recover the operator A on the whole set X. Further nontrivial examples are summarised below.

Example 2. Let μ_* be the weakest capacity, and $\otimes$ satisfies (RN) and (RA). Then the value of the (1)ChainC-operator is zero whenever $X \notin \mathcal{C}$. If $X \in \mathcal{C}$, then $(1)\mathrm{CC}_{\mathcal{C},\mathscr{A}}^{\otimes}(\mathbf{x},\mu_*) = \mathsf{A}(\mathbf{x}|X \setminus C_{m-1})$. Here the aggregation depends just on the penultimate set of the chain $\mathcal{C}$. On the other hand, for the strongest capacity μ^* we get $(1)\mathrm{CC}_{\mathcal{C},\mathscr{A}}^{\otimes}(\mathbf{x},\mu^*) = \mathsf{A}(\mathbf{x}|C_1)$, which depends only on the first (nonempty) set of the chain.

Now, we exemplify the (1)ChainC-operator w.r.t. a family of CAOs consisting of different CAOs.

Example 3. Consider the chain $\mathcal{C} = \{\varnothing, \{1\}, \{1,2,3\}\}$ in $X = [3]$, $\mu \in \mathbf{M}_3$ and $\mathbf{x} = (x_1, x_2, x_3) \in \mathbf{F}_3$ such that $x_2 \geq x_3$. Let $\mathscr{A}$ given by (1). Then the (1)ChainC-operator w.r.t. $\mathcal{C}$, $\mathscr{A}$ and $\otimes$ is of the form

$$(1)\mathrm{CC}_{\mathcal{C},\mathscr{A}}^{\otimes}(\mathbf{x},\mu) = \mathsf{A}^{\mathrm{Su}_\nu}(\mathbf{x}|\{1\}) \otimes \mu(\{1\}) + \mathsf{A}^{\mathrm{Ch}_\nu}(\mathbf{x}|\{2,3\}) \otimes (\mu(X) - \mu(\{1\}))$$

$$= \min\{x_1, \nu(\{1\})\} \otimes \mu(\{1\})$$
$$+ (x_2\nu(\{2\}) + x_3(\nu(\{2,3\}) - \nu(\{2\}))) \otimes (\mu(X) - \mu(\{1\})).$$

A chain $\mathcal{C}$ is called *maximal* in Σ_n, if there is no other chain in Σ_n which has $\mathcal{C}$ as a proper subset. The set of all maximal chains in Σ_n is denoted by **MaxChain**(Σ_n).

Example 4. Define a FCA $\mathscr{A} = \{\mathsf{A}(\cdot|E) : E \in \Sigma_n\}$ such that

(C3) $\mathsf{A}(\mathbf{x}|\{i\}) = x_i$ for each $\mathbf{x} \in \mathbf{F}_n$ and $i \in [n]$.

Many families of CAOs satisfy the above condition, e.g., $\mathscr{A}^{\mathrm{prod}}$, $\mathscr{A}^{\mathrm{sum}}$, and $\mathscr{A}^{\mathrm{min}}$. For any $\mathbf{x} \in \mathbf{F}_n$ with $n \geqslant 2$ and $\mathcal{C} = \{C_0, C_1, \ldots, C_m\} \in \mathbf{Chain}(\Sigma_n)$ such that $|C_i| = i$ for any $i \in [m]$ and $m \geqslant 2$, the (1)ChainC-operator w.r.t. $\mathscr{A}$ takes the form

$$(1)\mathrm{CC}_{\mathcal{C},\mathscr{A}}^{\otimes}(\mathbf{x},\mu) = x_1 \otimes \mu(\{1\}) + \sum_{i=2}^{m} x_i \otimes (\mu(C_i) - \mu(C_{i-1})). \qquad (2)$$

In particular, for $\mu(E) = i$ for $|E| = i$, we get

$$(1)\mathrm{CC}_{\mathcal{C},\mathscr{A}}^{\otimes}(\mathbf{x},\mu) = \sum_{i=1}^{m}(x_i \otimes 1).$$

Additionally, for a fixed $\mathbf{x} \in \mathbf{F}_n$ there exists a maximal chain $\mathcal{C} = \{C_0, C_1, \ldots, C_n\}$ for which operator (2) is the Choquet integral.

We now show the relationship to the IOWA. Recall the definition of the IOWA (see [1, Definition 8] or [12]):

Definition 3. *Given a weighting vector* $\mathbf{w} = (w_1, \ldots, w_n)$ *and an inducing variable* $\mathbf{y} = (y_1, \ldots, y_n)$ *the Induced Ordered Weighted Averaging (IOWA, for short) function is*

$$\text{IOWA}_{(\mathbf{y})}(\mathbf{x}, \mathbf{w}) = \sum_{i=1}^{n} x_{\eta(i)} w_i \tag{3}$$

for any $\mathbf{x} \in \mathbf{F}_n$, *where the* $\eta(\cdot)$ *notation denotes the inputs* (x_i, y_i) *reordered such that* $y_{\eta(1)} \geqslant y_{\eta(2)} \geqslant \ldots \geqslant y_{\eta(n)}$ *and the convention that if q of the* $y_{\eta(i)}$ *are tied, i.e.,* $y_{\eta(i)} = \ldots = y_{\eta(i+q-1)}$, *then*

$$x_{\eta(i)} = \frac{1}{q} \sum_{j=\eta(i)}^{\eta(i+q-1)} x_j.$$

In the following example we show the calculation of the IOWA for the fixed data and we compare it with the value of the (1)ChainC-operator.

Example 5. For $X = [4]$, we firstly compute the value of IOWA operator of the vector $\mathbf{x} = (5, 8, 9, 11)$ w.r.t. the weighting vector $\mathbf{w} = (0.4, 0.3, 0.2, 0.1)$ and inducing vector $\mathbf{y} = (1, 1, 2, 5)$. Since $\mathbf{y}_{\downarrow} = (5, 2, 1, 1)$, where $\mathbf{y}_{\downarrow}$ denotes the rearranged vector $\mathbf{y}$ in nonincreasing way, and there are two ties in the inducing vector, we get

$$\text{IOWA}_{(\mathbf{y})}(\mathbf{x}, \mathbf{w}) = 11 \cdot w_1 + 9 \cdot w_2 + \frac{5+8}{2} \cdot (w_3 + w_4) = 9.05.$$

Let $\mathscr{A} = \mathscr{A}^{\text{AM}}$, $\otimes = \text{Prod}$ and $\mu_{\mathbf{w}}(E) = \sum_{i=1}^{|E|} w_i$ for any E. Then for $\mathcal{C}_1 = \{\varnothing, \{4\}, \{1, 2, 4\}, X\}$, the (1)ChainC-operator takes the form

$$(1)\text{CC}_{\mathcal{C}_1, \mathscr{A}^{\text{AM}}}^{\text{Prod}}(\mathbf{x}, \mu_{\mathbf{w}}) = 11 \cdot \mu_{\mathbf{w}}(\{4\}) + \frac{5+8}{2} \cdot \big(\mu_{\mathbf{w}}(\{1, 2, 4\}) - \mu_{\mathbf{w}}(\{4\})\big)$$

$$+ 9 \cdot \big(\mu_{\mathbf{w}}(\{1, 2, 3, 4\}) - \mu_{\mathbf{w}}\{1, 2, 4\}\big)$$

$$= 11 \cdot w_1 + \frac{13}{2} \cdot (w_2 + w_3) + 9 \cdot w_4 = 8.55 \neq \text{IOWA}_{(\mathbf{y})}(\mathbf{x}, \mathbf{w}).$$

However, for the chain $\mathcal{C}_2 = \{\varnothing, \{4\}, \{3, 4\}, X\}$, the (1)ChainC-operator coincides with IOWA, since

$$(1)\text{CC}_{\mathcal{C}_2, \mathscr{A}^{\text{AM}}}^{\text{Prod}}(\mathbf{x}, \mu_{\mathbf{w}}) = 11 \cdot \mu_{\mathbf{w}}(\{4\}) + 9 \cdot \big(\mu_{\mathbf{w}}(\{3, 4\}) - \mu_{\mathbf{w}}(\{4\})\big)$$

$$+ \frac{5+8}{2} \cdot \big(\mu_{\mathbf{w}}(\{1, 2, 3, 4\}) - \mu_{\mathbf{w}}(\{3, 4\})\big)$$

$$= 11 \cdot w_1 + 9 w_2 + \frac{13}{2}(w_3 + w_4) = 9.05.$$

Example 5 exemplifies a way how to construct the chain for which IOWA takes the same value as the (1)ChainC-operator. We now describe the construction of such a chain in general. Let $\mathbf{y} \in \mathbf{F}_n$ and $\eta \colon [n] \to [n]$ be a permutation such that $y_{\eta(1)} \geqslant \dots \geqslant y_{\eta(n)}$. Let's choose k unique values in the sequence $(y_{\eta(i)})_{i=1}^n$ and form a k-element sequence $(a_i)_{i=1}^k$ in the following way: $a_1 > \dots > a_k$ with $k \geqslant 1$. Putting $C_j = \{\eta(i) \colon y_{\eta(i)} \geqslant a_j\}$ for any $j \in [k]$, we have constructed a chain $\mathcal{C}_{\mathbf{y}} = \{C_0, C_1, \dots, C_k\}$ with $C_0 = \varnothing$. Note that the sequence $(C_j)_{j=1}^k$ is the same, it is independent on the choice of the permutation η. For the data from Example 5 and permutation $\eta = (4, 3, 2, 1)$, we get

$$C_1 = \{\eta(1)\} = \{4\}, \quad C_2 = \{\eta(1), \eta(2)\} = \{3, 4\}, \quad C_3 = \{\eta(1), \eta(2), \eta(3), \eta(4)\} = X.$$

The same sets $(C_i)_{i=1}^k$ can be obtained when using the second possible permutation $\eta = (4, 3, 1, 2)$. Now put $D_j = C_j \setminus C_{j-1} = \{\eta(i) \colon a_j \leqslant y_{\eta(i)} < a_{j-1}\}$ for $j \geqslant 1$ under the convention $a_0 = \infty$. The set D_j consists of such indices i for which the values of y_i have the same value as $y_{\eta(j)}$, i.e., $y_i = y_{\eta(j)}$ for any $i \in D_j$. Thence, the value $\mathsf{A}^{\mathrm{AM}}(\mathbf{x}|D_i)$ corresponds to the arithmetic mean of all ties. Then

$$(1)\mathrm{CC}^{\mathrm{Prod}}_{\mathcal{C}_{\mathbf{y}}, \mathscr{A}^{\mathrm{AM}}}(\mathbf{x}, \mu_{\mathbf{w}}) = \sum_{i=1}^{k} \mathsf{A}^{\mathrm{AM}}(\mathbf{x}|C_i \setminus C_{i-1}) \cdot \varDelta_{\mu_{\mathbf{w}}}(C_i) = \mathrm{IOWA}_{(\mathbf{y})}(\mathbf{x}, \mathbf{w}).$$

Our consideration is summarised in the following proposition.

Proposition 1. *For each $\mathbf{x}, \mathbf{y} \in \mathbf{F}_n$ and each weighting vector $\mathbf{w}$, there exists $\mathcal{C}_{\mathbf{y}} \in \mathbf{Chain}(\Sigma_n)$ such that*

$$(1)\mathrm{CC}^{\mathrm{Prod}}_{\mathcal{C}_{\mathbf{y}}, \mathscr{A}^{\mathrm{AM}}}(\mathbf{x}, \mu_{\mathbf{w}}) = \mathrm{IOWA}_{(\mathbf{y})}(\mathbf{x}, \mathbf{w}),$$

where $\mu_{\mathbf{w}}(E) = \sum_{i=1}^{|E|} w_i$.

3.2 ChainC-operator of Type 2

We now consider yet another special case of the generalized Choquet-Sugeno-like operator, which enables us to cover the chain integral [11]. Let $\mathcal{C} = \{C_0, C_1, \dots, C_m\} \in \mathbf{Chain}(\Sigma_n)$. Putting $\mathcal{H} = \{\Sigma_n^0\}$, $\mathscr{A} = \widehat{\mathscr{A}}$, $\mu = \widehat{\mu}$, $\mathrm{L}(x, y, z, w) = x \otimes (z - w)_+$ and the quaternary relation $\mathcal{R} = \{(C_i, X, C_i, C_{i-1}) \colon i \in [m]\}$ on Σ_n in Definition 1, we get the *chain-based Choquet-like operator of type 2* (shortly, (2)ChainC-operator),

$$(2)\mathrm{CC}^{\otimes}_{\mathcal{C}, \mathscr{A}}(\mathbf{x}, \mu) = \sum_{i=1}^{m} \mathsf{A}(\mathbf{x}|C_i) \otimes \varDelta_{\mu}(C_i).$$

Observe that the aggregation of vector $\mathbf{x}$ depends only on sets from the chain $\mathcal{C}$.

Example 6. Consider $\mathscr{A} = \mathscr{A}^{\min}$. For a chain $\mathcal{C} = \{C_0, C_1, \ldots, C_m\}$, the (2)ChainC-operator takes the form

$$(2)\mathrm{CC}^{\otimes}_{\mathcal{C}, \mathscr{A}^{\min}}(\mathbf{x}, \mu) = \sum_{i=1}^{m} \min_{j \in C_i}\{x_j\} \otimes \Delta_\mu(C_i). \tag{4}$$

Regarding the product-based operator, by rearranging the terms of the sum, we get the chain-integral defined in [11]

$$(2)\mathrm{CC}^{\mathrm{Prod}}_{\mathcal{C}, \mathscr{A}^{\min}}(\mathbf{x}, \mu) = \sum_{k=1}^{m} \big(\min_{j \in C_k}\{x_j\} - \min_{j \in C_{k+1}}\{x_j\}\big)\mu(C_k)$$

under the convention $\min_{j \in C_{m+1}} x_j = 0$.

3.3   Basic Properties of ChainC-operator of Type 1 and 2

Some elementary properties of the (j)ChainC-operator, $j \in [2]$, are summarised in the following proposition. Recall that for two families of CAOs $\mathscr{A}_1$ and $\mathscr{A}_2$ we write $\mathscr{A}_1 \leqslant \mathscr{A}_2$ if $A_1(\mathbf{x}|E) \leqslant A_2(\mathbf{x}|E)$ for any $A_1 \in \mathscr{A}_1, A_2 \in \mathscr{A}_2$, any $\mathbf{x} \in \mathbf{F}_n$ and any $E \in \Sigma_n^0$. Similarly, we write $\otimes_1 \leqslant \otimes_2$ whenever $x \otimes_1 y \leqslant x \otimes_2 y$ for any $x, y \in [0, \infty)$.

Notation. To shorten the notations, we will write

$$(j)\mathrm{CC}^{\otimes}_{\mathcal{C}, \mathscr{A}}(\mathbf{x}, \mu) = \sum_{i=1}^{m} A(\mathbf{x}|D_i) \otimes \Delta_\mu(C_i)$$

for $j \in [2]$, where $D_i = C_i \setminus C_{i-1}$ for $j = 1$ and $D_i = C_i$ for $j = 2$.

Proposition 2. *Let $j \in [2]$, $\mathcal{C} \in \mathbf{Chain}(\Sigma_n)$, $\mathscr{A}, \mathscr{A}_i$ be families of CAOs, $\mu, \mu_i \in \mathbf{M}_n$, $\mathbf{x}, \mathbf{x}_i \in \mathbf{F}_n$ and $\otimes, \otimes_i \colon [0, \infty)^2 \to [0, \infty)$ for each $i = 1, 2$.*

- (i) *If $\otimes$ satisfies (nD1), then $(j)\mathrm{CC}^{\otimes}_{\mathcal{C}, \mathscr{A}}(\mathbf{x}_1, \mu) \leqslant (j)\mathrm{CC}^{\otimes}_{\mathcal{C}, \mathscr{A}}(\mathbf{x}_2, \mu)$ whenever $\mathbf{x}_1 \leqslant \mathbf{x}_2$.*
- (ii) *If $\otimes$ satisfies (nD1), then $(j)\mathrm{CC}^{\otimes}_{\mathcal{C}, \mathscr{A}_1}(\mathbf{x}, \mu) \leqslant (j)\mathrm{CC}^{\otimes}_{\mathcal{C}, \mathscr{A}_2}(\mathbf{x}, \mu)$ whenever $\mathscr{A}_1 \leqslant \mathscr{A}_2$.*
- (iii) *If $\otimes_1 \leqslant \otimes_2$, then $(j)\mathrm{CC}^{\otimes_1}_{\mathcal{C}, \mathscr{A}}(\mathbf{x}, \mu) \leqslant (j)\mathrm{CC}^{\otimes_2}_{\mathcal{C}, \mathscr{A}}(\mathbf{x}, \mu)$.*
- (iv) *If $\mathscr{A}$ is homogeneous of degree θ and $\otimes$ satisfies (H1), then $(j)\mathrm{CC}^{\otimes}_{\mathcal{C}, \mathscr{A}}(\lambda^\theta \mathbf{x}, \mu) = \lambda^\theta \cdot (j)\mathrm{CC}^{\otimes}_{\mathcal{C}, \mathscr{A}}(\mathbf{x}, \mu)$ for each $\lambda \geqslant 0$.*
- (v) *If $\otimes$ satisfies (LA), then $(j)\mathrm{CC}^{\otimes}_{\mathcal{C}, \mathscr{A}}(\mathbf{0}, \mu) = 0$.*
- (vi) *Let $X \in \mathcal{C}$. If $\mathscr{A}^{\min} \leqslant \mathscr{A}$ and $\otimes$ satisfies (nD1) and (LD), then $A^{\min}(\mathbf{x}|X) \otimes \mu(X) \leqslant (j)\mathrm{CC}^{\otimes}_{\mathcal{C}, \mathscr{A}}(\mathbf{x}, \mu)$.*
- (vii) *Let $X \in \mathcal{C}$. If $\mathscr{A} \leqslant \mathscr{A}^{\max}$ and $\otimes$ satisfies (nD1) and (LD), then $A^{\max}(\mathbf{x}|X) \otimes \mu(X) \geqslant (j)\mathrm{CC}^{\otimes}_{\mathcal{C}, \mathscr{A}}(\mathbf{x}, \mu)$.*

Proof. Proofs of (i), (ii) and (iii) are immediate by definition, and therefore omitted.

(iv) Under the assumptions of homogeneity of FCA $\mathscr{A}$ and $(\alpha \cdot \beta) \otimes \gamma = \alpha \cdot (\beta \otimes \gamma)$ for each $\alpha, \beta, \gamma \geq 0$, we get

$$(j)\mathrm{CC}^{\otimes}_{\mathcal{C},\mathscr{A}}(\lambda^{\theta}\mathbf{x}, \mu) = \sum_{i=1}^{m} \left(\lambda^{\theta} \cdot \mathsf{A}(\mathbf{x}|D_i)\right) \otimes \Delta_{\mu}(C_i) = \lambda^{\theta} \cdot \sum_{i=1}^{m} \mathsf{A}(\mathbf{x}|D_i) \otimes \Delta_{\mu}(C_i)$$

$$= \lambda^{\theta} \cdot (j)\mathrm{CC}^{\otimes}_{\mathcal{C},\mathscr{A}}(\mathbf{x}, \mu).$$

(v) From the fact that 0 is the left annihilator of $\otimes$ and $\mathsf{A}(\mathbf{0}|E) = 0$ for any $E \in \Sigma_n^0$ (see [2, Proposition 3.3 (c)]), we get the sum of zeros.

(vi) From the assumptions we immediately get

$$(j)\mathrm{CC}^{\otimes}_{\mathcal{C},\mathscr{A}}(\mathbf{x}, \mu) \geqslant \sum_{i=1}^{m} \mathsf{A}^{\min}(\mathbf{x}|D_i) \otimes \Delta_{\mu}(C_i) \geqslant \sum_{i=1}^{m} \mathsf{A}^{\min}(\mathbf{x}|X) \otimes \Delta_{\mu}(C_i)$$

$$= \mathsf{A}^{\min}(\mathbf{x}|X) \otimes \sum_{i=1}^{m} \Delta_{\mu}(C_i) = \mathsf{A}^{\min}(\mathbf{x}|X) \otimes \mu(X).$$

(vii) Similarly as above we have

$$(j)\mathrm{CC}^{\otimes}_{\mathcal{C},\mathscr{A}}(\mathbf{x}, \mu) \leqslant \sum_{i=1}^{m} \mathsf{A}^{\max}(\mathbf{x}|D_i) \otimes \Delta_{\mu}(C_i)$$

$$\leqslant \sum_{i=1}^{m} \mathsf{A}^{\max}(\mathbf{x}|X) \otimes \Delta_{\mu}(C_i) = \mathsf{A}^{\max}(\mathbf{x}|X) \otimes \mu(X),$$

which gives the desired result. □

Remark 2. – Let $j = 1$ in (i). Fixing a chain $\mathcal{C}$, we can weaken the condition $\mathbf{x} \leqslant \mathbf{y}$ to compare the vectors only on differences of sets from $\mathcal{C}$.
- Regarding the condition (H1) in (iv), for $\otimes = \mathrm{Prod}$ the identity $(\alpha \cdot \beta) \otimes \gamma = \alpha \cdot (\beta \otimes \gamma)$ is nothing but the associativity of the standard product. The next operation satisfying (H1) is any operation of the form $x \otimes_g y = x \cdot g(y)$ with $g \colon [0, \infty) \to [0, \infty)$. For $g(t) = 1$ we get the first canonical projection $\mathrm{Proj}_1(x, y) = x$.
- Note also that in (vi) the condition (LD) can be weakened to *left subdistributivity* $x \otimes (y + z) \leqslant (x \otimes y) + (x \otimes z)$, and in (vii) to *left superdistributivity* $x \otimes (y + z) \geqslant (x \otimes y) + (x \otimes z)$ for each $x, y, z \in [0, \infty)$.

As a corollary we get the mean behaviour of the (j)ChainC-operator. Since the compensation property $\mathsf{A}^{\min} \leqslant \mathsf{A} \leqslant \mathsf{A}^{\max}$ is, in fact, equivalent to the idempotency[1] of A, see [2, Proposition 3.10 and Remark 3.11], we get the following consequence.

---

[1] The CAO $\mathsf{A}(\cdot|E)$ is idempotent if $\mathsf{A}(b \cdot \mathbf{1}|E) = b$ for any $b \geqslant 0$.

Corollary 1. *Let* $\mathcal{C} \in \mathbf{Chain}(\Sigma_n)$, $X \in \mathcal{C}$, $\mathscr{A}$ *be an idempotent FCA and* $\mu \in \mathbf{M}_n$ *be a capacity. If* $\otimes$ *satisfies* (nD1), (LD) *and* (RN), *then the* (j)*ChainC-operator,* $j \in [2]$, *is a mean, i.e.,*

$$\mathsf{A}^{\min}(\mathbf{x}|X) \leqslant (j)\mathrm{CC}^{\otimes}_{\mathcal{C},\mathscr{A}}(\mathbf{x},\mu) \leqslant \mathsf{A}^{\max}(\mathbf{x}|X).$$

3.4   Linearity Property

Linearity of nonadditive integrals usually holds under some restrictive conditions on monotone measures or input vectors. However, the (j)ChainC-operator w.r.t. a fixed chain is a linear functional (in vectors as well as monotone measures) under some mild conditions. In what follows, $\widehat{\mathbf{F}}_n^2 \subseteq \mathbf{F}_n^2$ is a nonempty set.

Proposition 3. *Let* $\mathcal{C} = \{C_0, C_1, \ldots, C_m\} \in \mathbf{Chain}(\Sigma_n)$ *and* $\mathcal{D} = \{D_1, \ldots, D_m\}$ *be either* $D_i = C_i \setminus C_{i-1}$ *for any* i *or* $D_i = C_i$ *for any* i. *Assume that* $\mathscr{A}$ *is a FCA such that* $\mathsf{A}(\cdot|E)$ *is homogeneous of degree 1 for any* $E \in \mathcal{D}$ *and* $\mathsf{A}(\mathbf{x}|E) + \mathsf{A}(\mathbf{y}|E) = \mathsf{A}(\mathbf{x}+\mathbf{y}|E)$ *for any* $(\mathbf{x},\mathbf{y}) \in \widehat{\mathbf{F}}_n^2$ *and any* $E \in \mathcal{D}$. *If* $\otimes$ *satisfies* (RD) *and* (H1), *then*

$$(j)\mathrm{CC}^{\otimes}_{\mathcal{C},\mathscr{A}}(\alpha\mathbf{x} + \beta\mathbf{y}, \mu) = \alpha \cdot (j)\mathrm{CC}^{\otimes}_{\mathcal{C},\mathscr{A}}(\mathbf{x},\mu) + \beta \cdot (j)\mathrm{CC}^{\otimes}_{\mathcal{C},\mathscr{A}}(\mathbf{y},\mu) \qquad (5)$$

for any $j \in [2]$, *any* $\alpha, \beta \geq 0$, *any* $(\mathbf{x},\mathbf{y}) \in \widehat{\mathbf{F}}_n^2$ *and any* $\mu \in \mathbf{M}_n$.

Proof. Using the assumption of $\mathscr{A}$, and then (RD) and (H1) we get

$$(j)\mathrm{CC}^{\otimes}_{\mathcal{C},\mathscr{A}}(\alpha\mathbf{x} + \beta\mathbf{y}, \mu) = \sum_{i=1}^{m} \big(\alpha\mathsf{A}(\mathbf{x}|D_i) + \beta\mathsf{A}(\mathbf{y}|D_i)\big) \otimes \Delta_\mu(C_i)$$

$$= \alpha \cdot (j)\mathrm{CC}^{\otimes}_{\mathcal{C},\mathscr{A}}(\mathbf{x},\mu) + \beta \cdot (j)\mathrm{CC}^{\otimes}_{\mathcal{C},\mathscr{A}}(\mathbf{y},\mu),$$

which completes the proof. $\square$

Corollary 2. *If* $\mathcal{C} \in \mathbf{MaxChain}(\Sigma_n)$, *any CAO from* $\mathscr{A} = \{\mathsf{A}(\cdot|E) \colon E \in \Sigma_n\}$ *satisfies* (C3), $\otimes$ *satisfies* (RD) *and* (H1), *then*

$$(1)\mathrm{CC}^{\otimes}_{\mathcal{C},\mathscr{A}}(\alpha\mathbf{x} + \beta\mathbf{y}, \mu) = \alpha \cdot (1)\mathrm{CC}^{\otimes}_{\mathcal{C},\mathscr{A}}(\mathbf{x},\mu) + \beta \cdot (1)\mathrm{CC}^{\otimes}_{\mathcal{C},\mathscr{A}}(\mathbf{y},\mu) \qquad (6)$$

for any $\alpha, \beta \geq 0$, *any* $(\mathbf{x},\mathbf{y}) \in \mathbf{F}_n^2$ *and any* $\mu \in \mathbf{M}_n$.

Recall that the Choquet integral is additive either for all vectors (if and only if $\mu \in \mathbf{M}_n$ is additive, cf. [5, Proposition 5.41], thus the terminology *additivity* of the integral), or for all monotone measures (whenever $\mathbf{x}, \mathbf{y} \in \mathbf{F}_n$ are comonotone, thus the terminology *comonotone additivity*, see [5, Proposition 5.36(ii)]). In other words, according to Example 4, for $\otimes = \mathrm{Prod}$, arbitrary vectors $\mathbf{x}, \mathbf{y} \in \mathbf{F}_n$ and monotone measure $\mu \in \mathbf{M}_n$, if the operator on the left-hand side of (6) is the Choquet integral, the operators on the right-hand side of (6) need not be the Choquet integrals.

From the fact that the FCA $\mathscr{A}^{\min}$ is additive for any comonotone vectors (see [7, Theorem 2.7]), the following consequence is obtained.

Corollary 3. *Let* $\mathcal{C} \in \mathbf{Chain}(\Sigma_n)$. *If* $\otimes$ *satisfies* (RD) *and* (H1), *then*

$$(2)\mathrm{CC}^{\otimes}_{\mathcal{C},\mathscr{A}\min}(\alpha\mathbf{x} + \beta\mathbf{y}, \mu) = \alpha \cdot (2)\mathrm{CC}^{\otimes}_{\mathcal{C},\mathscr{A}\min}(\mathbf{x}, \mu) + \beta \cdot (2)\mathrm{CC}^{\otimes}_{\mathcal{C},\mathscr{A}\min}(\mathbf{y}, \mu)$$

for any $\alpha, \beta \geq 0$, *any comonotone vectors* $\mathbf{x}, \mathbf{y} \in \mathbf{F}_n$ *and any* $\mu \in \mathbf{M}_n$.

The linearity of (j)ChainC-operators (in monotone measures) is the result of the next proposition.

Proposition 4. *Let* $j \in [2]$ *and* $\mathcal{C} \in \mathbf{Chain}(\Sigma_n)$. *If* $\otimes$ *satisfies* (LD) *and* (H2), *then*

$$(j)\mathrm{CC}^{\otimes}_{\mathcal{C},\mathscr{A}}(\mathbf{x}, \alpha\mu + \beta\nu) = \alpha \cdot (j)\mathrm{CC}^{\otimes}_{\mathcal{C},\mathscr{A}}(\mathbf{x}, \mu) + \beta \cdot (j)\mathrm{CC}^{\otimes}_{\mathcal{C},\mathscr{A}}(\mathbf{x}, \nu)$$

for any $\alpha, \beta \geq 0$, *any* $\mathbf{x} \in \mathbf{F}_n$ *and any* $\mu, \nu \in \mathbf{M}_n$.

Proof. For $\mathcal{C} = \{C_0, C_1, \ldots, C_m\} \in \mathbf{Chain}(\Sigma_n)$, we immediately have the equalities

$$\begin{aligned}
(j)\mathrm{CC}^{\otimes}_{\mathcal{C},\mathscr{A}}(\mathbf{x}, \alpha\mu + \beta\nu) &= \sum_{i=1}^{m} \mathsf{A}(\mathbf{x}|D_i) \otimes \left(\alpha \cdot \Delta_\mu(C_i) + \beta \cdot \Delta_\nu(C_i)\right) \\
&\overset{(\mathrm{LD})}{=} \sum_{i=1}^{m} \left(\mathsf{A}(\mathbf{x}|D_i) \otimes (\alpha \cdot \Delta_\mu(C_i)) + \mathsf{A}(\mathbf{x}|D_i) \otimes (\beta \cdot \Delta_\nu(C_i))\right) \\
&\overset{(\mathrm{H2})}{=} \alpha \cdot \sum_{i=1}^{m} \mathsf{A}(\mathbf{x}|D_i) \otimes \Delta_\mu(C_i) + \beta \cdot \sum_{i=1}^{m} \mathsf{A}(\mathbf{x}|D_i) \otimes \Delta_\nu(C_i) \\
&= \alpha \cdot (j)\mathrm{CC}^{\otimes}_{\mathcal{C},\mathscr{A}}(\mathbf{x}, \mu) + \beta \cdot (j)\mathrm{CC}^{\otimes}_{\mathcal{C},\mathscr{A}}(\mathbf{x}, \nu),
\end{aligned}$$

which prove the result. $\square$

3.5 (j)ChainC-Operator as Monotone Measure Extension

Many important nonadditive integrals (e.g., Choquet, Shilkret, Sugeno, Imaoka, Weber, etc.) return the values of monotone measure on Σ_n being an extension of the underlying monotone measure. In this section we discuss this question w.r.t. (j)ChainC-operator in details.

Proposition 5. *Let* $\mathcal{C} \in \mathbf{Chain}(\Sigma_n)$ *and* $\mathscr{A}$ *be an idempotent FCA.*

(a) *If* $\otimes$ *satisfies* (LA) *and* (LD), *then for each* $B \in \mathcal{C}$ *and* $c \geqslant 0$ *we have*
    $(1)\mathrm{CC}^{\otimes}_{\mathcal{C},\mathscr{A}}(c \cdot \mathbb{1}_B, \mu) = c \otimes \mu(B)$.
(b) *If* $\otimes$ *satisfies* (LA) *and* (LN), *then for each* $B \in \mathcal{C}$ *we have*
    $(1)\mathrm{CC}^{\otimes}_{\mathcal{C},\mathscr{A}}(\mathbb{1}_B, \mu) = \mu(B)$.

Proof. Since $B \in \mathcal{C} = \{C_0, C_1, \ldots, C_m\}$, there exists $k \in [m]$ such that $B = C_k \in \mathcal{C}$. Clearly, for any $i \in [m]$ with $i \leq k$ we have $C_i \setminus C_{i-1} \subseteq C_k$, and $(C_i \setminus C_{i-1}) \cap C_k = \varnothing$ whenever $i > k$. Then, by [2, Proposition 3.3], we get

$A(c \cdot \mathbb{1}_{C_k}|C_i \setminus C_{i-1}) = c$ for $i \leqslant k$, and 0 otherwise. So, by the idempotency of $\mathscr{A}$, we have

$$(1)CC^{\otimes}_{C,\mathscr{A}}(c \cdot \mathbb{1}_B, \mu) = \sum_{i=1}^{k} c \otimes \Delta_\mu(C_i) + \sum_{i=k+1}^{m} 0 \otimes \Delta_\mu(C_i).$$

(a) By the left distributivity of $\otimes$ and (LA) we get

$$(1)CC^{\otimes}_{C,\mathscr{A}}(c \cdot \mathbb{1}_B, \mu) = c \otimes \sum_{i=1}^{k} \Delta_\mu(C_i) = c \otimes \mu(C_k) = c \otimes \mu(B).$$

(b) By (LA) and (LN) we obtain

$$(1)CC^{\otimes}_{C,\mathscr{A}}(\mathbb{1}_B, \mu) = \sum_{i=1}^{k} \Delta_\mu(C_i) = \mu(C_k) = \mu(B),$$

which completes the proof. $\qquad\square$

Remark 3. Observe that for $B = [n] \in C$ the assumption (LA) in Proposition 5 (b) is superfluous. In the case of (1)ChainC-operator, we can reconstruct only sets from the chain which the integral is related to. In general, it is not possible to get back the monotone measure of a set outside the chain. On the other hand, as is well-known, the monotone measure reconstruction for the Choquet integral is true for each set from Σ_n, see [5, Proposition 5.36(i)]. The reason is that for the characteristic vector $\mathbb{1}_B$ of a set $B \in \Sigma_n$ the chain $C_\downarrow$ (which corresponds to a permutation rearranging an input vector in nonincreasing way) is constructed, in which the set B is included, and its reconstruction can be done by Proposition 5 (b). If we change the set (in general, from Σ_n), we change the chain and correspondingly we compute a different (1)ChainC-operator (which need not be the Choquet one!).

Proposition 6. *Let* $C = \{C_0, C_1, \ldots, C_m\}$, $d \geqslant 0$ *and* $\mathscr{A}$ *be an idempotent FCA such that* $A(c \cdot \mathbb{1}_{C_k}|C_i) = d$ *for* $i > k$. *If* $\otimes$ *satisfies* (LD)*, then for each* $C_k \in C$ *with* $k < m$ *and* $c \geqslant 0$ *we have* $(2)CC^{\otimes}_{C,\mathscr{A}}(c \cdot \mathbb{1}_{C_k}, \mu) = c \otimes \mu(C_k) + d \otimes (\mu(C_m) - \mu(C_k))$.

Proof. By the idempotency and [2, Proposition 3.3], we get $A(c \cdot \mathbb{1}_{C_k}|C_i) = c$ for $i \leqslant k$. By (LD) and assumptions, we have

$$(2)CC^{\otimes}_{C,\mathscr{A}}(c \cdot \mathbb{1}_{C_k}, \mu) = \sum_{i=1}^{k} c \otimes \Delta_\mu(C_i) + \sum_{i=k+1}^{m} d \otimes \Delta_\mu(C_i)$$
$$= c \otimes \mu(C_k) + d \otimes (\mu(C_m) - \mu(C_k)),$$

which completes the proof. $\qquad\square$

Putting $\mathscr{A}^{\min}$ in Proposition 6, we get $d = 0$ and

$$(2)CC^{\otimes}_{C,\mathscr{A}^{\min}}(\mathbb{1}_{C_k}, \mu) = \mu(C_k)$$

whenever (LA) and (LN) holds.

4   Conclusion

In this contribution, we have introduced two types of Choquet-like operators based on a chain in the algebra of power sets of a finite set. Starting from the generalized Choquet-Sugeno-like operator defined in [3] we were able to describe broader frameworks including the IOWA operator and the chain integral discussed in [11,12], respectively. We have also proved several basic properties of these operators. The most surprising property is the linearity of both operators w.r.t. vectors. Furthermore, both operators have been studied in connection with the monotone measure reconstruction.

References

1. Beliakov, G., James, S.: Induced ordered weighted averaging operators. In: Yager, R.R., Kacprzyk, J., Beliakov, G. (eds.) Recent Developments in the Ordered Weighted Averaging Operators: Theory and Practice. Studies in Fuzziness and Soft Computing, vol. 265, pp. 29–47. Springer, Heidelberg (2011)
2. Boczek, M., Halčinová, L., Hutník, O., Kaluszka, M.: Novel survival functions based on conditional aggregation operators. Inform. Sci. **580**, 705–719 (2021). https://doi.org/10.1016/j.ins.2020.12.049
3. Boczek, M., Hutník, O., Kaluszka, M.: Choquet-Sugeno-like operator based on relation and conditional aggregation operators. Inform. Sci. **582**, 1–21 (2022). https://doi.org/10.1016/j.ins.2021.07.063
4. Boczek, M., Kałuszka, M.: On the extended Choquet-Sugeno-like operator. Int. J. Approx. Reason. **154**, 48–55 (2023). https://doi.org/10.1016/j.ijar.2022.12.006
5. Grabisch, M., Marichal, J-L., Mesiar, R., Pap, E.: Aggregation Functions. Cambridge University Press (2009)
6. Honda, A., Okazaki, Y.: Theory of inclusion-exclusion integral. Inform. Sci. **376**, 136–147 (2017). https://doi.org/10.1016/j.ins.2016.09.063
7. Hutník, O., Pócs, J.: On ⋆-associated comonotone functions. Kybernetika **54** (2018), 268–278. http://doi.org/10.14736/kyb-2018-2-0268
8. Klement, E.P., Mesiar, R., Pap, E.: A universal integral as common frame for Choquet and Sugeno integral. IEEE Trans. Fuzzy Syst. **18**, 178–187 (2010). https://doi.org/10.1109/TFUZZ.2009.2039367
9. Murofushi, T., Sugeno, M.: Fuzzy t-conorm integral with respect to fuzzy measures: generalization of Sugeno integral and Choquet integral. Fuzzy Sets Syst. **4**, 57–71 (1991). https://doi.org/10.1016/0165-0114(91)90089-9
10. Narukawa, Y., Torra, V.: Twofold integral and multi-step Choquet integral. Kybernetika **40**, 39–50 (2004)
11. Šeliga, A.: Decomposition integral without alternatives, its equivalence to Lebesgue integral, and computational algorithms. J. Autom. Mob. Robot. Intell. Syst. **13**(3), 2019, pp. 41–48. https://doi.org/10.14313/JAMRIS/3-2019/26
12. Yager, R., Filev, D.: Induced ordered weighted averaging operators. IEEE Trans. Syst. Man. Cybern. B **29**(2), 141–150 (1999). https://doi.org/10.1109/3477.752789

On a New Generalization
of Decomposition Integrals

Adam Šeliga$^{(\boxtimes)}$ (iD)

Department of Mathematics and Descriptive Geometry, Faculty of Civil Engineering,
Slovak University of Technology in Bratislava, Radlinského 11,
810 05 Bratislava, Slovakia
adam.seliga@stuba.sk

Abstract. In the few past years, decomposition integrals show a prolific interest of researchers. Some modifications and generalizations of these integrals were proposed, including the so-called minimax integrals. In the presented work, we introduce a new generalization of decomposition integrals based on set-based extended aggregation functions, which unifies the classical decomposition integrals and the minimax integrals into one framework of integrals called S-decomposition integrals. Some examples are given and future research outlined.

Keywords: decomposition integrals · set-based extended aggregation functions · minimax integrals

1 Introduction

Non-linear integrals are a special sub-class of aggregation functions which are heavily used in decision making. A special class of non-linear integrals is the class of decomposition integrals introduced by Even and Lehrer in [2] and further examined in [14]. This framework of integrals includes some widely used integrals in practice such as the Choquet integral [1], the Shilkret integral [18], the concave integral [10] and the PAN integral [19,20]. Observe that some of these integrals can be seen as universal integrals proposed in [9], such as the Choquet and Shilkret integrals, but some of them are out of the universal integrals framework, such as the concave and the PAN integrals. Another related class of integrals proposed and examined by Honda and Okazaki [7] is formed by inclusion-exclusion integrals, see also [6].

Since the introduction of decomposition integrals many modifications and extensions of them were introduced. To note some: the super-decomposition integrals [13], the modification of the product operator in the definition of decomposition integrals [8]. An extension of decomposition integrals for interval-valued functions was examined in [16]. Our contribution was inspired by a recent idea of minimax integrals [17], where the supremum of collection integrals considered for decomposition integrals is replaced by infimum.

In this contribution we introduce a new generalization of decomposition integrals that unifies the classical decomposition integrals and minimax integrals.

V. Torra and Y. Narukawa (Eds.): MDAI 2023, LNAI 13890, pp. 96–105, 2023.
https://doi.org/10.1007/978-3-031-33498-6_6

This generalization is based on set-based extended aggregation functions introduced in [11].

The rest of the paper is organized as follows: In the second section we introduce some basic notions, definitions and results used in the following. Section three is devoted to the extension of decomposition integrals based on the set-based extended aggregation functions and the examination of their properties. The last section remarks some conclusions and lays out a potential future research of the topic.

2   Preliminaries

Let $X = \{1, 2, \ldots, n\} \subsetneq \mathbb{N}$, where $n \in \mathbb{N}$ is some natural number, be a finite non-empty set fixed throughout the paper and referred to as a *space*. A *function* is any mapping $f\colon X \to [0, \infty[$ and a *monotone measure* is a mapping $\mu\colon 2^X \to [0, \infty[$ that is grounded and non-decreasing, i.e., $\mu(\emptyset) = 0$ and if $A \subseteq B \subseteq X$ then $\mu(A) \leq \mu(B)$. The set of all functions will be denoted by $\mathbb{F}$ and the set of all monotone measures by $\mathbb{M}$.

A k-ary *aggregation function* [5, 12] is a mapping $B\colon [0, \infty[^k \to [0, \infty[$ (with $k \in \mathbb{N}$ being some natural number) respecting the boundary condition $B(\mathbf{0}) = 0$ (where $\mathbf{0}$ denotes the k-dimensional zero vector) and B is non-decreasing with respect to the partial order of k-dimensional vectors, i.e., if $\mathbf{x}, \mathbf{y} \in [0, \infty[^k$ are such that $\mathbf{x} \leq \mathbf{y}$, then $B(\mathbf{x}) \leq B(\mathbf{y})$. An aggregation function B is called *idempotent* if and only if $B(\beta\mathbf{1}) = \beta$ for all $\beta \geq 0$ (where $\mathbf{1}$ is the k-dimensional vector of ones).

An *extended aggregation function* is a mapping

$$A\colon \bigcup_{k \in \mathbb{N}} [0, \infty[^k \to [0, \infty[$$

such that $A(\mathbf{0}) = 0$ for all zero vectors $\mathbf{0}$ of any length and such that A is non-decreasing with respect to the partial order of vectors of the same length, i.e., if $\mathbf{x}, \mathbf{y} \in [0, \infty[^k$, where $k \in \mathbb{N}$, are such that $\mathbf{x} \leq \mathbf{y}$ then $A(\mathbf{x}) \leq A(\mathbf{y})$. It is convenient to assume that $A(\mathbf{x}) = x$ if $\mathbf{x} = (x)$ is one-dimensional vector. We will consider this convention in what follows. Evidently, A is an extended aggregation function if and only if $A\!\upharpoonright_{[0,\infty[^k}$ is a k-ary aggregation function for any $k \in \mathbb{N}$.

A special sub-class of extended aggregation functions is the class of the set-based extended aggregation functions [11]. Let us define a map

$$\mathrm{set}\colon \bigcup_{k \in \mathbb{N}} [0, \infty[^k \to \{E \subseteq [0, \infty[\colon E \text{ is finite}\},$$

which assigns to a vector $\mathbf{x}$ the set of its pair-wise different elements. In other words, if $\mathbf{x} \in [0, \infty[^k$ then $\mathbf{x} = (x_1, x_2, \ldots, x_k)$ is a k-tuple (with possibly repeated numbers), and $\mathrm{set}(\mathbf{x}) = \{x_1, x_2, \ldots, x_k\}$ is the set of its members with cardinality between 1 and k. A *set-based extended aggregation function* is an extended aggregation function S satisfying the property that if $\text{set}(\mathbf{x}) = \text{set}(\mathbf{y})$ then $S(\mathbf{x}) = S(\mathbf{y})$ for all $\mathbf{x}, \mathbf{y}$ belonging to the domain of S. Note that every set-based extended aggregation function is symmetric. It can be shown that any set-based extended aggregation function S can be constructed using an appropriate idempotent binary aggregation function $B \colon [0, \infty[^2 \to [0, \infty[$ by

$$S(\mathbf{x}) = B\left(\min_{i=1}^{k} x_i, \max_{i=1}^{k} x_i\right),$$

where $\mathbf{x} = (x_1, x_2, \ldots, x_k) \geq \mathbf{0}$.

Example 1. A classical example of a set-based extended aggregation function is a statistical measure of central tendency called midrange, which is given by

$$\text{midrng}(\mathbf{x}) = \frac{1}{2}\left(\min_{i=1}^{k} x_i + \max_{i=1}^{k} x_i\right)$$

for all $\mathbf{x} = (x_1, x_2, \ldots, x_k) \geq \mathbf{0}$, where $k \in \mathbb{N}$ is arbitrary natural number.

Example 2. An α-median [3,4], where $\alpha \in [0, \infty]$, is an idempotent binary aggregation function given by

$$\text{med}_\alpha(x, y) = \text{med}(x, \alpha, y),$$

where med is the standard median. Note that $\text{med}_0 = \wedge$ and $\text{med}_\infty = \vee$ are minimum and maximum, respectively. This leads to the set-based extended aggregation function A_α given by

$$A_\alpha(\mathbf{x}) = \left(\alpha \wedge \max_{i=1}^{k} x_i\right) \vee \min_{i=1}^{k} x_i,$$

where $\mathbf{x} = (x_1, x_2, \ldots, x_k) \geq \mathbf{0}$.

A *collection* is any non-empty subset of $2^X \setminus \{\emptyset\}$ and a *decomposition system* is a non-empty set of collections. The set of all collections is denoted by $\mathbb{D}$ and the set of all decomposition systems by $\mathbb{H}$.

A *decomposition integral* [2,14] *with respect to a decomposition system* $\mathcal{H} \in \mathbb{H}$ is an operator $\text{dec}_\mathcal{H} \colon \mathbb{F} \times \mathbb{M} \to [0, \infty[$ given by

$$\text{dec}_\mathcal{H}(f, \mu) = \bigvee_{\mathcal{D} \in \mathcal{H}} \bigvee \left\{ \sum_{A \in \mathcal{D}} \beta_A \mu(A) \colon \sum_{A \in \mathcal{D}} \beta_A 1_A \leq f, \beta_A \geq 0 \text{ for all } A \in \mathcal{D} \right\},$$

for all functions $f \in \mathbb{F}$ and all monotone measures $\mu \in \mathbb{M}$, where 1_A denotes the characteristic function of the set A, i.e.,

$$1_A(x) = \begin{cases} 1, & \text{if } x \in A, \\ 0, & \text{otherwise.} \end{cases}$$

3 Decomposition Integrals Generalized by Set-Based Extended Aggregation Functions

Note that the definition of the decomposition integral with respect to a decomposition system $\mathcal{H} \in \mathbb{H}$ can be rewritten in the following form: For a given function $f \in \mathbb{F}$ and a given monotone measure $\mu \in \mathbb{M}$ we can construct a k-dimensional vector $\mathbf{d}$, where $k = \text{card}(\mathcal{H})$, by

$$d_i = \bigvee \left\{ \sum_{A \in \mathcal{D}_i} \beta_A \mu(A) : \sum_{A \in \mathcal{D}_i} \beta_A 1_A \leq f, \beta_A \geq 0 \text{ for all } A \in \mathcal{D}_i \right\},$$

where $\{\mathcal{D}_i\}_{i=1}^{k}$ is some enumeration of the decomposition system $\mathcal{H}$. Then

$$\text{dec}_{\mathcal{H}}(f, \mu) = \vee(\mathbf{d}) = \max_{i=1}^{k} d_i.$$

Noticing that $\vee$ is a set-based extended aggregation function, we propose the following generalization of decomposition integrals.

Definition 1. *Let S be a set-based extended aggregation function and $\mathcal{H} \in \mathbb{H}$ be a decomposition system. An S-decomposition integral with respect to the decomposition system $\mathcal{H}$ is an operator $S\text{dec}_{\mathcal{H}} \colon \mathbb{F} \times \mathbb{M} \to [0, \infty[$ given by*

$$S\text{dec}_{\mathcal{H}}(f, \mu) = S(\mathbf{d}^{f, \mu}),$$

where $\mathbf{d}^{f,\mu}$ is a k-dimensional vector, with $k = \text{card}(\mathcal{H})$, whose ith coordinate is given by

$$d_i^{f,\mu} = \bigvee \left\{ \sum_{A \in \mathcal{D}_i} \beta_A \mu(A) : \sum_{A \in \mathcal{D}_i} \beta_A 1_A \leq f, \beta_A \geq 0 \text{ for all } A \in \mathcal{D}_i \right\},$$

where $\{\mathcal{D}_i\}_{i=1}^{k}$ is some enumeration of the decomposition system $\mathcal{H}$.

Remark 1. Note that the S-decomposition integral is well-defined and the choice of the enumeration of the decomposition system does not matter thanks to symmetry of set-based extended aggregation functions.

Remark 2. The coordinates of the vector $\mathbf{d}^{f,\mu}$ are collection integrals introduced in [15] of the function f and the monotone measure μ with respect to collections belonging to the chosen decomposition system. Recall that, for a collection $\mathcal{D} \in \mathbb{D}$, $f \in \mathbb{F}$ and $\mu \in \mathbb{M}$, the related collection integral $d^{f,\mu}$ is given by

$$d_{\mathcal{D}}^{f,\mu} = \bigvee \left\{ \sum_{A \in \mathcal{D}} \beta_A \mu(A) : \sum_{A \in \mathcal{D}} \beta_A 1_A \leq f, \beta_A \geq 0 \text{ for all } A \in \mathcal{D} \right\}.$$

The S-decomposition integral is thus aggregation of these collections integrals using the chosen set-based extended aggregation function S.

Example 3. Choosing the maximum as the set-based extended aggregation function in the definition of S-decomposition integral, i.e., $S = \vee$, we recover the original decomposition integral introduced in [2,14].

Example 4. The choice of $S = \wedge$, i.e., the set-based extended aggregation function is minimum, we obtain a so-called minimax integral introduced in [17].

It is easy to notice that if the function f is the zero function, i.e., $f(x) = 0$ for all $x \in X$ (for future references denoted by f_0), then $\mathbf{d}^{f,\mu} = \mathbf{0}$ and thus also the S-decomposition integral of such function is always zero. If f and g are functions such that $f \leq g$, then also $\mathbf{d}^{f,\mu} \leq \mathbf{d}^{g,\mu}$ which implies that the S-decomposition integral of f is less or equal to the S-decomposition integral of g. We have just shown the next important result.

Theorem 1. *Let $\mu \in \mathbb{M}$ be a monotone measure and let $\mathcal{H} \in \mathbb{H}$ be a decomposition system. Let S be an arbitrary set-based extended aggregation function. Then*

$$Sdec_{\mathcal{H}}(f_0, \mu) = 0$$

and for all functions $f, g \in \mathbb{F}$ such that $f \leq g$ one has

$$Sdec_{\mathcal{H}}(f, \mu) \leq Sdec_{\mathcal{H}}(g, \mu).$$

In other words, we can assign an n-ary vector $\mathbf{f}$, where $n = \mathrm{card}(X)$, to any function $f \in \mathbb{F}$, whose coordinates are $f_i = f(i)$. Thus, the vectors of $[0, \infty[^n$ are in one-to-one correspondence with the functions from $\mathbb{F}$. The previous theorem thus says that the operator $Sdec\colon [0, \infty[^n \to [0, \infty[$, defined by $Sdec(\mathbf{f}) = Sdec_{\mathcal{H}}(f, \mu)$, is an aggregation function for all decomposition systems $\mathcal{H} \in \mathbb{H}$, all monotone measures $\mu \in \mathbb{M}$ and all set-based extended aggregation functions S.

Example 5. Consider a decomposition system $\mathcal{H} = \left\{ \{\{1,2\}\}, \{\{1\}, \{2\}\} \right\}$ on the space $X = \{1, 2\}$. Let $\mu \in \mathbb{M}$ be a monotone measure given by $\mu(\emptyset) = 0$, $\mu(\{1\}) = 1/3$, $\mu(\{2\}) = 2/3$ and $\mu(X) = 1$. For an arbitrary function $f \in \mathbb{F}$ with $f(1) = x$ and $f(2) = y$, where $x, y \geq 0$, we obtain that

$$Sdec_{\mathcal{H}}(f, \mu) = S \left(\min\{x, y\}, \frac{x + 2y}{3} \right),$$

where S is an arbitrary set-based extended aggregation function. In Fig. 1, the graphs of $Sdec_{\mathcal{H}}$ are indicated for the choice $S = \mathrm{med}_0 = \wedge$, $S = \mathrm{med}_{1/2}$ and $S = \mathrm{med}_\infty = \vee$.

Example 6. If we consider the space X, the decomposition system $\mathcal{H}$ and the function $f \in \mathbb{F}$ from the previous example, i.e., Example 5, with a set-based extended aggregation function $S = \mathrm{med}_1$ and $\mu \in \mathbb{M}$ is given by: (i) $\mu(\emptyset) = 0$, $\mu(\{1\}) = 1/4$, $\mu(\{2\}) = 1/2$ and $\mu(X) = 1$, i.e., μ is sub-additive monotone measure, then we obtain

$$Sdec_{\mathcal{H}}(f, \mu) = \mathrm{med} \left(\min\{x, y\}, 1, \frac{x + 2y}{4} \right);$$

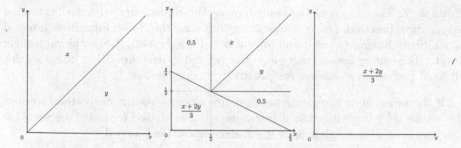

Fig. 1. Graphs of the S-decomposition integral from Example 5. The choice $S = \wedge$ is visualized on the left, $S = \mathrm{med}_{0.5}$ is in the middle and $S = \vee$ is on the right.

(ii) if μ is given by $\mu(\emptyset) = 0$, $\mu(\{1\}) = \mu(\{2\}) = 2/3$, $\mu(X) = 1$, i.e., μ is super-additive and symmetric, then we obtain

$$S\mathrm{dec}_{\mathcal{H}}(f, \mu) = \mathrm{med}\left(\min\{x, y\}, 1, \frac{2(x+y)}{3}\right).$$

The graphs of these two functions can be found in Fig. 2.

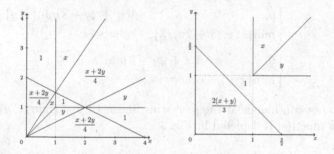

Fig. 2. Graphs of the S-decomposition integral from Example 6; (i) on the left and (ii) on the right.

Note that for any function $f \in \mathbb{F}$ and a non-negative number $\beta \geq 0$, one obtains that $\mathbf{d}^{\beta f, \mu} = \beta \mathbf{d}^{f, \mu}$, in general, for any monotone measure $\mu \in \mathbb{M}$. Also, the equality $\mathbf{d}^{f, \beta\mu} = \beta \mathbf{d}^{f, \mu}$ holds. This implies that if the underlying set-based extended aggregation function S is positively homogeneous, then so is the S-decomposition integral.

Theorem 2. *If S is positively homogeneous set-based extended aggregation function, then the S-decomposition integral is also positively homogeneous operator.*

102   A. Šeliga

Example 7. The choice of the α-median as the underlying set-based extended aggregation function, i.e., $S = \text{med}_\alpha$, implies that the S-decomposition integral is positively homogeneous if and only if $\alpha \in \{0, \infty\}$. Also, if S is the midrange, due to its positive homogeneity also the related S-decomposition integrals, for all fixed monotone measures, are positively homogeneous.

If the function or the monotone measure changes continuously, then so does the vector $\mathbf{d}^{f,\mu}$ implying that if the underlying set-based extended aggregation function is continuous then so is the S-decomposition integral.

Theorem 3. *If S is continuous set-based extended aggregation function, then the S-decomposition integral is also continuous, both in functions and in monotone measures.*

Example 8. Consider a set-based extended aggregation function S given by

$$S(\mathbf{x}) = \begin{cases} 0, & \text{if } \wedge(\mathbf{x}) + \vee(\mathbf{x}) \leq 1, \\ \wedge(\mathbf{x}), & \text{otherwise,} \end{cases}$$

which is discontinuous along the line $\wedge(\mathbf{x}) + \vee(\mathbf{x}) = 1$, i.e., in two dimensions, if $\mathbf{x} = (x, y)$, along the line $x + y = 1$. Consider the space, the decomposition system, the monotone measure, and the function from Example 5. The corresponding S-decomposition integral is then given by

$$S\text{dec}_{\mathcal{H}}(f, \mu) = \begin{cases} 0, & \text{if } x + 2y + 3\min\{x, y\} \leq 3, \\ \min\{x, y, (x + 2y)/3\}, & \text{otherwise,} \end{cases}$$
$$= \begin{cases} 0, & \text{if } x + 2y + 3\min\{x, y\} \leq 3, \\ \min\{x, y\}, & \text{otherwise,} \end{cases}$$

which is also not continuous at the piecewise line $x + 2y + 3\min\{x, y\} = 3$. The graph of this function is depicted in Fig. 3.

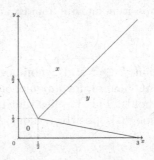

Fig. 3. Graph of the S-decomposition integral from Example 8.

Remark 3. See that the choice of not positively homogeneous set-based extended aggregation function can lead to a positively homogeneous S-decomposition integral and, analogously, a choice of discontinuous set-based extended aggregation function can also lead to a continuous S-decomposition integral. This can be seen, e.g., by choosing the zero monotone measure $\mu \equiv 0$.

In general, S-decomposition integrals are not symmetric. However, if the considered monotone measure μ is symmetric (i.e., $\mu(G) = \mu(H)$ for any $G, H \subseteq X$ such that $\mathrm{card}(G) = \mathrm{card}(H)$), then for any $\mathcal{H} \in \mathbb{H}$ and any set-based extended aggregation function S, the n-ary aggregation function $S\mathrm{dec}$ is symmetric.

4   Concluding Remarks

In this work, we have proposed a generalization of the decomposition integrals introduced by Even and Lehrer in [2]. This generalization is based on replacing the outer maximum operator by an arbitrary set-based extended aggregation function which unifies decomposition integrals and recently introduced minimax integrals [17] into one framework of integrals, called S-decomposition integrals.

It was proved that the S-decomposition integral is again an aggregation function, i.e., it respects the boundary condition of aggregation functions and is monotonic. If the underlying set-based extended aggregation function is positively homogeneous then so is the S-decomposition integral.

Some examples of S-decomposition integrals are given leading back to the original decomposition integrals, the minimax integrals and to new integrals based on the α-medians.

The properties of the S-decomposition integrals and their possible use in practice are future topics of the research of the author. As a further generalization of decomposition integrals we aim to consider symmetric extended aggregation functions, following the spirit of Definition 1. In particular, one can consider the quasi-arithmetic means, with a distinguished example AM (the arithmetic mean). The related AM-decomposition integrals are given by

$$\mathsf{AMdec}_{\mathcal{H}}(f, \mu) = \frac{1}{k} \sum_{i=1}^{k} d_i^{f, \mu}.$$

More, our ideas from this contribution and those sketched above could be considered for the case of super-decomposition integrals, too. Note that there one should not forget the infinity as a possible value of integrals, violating the possible duality of both types of integrals.

Acknowledgements. The author was supported by the Slovak Research and Development Agency under the contract no. APVV-18-0052. Also the support of the grant VEGA 1/0036/23 is kindly announced.

References

1. Choquet, G.: Theory of capacities. Annales de l'Institut Fourier **5**, 131–295 (1954). https://doi.org/10.5802/aif.53
2. Even, Y., Lehrer, E.: Decomposition-integral: unifying Choquet and the concave integrals. Econ. Theor. **56**(1), 33–58 (2013). https://doi.org/10.1007/s00199-013-0780-0
3. Fodor, J.C.: An extension of Fung-Fu's theorem. Internat. J. Uncertain. Fuzziness Knowl.-Based Syst. **4**(3), 235–243 (1996). https://doi.org/10.1142/S0218488596000147
4. Fung, L.W., Fu, K.S.: An axiomatic approach to rational decision making in a fuzzy environment. In: Zadeh, L.A., Fu, K.S., Tanaka, K., Shimura, M. (eds.) Fuzzy Sets and Their Applications to Cognitive and Decision Processes, pp. 227–256. Academic Press, New York (1975). https://doi.org/10.1016/B978-0-12-775260-0.50015-3
5. Grabisch, M., Marichal, J.-L., Mesiar, R., Pap, E.: Aggregation functions. Encyclopedia of Mathematics and Its Applications 127. Cambridge University Press (2009). ISBN 978-0-521-51926-7
6. Honda, A., James, S., Rajasegarar, S.: Orness and cardinality indices for averaging inclusion-exclusion integrals. In: Torra, V., Narukawa, Y., Honda, A., Inoue, S. (eds.) MDAI 2017. LNCS (LNAI), vol. 10571, pp. 51–62. Springer, Cham (2017). https://doi.org/10.1007/978-3-319-67422-3_6
7. Honda, A., Okazaki, Y.: Theory of inclusion-exclusion integral. Inf. Sci. **376**, 136–147 (2017). https://doi.org/10.1016/j.ins.2016.09.063
8. Horanská, Ľ, Bustince, H., Fernandez, J., Mesiar, R.: Generalized decomposition integral. Inf. Sci. **538**, 415–427 (2020). https://doi.org/10.1016/j.ins.2020.05.081
9. Klement, E.P., Mesiar, R., Pap, E.: A universal integral as common frame for Choquet and Sugeno integral. IEEE Trans. Fuzzy Syst. **18**(1), 178–187 (2010). https://doi.org/10.1109/TFUZZ.2009.2039367
10. Lehrer, E.: A new integral for capacities. Econ. Theor. **39**, 157–176 (2009). https://doi.org/10.1007/s00199-007-0302-z
11. Mesiar, R., Kolesárová, A., Gómez, D., Montero, J.: Set-based extended aggregation functions. Int. J. Intell. Syst. **34**(9), 2039–2054 (2019). https://doi.org/10.1002/int.22128
12. Mesiar, R., Kolesárová, A., Stupňanová, A.: Quo vadis aggregation? Int. J. Gen. Syst. **47**(2), 97–117 (2018). https://doi.org/10.1080/03081079.2017.1402893
13. Mesiar, R., Li, J., Pap, E.: Superdecomposition integrals. Fuzzy Sets Syst. **259**, 3–11 (2015). https://doi.org/10.1016/j.fss.2014.05.003
14. Mesiar, R., Stupňanová, A.: Decomposition integrals. Int. J. Approximate Reasoning **54**(8), 1252–1259 (2013). https://doi.org/10.1016/j.ijar.2013.02.001
15. Šeliga, A.: Decomposition integral without alternatives, its equivalence to Lebesgue integral, and computational algorithms. J. Automation Mob. Robot. Intell. Syst. **13**(3), 41–48 (2019). https://doi.org/10.14313/JAMRIS/3-2019/26
16. Šeliga, A.: Decomposition integrals for interval-valued functions. In: Cornejo, M.E., Kóczy, L.T., Medina-Moreno, J., Moreno-García, J. (eds.) Computational Intelligence and Mathematics for Tackling Complex Problems 2. SCI, vol. 955, pp. 183–189. Springer, Cham (2022). https://doi.org/10.1007/978-3-030-88817-6_21
17. Šeliga, A., Mesiar, R., Ouyang, Y., Li, J.: Minimax decomposition integrals. Submitted

18. Shilkret, N.: Maxitive measure and integration. Indag. Math. **33**, 109–116 (1971). https://doi.org/10.1016/S1385-7258(71)80017-3
19. Wang, Z., Klir, G.J.: Generalized Measure Theory. Springer (2009). ISBN 9780387768526
20. Yang, Q.: The PAN-integral on the fuzzy measure space. Fuzzy Math. **3**, 107–114 (1985). In Chinese

Bipolar OWA Operators with Continuous Input Function

Martin Kalina[(✉)] [iD]

Faculty of Civil Engineering, Slovak University of Technology,
Radlinského 11, 810 05 Bratislava, Slovakia
martin.kalina@stuba.sk

Abstract. Mesiar et al. in 2020 introduced discrete bipolar OWA operators and in 2022 a further investigation on discrete bipolar OWA operators was published by the same authors. They introduced also the abbreviation BIOWA. In the paper, BIOWA operators with continuous input functions are proposed and studied. Also the orness measure of continuous BIOWA is introduced.

Keywords: Aggregation function · Bipolar OWA · Bipolar Choquet integral · Orness measure

1 Introduction

Ordered weighted averaging (OWA) operators were introduced by Yager [20]. Since then they have proved their usefulness in several areas, see e.g., [8]. Grabisch [6] has shown that OWA operators are Choquet integrals with respect to symmetric capacities.

Grabisch and Labreuche introduced bi-capacities [9,10] as a tool for decision-makers, where they can assign both, positive and negative score in multi-criteria decision problems. Mesiar et al. [15,16] to treat the bipolar scales in multicriteria decision-making problems, introduced BIOWA (bipolar OWA) operators in case of finitely many criteria. For possible applications of bipolarity see, e.g., Grabish et al. [7]. It is a natural generalization of the OWA operators introduced by Yager.

If there are too many input values, it may be easier to model the situation using continuous input functions. This situation is studied in Jin et al. [12] where OWA operators for continuous input functions are proposed. The results in this paper were further generalized by Kalina [13]. Some of the ideas in papers [12,13] can be found in Torra [19] and also in the monograph Denneberg [3].

The papers [15,16] on one hand, and [12,13] on the other hand, were the main motivation of the author for the research presented in this contribution. Some of the ideas from [12,13] will be used also in this paper. However, handling

Supported by the VEGA grant agency, grant No. 2/0142/20 and by the Science and Technology Assistance Agency under contract No. APVV-18-0052.

bi-polarity of evaluations means facing a new problem. Namely, for positive and negative evaluations different measures are used. This means the decreasing form of an input function as defined in [12] (Definition 7), has to be modified.

The paper is organized as follows. Some necessary known notions and results are provided in Sect. 2. Section 3 is devoted to BIOWA operators with continuous input functions. Orness measures are introduced in Sect. 4. Finally, conclusions are formulated in Sect. 5.

2   Basic Notations and Some Known Facts

To increase comfort for readers, in this section we provide some notions and known facts which will be important for our considerations. The reader is assumed to be familiar with basic properties of aggregation functions. To get some information on aggregation functions, we recommend monographs [1,11]. Concerning measurability and measurable spaces, the reader is advised to read monographs [17,18].

2.1   OWA Operators, Choquet Integral and Bipolar Capacities

As introduced in [20], for an n-dimensional input vector $\mathbf{v} = (v_1, \ldots, v_n)$ and an n-dimensional weighting vector $\mathbf{w} = (w_1, \ldots, w_n)$, the OWA is given by $\mathrm{OWA}_{\mathbf{w}}(\mathbf{v}) = \sum_{i=1}^{n} w_i \cdot v_{\pi(i)}$ where π is a permutation of the set $\{1, 2, \ldots, n\}$ such that $v_{\pi(1)} \geq v_{\pi(2)} \geq \cdots \geq v_{\pi(n)}$.

Definition 1 ([17]). *Let $(X, \mathcal{S})$ be a measurable space and $\mu : \mathcal{S} \to [0,1]$ be a monotone set-function such that $\mu(\emptyset) = 0$ and $\mu(X) = 1$. Further assume that for arbitrary system of measurable sets $A_1 \subset A_2 \subset \cdots \subset A_i \subset \ldots$ the following holds*

$$\mu\left(\bigcup_{i=1}^{\infty} A_i\right) = \lim_{i \to \infty} \mu(A_i). \tag{1}$$

Then μ is called a capacity.
If moreover for all $A, B \in \mathcal{S}$ if $\mu(B) = 0$ then $\mu(A \cup B) = \mu(A)$ holds, then μ is a null-additive *capacity.*

The triplet $(X, \mathcal{S}, \mu)$ will be called a *capacity space*. Recall that for every capacity μ, $\mu^d(A) = 1 - \mu(A^c)$ (for $A \in \mathcal{S}$) is the *dual capacity*.

Definition 2 (see, e.g., [18]). *Let $(X, \mathcal{S}, \mu)$ be a capacity space. Capacity μ is said to be* semi-continuous from above *if for arbitrary system of measurable sets $A_1 \supset A_2 \supset \cdots \supset A_i \supset \ldots$ the following holds*

$$\mu\left(\bigcap_{i=1}^{\infty} A_i\right) = \lim_{i \to \infty} \mu(A_i). \tag{2}$$

Notation 1. For arbitrary function $f : X \to \mathbb{R}$ we denote

$$f^+(x) = f(x) \vee 0 \quad \text{and} \quad f^-(x) = (-f)^+(x).$$

Definition 3 ([18]). *Let $f : X \to \mathbb{R}$ be a function and $\mathrm{rng}(f)$ be its range (called also co-domain). If $\mathrm{rng}(f)$ is a finite set, then f is said to be a simple function. If f is simple and moreover $\{x \in X; f(x) = a\} \in \mathcal{S}$ for all $a \in \mathrm{rng}(f)$, then we say that f is a simple measurable function. The set of all simple measurable functions on $(X, \mathcal{S})$ will be denoted by $\mathrm{SM}_{(X,\mathcal{S})}$.*

Definition 4 ([18]). *A function $f : X \to \mathbb{R}$ is said to be measurable if there exists a function $F : \mathbb{N} \to \mathrm{SM}_{(X,\mathcal{S})}$ such that, for all $x \in X$,*

$$F(x) = \lim_{i \to \infty} F_i(x),$$

where $\mathbb{N}$ denotes the set of all natural numbers and F_i denotes the function $F(i)$.

Definition 5 (see, e.g., [2,3,17]). *Let $f : X \to [0, \infty[$ be a measurable function and μ be a capacity. The functional*

$$(C) \int f \, d\mu = \int_0^\infty \mu(\{x \in X; f(x) \geq t\}) \, dt,$$

where the right-hand-side integral is the Riemann one, is called the Choquet integral.

Remark 1. Since the function f in Definition 5 is measurable, function $\tilde{f} : [0, \infty[\to [0, 1]$ defined by $\tilde{f}(t) = \mu(\{x; f(x) \geq t\})$ is well defined. Moreover, it is decreasing and thus Riemann integrable. This justifies the definition of Choquet integral. The Choquet integral can be expressed also by

$$(C) \int f \, d\mu = \int_0^\infty \mu(\{x \in X; f(x) > t\}) \, dt,$$

see [17].

The paper [8] is a nice overview of applications of the Choquet integral in decision-making under uncertainty.

2.2   OWA with Continuous Input Functions

In [12], the authors extended the theory of OWA operators to OWA with continuous input functions. The mentioned paper is written in the language of measure (capacity) spaces.

Definition 6 ([12]). *Let $(X, \mathcal{S})$ be a measurable space. Any bounded measurable function $f : X \to \mathbb{R}$ is said to be an input function. The set of all input functions will be denoted by $\mathfrak{F}_{(X,\mathcal{S})}$.*

Definition 7 ([12]). *Let* $\mathcal{M} = (X, \mathcal{S}, \mu)$ *be a capacity space and* $f \in \mathfrak{F}_{(X,\mathcal{S})}$. *Function* $g_{(f,\mu)} \in \mathfrak{F}_{(X,\mathcal{S})}$ *is a decreasing form of* f *in* $\mathcal{M}$ *if the following constraints are fulfilled:*

(a) $g_{(f,\mu)}(x_1) \geq g_{(f,\mu)}(x_2)$ *whenever* $x_1 \geq x_2$ *for all* $x_1, x_2 \in X$,
(b) $\mu(\{z \in X; g_{(f,\mu)}(z) \geq t\}) = \mu(\{z \in X; f(z) \geq t\})$ *for all* $t \in \mathbb{R}$.

Of course, in some cases the decreasing form $g_{(f,\mu)}$ of an input function f is not given uniquely. On the other hand, for some capacity spaces $(X, \mathcal{S}, \mu)$, there exist input functions with no decreasing form. The most important is the question of the existence of a decreasing form.

Assumption 1 *The triplet* $(X, \mathcal{S}, \mu)$ *will denote a capacity space fulfilling*

1. $X \subset \mathbb{R}$, *there exist* $x_m = \min(X)$, $x_M = \max(X)$, $x_m, x_M \in [0,1]$,
2. $\mathcal{S} \subset 2^X$ *is a* σ-*algebra such that* $[x_m, x] \cap X \in \mathcal{S}$ *for all* $x \in X$,
3. μ *is a null-additive capacity such that for any disjoint* $A, B \in \mathcal{S}$

$$\mu(A \cup B) = \mu(A) \quad \Leftrightarrow \quad \mu(B) = 0. \tag{3}$$

Proposition 1 ([12]). *Let* $\mathcal{M} = (X, \mathcal{S}, \mu)$ *be a capacity space fulfilling Assumption 1 and the capacity* μ *is semicontinuous from above. Then for every* $f \in \mathfrak{F}_{(X,\mathcal{S})}$ *there exists a decreasing form* $g_{(f,\mu)}$ *in* $\mathcal{M}$ *if and only if for every* $E \in \mathcal{S}$ *such that* $\mu(E) \neq 0$ *there exist* $a_1, a_2 \in X$ *such that*

$$\mu(E) = \mu(X \cap [x_m, a_1]) = \mu^d(X \cap [a_2, x_m]).$$

Moreover, if g_1, g_2 *are two different decreasing forms of* f *in* $\mathcal{M}$ *then*

$$(C) \int g_1 \, d\mu = (C) \int g_2 \, d\mu. \tag{4}$$

Remark 2. The input function f in Proposition 1 may achieve both positive as well as negative values. This is the reason why we need also the dual capacity μ^d in equality (4). In case we know that the input function is non-negative, we can skip the most right-hand-side (the part with μ^d) in equality (4).

2.3   Bipolar Capacity and Bipolar OWA (BIOWA) Operators

Grabisch and Labreuche introduced a bi-polar capacity (bicapacity) [9]. We will slightly modify (generalize) their definition for the case of arbitrary measurable space.

Definition 8. *For a measurable space* $(X, \mathcal{S})$ *denote* $L = \{(A, B) \in \mathcal{S}^2; B \subset A^c\}$. *A function* $h : L \to [-1, 1]$ *is said to be a bipolar capacity if*

1. $h(\emptyset, \emptyset) = 0$, $h(X, \emptyset) = 1$, $h(\emptyset, X) = -1$,
2. $h(\cdot, \emptyset)$ *is increasing and semicontinuous from above,*
3. $h(\emptyset, \cdot)$ *is decreasing and semicontinuous from above.*

The Choquet integral with respect to a bicapacity h is defined as follows [9].

$$(C) \int f \, dh = \int_0^\infty h(f^+ > t, f^- > t) \, dt.$$

Let X be a finite set. A bicapacity $h : L \to [-1,1]$ is symmetric if

$$h(A, B) = \chi(\text{card}(A), \text{card}(B)),$$

where χ is a function increasing in the first and decreasing in the second variable and $\chi(0,0) = 0$, $\chi(1,0) = 1$ and $\chi(0,1) = -1$,
i.e., if the bicapacity is a function of the cardinalities of the input sets.

Definition 9 ([16]). *Let X be a finite set and h be a symmetric bipolar capacity. Then* $\text{BIOWA}_h(f) = (C) \int f \, dh$ *is the bipolar OWA (BIOWA) operator.*

2.4   Orness Measures

Orness measure was originally introduced by Dujmović [4,5]. Now, we repeat the definition of the measure of orness from [20]. For an OWA operator with a weighting vector $\omega = \{w_1, \ldots, w_n\}$ is its orness defined by (see [20])

$$\text{orness}^Y(\omega) = \sum_{i=1}^n \frac{n-i}{n-1} w_i. \tag{5}$$

Later the orness measure was studied by several authors and some other orness measures were introduced. Just briefly, in [14] the orness measure was axiomatized.

Definition 10 (see [14]). *Let ω be a weighting vector corresponding to a discrete OWA operator. An orness function, denoted by ^{A}orness, satisfies the following properties.*

(A1) $^A\text{orness}(\omega^*) = 1$, where $\omega^* = (1, 0, \ldots, 0)$.
(A2) $^A\text{orness}(\omega_*) = 0$, where $\omega_* = (0, 0, \ldots, 1)$.
(A3) $^A\text{orness}(\omega_A) = \frac{1}{2}$, where $\omega_A = (\frac{1}{n}, \frac{1}{n}, \ldots, \frac{1}{n})$.
(A4) *Let* $\omega = (w_1, w_2, \ldots, w_n)$ $\omega_\varepsilon = (w_1, \ldots, w_j - \varepsilon, \ldots, w_k + \varepsilon, \ldots, w_n)$, *for* $\varepsilon > 0$ *and* $j < k$, *be weighting n-tuples. Then* $^A\text{orness}(\omega) > {}^A\text{orness}(\omega_\varepsilon)$.

Finally, we provide the definition of orness measure for OWA operators from [12]. First, we recall the definition of absolute continuity of a capacity ν with respect to μ.

Definition 11 ([18]). *Let A be a measurable set. We say that ν is absolutely continuous with respect to μ if $\mu(A) = 0$ implies $\nu(A) = 0$, notation $\nu \ll \mu$.*

Definition 12. *Let μ be a capacity fulfilling Assumption 1 with $\mu(\{x\}) = 0$ for all $x \in X$ and $\mathbf{w} \ll \mu$ be a probability measure (weighting function). Denote*

$$G(x) = \mu([x_m, x] \cap X). \tag{6}$$

Measure of orness of $\mathbf{w}$ *with respect to G is given by*

$$\text{orness}^G(\mathbf{w}) = (C) \int (1 - G(x)) \, d\mathbf{w}. \tag{7}$$

3   BIOWA with Continuous Input Functions

As we have already pointed out, this part is based on the papers [12,16]. We will assume that $(X, \mathcal{S})$ is a measurable space fulfilling Assumption 1 and such that $\min(X) = 0$, $\max(X) = 1$.

Definition 13. *For a measurable space $(X, \mathcal{S})$ denote $L = \{(A, B) \in \mathcal{S}^2; B \subset A^c\}$. A function $h : L \to [-1, 1]$ is said to be a bipolar capacity if*

1. $h(\emptyset, \emptyset) = 0$, $h(X, \emptyset) = 1$, $h(\emptyset, X) = -1$,
2. $h(\cdot, \emptyset)$ *is increasing and semicontinuous from above,*
3. $h(\emptyset, \cdot)$ *is decreasing and semicontinuous from above.*

Unlike the re-ordering of an input vector used in [16], we will construct a decreasing form of f^+ and an increasing form of f^-. The reason for this is that we want to keep capacities μ and ν as general as possible, where μ and ν are capacities with respect to which we construct the monotone forms of f^+ and f^- for an input function f, respectively. For this reason we modify Proposition 1 into the following form.

Proposition 2. *Let $(X, \mathcal{S})$ be a measurable space fulfilling Assumption 1 and $\mu : \mathcal{S} \to [0, 1]$, $\nu : \mathcal{S} \to [0, 1]$ be two capacities semicontinuous from above. Let $f \in \mathfrak{F}_{(X, \mathcal{S})}$ be arbitrarily chosen. Then there exists a decreasing form $g_{(f^+, \mu)}$ of f^+ and an increasing form $g^{(f^-, \nu)}$ of f^- if and only if for every disjoint $A, B \in \mathcal{S}$ there exist $a, b \in [0, 1]$, $a \leq b$, such that*

$$\mu(A) = \mu([0, a] \cap X), \quad \nu(B) = \nu([b, 1] \cap X). \tag{8}$$

Proof. The left-hand-side equality in formula (8) is due to Proposition 1. The right-hand-side equality is in a sense dual to the left one.

Assumption 2 *In what follows, we will assume that a pair of capacities (μ, ν) fulfilling Assumption 1, fulfils the following*

– *for measurable A, B such that $B \subset A^c$ there exist $a, b \in [0, 1]$, $a \leq b$ such that equalities (8) hold.*

Proposition 3. *Assume (μ, ν) is a pair of capacities fulfilling Assumption 1. The pair (μ, ν) fulfils Assumption 2 if and only for arbitrary measurable sets A, B, $B \subset A^c$, there exist numbers $a, b_1, b_2 \in [0, 1]$ such that $a \leq b_1 \leq b_2$ with*

$$\mu(A) = \mu([0, a] \cap X), \quad \nu(B) = \nu([b_2, 1] \cap X), \quad \mu^c(B) = \mu^c([b_1, 1] \cap X). \tag{9}$$

Proof. It is immediate that formula (8) implies formula (9).

The next example illustrates the role of the pair of capacities (μ, ν) that they play in the design of decreasing/increasing form of f^+ and f^-, respectively.

Example 1. Set $X = [0,1]$ and $\mathcal{S} = \mathcal{B} \cap [0,1]$. For simplicity reasons, we set capacities μ_1 and ν_1 to be probability distributions given by distribution functions Φ_1 and Ψ_1, respectively, restricted to the unit interval:

$$\Phi_1(x) = \begin{cases} 2x & \text{for } x \in [0,\frac{1}{4}], \\ \frac{1}{2} & \text{for } x \in]\frac{1}{4},\frac{1}{2}[, \\ x & \text{for } x \in [\frac{1}{2},1], \end{cases} \quad \Psi_1(x) = \begin{cases} 0 & \text{for } x \in [0,\frac{1}{2}], \\ 2x-1 & \text{for } x \in]\frac{1}{2},1]. \end{cases}$$

We will consider yet another pair of probability distributions (μ_2,ν_2) given by distribution functions Φ_2 and Ψ_2, respectively, restricted to the unit interval:

$$\Phi_2(x) = \begin{cases} 2x & \text{for } x \in [0,\frac{1}{8}], \\ x+\frac{1}{8} & \text{for } x \in]\frac{1}{8},\frac{7}{8}[, \\ 1 & \text{for } x \in [\frac{7}{8},1], \end{cases} \quad \Psi_2(x) = \begin{cases} 0 & \text{for } x \in [0,\frac{1}{4}], \\ 2x-\frac{1}{2} & \text{for } x \in]\frac{1}{4},\frac{1}{2}[, \\ \frac{1}{2} & \text{for } x \in [\frac{1}{2},\frac{3}{4}[, \\ 2x-1 & \text{for } x \in [\frac{3}{4},1]. \end{cases}$$

Let

$$f(x) = \begin{cases} x & \text{for } x \in [0,\frac{1}{4}], \\ 0 & \text{for } x \in]\frac{1}{4},\frac{1}{2}[, \\ -1 & \text{for } x \in [\frac{1}{2},\frac{3}{4}[, \\ -x & \text{for } x \in [\frac{3}{4},1]. \end{cases}$$

Now, we provide decreasing forms $g_{(f^+,\mu_1)}, g_{(f^+,\mu_2)}$ of f^+ and increasing forms $g^{(f^-,\nu_1)}, g^{(f^-,\nu_2)}$ of f^-

$$g_{(f^+,\mu_1)}(x) = \begin{cases} \frac{1}{4}-x & \text{for } x \in [0,\frac{1}{4}], \\ 0 & \text{otherwise,} \end{cases} \quad g_{(f^+,\mu_2)}(x) = \begin{cases} \frac{1}{4}-2x & \text{for } x \in [0,\frac{1}{16}], \\ \frac{3}{16}-x & \text{for } x \in]\frac{1}{16},\frac{1}{8}[, \\ \frac{1}{8}-\frac{1}{2}x & \text{for } x \in [\frac{1}{8},\frac{1}{4}], \\ 0 & \text{otherwise,} \end{cases}$$

$$g^{(f^-,\nu_1)}(x) = \begin{cases} 1 & \text{for } x \in [\frac{3}{4},1], \\ x+\frac{1}{4} & \text{for } x \in [\frac{1}{2},\frac{3}{4}[, \\ 0 & \text{otherwise,} \end{cases} \quad g^{(f^-,\nu_2)}(x) = \begin{cases} x & \text{for } x \in]\frac{3}{4},1], \\ 0 & \text{otherwise.} \end{cases}$$

Since $\nu_2([\frac{1}{2},\frac{3}{4}]) = 0$, another option for $g^{(f^-,\nu_2)}$ is

$$\bar{g}^{(f^-,\nu_2)}(x) = \begin{cases} x & \text{for } x \in [\frac{1}{2},1], \\ 0 & \text{otherwise.} \end{cases}$$

This means that the decreasing (increasing) forms of f^+ (f^-) are not given uniquely. Particularly, it is possible to change the values of the corresponding functions on a set of zero capacity, keeping in kind the monotonocity of those modified decreasing (increasing) forms.

Definition 14. *Denote* $\mathcal{A} = \{(x,y) \in [0,1]^2; x+y \leq 1\}$. *A function* $\chi \colon \mathcal{A} \to [-1,1]$ *is said to be a* bipolar distribution function *if it is increasing in the first and decreasing in the second variable and such that* $\chi(0,0) = 0$, $\chi(1,0) = 1, \chi(0,1) = -1$.

Notation 2. *For any bipolar distribution function* χ *and a pair of capacities* (μ, ν) *we denote*

$$H_{(\chi,\mu,\nu)}(A,B) = \chi\big(\mu(A), \nu(B)\big) \quad for\ (A,B) \in L. \tag{10}$$

Lemma 1. *For arbitrary bipolar distribution function* χ *and any pair of capacities* (μ, ν), *the function* $H_{(\chi,\mu,\nu)}$ *given by formula* (10), *is a bipolar capacity.*

The proof of Lemma 1 is straightforward by properties of bipolar distribution functions and by formula (10). That is why it is omitted.

Definition 15. *Assume a measurable space* $(X, \mathcal{S})$ *and capacities* μ, ν *fulfilling Assumptions 1 and 2. Let* $h : L^2 \to [-1,1]$ *be a bipolar capacity. We say that* h *is* absolutely continuous with respect to the pair (μ, ν), *notation* $h \ll (\mu, \nu)$, *if for arbitrary* $A \in \mathcal{S}$ *and* $B, C \in \mathcal{S}$ *such that* $C \subset (B \cup A)^c$ *the following constraints are satisfied:*

(a) *if* $\mu(A) = 0$ *then* $h(B,C) = h(B \cup A, C)$,
(b) *if* $\nu(A) = 0$ *then* $h(C,B) = h(C, B \cup A)$.

Lemma 2. *Assume* χ *is a bipolar distribution function. For a pair of capacities* (μ, ν) *that satisfy Assumption 1 and 2, let function* $H_{(\chi,\mu,\nu)}$ *be defined by formula* (10). *Then* $H_{(\chi,\mu,\nu)} \ll (\mu, \nu)$.

Proof. Since $H_{(\chi,\mu,\nu)}$ depends just on the values of the capacities μ and ν, and not on the choice of particular pair of sets $(A,B) \in L$, the absolute continuity of $H_{(\chi,\mu,\nu)}$ is straightforward.

Proposition 4. *Let* $f \in \mathfrak{F}_{(X,\mathcal{S})}$ *and assume there exists a decreasing form* $g_{(f^+,\mu)}$ *of* f^+ *in a capacity space* $\mathcal{M} = (X, \mathcal{S}, \mu)$ *and an increasing form* $g^{(f^-,\nu)}$ *of* f^- *in a capacity space* $\mathcal{N} = (X, \mathcal{S}, \nu)$. *Denote* $g = g_{(f^+,\mu)} + g^{(f^-,\nu)}$. *Let* χ *be a bipolar distribution function and* $H_{(\chi,\mu,\nu)}$ *be given by formula* (10). *Then*

$$(C) \int |f| \, \mathrm{d}H_{(\chi,\mu,\nu)} = (C) \int g \, \mathrm{d}H_{(\chi,\mu,\nu)}.$$

Proof. The idea of the proof is based in the fact that all cuts of $|f|$ as well as of g have the same bipolar capacity $H_{(\chi,\mu,\nu)}$. For this reason the corresponding bipolar Choquet integrals coincide.

Remark 3. In Proposition 4 we use the bipolar capacity $H_{(\chi,\mu,\nu)}$ to compute the corresponding Choquet integrals. For a general bipolar capacity h we have no guarantee that the bipolar capacities of cuts of $|f|$ and g coincide.

Definition 16. *Assume (μ, ν) is a pair of capacities fulfilling Assumptions 1 and 2. We say that a bipolar capacity h is symmetric with respect to (μ, ν), if for arbitrary $A_1, B_1, A_2, B_2 \in S$ such that $B_1 \subset A_1^c$ and $B_2 \subset A_2^c$, we have that for $\mu(A_1) = \mu(A_2)$, $\nu(B_1) = \nu(B_2)$ imply $h(A_1, B_1) = h(A_2, B_2)$.*

Proposition 5. *Assume (μ, ν) is a pair of capacities fulfilling Assumptions 1 and 2, and χ is a bipolar distribution function. Then the bipolar capacity $H_{(\chi, \mu, \nu)}$ is symmetric with respect to (μ, ν).*

Proof. The arguments are the same as those in the proof of Lemma 2.

Definition 17. *Let (μ, ν) be a pair of capacities fulfilling Assumptions 1 and 2, and χ be a bipolar distribution function. For $f \in \mathfrak{F}_{(X,S)}$, the bipolar OWA operator (BIOWA) is defined by*

$$\text{BIOWA}(f) = (C) \int g \, dH_{(\chi, \mu, \nu)},$$

where $g_{(f^+, \mu)}$ is a decreasing form of f^+ in the capacity space (X, S, μ), $g^{(f^-, \nu)}$ is an increasing form of f^- in the capacity space (X, S, ν) and $g = g_{(f^+, \mu)} + g^{(f^-, \nu)}$.

Proposition 6. *Let (μ, ν) be a pair of capacities fulfilling Assumptions 1 and 2, and χ be a bipolar distribution function. BIOWA is an idempotent monotone operator. Moreover, if for $f_1, f_2 \in F_{(X,S)}$, for arbitrary $t \geq 0$ we have*

$$\mu(\{x \in [0,1]; f_1^+(x) \geq t\}) = \mu(\{x \in [0,1]; f_2^+(x) \geq t\}),$$
$$\nu(\{x \in [0,1]; f_1^-(x) \geq t\}) = \nu(\{x \in [0,1]; f_2^-(x) \geq t\}),$$

then $\text{BIOWA}(f_1) = \text{BIOWA}(f_2)$.

Example 2. Denote $\chi_{\text{ad}}(x, y) = x - y$. Consider function f defined by

$$f(x) = \begin{cases} x - \frac{1}{4} & \text{for } x \in [0, \frac{1}{2}], \\ \frac{1}{2} & \text{for } x \in]\frac{1}{2}, \frac{3}{4}[, \\ -\frac{1}{4} & \text{for } x \in [\frac{3}{4}, 1]. \end{cases}$$

We will consider the pairs of capacities (μ_1, ν_1) and (μ_2, ν_2) from Example 1. Then we get

$$g_{(f^+, \mu_1)}(x) = \begin{cases} \frac{1}{2} & \text{for } x \in [0, \frac{1}{8}], \\ 0 & \text{otherwise,} \end{cases} \quad g^{(f^-, \nu_1)}(x) = \begin{cases} \frac{1}{4} & \text{for } x \in [\frac{3}{4}, 1], \\ 0 & \text{otherwise,} \end{cases}$$

$$g_{(f^+, \mu_2)}(x) = \begin{cases} \frac{1}{2} & \text{for } x \in [0, \frac{1}{8}], \\ \frac{3}{8} - x & \text{for } x \in]\frac{1}{8}, \frac{3}{8}[, \\ 0 & \text{otherwise,} \end{cases} \quad g^{(f^-, \nu_2)}(x) = \begin{cases} \frac{1}{4} & \text{for } x \in [\frac{3}{4}, 1], \\ 0 & \text{otherwise.} \end{cases}$$

For the bipolar distribution function χ_{ad} and pairs of capacities (in fact, pairs of probability distributions) (μ_1, ν_1) and (μ_2, ν_2), we can compute the BIOWA operators as a difference of Lebesgue integrals with respect to the corresponding probability distributions. Then we get

$$\text{BIOWA}_{(\chi_{\text{ad}},\mu_1,\nu_1)}(f) = \frac{1}{2} \cdot \frac{1}{4} - \frac{1}{4} \cdot \frac{1}{2} = 0,$$

$$\text{BIOWA}_{(\chi_{\text{ad}},\mu_2,\nu_2)}(f) = \frac{1}{2} \cdot \frac{1}{4} - \frac{1}{4} \cdot \frac{1}{2} + \int_{\frac{1}{8}}^{\frac{3}{8}} \left(\frac{3}{8} - x \right) \phi_2(\mathrm{d}x) = \frac{1}{32}.$$

For

$$\chi^*(x,y) = \begin{cases} 0 & \text{for } x = 0 \text{ and } y < 1, \\ -1 & \text{for } y = 1, \\ 1 & \text{otherwise,} \end{cases}$$

we get

$$\text{BIOWA}_{(\chi^*,\mu_1,\nu_1)}(f) = \text{BIOWA}_{(\chi^*,\mu_1,\nu_1)}(f) = \frac{1}{2}.$$

For

$$\chi_*(x,y) = \begin{cases} 0 & \text{for } y = 0 \text{ and } x < 1, \\ 1 & \text{for } x = 1, \\ -1 & \text{otherwise,} \end{cases}$$

we get

$$\text{BIOWA}_{(\chi_*,\mu_1,\nu_1)}(f) = \text{BIOWA}_{(\chi_*,\mu_1,\nu_1)}(f) = -\frac{1}{4}.$$

For

$$\chi_0(x,y) = \begin{cases} 1 & \text{for } x = 1, \\ -1 & \text{for } y = 1, \\ 0 & \text{otherwise,} \end{cases}$$

we have

$$\text{BIOWA}_{(\chi_0,\mu_1,\nu_1)}(f) = \text{BIOWA}_{(\chi_0,\mu_1,\nu_1)}(f) = 0.$$

Remark 4. For a better illustration of BIOWA operators with continuous input functions we have transformed some of the BIOWA operators used in [16] using the notation from that paper. As we may see, for χ^* the BIOWA operator gives $\sup f$ as result, for χ_* the result is $\inf f$. For χ_0 the result is 0 unless f has only positive or only negative values.

4   Orness Measure for BIOWA

Yager [20] introduced orness measures for OWA operators to express, in a sense, a grade of 'or-like' property of OWA operators. Particularly, the higher weights have the greatest inputs, the higher is the measure of orness. In [12], we proposed measures of orness for OWA operators with continuous input functions. Now, we are going to propose an orness measure for BIOWA operators with continuous input functions.

By Γ we denote the set of all bipolar distribution functions. We will use the notation from Example 8.

116   M. Kalina

Lemma 3. *et (μ,ν) be a pair of capacities fulfilling Assumption 1. Then*

$$(C)\int\int \chi_0\,\mathrm{d}\nu\,\mathrm{d}\mu = 0, \quad (C)\int\int \chi^*\,\mathrm{d}\nu\,\mathrm{d}\mu = \frac{1}{2}, \quad (C)\int\int \chi_*\,\mathrm{d}\nu\,\mathrm{d}\mu = -\frac{1}{2}.$$

Moreover, $\sup \Gamma = \chi^*$ *and* $\inf \Gamma = \chi_*$.

Due to Lemma 3, we introduce the following definition.

Definition 18. *The orness measure of the BIOWA operator defined via the triple (χ,μ,ν), where χ is a bipolar distribution function and (μ,ν) is a pair of capacities fulfilling Assumptions 1 and 2, is defined by*

$$\mathrm{orness}(\mathrm{BIOWA}_{(\chi,\mu,\nu)}) = (C)\int\int \chi\,\mathrm{d}\nu\,\mathrm{d}\mu + \frac{1}{2}.$$

Example 3. Lemma 3 implies that regardless of the choice of (μ,ν) we have

$$\mathrm{orness}(\mathrm{BIOWA}_{(\chi^*,\mu,\nu)}) = 1, \quad \mathrm{orness}(\mathrm{BIOWA}_{(\chi_*,\mu,\nu)}) = 0,$$

$$\mathrm{orness}(\mathrm{BIOWA}_{(\chi_0,\mu,\nu)}) = 0.$$

For the pairs of capacities (μ_1,ν_1) and (μ_2,ν_2) from Example 1, we will compute the corresponding orness measure choosing χ_{ad} as the bipolar distribution function.

$$\mathrm{orness}(\mathrm{BIOWA}_{(\chi_{\mathrm{ad}},\mu_1,\nu_1)}) = (C)\int\int (x-y)\,\mathrm{d}\Psi_1\,\mathrm{d}\Phi_1$$

$$= \int_0^{\frac{1}{4}}\int_{\frac{1}{2}}^{1-x} (x-y)\cdot 2\cdot 2\,\mathrm{d}y\,\mathrm{d}x = -\frac{7}{32},$$

$$\mathrm{orness}(\mathrm{BIOWA}_{(\chi_{\mathrm{ad}},\mu_2,\nu_2)}) = (C)\int\int (x-y)\,\mathrm{d}\Phi_2\,\mathrm{d}\Psi_2 = -\frac{3}{64}.$$

5 Conclusions

In this contribution, we have introduced BIOWA operators for continuous input functions and exemplified the results. We have shown under which constraints put on a pair of capacities (μ,ν), it is possible to construct a decreasing form of f^+ and an increasing form of f^-, where f is the input function. Further, we have introduced an orness measure for BIOWA operators with continuous input functions.

References

1. Calvo, T., Kolesárová, A., Komorníková, M., Mesiar, R.: Aggregation operators: properties, classes and construction methods. In: Aggregation Operators, in: New Trends and Applications, vol. 97, Physica-Verlag, Heidelberg, pp. 3–104 (2002)
2. Choquet, G.: Theory of capacities. Ann. Inst. Fourier **5**, 131–295 (1953/54)

3. Denneberg, D.: Non-additive Measure and Integral. Kluwer Academic Publishers, Dordrecht (1994)
4. Dujmović, J.J.: Mixed averaging by levels (MAL)-A system and computer evaluation method, in Proc. Informatica Conf. (in Serbo- Croatian), Bled, Yugoslavia, paper d28 (1973)
5. Dujmović, J.J.: Weighted conjunctive and disjunctive means and their application in system evaluation, J. Univ. Belgrade, EE Dept., ser. Mathematics and Physics, no. 483, 147–158 (1974)
6. Grabisch, M.: Fuzzy integral in multicriteria decision making. Fuzzy Sets Syst. **69**(3), 279–298 (1995)
7. Grabisch, M., Greco, S., Pirlot, M.: Bipolar and bivariate models in multicriteria decision analysis: descriptive and constructive approaches. Int. J. Intell. Syst. **23**(9), 930–969 (2008)
8. Grabisch, M., Labreuche, C.: A decade of application of the Choquet and Sugeno integrals in multi-criteria decision aid. Ann. Oper. Res. **175**(1), 247–290 (2010)
9. Grabisch, M., Labreuche, C.: Bi-capacities-I: definition, Möbius transform and interaction. Fuzzy Sets Syst. **151**, 211–236 (2005)
10. Grabisch, M., Labreuche, C.: Bi-capacities-II: the Choquet integral. Fuzzy Sets Syst. **151**, 237–256 (2005)
11. Grabisch, M., Marichal, J.-L., Mesiar, R., Pap, E.: Aggregation functions. In: Encyclopedia of Mathematics and Its Applications, vol. 127. Cambridge University Press, Cambridge (2009)
12. Jin, L.S., Mesiar, R., Kalina, M., Yager, R.R.: Canonical form of ordered weighted averaging operators. Ann. Oper. Res. **295**(2), 605–631 (2020). https://doi.org/10.1007/s10479-020-03802-6
13. Kalina, M.: Continuous OWA operators, Atlantis Studies in Uncertainty Modelling, volume 3. Joint Proceedings of the 19th World Congress of the International Fuzzy Systems Association (IFSA), the 12th Conference of the European Society for Fuzzy Logic and Technology (EUSFLAT), and the 11th International Summer School on Aggregation Operators (AGOP), pp. 589–595 (2001)
14. Kishor, A., Singh, A.K., Pal, N.R.: Orness measure of OWA operators: a new approach. IEEE Trans. Fuzzy Syst. **22**(4), 1039–1045 (2014). https://doi.org/10.1109/tfuzz.2013.2282299
15. Stupňanová, A., Jin, L.S.: BIOWA operators. In: Lesot, M.-J., Vieira, S., Reformat, M.Z., Carvalho, J.P., Wilbik, A., Bouchon-Meunier, B., Yager, R.R. (eds.) IPMU 2020. CCIS, vol. 1238, pp. 419–425. Springer, Cham (2020). https://doi.org/10.1007/978-3-030-50143-3_32
16. Mesiar, R., Stupňanová, A., Jin, L.: Bipolar ordered weighted averages: BIOWA operators. Fuzzy Sets Syst. **433**, 108–121 (2022)
17. Pap, E.: Null-Additive Set Functions, Mathematics and Its Applications, vol. 337. Kluwer Academic Publishers Group, Dordrecht (1995)
18. Riečan, B., Neubrunn, T.: Integral, measure and ordering. Kluwer Acad. Publ, Dordrecht, Ister Science, Bratislava (1997)
19. Torra, V.: The weighted OWA operator. Int. J. Intell. Syst. **12**, 153–166 (1997)
20. R. R. Yager, R. R. On ordered weighted averaging aggregation operators in multicriteria decision making. IEEE Syst. Man Cybern. Soc. **18**(1), 183–190 (1988)

Machine Learning and Data Science

Cost-constrained Group Feature Selection Using Information Theory

Tomasz Klonecki[1]([✉])(iD), Paweł Teisseyre[1,2](iD), and Jaesung Lee[3,4](iD)

[1] Institute of Computer Science, Polish Academy of Sciences, Warsaw, Poland
{tomasz.klonecki,pawel.teisseyre}@ipipan.waw.pl
[2] Faculty of Mathematics and Information Science,
Warsaw University of Technology, Warsaw, Poland
[3] Department of Artificial Intelligence, Chung-Ang University, Seoul, South Korea
curseor@cau.ac.kr
[4] AI/ML Innovation Research Center, Seoul, South Korea

Abstract. A problem of cost-constrained group feature selection in supervised classification is considered. In this setting, the features are grouped and each group is assigned a cost. The goal is to select a subset of features that does not exceed a user-specified budget and simultaneously allows accurate prediction of the class variable. We propose two sequential forward selection algorithms based on the information-theoretic framework. In the first method, a single feature is added in each step, whereas in the second one, we select the entire group of features in each step. The choice of the candidate feature or group of features is based on the novel score function that takes into account both the informativeness of the added features in the context of previously selected ones as well as the cost of the candidate group. The score is based on the lower bound of the mutual information and thus can be effectively computed even when the conditioning set is large. The experiments were performed on a large clinical database containing groups of features corresponding to various diagnostic tests and administrative data. The results indicate that the proposed method allows achieving higher accuracy than the traditional feature selection method, especially when the budget is low.

Keywords: group feature selection · information theory · mutual information · costly features

1 Introduction

We consider the problem of cost-constrained feature selection which aims to select a subset of features relevant to the target variable while satisfying a user-specific maximal admissible budget. In the cost-constrained methods, it is necessary to find a trade-off between the relevancy of the feature subset and its cost. Unlike previous papers on cost-constrained feature selection [1,6,17,22], which assume that each feature is associated with the individual cost of acquiring its value, we consider costs assigned to entire groups of features. The costly groups

© The Author(s), under exclusive license to Springer Nature Switzerland AG 2023
V. Torra and Y. Narukawa (Eds.): MDAI 2023, LNAI 13890, pp. 121–132, 2023.
https://doi.org/10.1007/978-3-031-33498-6_8

of features naturally appear in many research domains. In medical diagnostics, groups may contain various parameters corresponding to a single diagnostic test. Incurring the test cost, we get feature values for the entire group. For example, a complete blood count (CBC) is a blood test providing various parameters (features) about cells in a person's blood. Moreover, the groups may consist of different statistics (such as mean, median, or standard deviation) corresponding to one medical parameter measured over a period of time, such as blood pressure during the patient's hospitalization. The costs can vary significantly between groups; for example, obtaining administrative data is usually much cheaper than performing advanced diagnostic tests. Costly groups also appear in other domains, e.g., in image segmentation, groups may correspond to different characteristics of an image [11], and the costs of the groups are associated with the difficulty in obtaining the values of the features due to the necessity of computationally intensive preprocessing.

In this paper, we consider the information-theoretic framework. The problem can be formally stated as follows. Let $X = (X_1, \ldots, X_p)$ be a vector of features, Y be discrete target variable and $F = \{1, \ldots, p\}$. We assume that there are K disjoint groups of features $G_1, \ldots, G_K$ such that $F = G_1 \cup \ldots \cup G_K$ and the costs $c(G_1), \ldots, c(G_K)$ are associated with the groups. If we acquire the value of one feature from the group, then the values of the remaining features from the group are obtained for free. The mutual information (MI) between the target variable Y and the vector X_S corresponding to the feature subset $S \subset F$ is defined as $I(Y, X_S) = H(Y) - H(Y|X_S)$, where $H(Y)$ and $H(Y|X_S)$ are entropy and conditional entropy respectively [3]. MI quantifies how much uncertainty of Y is removed by knowing X_S, it measures the dependence strength between X_S and Y. The grouped cost-constrained problem of feature selection can be stated using the information-theoretic framework as

$$S_{opt} = \arg \max_{S:c(S) \leq B} I(Y, X_S), \tag{1}$$

where B is a user specified maximal admissible budget and $c(S)$ is the cost associated with subset $S \subset F$. Since the costs are associated with the groups and not single features, the cost of any subset S is defined as

$$c(S) = \sum_{k=1}^{K} c(G_k) \mathbb{1}\{\exists j \in S : j \in G_k\}, \tag{2}$$

where $\mathbb{1}$ is the indicator function. Direct solving of the problem (1) is challenging, and thus we propose two sequential forward selection algorithms. In the first method, a single feature is added in each step, whereas in the second one, we select the entire group of features in each step. The choice of the candidate feature or group of features is based on the novel score function that is based on the lower bound of the joint MI (JMI) and thus can be effectively computed even when the set of already selected features is large. Subsequently, we apply the methods to a large clinical database MIMIC [14], containing groups of features corresponding to various medical tests and administrative data. The experiments indicate that, for low budgets, the proposed methods allow choosing a subset of features for which the classification model achieves significantly better accuracy when compared to the subsets selected by traditional methods.

2   Related Work

Feature selection in supervised classification is one of the central problems in machine learning [4]. Among various approaches, methods based on information theoretic quantities such as MI and conditional MI (CMI) have attracted significant attention in recent years, mainly due to their model-free nature and the ability to detect interactions and non-linear dependencies. For a comprehensive review, we refer to [2,18]. Most of the considered methods are based on the sequential forward selection in which the candidate feature maximizing certain score function is chosen in each step [9,19,20]. The score function reflects the informativeness of the candidate feature in the context of already selected features. The natural choice of the score function is CMI; however, its estimation is challenging in practice [12]. Therefore, most score functions aim to approximate the CMI. Unfortunately, traditional methods ignore the costs of features which may lead to choosing the feature subset exceeding the assumed budget. Score functions can be modified by introducing a penalty for the cost of the candidate feature. In such an approach, the trade-off between feature relevance and its cost should be controlled by an additional parameter called the cost factor. The above idea is used in [1] and in a recent paper [17], where an algorithm for optimization of the cost factor is proposed. In addition to information-theoretic approaches, there are other feature selection methods that take feature costs into account. Examples include modifications of decision trees and Random Forests [22], AIC criterion [5] and lasso [16]. The idea of selecting entire groups of features has also attracted attention. The most extensively studied approach is group lasso and its variants [13,21], but there are also information-theoretic approaches [8]. Although these approaches use structural information among features, they ignore the costs of the groups. The costs of the groups are considered in [11] in the context of the segmentation of backscatter images in product analysis. The authors use the performance of a classifier on a validation set as a score function to evaluate the informativeness of the groups. Although straightforward, the approach requires significant computational cost and fitting the model several times, which can be prohibitive for large datasets. In our method, we overcome this problem by using a computationally effective feature selection score based on the lower bound of the JMI.

3   Proposed Methods

Since solving (1) requires the infeasible computational cost of an exhaustive search on 2^p of candidate feature subsets, most researchers use sequential forward procedures that allow evaluating the relevance of the candidate feature, given the set of already selected features. In such approaches, CMI $I(X_k,$

$Y|X_S) = H(Y|X_S) - H(Y|X_k, X_S)$ is a natural score function that allows assessing the informativeness of a candidate feature X_k in the context of already selected features X_k. We adopt this approach, additionally taking into account information about group costs.

3.1   Method 1: Single Feature Selection

The method is based on adding a single feature in each step. Assume that S is a set of features selected in previous steps. We define the cost of the candidate feature $k \in F \setminus S$ in the context of S as

$$c(k, S) = \begin{cases} 0 \text{ if } k \in G \text{ and } \exists j \in S : j \in G \\ c(G) \text{ if } k \in G \text{ and } \nexists j \in S : j \in G. \end{cases}$$

If the candidate feature X_k belongs to the group G, from which some feature has already been selected, then the cost of adding X_k is zero. Otherwise, we pay the cost of the group G. We start from empty set $S = \emptyset$ and in each step we add a candidate feature $S \leftarrow S \cup \{k^*\}$ such that

$$k^* = \arg \max_{k \in F \setminus S} [I(X_k, Y|X_S) - \lambda c(k, S)], \tag{3}$$

where $\lambda > 0$ is a parameter controlling the trade-off between feature relevance and its cost. The candidate features are added until we exceed the budget, i.e., $c(S) > B$, where $c(S)$ is defined in (2).

3.2   Method 2: Group Feature Selection

The method utilizes the group structure of the features and is based on adding a whole group of features in each step instead of a single feature. We start from empty set $S = \emptyset$ and in each step we add a candidate group $S \leftarrow S \cup \{G^*\}$ such that

$$G^* = \arg \max_G [I(X_G, Y|X_S) - \lambda c(G)], \tag{4}$$

where $\lambda > 0$ is a parameter controlling the trade-off between the relevance of the group of features and its cost. The candidate groups are added until we exceed the budget, i.e., $c(S) > B$. Adding groups of features instead of single features has both advantages and disadvantages. The main advantage is that we can detect synergistic interactions among features belonging to one group. For example, let us consider the group $G = \{1, 2\}$, such that $Y = XOR(X_1, X_2)$. In this case $I(X_1, Y) = I(X_2, Y) = 0$ and thus neither X_1 nor X_2 will be selected as relevant by the first method (3). On the other hand, we have $I(X_G, Y) > 0$, and therefore group G will be selected as relevant by the second method (4). Although appealing, the group selection method also carries some risks. For example, the group may contain only one relevant feature, whereas the rest are noisy features. Moreover, including an entire group of features may result in the inclusion of some redundant features, e.g., when the group contains features that are strongly correlated. Finally, some features from the candidate group may be strongly correlated with the already selected features. Including too many redundant and irrelevant features may result in the deterioration of model performance. In view of this, it is necessary to add an elimination step to remove redundant features from the set selected by (4). The natural approach is to remove from set S feature $r \in S$ such that

$$I(X_r, Y | X_{S \setminus \{r\}}) = 0, \tag{5}$$

i.e., remove the feature that brings no additional information in the context of the remaining features. Unfortunately, checking (5) is challenging for many reasons. First, the true value of the CMI is unknown and has to be estimated, which is challenging when S is large. Secondly, checking (5) requires using statistical hypothesis testing which is also challenging, especially for small sample sizes and large conditioning sets. The possible solution is to replace (5) with some simpler condition that can be effectively computed. The simplest approach is to remove feature r which is strongly associated with one of the remaining features, i.e., we remove r when

$$\frac{I(X_r, X_j)}{H(X_r)} > \tau, \tag{6}$$

for some $j \in S \setminus \{r\}$, where $\tau \in [0, 1]$ is a threshold (we set $\tau = 0.8$ in our experiments). The following Lemma formally justifies using (6) as a surrogate for (5).

Lemma 1. *Let $r \in S$. Assume that $I(X_r, X_j)/H(X_r) \approx 1$ for $j \in S \setminus \{r\}$ and $H(X_r) > 0$. Then $I(X_r, Y | X_{S \setminus \{r\}}) \approx 0$.*

Proof. Since conditioning on a smaller subset of features increases the entropy, we have

$$I(X_r, Y | X_{S \setminus \{r\}}) = H(X_r | X_{S \setminus \{r\}}) - H(X_r | X_{S \setminus \{r\}}, Y)$$
$$\leq H(X_r | X_{S \setminus \{r\}}) \leq H(X_r | X_j). \tag{7}$$

Moreover, observe that

$$\frac{I(X_r, X_j)}{H(X_r)} = \frac{H(X_r) - H(X_r | X_j)}{H(X_r)} = 1 - \frac{H(X_r | X_j)}{H(X_r)}$$

and thus $I(X_r, X_j)/H(X_r) \approx 1$ is equivalent to $H(X_r | X_j) \approx 0$, which combined with (7) gives the assertion.

3.3   Approximating the Relevance Terms

Estimation of the CMI term $I(X_G, Y | X_S)$ appearing in (4) is a challenging task due to the dimensionality of both G and S. A possible solution is to replace the CMI with the function of lower dimensional terms which are easier to estimate. Observe that since $I(X_G, Y | X_S) = I(X_{S \cup G}, Y) - I(X_S, Y)$, maximization of $I(X_G, Y | X_S)$ with respect to G is equivalent to maximization of $I(X_{S \cup G}, Y)$

as the term $I(X_S, Y)$ does not depend on candidate group G and thus can be omitted. In this work, we use the lower bounds of the terms $I(X_{S \cup \{k\}}, Y)$ and $I(X_{S \cup G}, Y)$, which are denoted as $I_{\mathrm{LB}}(X_{S \cup \{k\}}, Y)$ and $I_{\mathrm{LB}}(X_{S \cup G}, Y)$, respectively.

The following Theorem shows that the lower bound $I_{\mathrm{LB}}(X_{S \cup G}, Y)$ is proportional to the quantity, consisting of lower dimensional terms, which are relatively easy to estimate.

Theorem 1. *The following property holds*

$$I_{LB}(X_{S \cup G}, Y) \propto \sum_{i,j \in G: i<j} I(Y, (X_i, X_j)) + \sum_{i \in G, j \in S} I(Y, (X_i, X_j)), \qquad (8)$$

where $\propto$ denotes equality after omitting the terms which are independent of candidate group G.

Proof. Using Theorem 2 from Appendix with $|A| = 2$ we can write

$$
\begin{aligned}
I_{\mathrm{LB}}(X_{G \cup S}, Y) \propto \sum_{i,j \in G \cup S: i<j} I(Y, (X_i, X_j)) &= \sum_{i,j \in G: i<j} I(Y, (X_i, X_j)) \\
&+ \sum_{i \in G, j \in S} I(Y, (X_i, X_j)) + \sum_{i,j \in S: i<j} I(Y, (X_i, X_j)) \\
\propto \sum_{i,j \in G: i<j} I(Y, (X_i, X_j)) &+ \sum_{i \in G, j \in S} I(Y, (X_i, X_j)), \qquad (9)
\end{aligned}
$$

as the term $\sum_{i,j \in S: i<j} I(Y, (X_i, X_j))$ does not depend on the candidate group G and thus can be treated as constant.

Corollary 1. *The following property holds*

$$I_{LB}(X_{S \cup \{k\}}, Y) \propto \sum_{j \in S} I(Y, X_k | X_j) \qquad (10)$$

Proof. Note that $I(X_{S \cup \{k\}}, Y)$ is a special case of $I(X_{G \cup S}, Y)$, obtained for $G = \{k\}$. Thus, using Theorem 1 we can write $I_{\mathrm{LB}}(X_{S \cup \{k\}}, Y) \propto \sum_{j \in S} I(Y, (X_k, X_j))$. Using the chain rule for mutual information we get $\sum_{j \in S} I(Y, (X_k, X_j)) = \sum_{j \in S} I(Y, X_k | X_j) + \sum_{j \in S} I(Y, X_j) \propto \sum_{j \in S} I(Y, X_k | X_j)$ as $I(Y, X_j)$ does not depend on candidate feature X_k. This gives the assertion.

The score function given in Corollary (10) is well-known as joint MI criterion [20], we refer to [7,15] where further theoretical properties of JMI are discussed. The score function, given in (8) can be treated as a generalization of joint MI to group feature selection. To the best of our knowledge, such generalization has not yet been considered in previous papers.

Algorithm 1: Cost-constrained single feature selection (CC-SFS)

Input   : $Y, X_1, \ldots, X_p, \lambda, B, c(G_1), \ldots, c(G_K)$
$S = \emptyset$
while $c(S) \leq B$ **do**
    $k^* = \arg\max_{k \in F \setminus S}[\sum_{j \in S} I(X_k, Y | X_j) - \lambda c(k, S)],$
    $S \leftarrow S \cup \{k^*\}.$
end
Output   : S

Algorithm 2: Cost-constrained group feature selection (CC-GFS)

Input   : $Y, X_1, \ldots, X_p, \lambda, B, c(G_1), \ldots, c(G_K), \tau$
$S = \emptyset$
while $c(S) \leq B$ **do**
    Add optimal candidate group:
    $G^* = \arg\max_G[\sum_{i,j \in G: i<j} I(Y, (X_i, X_j)) + \sum_{i \in G, j \in S} I(Y, (X_i, X_j)) - \lambda c(G)]$
    $S \leftarrow S \cup \{G^*\}.$
    Remove redundant features:
    for $r \in S$ **do**
        for $j \in S \setminus \{r\}$ **do**
            if $I(X_r, X_j)/H(X_r) > \tau$ *and* $I(Y, X_r) < I(Y, X_j)$ **then**
                $S \leftarrow S \setminus \{r\}$
            end
        end
    end
end
Output   : S

3.4 Algorithms

Taking into account the issues discussed in the above sections leads to two feature selection algorithms, called CC-SFS (cost-constrained single feature selection) and CC-GFS (cost-constrained group feature selection), respectively. They are based on (3) and (4) and use approximations described in Sect. 3.3. In Algorithm 1, the algorithm adds a single feature in each step. In Algorithm 2, the algorithm adds the entire group of features in each step and also removes the redundant features from the current set of features.

An important issue in both algorithms is the choice of parameter λ as it controls the trade-off between the informativeness of the candidate features and the costs of the groups. We first describe the procedure for Method 1. Note that for $\lambda = 0$ the costs are not considered, whereas for a sufficiently large value of λ only the costs will affect the order of selecting features. We denote such value by $\lambda_{\max}$. To determine its value, we use the following approach. Let $c_{(1)} \leq c_{(2)} \leq \ldots \leq c_{(K)}$ be the group costs sorted in ascending order and let $I_{\max} = \max_k I(Y, X_k)$ and $I_{\min} = \min_k I(Y, X_k)$. For $\lambda = \lambda_{\max}$, we should select the feature belonging to the cheapest group in the first step, regardless

Table 1. Selected feature groups and their costs.

Group Name	Description	Cost	# Features
A	Administrative data from the interview (e.g., age, gender)	1.0	9
NBP	Non-invasive blood pressure	3.0	8
RL	RLL & RUL lung sounds frequency	9.0	4
UN	Urea nitrogen in serum or plasma	12.0	4
VR	Verbal response	2.0	3
HR	Heart rate	1.5	4
P	Platalets in blood	2.0	4

of feature relevance. Therefore, when we consider the first step in Method 1, value $\lambda_{\max}$ should satisfy $I_{\max} - \lambda c_{(2)} \leq I_{\min} - \lambda c_{(1)}$ as the feature from the cheapest group with cost $c_{(1)}$ should be selected regardless of its informativeness. It is easy to see that $\lambda_{\max} := (I_{\max} - I_{\min})/(c_{(2)} - c_{(1)})$ satisfies the above inequality. Subsequently, we run Method 1 for different values of λ from the range $0, \ldots, \lambda_{\max}$ and select the value for which the corresponding classification model maximizes the accuracy calculated for the validation set. In the case of Method 2, we use $I_{\max} := \max_G I_{LB}(Y, X_G)$, $I_{\min} := \min_G I_{LB}(Y, X_G)$ and perform the same steps. The number of values in the grid $0, \ldots, \lambda_{\max}$ depends on the user preferences and computational resources. For a denser grid, the optimal value can be chosen more precisely, although the computational cost of the procedure increases. Let us also mention that the MI terms are estimated using plug-in estimators in which the probabilities are estimated by fractions for discretized features.

4   Experiments

The main goal of the experiments was to compare the performance of the proposed cost-constrained methods CC-SFS and CC-GFS. As a baseline, we use the traditional feature selection approach that does not take into account the costs of the groups. As a representative of traditional methods, we use JMI criterion [20], which directly corresponds to CC-SFS with $\lambda = 0$.

4.1   Data

We performed experiments on a large medical dataset MIMIC [14], containing information about the medical conditions of over $19,773$ patients from the intensive care units (ICUs). Although the patients are diagnosed with multiple diseases, we focus on predicting hypertension disease using $p = 305$ features in this work, mostly corresponding to the results of diagnostic tests. The dataset

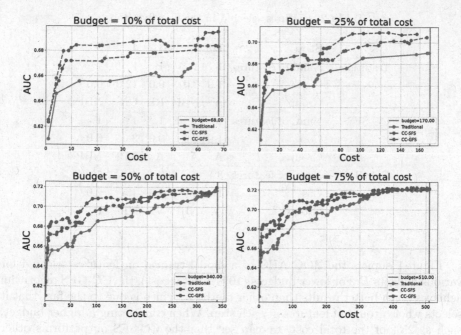

Fig. 1. Feature selection for MIMIC-II dataset (hypertension).

was already used in related studies, we refer to [23], where more details about feature extraction and data cleansing can be found. Importantly, the costs of the original features have been assigned by the experts, and the complete list of the features along with the costs is described in [16]. In the current work, we extend this approach, and we group features having similar origins and assign costs to the groups. Most groups consist of four different statistics (mean, median, standard deviation, and range) of one medical parameter measured over a period of time, examples include creatinine or glucose in Serum or Plasma. The other natural group (administrative data) contains basic information such as age, gender, or marital status that can be obtained during a medical interview. Group costs assignment can be found in our GitHub repository[1]. The selected groups and their costs are described in Table 1. Before running the algorithms, all costs are normalized to $[0, 1]$.

4.2 Results

To assess the quality of the selected subset of features we use a logistic regression model. The feature selection methods and the model are launched on training data (80%), and the ROC AUC evaluation metric is calculated on the test dataset (20%). The 5-fold cross-validation was used to select the optimal value of λ.

---

[1] MIMIC-II group costs: https://github.com/Kaketo/mimic-II-group-costs.

130   T. Klonecki et al.

Table 2. Features selected in the first five steps.

	Step	1	2	3	4	5
Traditional	Num. of features	1	1	1	1	1
	Cost	1.0	3.0	9.0	12.0	0.0
	Group	A	NBP	RL	UN	NBP
CC-SFS	Num. of features	1	1	1	1	1
	Cost	1.0	0.0	0.0	3.0	0.0
	Group	A	A	A	NBP	NBP
CC-GFS	Num. of features	8	8	2	4	4
	Cost	1.0	3.0	2.0	1.5	2.0
	Group	A	NBP	VR	HR	P

Figure 1 depicts the ROC AUC of a model trained on features selected for various budgets B. For lower budgets (10% of total cost), the CC-GFS algorithm achieves much better results than other methods, which is due to the fact that it selects whole groups of features at each step. When considering a higher budget, such as 25% of the total cost, we can see that the CC-SFS outperforms other methods. For a budget of 50% of the total cost, cost-constrained methods even out but still have a larger AUC than the traditional method. For the highest considered budget (75%), all methods perform equally, which indicates that all informative features have already been selected.

Table 2 presents features/groups selected in the first five steps for all three algorithms. First, the experimental results indicate that all algorithms have selected features from administrative and non-invasive blood pressure groups. It is reasonable since hypertension is a disease usually correlated with age and elevated blood pressure. In the next steps, the selected groups diverge significantly; the traditional method selects informative, but at the same time, expensive medical tests. The CC-SFS algorithm prefers features from already selected groups, and hence the cumulative cost does not increase rapidly. In addition, the CC-GFS method selects the whole group in each step; thus it consistently adds multiple informative and usually cheap features.

We measured the computational time for all methods on a computer (AMD Ryzen 7 3700X 8-Core 32GB RAM). With the budget set to 10% of the total cost, the traditional method took 29 minutes to compute, the CC-SFS and the CC-GFS methods took 1 hour 20 minutes and 2 hours and 30 minutes respectively.

5   Conclusions

The problem of feature selection with costs assigned to a group of features was discussed. We proposed two methods called CC-SFS and CC-GFS that are based on the sequential selection of candidate features or groups of features. The results, performed on a large clinical database MIMIC indicate that both methods significantly outperform the traditional approach which ignores the group structure of the features and the costs. The proposed methods can be recommended when the budget is small, as in such cases their superiority is most pronounced. The CC-GFS usually selects more features than CC-SFS and works slightly better than CC-SFS when the budget is low. There are some interesting issues left for future research. The discussed methods can be extended to solve the multi-output tasks, where Y is a multi-dimensional vector. Moreover, applying Theorem 2 with different size of set A makes it possible to consider more general relevance term, which takes into account higher-order terms and in this way detect complex interactions among features. Finally, it would be interesting to consider the relationships between the costs of the groups, e.g., when the features from one group are acquired, the cost of the other group is reduced.

Acknowledgment. This research was supported by Institute of Information & communications Technology Planning & Evaluation (IITP) grant funded by the Korea government (MSIT) (2021-0-01341, Artificial Intelligence Graduate School Program (Chung-Ang University)).

Appendix

The Theorem can be found in [10], but for completeness, we give the proof below.

Theorem 2. *Let $A \subset G$. Then the following inequality holds*
$$I(Y, X_G) \geq \binom{|G|}{|A|}^{-1} \sum_{(i,j) \in G} I(Y, X_A).$$

Proof. Since conditioning on a larger set can only decrease the entropy, we have $I(Y, X_A) = H(Y) - H(Y|X_A) \leq H(Y) - H(Y|X_G) = I(Y, X_G)$. By averaging over all subsets A, we get the assertion.

References

1. Bolón-Canedo, V., Porto-Díaz, I., Sánchez-Maroño, N., Alonso-Betanzos, A.: A framework for cost-based feature selection. Pattern Recogn. **47**(7), 2481–2489 (2014)
2. Brown, G., Pocock, A., Zhao, M.J., Luján, M.: Conditional likelihood maximisation: a unifying framework for information theoretic feature selection. J. Mach. Learn. Res. **13**(1), 27–66 (2012)
3. Cover, T.M., Thomas, J.A.: Elements of Information Theory (Wiley Series in Telecommunications and Signal Processing). Wiley-Interscience (2006)
4. Guyon, I., Elisseeff, A.: An introduction to variable and feature selection. J. Mach. Learn. Res. **3**, 1157–1182 (2003)
5. Jagdhuber, R., Lang, M., Stenzl, A., Neuhaus, J., Rahnenfuhrer, J.: Cost-constrained feature selection in binary classification: adaptations for greedy forward selection and genetic algorithms. BMC Bioinform. **21**(2), 307–333 (2020)

6. Jagdhuber, R., Lang, M., Stenzl, A., Neuhaus, J., Rahnenführer, J.: Cost-constrained feature selection in binary classification: adaptations for greedy forward selection and genetic algorithms. BMC Bioinform. **21**(1), 1–21 (2020)
7. Łazęcka, M., Mielniczuk, J.: Multiple testing of conditional independence hypotheses using information-theoretic approach. In: Torra, V., Narukawa, Y. (eds.) MDAI 2021. LNCS (LNAI), vol. 12898, pp. 81–92. Springer, Cham (2021). https://doi.org/10.1007/978-3-030-85529-1_7
8. Li, H., Wu, X., Li, Z., Ding, W.: Group feature selection with streaming features. In: Proceedings of the 13th IEEE International Conference on Data Mining, pp. 1109–1114. ICDM'2013 (2013)
9. Lin, D., Tang, X.: Conditional infomax learning: an integrated framework for feature extraction and fusion. In: Proceedings of the 9th European Conference on Computer Vision - Volume Part I, pp. 68–82. ECCV'06 (2006)
10. Meyer, P., Schretter, C., Bontempi, G.: Information-theoretic feature selection in microarray data using variable complementarity. IEEE J. Selected Top. Sig. Process. **2**(3), 261–274 (2008)
11. Paclík, P., Duin, R., van Kempen, G., Kohlus, R.: On feature selection with measurement cost and grouped features. In: Proceedings of Joint IAPR International Workshops on Statistical Techniques in Pattern Recognition and Structural and Syntactic Pattern Recognition, pp. 461–469 (2002)
12. Paninski, L.: Estimation of entropy and mutual information. Neural Comput. **15**(6), 1191–1253 (2003)
13. Roth, V., Fisher, B.: The group-lasso for generalized linear models: uniqueness of solutions and efficient algorithms. In: Proceedings of the 25th International Conference on Machine Learning, pp. 848–855. ICML'2008 (2008)
14. Saeed, M., et al.: Multiparameter intelligent monitoring in intensive care II: a public-access intensive care unit database. Critical Care Med. **39**(5), 952–960 (2011)
15. Sechidis, K., Nikolaou, N., Brown, G.: Information theoretic feature selection in multi-label data through composite likelihood. In: Fränti, P., Brown, G., Loog, M., Escolano, F., Pelillo, M. (eds.) S+SSPR 2014. LNCS, vol. 8621, pp. 143–152. Springer, Heidelberg (2014). https://doi.org/10.1007/978-3-662-44415-3_15
16. Teisseyre, P., Zufferey, D., Słomka, M.: Cost-sensitive classifier chains: selecting low-cost features in multi-label classification. Pattern Recogn. **86**, 290–319 (2019)
17. Teisseyre, P., Klonecki, T.: Controlling costs in feature selection: information theoretic approach. In: Proceedings of the International Conference on Computational Science, pp. 483–496. ICCS'21 (2021)
18. Vergara, J.R., Estévez, P.A.: A review of feature selection methods based on mutual information. Neural Comput. Appl. **24**(1), 175–186 (2014)
19. Vinh, N., Zhou, S., Chan, J., Bailey, J.: Can high-order dependencies improve mutual information based feature selection? Pattern Recogn. **53**, 45–58 (2016)
20. Yang, H.H., Moody, J.: Data visualization and feature selection: new algorithms for non Gaussian data. Adv. Neural. Inf. Process. Syst. **12**, 687–693 (1999)
21. Yuan, M., Lin, Y.: Model selection and estimation in regression with grouped variables. J. Royal Statist. Soc.: Ser. B **68**(1), 49–67 (2006)
22. Zhou, Q., Zhou, H., Li, T.: Cost-sensitive feature selection using random forest: selecting low-cost subsets of informative features. Knowl.-Based Syst. **95**, 1–11 (2016)
23. Zufferey, D., Hofer, T., Hennebert, J., Schumacher, M., Ingold, R., Bromuri, S.: Performance comparison of multi-label learning algorithms on clinical data for chronic diseases. Comput. Biol. Med. **65**, 34–43 (2015)

Conformal Prediction for Accuracy Guarantees in Classification with Reject Option

Ulf Johansson[1(✉)], Tuwe Löfström[1], Cecilia Sönströd[1], and Helena Löfström[2,3]

[1] Department of Computing, Jönköping University, Jönköping, Sweden
{ulf.johansson,tuwe.lofstrom,cecilia.sonstrod}@ju.se
[2] Jönköping International Business School, Jönköping, Sweden
helena.lofstrom@ju.se
[3] Department of Information Technology, University of Borås, Borås, Sweden

Abstract. A standard classifier is forced to predict the label of every test instance, even when confidence in the predictions is very low. In many scenarios, it would, however, be better to avoid making these predictions, maybe leaving them to a human expert. A classifier with that alternative is referred to as a *classifier with reject option*. In this paper, we propose an algorithm that, for a particular data set, automatically suggests a number of accuracy levels, which it will be able to meet perfectly, using a classifier with reject option. Since the basis of the suggested algorithm is conformal prediction, it comes with strong validity guarantees. The experimentation, using 25 publicly available two-class data sets, confirms that the algorithm obtains empirical accuracies very close to the requested levels. In addition, in an outright comparison with probabilistic predictors, including models calibrated with Platt scaling, the suggested algorithm clearly outperforms the alternatives.

1 Introduction

Classification is a well-established predictive task in data science, where the objective is to approximate the function $\theta(\mathbf{x}, y)$ from an input vector $\mathbf{x}$ to a target variable y, which take its values from a predefined set C of class labels $\{c_0, c_1, \ldots, c_m\}$. For $C = \{0, 1\}$, the task is called binary classification. Simple as though this may seem, there are some noteworthy observations to make, from a decision-support perspective. First of all, it must be noted that all predictions are not equal – most notably they vary in difficulty, where some instances are easy for the model and some are harder. The difficulty of predicting a particular

The authors acknowledge the Swedish Knowledge Foundation, Jönköping University, and the industrial partners for financially supporting the research through the AFAIR project with grant no. 20200223, as part of the research and education environment SPARK at Jönköping University. Helena Löfström is a PhD student in the Industrial Graduate School in Digital Retailing (INSiDR) at the University of Borås, funded by the Swedish Knowledge Foundation, grant no. 20160035.

V. Torra and Y. Narukawa (Eds.): MDAI 2023, LNAI 13890, pp. 133–145, 2023.
https://doi.org/10.1007/978-3-031-33498-6_9

instance is reflected in the *probability estimates* that most machine learning models can output to accompany their predictions. Indeed, for most classifiers, these probability estimates are the mechanism underlying the prediction. To be useful, probability estimates should be *well-calibrated*, i.e., correspond to the actual (true) probability of a particular instance belonging to the predicted class.

In the usual formulation of the classification task, models are forced to make predictions, even on instances where the model is uncertain about the class label. When the model is used for decision support, either by a human decision-maker, or as part of an automated system, this poses problems. Normally, the performance of the model is measured using some variant of accuracy across an entire set of predictions, making it hard, or even impossible, for a user to identify which instances the model is uncertain about. If the prediction probability is made available to the user, this can somewhat alleviate the problem by giving additional information about single predictions, provided of course that prediction probabilities are well-calibrated. Chow, in [3], introduced the *classification with reject option* framework, where a model is allowed to refrain from making predictions. A typical scenario for using classification with reject option is to refer instances rejected by the model to a human expert, for manual decisions, possibly aided by the model and/or accompanying explanations. In these cases, the trade-off between rejection rate and classification accuracy is a key issue, since there can be costs associated both with mis-classification errors and with human processing.

Conformal classifiers [18], which are built on top of machine learning models, associate their predictions with statistically valid measures of confidence. In the standard setting, the predictions are *set predictions*, i.e., for a test example x_{k+1}, the conformal predictor outputs a subset of the labels, Γ_{k+1}^{ϵ}. Under exchangeability, which is a weaker assumption than the standard i.i.d., these label sets contain the true label y_{k+1} with probability $1-\epsilon$, where $\epsilon \in (0,1)$ is a predefined (user-provided) significance level. Conformal classification can also produce so-called *confidence-credibility* predictions [13]. In that setting, the predicted label is accompanied by two values representing the belief in that prediction. This confidence measure is similar to a probability estimate from a probabilistic predictor, but with a key difference; the probability estimates are guaranteed to be well-calibrated not for the individual instance, but instead for all instances with that confidence or higher.

In this paper, we build on the work of Linusson et al. [11], where conformal prediction was suggested as a way of producing classifiers with reject option. In that approach, a user would provide the acceptable number of errors, and then classifier would output as many predictions as possible, given that constraint. Here, we suggest and evaluate a new algorithm that gives accuracy guarantees, which we argue is more intuitive than requesting the number of acceptable errors. In fact, the algorithm – which is only applicable to batch predictions – automatically suggests a number of accuracy levels that it can meet perfectly by using the reject option. One example could be that for a certain data set, the algorithm can guarantee 90% accuracy if rejecting 8.5% of the test instances, and 95% accuracy if rejecting 52.3%. The final selection of which accuracy level to use, would then be made by a user. Obviously, the algorithm operates without access to any test set labels. In the experimental evaluation, we also compare the suggested methodology to probabilistic prediction, using standard probability estimates (both uncalibrated and calibrated) directly from the machine learning model.

2 Background

2.1 Probabilistic Prediction and Calibration

Probabilistic predictors output a probability distribution over the possible labels. The probabilistic predictor is *well-calibrated* if:

$$p(c_j \mid p^{c_j}) = p^{c_j}. \tag{1}$$

where p^{c_j} is the probability estimate for class j. In practice, the probability estimate for the predicted label should correspond to the empirical accuracy. If we, for example, make a number of predictions with the probability estimate 0.9, we would expect 90% of these to be correct and 10% incorrect.

While almost all classifiers can accompany the predicted label with such probability estimates, these are normally not well-calibrated. In fact, techniques like naive Bayes [12] and decision trees [16] are notorious for producing very poorly calibrated models. In addition, more recent studies show that even modern (i.e., deep) neural networks [5] and traditional neural networks [9] are typically not well-calibrated either. With this in mind, there is a need for external calibration methods that transform the scores outputted from the classifiers into better calibrated probability estimates. The most well-know calibration technique is arguably *Platt scaling* [15], which calibrates the underlying model by fitting a sigmoid function to the scores, using a specific calibration set. The function is

$$\hat{p}(c \mid s) = \frac{1}{1 + e^{As+B}}, \tag{2}$$

where $\hat{p}(c \mid s)$ gives the probability that an example belongs to class c, given that it has obtained the score s. A and B are found by a gradient descent search, minimizing a specific loss function, for details see [15].

2.2 Conformal Classification

Conformal prediction utilizes *nonconformity functions* $A : X \times Y \rightarrow \mathbb{R}$ for measuring the relative strangeness of an instance (x, y) compared to a set of instances with known target values. In the standard conformal classification setting, a test instance is tentatively labeled $(x_{k+1}, \tilde{y})$, and then a p-value statistic is calculated from the nonconformity scores to attempt to reject the hypothesis that $\tilde{y}$ is the true label y_{k+1} at the significance level ϵ. This procedure is repeated for all possible labels, resulting in the set of labels $\tilde{y} \subseteq Y$ that were not rejected. This set, per construction and under exchangeability, contains the true target y_{k+1} with a probability of $1 - \epsilon$.

In classification, the nonconformity function is most often based on the prediction error of an underlying machine learning model. One obvious option, also used in this study, is the *hinge loss* function,

$$\Delta[h(\boldsymbol{x}_i), \tilde{y}] = 1 - \hat{P}_h(\tilde{y} \mid \boldsymbol{x}_i),\tag{3}$$

where $\hat{P}_h(\tilde{y} \mid \boldsymbol{x})$ is the probability estimate provided by the machine learning model h that the instance $\boldsymbol{x}_i$ has label $\tilde{y}$.

While conformal classification was originally suggested in a transductive setting, the inductive version is now more commonly used. An *inductive conformal classifier* [13,14,18], is constructed using some machine learning algorithm and a nonconformity measure, in the following way:

1. Divide the training data Z into two disjoint subsets: a proper training set Z^t and a calibration set Z^c, where $|Z^c| = q$.
2. Use the machine learning algorithm and the proper training set Z^t, to induce the underlying model h.
3. Use the chosen nonconformity function, e.g., Eq. 3, to calculate the nonconformity of the calibration examples in Z^c to produce a list of calibration scores $\alpha_1, \ldots, \alpha_q$.

When predicting a test instance $\boldsymbol{x}_{k+1}$:

1. Obtain the prediction $h(\boldsymbol{x}_{k+1})$ from the underlying model.
2. Tentatively assign the label $\tilde{y} \in Y$ as the label for $\boldsymbol{x}_{k+1}$, and measure the nonconformity of the resulting instance, $(\boldsymbol{x}_{k+1}, \tilde{y})$.
3. Calculate the resulting p-value according to

$$p_{k+1}^{\tilde{y}} = \frac{\left|\left\{z_i \in Z^c : \alpha_i \geq \alpha_{k+1}^{\tilde{y}}\right\}\right| + 1}{q + 1}.\tag{4}$$

4. Repeat the steps 2–3 for each possible label $\tilde{y} \in Y$.

In the standard setting, a set prediction would then be created by comparing the p-values to a chosen significance level ϵ, rejecting all labels $\tilde{y}$ where $p_{k+1}^{\tilde{y}} < \epsilon$. Labels not rejected are included in the final predicted label set Γ_{k+1}^{ϵ}.

We will, however, instead use confidence-credibility predictions, which are also based on the p-values calculated as per above. Here, for each test instance $\boldsymbol{x}_j$ we get the following three values:

– The most likely class label $\hat{y}_j$, i.e., the label with the highest $p_j^{\tilde{y}}$.
– The *confidence*, calculated as one minus the second largest p-value.
– The *credibility*, which is the largest p-value.

The connection to the set predictor is that the confidence represents the highest significance level where we get a singleton prediction, and the credibility corresponds to the significance level where all labels are rejected. More importantly for the purpose of this paper, we can use the confidence measures to produce statistical guarantees for the predictions, as long as we have a set of test predictions, i.e., the suggested procedure can not be used in a streaming scenario. To understand the guarantees provided, we give a synthetic example, for a tiny test set, where we have sorted the ten predictions based on their confidence, see Table 1 below. The correct way of interpreting these confidence scores is that all predictions with a confidence of at least c will contain (on average) $n(1-c)$ errors, where n is the total number of predictions made, here ten. So, in this example, we should expect approximately three errors in total, two errors among the predictions for idx 2–9 and one error among the predictions for idx 5–9.

Table 1. Example of confidence predictions. Confidence values represent the expected accuracy for instances with at least that confidence, over the entire test set.

idx	0	1	2	3	4	5	6	7	8	9
$\hat{y}$	0	0	1	1	0	1	0	1	0	1
confidence	0.70	0.75	0.80	0.83	0.87	0.90	0.93	0.95	0.97	0.99

2.3 Related Work

Since the framework for classification with reject option was introduced, in the context of studying the trade-off between error rate and reject for binary classification systems [3], multiple studies have both extended the theoretical framework and applied it in different domains. For example, in [8], the statistical framework is generalized and risk functions are included to further inform the trade-off between errors and rejections. Applications of classification with reject are mainly within the medical domain, see e.g. [4,6,7]. In [10] a methodology, called confidence-based classifier design, is proposed and evaluated. This methodology has the same approach as this study, i.e. to control the error rate of the classifier via reject option, but does not employ conformal classification to achieve this. Instead, a dynamic bin width allocation method is used to estimate probabilities and an empirical cumulative density function estimates the error rate. This approach does not yield any optimality guarantees, but is reported to perform well in empirical tests. Similarly, [7] develops an approach where the user can set the desired accuracy, and the classifier then tries to identify a minimal rejection region in the feature space, whilst observing the bound on accuracy.

3 Method

As described in the introduction, the overall purpose is to investigate whether conformal classification can be used as the basis for a classifier with reject option. Specifically, we want the classifier to present a number of accuracy levels accompanied with the prediction rate, i.e., the proportion of all instances that it will predict, with that accuracy requirement. For this to be useful, the accuracy levels suggested by the algorithm must be well-calibrated, i.e., close to the empirical accuracy obtained. Given this, a decision-maker will be able to request an exact accuracy level from the classifier, and know which proportion of instances the model will then predict. In the experimentation, we compare the following three setups:

- Conformal (C): Here a conformal classifier is generated and calibrated on a calibration set, before predicting the test set and producing confidence scores, as described above.
- Platt (P): The scores from the underlying model are calibrated using Platt scaling. The calibration is done using the same calibration set as for (C).
- Uncalibrated (U): The scores from the underlying model are used without external calibration.

When deciding which instances to reject, given the chosen accuracy level, the P and U setups operate in an identical fashion; first all probability estimates for the predicted class are sorted, before finding the lowest estimate where the average probability of all instances with a higher probability is larger than the chosen accuracy level. With well-calibrated probability estimates, this simple procedure should lead to valid predictors.

For the C setup, the principle is the same, but it should again be noted that the confidence values have a different meaning than the probability estimates. Referring back to Table 1 and the example, the instance with idx 2 would be picked as the threshold if the requested accuracy level is 75%; we would then make eight predictions, and expect two of them to be incorrect. More generally, if we have n predicted instances sorted on their confidences, and a is the requested accuracy, we pick the instance with the lowest index i where:

$$1 - \frac{n \cdot (1 - \text{conf}(i))}{(n - i)} \geq a \qquad (5)$$

Every setup will try the following accuracy levels for all data sets: {0.7, 0.75, 0.8, 0.85, 0.9, 0.95, 0.99}, while predicting between 5% and 95% of all test instances. Here it must be noted that the goal of the setups is to match the requested accuracy as well as possible, while rejecting sufficiently many instances for this. Specifically, the setups must also avoid a higher accuracy than requested. Consequently, the setups will not make any predictions on a certain accuracy level if the probability estimates or confidences do not allow this. Simply put, a setup will not predict on a certain accuracy level if it cannot match it, either because the top five percent of the instances are expected to have a lower accuracy, or the top 95 percent are expected to have a higher accuracy.

For the modeling, decision trees and random forests [2] were used. Here, all parameters were left at the default values in scikit-learn, with the exception of having 300 trees in the random forest, and at least six instances in each leaf of the decision trees. The testing protocol was 10×10-fold stratified cross-validation, so all results are averaged over the 100 folds. For the calibrated models, the proper training set consisted of 2/3 of the training instances, and the calibration set of

1/3. For the non-calibrated models, all training data was used for inducing the model. Accuracy and the area under the ROC curve (AUC) are used to measure the predictive performance of the underlying models, whilst calibration quality is measured using the expected calibration error (ECE) measure.

Table 2 below shows the 25 two-class benchmarking data sets used. All data sets are publicly available from either the UCI repository [1] or the PROMISE Software Engineering Repository [17].

Table 2. Benchmark data sets.

Data set	Instances	Attributes	Source	Data set	Instances	Attributes	Source
colic	328	23	UCI	kc2	522	22	Promise
creditA	690	16	UCI	kc3	325	39	Promise
diabetes	768	9	UCI	liver	345	7	UCI
german	1000	21	UCI	pc1req	320	9	Promise
haberman	306	4	UCI	pc4	1458	38	Promise
heartC	303	13	UCI	sonar	208	61	UCI
heartH	270	12	UCI	spect	218	22	UCI
heartS	270	14	UCI	spectf	348	45	UCI
hepati	155	20	UCI	transfusion	748	5	UCI
iono	351	35	UCI	ttt	958	10	UCI
je4042	274	9	Promise	vote	435	17	UCI
je4243	363	8	Promise	wbc	699	10	UCI
kc1	2109	22	Promise				

4   Results

Table 3 below summarizes the predictive performance of the underlying models and the calibration. Due to space limitations, only averaged values over the 25 data sets are shown. First we notice that the random forests, as expected, outperform the decision trees with regard to accuracy. Comparing the three setups, there are, however, only small differences in the predictive performance.

Table 3. Predictive performance and calibration for the three setups using (C)onformal, (P)latt scaling and (U)ncalibrated models.

	Accuracy			AUC			ECE		
	C	P	U	C	P	U	C	P	U
Decision trees	.760	.774	.763	.745	.734	.747	.146	.028	.154
Random forests	.806	.809	.814	.824	.814	.833	.060	.028	.064

Looking at the calibration results, we see that the decision trees are very poorly calibrated off-the-shelf, but that using Platt scaling reduces the ECE significantly. While the random forests are reasonably well-calibrated, Platt scaling is again able to reduce the ECE substantially. Regarding the conformal setup, it must be noted that it does not calibrate the probability estimates, but instead uses the probability estimates from the underlying model. So, the ECE results for the conformal setup are as expected, reflecting the probability estimate bias of the underlying models.

The main results of the study are summarized in Table 4 below. Again, due to space limitations, we only show the mean results over all data sets here. Detailed results, i.e., on the data set level, are presented in Tables 5–6 last in the paper, but only for random forests. Please note that if there are no results for a certain setup on a specific accuracy level, this means that the algorithm was not able to meet that accuracy level by rejecting between 5% and 95% of all test instances.

Table 4. Aggregated results presented for the three setups (C)onformal, (P)latt scaling and (U)ncalibrated models on the different required accuracy levels. For each accuracy level, *data sets* is the number of data sets predicted, *mean acc* is the average empirical accuracy and *mean pr* is the proportion of all test instances predicted.

	DT C	DT P	DT U	RF C	RF P	RF U		DT C	DT P	DT U	RF C	RF P	RF U
0.7							**0.9**						
data sets	7	3		4	2	1	data sets	5	12	8	14	14	20
mean acc	.699	.667		.701	.689	.746	mean acc	.900	.884	.699	.900	.886	.883
mean pr	.597	.590		.820	.848	.941	mean pr	.715	.454	.815	.637	.573	.549
0.75							**0.95**						
data sets	8	9		7	6	3	data sets	1	7	16	13	13	22
mean acc	.753	.723		.751	.738	.789	mean acc	.956	.928	.766	.951	.957	.926
mean pr	.765	.615		.677	.723	.796	mean pr	.858	.224	.766	.503	.384	.392
0.8							**0.99**						
data sets	9	13		10	9	10	data sets			24	3	5	18
mean acc	.796	.769		.800	.792	.787	mean acc			.820	.990	.993	.968
mean pr	.662	.530		.537	.544	.800	mean pr			.698	.781	.293	.234
0.85													
data sets	7	14	3	13	14	18							
mean acc	.849	.821	.671	.852	.833	.845							
mean pr	.697	.457	.853	.657	.576	.718							

Starting with the decision trees, we see that the U setup is extremely overconfident, while also rejecting very few instances, even when a high accuracy is requested. Unfortunately, the actual accuracies obtained are much lower than requested. As an example, when the U setup elects to predict sixteen data sets on the 0.95 level, the average actual accuracy is only 0.766. The overconfidence of uncalibrated decision trees also produces the effect that, for most data sets, no predictions are given for accuracy levels below 0.9. The P setup is clearly better, but it is still systematically overconfident, as seen by the fact that the mean actual accuracy is lower than the requested accuracy for all levels. The mean accuracy of the C setup, on the other hand, is most often very close to the requested accuracy. As an example, the mean empirical accuracies for the levels 0.75, 0.8, 0.85, and 0.9 are 0.753, 0.796, 0.849, and 0.900. In a direct comparison, we see that the C setup is more conservative than P, often electing to predict on the lower accuracy levels. When both setups predict a data set on the same accuracy level, and with similar empirical accuracies, however, C does not reject more instances. As an interesting side note, it could be noted that no setup predicts the *wbc* data set on any accuracy level.

Summarizing the decision tree results, it is obvious that uncalibrated decision trees cannot be used as probabilistic predictors. Most importantly, the C setup clearly outperforms even P when it comes to matching the requested accuracy.

Turning to the random forest results in Tables 5–6, the overall picture is that all three setups are able to make predictions on more accuracy levels.

Comparing empirical and requested accuracies, all setups are often reasonably close. U is overconfident for the lower accuracy levels, and underconfident for the higher levels. P is better, but actually shows the opposite pattern to U, overestimating the accuracy on the lower levels, and underestimating on the higher. C does, however, again match the requested accuracy levels almost perfectly on average. In addition, empirical accuracies closely match the requested accuracy for individual data sets, being within 1 percentage point on 59 of the 64 data sets and accuracy level combinations that predictions are made for. Looking at the prediction rates, we find that all three setups often only need to reject relatively few instances, even when the requested accuracy is very high. As an example, on the 0.95-level, C rejects on average about half of the instances, on the thirteen data sets predicted.

Turning to observations on some specific data sets, it is seen that when using random forests, all three setups actually predict the *wbc* data set on the 0.99-level, matching the requested accuracy almost perfectly, see Tables 5–6. A more general, and quite interesting result, can be found by comparing C to P in these tables. Here, P is not able to match the requested accuracy levels 0.95 and 0.99, obtaining substantially higher mean empirical accuracies, 0.957 and 0.993, respectively. While this may appear to not be a problem, the consequence is, of course, that significantly fewer instances are predicted. For the *wbc* data set, C predicts 80.3% of the instances, compared to 32.1% for P, on the 99% level. Similarly, for the *pc4* data set, also on the 99% level, the corresponding prediction rates are 65.0% for C and 9.2% for P. Indeed, for the 27 data sets on accuracy levels of 90% and upwards, where both C and P predict, C has the higher prediction rate on 22 data sets.

In summary then, the results show that the C setup, using conformal classification to produce well-calibrated confidence-credibility predictions, are able to match requested accuracy levels to a much better degree than classifiers calibrated using Platt scaling. This holds both for decision tree models and random forests, and for accuracy levels ranging from 70% up to 99%.

Table 5. Detailed results for Random forests: Accuracy

Data set	0.70			0.75			0.80			0.85			0.90			0.95			0.99		
	C	P	U	C	P	U	C	P	U	C	P	U	C	P	U	C	P	U	C	P	U
colic									.868	.851	.858	.912	.904	.908	.932	.950	.931	.915			.957
creditA							.797	.794	.797	.848	.843	.901	.900	.907	.945	.951	.949	.954			.987
diabetes	.701						.796	.829	.706	.849	.843	.839	.899	.917	.893		.950	.950			.967
german				.754	.743		.826	.808	.692	.878	.856	.742	.889	.889	.792			.860			
haber	.705			.754	.735					.859	.862	.759									
heartC										.853	.844	.886	.910	.921	.928	.945	.955	.954			.960
heartH										.852	.858	.848	.897	.905	.892	.947	.967	.962			.978
heartS									.848			.881	.898	.907	.941	.947	.945	.966			.990
hepati										.868		.879	.902	.901	.925	.959	.961	.965			1.00
iono																.950	.960	.993		.983	.991
je4042				.749	.746		.794	.796	.783	.848	.837	.809	.863	.851	.830			.896			.899
je4243	.704	.695		.752	.747	.706	.812	.795	.731	.835	.835	.789						.868			
kc1							.806	.799	.783	.850	.844	.816	.894		.846		.966	.869			.900
kc2							.798			.841	.832	.810	.900	.912	.841	.953	.966	.910			.974
kc3													.910	.901	.890	.956	.971	.948			.968
liver			.746	.760	.764	.779	.803	.810	.813	.825	.825	.835	.852	.852	.833						
pc1req	.693	.682		.744	.691		.775	.711	.694		.691	.753	.682		.773			.783			
pc4						.881							.897	.915	1.00	.949	.940	.975	.989	.998	1.00
sonar										.849	.850	.939	.900		.989	.953	.973	1.00		.995	.980
spect													.900			.933	.933	.918			
spectf				.741						.849	.828	.870	.902	.894	.927	.957	.984	.988			1.00
transf							.796	.788		.838	.831	.740						.808			.887
ttt															.998			1.00			
vote													.901	.898	.913	.944	.959	.951	.990	.997	.993
wbc																			.990	.991	.990
Mean	.701	.689	.746	.751	.738	.789	.800	.792	.787	.852	.833	.845	.900	.886	.883	.951	.957	.926	.990	.993	.968

Table 6. Detailed results for Random forests: Prediction rate

Data set	0.70			0.75			0.80			0.85			0.90			0.95			0.99		
	C	P	U	C	P	U	C	P	U	C	P	U	C	P	U	C	P	U	C	P	U
colic									.924	.922	.906	.674	.630	.614	.345	.477	.155	.069			.050
creditA							.849	.874	.861			.917	.915	.894	.701	.484		.371			.068
diabetes							.337	.164	.762	.633	.647	.663	.432	.346	.461	.209		.256			
german				.710	.901		.453	.511	.947	.186	.145	.558	.092								.108
haber	.775									.272		.757									
heartC	.921									.862	.861	.791	.654	.616	.578	.269	.219	.315			.067
heartH										.873	.904	.913	.691	.662	.740	.455	.199	.490			.157
heartS										.891	.880	.761	.673	.651	.550	.278	.269	.297			.073
hepati																.486	.452	.568			.230
iono										.946		.930	.829	.828	.770	.940	.909	.775		.085	.367
je4042	.780			.939	.943		.727	.717	.904	.464	.440	.727	.159		.523			.281			.096
je4243		.804		.549	.513		.192	.263	.645		.092	.440			.252						.077
kc1							.714	.770	.906	.373	.413	.709	.069		.491			.077			
kc2							.920			.763	.801	.909	.575	.511	.738	.382	.064	.547			.313
kc3						.873			.634				.842	.884	.921	.505	.231	.718			.409
liver						.670	.457	.462	.431			.236	.067		.095						
pc1req	.806	.892	.941	.777	.723		.107	.379	.838		.187	.630		.063	.407			.168			
pc4				.424	.618											.851	.883	.785			
sonar						.845				.858	.867	.438	.708	.676	.248	.530	.430	.074			.532
spect													.855					.206			.210
spectf										.855	.925	.816	.704	.729	.628	.527	.372	.381			.098
transf				.837			.610	.759		.305	.338	.894						.484			.190
ttt															.883				.891	.878	.273
vote																.630	.504	.630			.303
wbc													.881	.889	.841				.803	.321	.860
Mean	.820	.848	.941	.677	.723	.796	.537	.544	.800	.657	.576	.718	.637	.573	.549	.503	.384	.392	.781	.293	.234

5 Concluding Remarks

We have in this paper demonstrated how conformal classification can be used to produce a perfectly calibrated classifier with reject option. Specifically, we designed and evaluated an algorithm automatically suggesting a number of accuracy levels depending on the underlying model and how hard the data set is. The empirical evaluation confirmed that the procedure, even for the relatively small data sets used here, obtained empirical accuracies very close to the requested levels. In an outright comparison with probabilistic predictors, the suggested algorithm clearly outperformed the alternatives, including Platt scaling.

References

1. Bache, K., Lichman, M.: UCI machine learning repository (2013)
2. Breiman, L.: Random forests. Mach. Learn. **45**(1), 5–32 (2001)
3. Chow, C.: On optimum recognition error and reject tradeoff. IEEE Trans. Inf. Theory **16**(1), 41–46 (1970)
4. Guan, H., Zhang, Y., Cheng, H.D., Tang, X.: Bounded-abstaining classification for breast tumors in imbalanced ultrasound images. Int. J. Appl. Math. Comput. Sci. **30**(2), 325–336 (2020)
5. Guo, C., Pleiss, G., Sun, Y., Weinberger, K.Q.: On calibration of modern neural networks. In: ICML, pp. 1321–1330. PMLR (2017)
6. Hamid, K., Asif, A., Abbasi, W., Sabih, D., Minhas, F.U.A.A.: Machine learning with abstention for automated liver disease diagnosis. In: 2017 International Conference on Frontiers of Information Technology (FIT), pp. 356–361 (2017)
7. Hanczar, B., Dougherty, E.R.: Classification with reject option in gene expression data. Bioinform. **24**(17), 1889–1895 (2008)
8. Herbei, R., Wegkamp, M.H.: Classification with reject option. Can. J. Statist. **34**(4), 709–721 (2006)
9. Johansson, U., Gabrielsson, P.: Are traditional neural networks well-calibrated? In: 2019 International Joint Conference on Neural Networks (IJCNN), pp. 1–8 (2019)
10. Li, M., Sethi, I.K.: Confidence-based classifier design. Pattern Recogn. **39**(7), 1230–1240 (2006)
11. Linusson, H., Johansson, U., Boström, H., Löfström, T.: Classification with reject option using conformal prediction. In: Phung, D., Tseng, V.S., Webb, G.I., Ho, B., Ganji, M., Rashidi, L. (eds.) PAKDD 2018. LNCS (LNAI), vol. 10937, pp. 94–105. Springer, Cham (2018). https://doi.org/10.1007/978-3-319-93034-3_8
12. Niculescu-Mizil, A., Caruana, R.: Predicting good probabilities with supervised learning. In: ICML, pp. 625–632 (2005)
13. Papadopoulos, H.: Inductive conformal prediction: theory and application to neural networks. Tools Artif. Intell. **18**, 315–330 (2008)
14. Papadopoulos, H., Proedrou, K., Vovk, V., Gammerman, A.: Inductive confidence machines for regression. In: Elomaa, T., Mannila, H., Toivonen, H. (eds.) ECML 2002. LNCS (LNAI), vol. 2430, pp. 345–356. Springer, Heidelberg (2002). https://doi.org/10.1007/3-540-36755-1_29
15. Platt, J.C.: Probabilistic outputs for support vector machines and comparisons to regularized likelihood methods. In: Advances in Large Margin Classifiers, pp. 61–74. MIT Press (1999)

16. Provost, F., Domingos, P.: Tree induction for probability-based ranking. Mach. Learn. **52**(3), 199–215 (2003)
17. Sayyad Shirabad, J., Menzies, T.: The PROMISE Repository of Software Engineering Databases. University of Ottawa, Canada, School of IT and Engineering (2005)
18. Vovk, V., Gammerman, A., Shafer, G.: Algorithmic Learning in a Random World. Springer-Verlag, New York, Inc (2005)

Adapting the Gini's Index for Solving Predictive Tasks

Eva Armengol[(✉)]

Artificial Intelligence Research Institute, (IIIA, CSIC) Campus UAB,
Camí de Can Planes, s/n, Bellaterra, 08193 Barcelona, Spain
`eva@iiia.csic.es`

Abstract. The most used technique for solving prediction tasks is regression analysis which approximates the data at hand using a polynomial function. To construct a regression model is necessary either to have a deep knowledge of the domain or to use some attribute selection method to select the appropriate variables that will form the model. In the present paper, we introduce P-LID, a new predictive method based on ideas coming from both lazy and inductive learning methods. P-LID takes two ideas from inductive models: one is to select the relevant attributes to classify new objects and the other is to justify the classification. A technique for selecting relevant attributes is to use Gini's index, but this is only applicable when attributes have continuous values and the class is categoric. In P-LID we propose an adaptation of the Gini's index to use it when the values of the classes are continuous.

Keywords: Machine Learning · Prediction · Gini's index

1 Introduction

Nowadays there is an enormous quantity of data from which experts want to extract knowledge. Many times the goal is to use all the available data to construct models that allow making predictions (i.e., to predict temperatures, to predict possible failures, etc.). Multivariate regression is the most used technique for predicting values. The idea of regression is to construct a polynomial function using a (sub)set of variables, called *independents*, that approximate the value of another variable, called *dependent*. Using all the variables at hand is useful for approaching and analysing the database. In this situation, the obtained regression model approaches well the known data, however, it is possible that the models will not be good for prediction. For this reason, it is usual to select a subset of relevant independent variables in a way that the regression model approaches good enough the known data but is also will be capable to predict the value of unseen data.

Regression models have the form of an equation with general form $Y = a + b_1 * X_1 + b_2 * X_2 + \cdots + b_n * X_n$, where Y is the variable to be predicted. The regression model has a global error in the predictions that can be assessed from an experimental procedure.

V. Torra and Y. Narukawa (Eds.): MDAI 2023, LNAI 13890, pp. 146–156, 2023.
https://doi.org/10.1007/978-3-031-33498-6_10

In machine learning two kinds of predictions can be made: 1) the prediction of the class to which an object belongs, and 2) the prediction of the value of a variable. Problems of the first type are known as *classification problems*. The goal is to predict values of categoric variables, called *classes* (for instance, the animal X is a *mammal*).

The second type of problem is known as *prediction problems*. The goal is to predict the value of continuous variables (for instance, the temperature for tomorrow will be 30°C). Classification problems can be seen as a special case of prediction problems since the difference between both kinds of problems is the type of variable of interest.

There are two main families of machine learning methods for classification tasks. *Lazy learning methods* that, given an input object O, they retrieve a subset S of similar objects and classify O according the classes of the objects in S [2,5]. Techniques included in this family of methods are similarity-based methods [7] and case-based reasoning methods [1,4,10]. *Inductive learning methods* take a set of objects (with known classification) and construct a general model that will be used to classify unseen objects. The most used techniques of this family are decision and regression trees [6,13,14].

In regression models, the only available knowledge is the equation and the variables involved, but any deduction can be done from it. Instead, machine learning methods can give a justification for the proposed classification. The explanation given by the 'lazy' method is the set of objects similar to the input object since the user can explore them and evaluate the validity of the final classification. Inductive learning methods, by construction, produce explanations that are general and understandable. These explanations are based on the attributes that have been considered the most relevant during the construction of the domain model.

Feature selection techniques [11] are useful to determine a subset of relevant attributes. These techniques are used as a preprocessing step in both regression and machine learning methods. Its goal is the rejection of attributes that will not be useful to construct the domain model. For instance, in regression is very common to use some techniques such as regularization [9], LASSO [15] or Elastic Net [17] to determine which are the independent variables that are more related to the dependent variable (i.e., the one to be predicted). In addition to these kinds of techniques, in machine learning and, particularly, in inductive learning methods there are several criteria to select the most relevant attributes: Quinlan Gain [14], López de Mántaras' distance [12] and the Gini's index [14]. Gini's index measures the impurity of a partition of the dataset with respect to the correct class and it is useful when the values of the attributes are continuous and the class is categoric.

The focus of this paper is prediction problems and we want to solve them using machine learning techniques. We propose a new predictive method called P-LID based on a lazy learning method called LID [3]. LID is useful for classification tasks, and it handles attributes with categorical values. The selection of relevant attributes in LID is made using the López de Mántaras' distance although also the Gini's index could be used. However, the result is a categorical class instead of a continuous value. What we propose is to adapt Gini's index to be able to handle numerical classes instead of categoric ones.

P-LID is based on the ideas coming from both lazy and inductive learning methods. On one hand, P-LID, same as LID, predicts an object taking into account the values of the attributes of the input examples. On the other hand, as inductive learning methods do, during the process of prediction P-LID constructs an explanation that justifies the prediction.

The paper is organized as follows. Section 2 introduces notation and some basic concepts that are useful to understand the rest of the paper. Particularly, Sect. 2.2 introduces the LID algorithm on which P-LID is based, and Sect. 2.3 introduces the algorithm to calculate the Gini's index. Section 3 introduces the new predictive method called P-LID, and Sect. 4 describes the experimentation with P-LID comparing it with regression models. The last section is devoted to conclusions and future work.

2   Preliminaries

Before explaining the approach introduced in the present paper, we will explain some important basics on which our approach is based.

2.1   Notation

Let DB be a database with objects described by a set of attributes $A = \{a_1, ..., a_n\}$ and let C_p be the *class* to be predicted. The values of all the attributes can be *categoric* (i.e. labels) or *numeric* (i.e. continuous values).

Our approach focuses on prediction problems, however, it is based on LID, which is a method useful for solving classification tasks.

To simplify the explanation, we will refer to the value v that the object O_k takes on an attribute a_h as $O_k.a_h$. Alternatively, we will use the notation (a_j, v_j) to indicate that the attribute a_j takes the value v_j in the object O_k. Thus, descriptions of objects or similitude terms (see below the definition) will be denoted as $\{(a_1, v_1), ..., (a_n, v_n)\}$.

2.2   The Lazy Induction of Descriptions Method

Lazy Induction of Descriptions (LID) [3] is a lazy learning method for classification tasks. Given an object O to be classified, LID determines which are the most relevant attributes for classifying O and searches in the database for objects sharing these relevant attributes. The new object O is classified when LID finds a set of relevant attributes shared by a subset of cases S_D all belonging to the same class C_i. Then LID classifies O as belonging to C_i. We call *similarity term* the description D formed by these relevant attributes and *support set* the set S_D of objects satisfying a similarity term. The values of all the attributes (including the class) are categorical (i.e. labels).

Function LID (O, S_D, D, C)
    $S_D :=$ Discriminatory-set (D)
    if stopping-condition(S_D)
        then return $class(S_D)$
        else $a_d :=$ Select-attribute (O, S_D, C)
            $D' :=$ Add-attribute(a_d, D)
            $S_{D'} :=$ Support-set (D', S_D)
            LID $(S_{D'}, p, D', C)$
    end-if
end-function

Fig. 1. The LID algorithm: O is the object to be classified, D is the similarity term, S_D is the support set associated with D, C is the set of classes, $class(S_D)$ is the class $C_i \in C$ to which all elements in S_D belong.

Figure 1 shows the LID algorithm (see a more detailed explanation of LID in [3]). There are two key issues in the LID algorithm: 1) the selection of the most relevant attribute; and 2) the similarity term.

The selection of the most relevant attribute is heuristically done using the López de Mántaras' distance [12] over the candidate attributes. The LM distance assesses how similar two partitions are in the sense that the lesser the distance the more similar they are. In LID the partitions to be compared are: 1) the *correct partition* P_c; and, 2) each one of the partitions P_{a_i} induced by $a_i \in A$. The *correct partition* P_c is the one where all the objects of a partition set belong to the same class. The partition P_{a_i} induced by the attribute a_i is one where each set of P_{a_i} contains objects having the same categorical value in a_i. Therefore, there are n partitions of a database, one for each attribute. LID selects as the most relevant the attribute a_k such that the value of $LM(P_{a_k}, P_c)$ is minimum.

The attributes of the *similarity term* D are the ones considered as the relevant ones during the process of classifying the object O. These attributes in D take the same categorical value as the object O. This is important because using D, LID can explain the classification of a new object. Because LID is a lazy learning method, the explanation of the classification is different depending on the values of the input object.

As an example, let us suppose that in classifying the object

$$O = \{(a_1, v_1), (a_2, v_2), (a_3, v_3), (a_4, v_4), (a_5, v_5)\}$$

LID has considered a_2, a_4, and a_5 as the most relevant attributes, in such situation the similitude term justifying the classification is the following:

$$D = \{(a_2, v_2), (a_4, v_4), (a_5, v_5)\}$$

2.3   The Gini's Index

Gini's index [6] is the most common technique for selecting relevant attributes when their value is continuous and the class is categorical. The Gini's index measures the impurity degree of a set where 0 means the set is pure (all the elements belong to the same class); 1 is the maximum impurity (random distribution of the elements among the classes); and 0.5 means an equal distribution of elements over some classes. The best attribute is the one with a lower Gini's index.

The formula to calculate the Gini's index is the following:

$$G = 1 - \sum_{i=1}^{n} (P_{C_i})^2$$

where P_{C_i} is the probability of an object being classified as belonging to the class C_i.

Let us explain in detail how to calculate the Gini's index for an attribute a_j. For the sake of simplicity, we will consider that there are only two classes C_1 and C_2. Let $V = \{v_1, ..., v_n\}$ be the set of all the values that a_j takes in the objects of DB. The algorithm is the following:

1. Sort the values of V in ascending order.
2. Form the set $M = \{m_h : m_h = mean(v_i, v_{i+1}) \; \forall v_i \in V\}$ (we will call *cuts* the elements of M).
3. For each $m_h \in M$:
   (a) Let L be the subset O_L of objects such that $o_t.a_j \leq m_h \; \forall o_t \in O_L$
   (b) Let U be the subset O_U of objects such that $o_t.a_j \geq m_h \; \forall o_t \in O_U$
   (c) $G_L = 1 - P_{C_1}^2 - P_{C_2}^2$ for elements in L
   (d) $G_U = 1 - P_{C_1}^2 - P_{C_2}^2$ for elements in U
   (e) $G_{T_{(a_j, m_h)}} = \frac{Card(L)}{Card(V)} * G_L + \frac{Card(U)}{Card(V)} * G_U$ (value of the Gini's index for the attribute a_j)

Notice that for each attribute a_j there is a value of the Gini's index for each cut $m_h \in M$, therefore the best cut for an attribute will be the one having the lowest value of the Gini's index.

The procedure above has to be carried out for each one of the attributes in A. In the end, we will have a value of Gini's index associated with each attribute. Therefore, the best attribute will be the one having the lowest index.

3   P-LID: Lazy Induction of Description for Prediction

Our goal is to modify LID to convert it from a classification method into a prediction method that we call P-LID. To do such a transformation it is necessary to make LID capable to handle continuous values of both the attributes and the class. Focusing on classification tasks (i.e., the class is categorical), LID can easily deal with continuous values of the attributes only by replacing the LM distance with the Gini's index. Notice that in such a situation, the algorithm shown in Fig. 1 is still valid, however, the similarity term will have a different format.

When the values of attributes are continuous it has no sense the expression (a_i, v_i) meaning that the attribute a_i takes exactly the value v_i. In addition, the Gini's index gives *cuts*, i.e., a threshold that separates the (sub)set of objects in two. For this reason, when the attributes have continuous values, LID produces similitude terms that have inequalities instead of equalities. Taking the same example used in Sect. 2.2, now the similitude term could have the following aspect: $D = \{(a_2 < v_2), (a_4 > v_4), (a_5 < v_5)\}$.

Finally, to predict a number it is necessary to replace categorical classes with numerical classes, since P-LID has to give as a solution an interval where the predicted value belongs. Therefore, first of all, it is necessary to introduce a new input parameter, namely ϵ, that is the error that the user is willing to accept. Thus, if P-LID predicts a value p, the interval of acceptability is $[p - \epsilon, p + \epsilon]$ meaning that the correct value will be inside the such interval. How P-LID can produce such an interval? The idea is to adapt Gini's index to deal with continuous classes. Let O be the object for which we want to predict the value of the attribute C_p with error ϵ. Let us focus on the attribute a_j. Let $V = \{v_1, ..., v_n\}$ be the set of all the values that a_j takes in a set of objects S and let be $VRef = O.a_j$. The algorithm we propose is the following one:

1. Sort the values of V in ascending order
2. Form the set $M = \{m_h : m_h = mean(v_i, v_{i+1}) \ \forall v_i \in V\}$
3. Select m_h and m_{h+1} such that $VRef \in [m_h, m_{h+1}]$
4. Let L be the subset of objects such that $o_t.a_j \in [m_h, m_{h+1}]$
5. Let U be the subset of objects such that $o_t.a_j \notin [m_h, m_{h+1}]$
6. Let $m_t = mean(O.C_p) \ \forall O \in S$.
7. $In_L = \{obj \in L : obj.C_p \in [m_t - \epsilon, m_t + \epsilon]\}$
8. $Out_L = \{obj \in L : obj.C_p \notin [m_t - \epsilon, m_t + \epsilon]\}$
9. $G_L = 1 - P_{In_L}^2 - P_{Out_L}^2$
10. $In_U = \{obj \in U : obj.C_p \in [m_t - \epsilon, m_t + \epsilon]\}$
11. $Out_U = \{obj \in U : obj.C_p \notin [m_t - \epsilon, m_t + \epsilon]\}$
12. $G_U = 1 - P_{In_U}^2 - P_{Out_U}^2$
13. $G_{T_{(a_j, m_h)}} = \frac{Card(L)}{Card(V)} * G_L + \frac{Card(U)}{Card(V)} * G_U$

Steps 1 and 2 of the algorithm above are the same that the one of the standard Gini's index (see Sect. 2.3). We have introduced Step 3 for two reasons. The first one is to conserve the lazy approach of LID, that is to say, we do not want to construct a general model but the goal is to predict a value for a particular object O and the justification of such value has to be done according to the characteristics of O. The second reason is the computational cost of Gini's index. The algorithm should be used for each attribute and each cut but in our approach, we are only interested in those objects that are similar to O, i.e., those having similar values in the attributes.

In Steps 4 and 5 the objects are separated according to their value in the attribute a_j. Thus, those objects having a value similar to $VRef$ (i.e., $o_t.a_j \in$

Table 1. Datasets from the UCI Repository used in the experiments. The value ϵ is the maximum error that would be acceptable for the prediction.

Dataset	Name	Total	Attributes	ϵ
AirFoil	AF	1503	6	7
Bias Correction Max	BCmax	7750	25	3
Bias Correction Min	BCmin	7750	25	3
Concrete Compressive	CC	1030	9	13
QSAR Fish	QF	908	7	2
QSAR Toxic	QT	908	9	2
Superconduct	SC	21263	81	17
Red Wine	RW	1559	12	1.5
White Wine	WW	4898	12	1.5
Yatch	YA	308	7	14

$[m_h, m_{h+1}]$) will be included in the subset L, otherwise, they will be included in the subset U. Step 6 calculates the mean value m_t of the attribute C_p to be predicted.

Steps 7 and 8 divide L in two subsets: In_L, with objects O_k such that $O_k.C_p \in [m_t - \epsilon, m_t + \epsilon]$; and Out_L with objects O_k such that $O_k.C_p \notin [m_t - \epsilon, m_t + \epsilon]$. Notice that these two sets represent the two classes C_1 and C_2 we considered in the explanation of the standard Gini's index (see Sect. 2.3). Step 7 is equivalent to step 3.c and step 8 is equivalent to step 3.d. Step 9 calculates the impurity of L as in the standard procedure. Steps 10, 11 and 12 are the same as 7, 8 and 9 respectively but using the objects of the set U. Finally, Step 13 is the same as Step 3.e.

What we do is construct the classes C_1 and C_2 considering those objects that have a value around the mean of C_p ($\pm\epsilon$). The rest of the algorithm is similar to the standard one repeated two times: one for the objects with a_j having a value around $VRef$ and another for the remaining ones. This separation is necessary to maintáin the same meaning as in the original Gini's index, where the whole set of objects is separated into two subsets according to a cut c and both subsets are taken into account to calculate the total Gini's index.

With this modification on the calculus of the Gini's index, P-LID is capable to predict the value of an attribute C_p with a maximum error of ϵ using the same algorithm as LID.

Concerning the justification of the prediction, the similitude term produced by P-LID has the same format as the one produced by LID but, in this case, the values of the attributes are numeric.

4   Experiments

We conducted several experiments to show the feasibility of P-LID. We have used the datasets shown in Table 1, all of them coming from the UCI Repository [8]. For all the datasets we have constructed a Multivariate Regression Model taking

Table 2. Comparison of accuracy (in %) of the regression model and P-LID.

Dataset	Regression (%)	P-LID (%)	dif (%)
AF	**79.05**	77.40	1.65
BCmax	**84.14**	71.23	12.91
BCmin	73.59	**89.06**	15.47
CC	70.84	**77.26**	6.42
QF	**95.38**	84.80	10.58
QT	**90.66**	78.54	12.12
SC	57.78	**82.63**	24.85
RW	**96.87**	86.20	10.67
WW	**95.04**	86.21	8.83
YA	82.45	**95.06**	12.61

into account the subset of variables that have been considered relevant using
LASSO Regression [15,16]. In that way, we can compare the results of regression
and the ones of P-LID. We have taken for each dataset an acceptable error ϵ that
seems adequate according to our knowledge of the dataset. For instance, for the
datasets BCmax and BCmin the goal is to predict a temperature, therefore,
we think that a difference of three degrees (i.e., $\epsilon = 3$) on the prediction is an
acceptable error. In any case, this does not influence the comparison between
methods since we have taken the same value of ϵ to evaluate the performance of
both the regression model and P-LID. Thus, we have considered that a prediction
p is correct when $p \in [p_c - \epsilon, p_c + \epsilon]$ being p_c the correct value.

We have evaluated both the regression prediction and the P-LID using one
trial of 10-fold cross-validation. We have randomly divided the dataset at hand
into 10 parts and such partition has been used for both methods. In that way,
both methods have been evaluated using the same objects. Table 2 shows the
results from the cross-validation. Columns *Regression* and P-LID show the accuracy of the methods. The column *dif* shows the mean difference in absolute value
between the predictions of both methods. This column gives us an idea of how
similar the predictions From 12 domains used in our experiments, the regression
model outperforms P-LID in 6 of them, with differences between 10%-12% meaning that the predictions of both methods are quite different. For the remaining
four datasets P-LID outperforms regression, with differences ranging from 12%
to 24%. These differences are high and could be interpreted as that in these cases
the regression model is not a good predictor.

In AF the difference between the two methods is low, less than 2%, meaning that in this case, both methods produce similar predictions. Globally, these
results suggest that P-LID is a good predictive method since their results that
can be compared with those of the regression models. It could be interesting
to analyze the domains to determine which situations are appropriate for each
method.

In observing the results, one could ask which could be the advantages of
using P-LID instead of a regression model. Both P-LID and the regression model

Table 3. Three regression models for BCmax and their corresponding accuracy after a trial of 10-fold cross-validation.

Model	Attributes	Accuracy
M1	LDAPS_Tmax_lapse, LDAPS_WS, lon, LDAPS_LH, Present_Tmax	87.02
M2	Present_Tmax, LDAPS_Tmax_lapse	84.14
M3	Present_Tmax, Solar radiation, LDAPS_PPT4, LDAPS_CC4	73.60

share the necessity of having as much data as possible to produce more accurate predictions. The main difference is that P-LID uses the data as they are given in the dataset whereas the construction of a regression model usually needs a previous step of attribute selection. In our case, we have used the LASSO regression to detect the most relevant attributes. P-LID handles all the available attributes, however, it is also possible to reject some of them if the user knows that some particular attribute is irrelevant. Therefore, one advantage of P-LID on the model regression model is that P-LID can be used directly on the available dataset without any preprocessing.

The attributes selected to construct the regression model should be selected carefully since the performance of the model can have different accuracy. As an example, let us focus on the dataset BCmax. We have experimented with several subsets of attributes to construct the regression model. Table 3 shows the models and their mean accuracy of prediction after one trial of 10-fold cross-validation. Notice that the difference in accuracy between M1 and M3 is high, and this proves the sensitivity of regression models to the selection of attributes. Conversely, P-LID does not depend on any selection and the accuracy is always the same.

The prediction made by the regression model is based on the equation of linear regression without any other justification. Instead, P-LID explains the prediction. For instance, as already has been explained before, the BCmax dataset is used to predict the maximum temperature for the next day. Objects in this dataset are described using 25 attributes. From these attributes, only 5 of them ('station', 'date', 'Next_Tmax', and 'Next_Tmin') have not been taken into account by P-LID and the remaining ones have been used to make the prediction. For a particular object O_1, P-LID has predicted the value of Nex_Tmax as belonging to the interval $[30.0775, 36.0775]$, whereas the regression model M2 (see Table 3) has predicted a value of 30.61. For the object O_1, the correct value is 33.1. Notice that taking $\epsilon = 3$ both methods predict an acceptable value of Next_Tmax. However, P-LID justifies the prediction with the following similitude term:

[['LDAPS_PPT4', ['inf', $5*10^{-5}$]], ['Present_Tmin', [25.25, 25.35]],
['LDAPS_PPT3', ['inf', 0.0013]]], 54]]

This means that there are 54 objects in the dataset with LDAPS_PPT4 $\leq$ $5*10^{-5}$, Present_Tmin $\in [25.25, 25.35]$, and LDAPS_PPT3 ≤ 0.0013, conditions that are also satisfied by the object O_1, and this also means that all 54 objects have a value for Next_Tmax belonging to the interval $[30.0775, 36.0775]$. In that way, the domain expert can assess the validity of the result because he can analyze the attributes that have been used to make the prediction.

5   Conclusions

In the present paper, we have introduced P-LID, a predictive method that can be a good alternative to regression methods when the domain has a high number of attributes and it is difficult to select an appropriate subset to construct the regression model. P-LID is based on a lazy learning method called LID and takes two main ideas of learning methods. The first one is the idea of *lazy*, meaning that no model is constructed from the known data, but a new prediction is made taking into account the characteristics (values of the attributes) of the input example (the one to be predicted). The second idea comes from inductive learning methods such as decision trees, where the key issue is the selection of the attribute that best partitions the known examples. In particular, when the attributes have continuous values, the criteria used to select the attribute is Gini's index. In all these cases the class (the attribute to be predicted) is categoric. We have proposed a modification of the Gini's index allowing us to deal with continuous classes. P-LID uses such modification to make predictions. Results have proved that P-LID achieves an accuracy comparable to the regression models. However, the advantage of P-LID on regression models is that it is not necessary to make a selection of the attributes (although it is possible) and that, in addition to the value prediction, it also explains why such prediction has been proposed.

In the experimental part, we have detected that the prediction on some domains is much better using regression and for some others, the P-LID predictions are better. In future work, we plan to analyze the characteristics of several datasets to determine which of both methods, regression or P-LID, can be the most appropriate for each one of them. In that way, we can have a set of "rules" that will allow us to choose the most appropriate method for a given dataset.

Acknowledgments. This research is partially funded by the project Isinc PID2019-111544GB-C21 from the Spanish Ministry of Science and Innovation, and also by the European project K-HEALTHinAIR [ref. 101057693] from HORIZON-HLTH-2021-ENVHLTH-02. The author also thanks to Àngel García-Cerdaña his helpful comments.

References

1. Aamodt, A., Plaza, E.: Case-based reasoning: foundational issues, methodological variations, and system approaches. AI Communications 7, 39–59, 08 (2001)
2. Aha, D.W.: Lazy Learning, pp. 7–10. Kluwer Academic Publishers, USA (1997)

156   E. Armengol

3. Armengol, E., Plaza, E.: Lazy induction of descriptions for relational case-based learning. In: Proceedings 12th European Conference on Machine Learning (ECML-2001), Freiburg, Germany, September, pp. 13–24, 09 (2001)
4. Bergmann, R. (ed.): LNCS, vol. 2432. Springer, Heidelberg (2002). https://doi.org/10.1007/3-540-45759-3
5. Bontempi, G., Birattari, M., Bersini, H.: Lazy learning for local modelling and control design. Int. J. Control **72**(7–8), 643–658 (1999)
6. Breiman, L., Friedman, J., Stone, C.J., Olshen, R.A.: Classification and Regression Trees. Chapman and Hall/CRC (1984)
7. Chen, Y., Garcia, E.K., Gupta, M.R., Rahimi, A., Cazzanti, L.: Similarity-based classification: concepts and algorithms. J. Mach. Learn. Res. **10**, 747–776 (2009)
8. Dua, D., Graff, C.: UCI machine learning repository (2017)
9. Hastie, T., Tibshirani, R., Friedman, J.: The Elements of Statistical Learning. Springer Series in Statistics. Springer, New York Inc., New York, NY, USA (2001). https://doi.org/10.1007/978-0-387-21606-5
10. Janet, L.K.: Case-based Reasoning. Morgan Kaufmann, San Mateo, CA (1993)
11. Kuhn, M., Johnson, K.: Applied Predictive Modeling. Springer, New York (2013). https://doi.org/10.1007/978-1-4614-6849-3
12. López de Mántaras, R.: A distance-based attribute selection measure for decision tree induction. Mach. Learn. **6**, 81–92 (1991)
13. Quinlan, J.R.: Induction of decision trees. Mach. Learn. **1**(1), 81–106 (1986)
14. Rokach, L., Maimon., O.: Decision Trees, vol. 6, pp. 165–192. 01 (2005)
15. Santosa, F., Symes, W.W.: Linear inversion of band-limited reflection seismograms. SIAM J. Sci. Statist. Comput. **7**(4), 1307–1330 (1986)
16. Tibshirani, R.: Regression shrinkage and selection via the lasso. J. Royal Statist. Soc.: Ser. B (Methodol.) **58**(1), 267–288 (1996)
17. Zou, H., Hastie, T.: Regularization and variable selection via the elastic net. J. Royal Statist. Soc.: Ser. B (Statist. Methodol.) **67**(2), 301–320 (2005)

Bayesian Logistic Model for Positive and Unlabeled Data

Małgorzata Łazęcka[1,2]([✉]) [iD]

[1] Faculty of Mathematics, Informatics and Mechanics University of Warsaw,
Banacha 2, 02-097 Warsaw, Poland
[2] Institute of Computer Science Polish Academy of Sciences, Jana Kazimierza 5,
01-248 Warsaw, Poland
malgorzata.lazecka@ipipan.waw.pl

Abstract. In the paper, we introduce a novel method of estimating label frequency and parameters of the logistic model for positive and unlabeled (PU) data. Our approach is based on Gibbs sampler that uses Pólya-Gamma latent variables for Bayesian logistic model. In the paper, we focus on estimating label frequency, but the proposed method also provides estimated probabilities of being positive observation among the unlabeled ones.

Keywords: positive and unlabeled data · Selected Completely At Random · Bayesian logistic regression · Gibbs sampling · graphical model

1 Introduction

In standard binary classification, the data consists of positive and negative examples. However, in many applications, the assumption that the class is known for all observations might not be realistic. Consider e.g. medical data, in which usually one has information about patients with the diagnosed disease and the rest of patients might either be healthy or have a disease and remain undiagnosed. In positive and unlabeled (PU) learning we model that situation by assuming that we have access to some positive examples (diagnosed patients), and we do not know the true class of the others (undiagnosed) - they might be either positive or negative. Another example is a survey with sensitive questions e.g. about illegal behavior. Some people who broke the law would answer to that question truthfully, but among those, who would answer "no", there might be a group that actually broke the law but would not admit that in the survey. The next example considers advertisements e.g. the ads that appear on the visited websites. Positive and labeled examples in that scenario are clicks on the ads. However, the remaining ads also might be interesting to the user even though the user has not clicked on them. In the paper we focus on estimating the frequency of such events that the user clicks on the ad, thus we estimate how many of the positive examples are labeled. As a by-product of the proposed method, we obtain probabilities indicating which of the unlabeled observations might be positive.

V. Torra and Y. Narukawa (Eds.): MDAI 2023, LNAI 13890, pp. 157–168, 2023.
https://doi.org/10.1007/978-3-031-33498-6_11

The main contribution of this paper is to adapt the model introduced in [8] in such a way that it can be applied to PU data. In [8] the authors propose a framework for Bayesian inference for the logistic model using the idea of data augmentation. Since the vector of classes is not observed in PU setting, the model proposed in [8] cannot be used directly, thus we extend it with new variables so the new model can cope with data censored as described above. That approach allows for estimating label frequency with high accuracy.

1.1 Notation and Assumptions in PU Learning

In PU learning, we consider a triple of variables (X, Y, S), where $X \in \mathbb{R}^p$ is a random variable corresponding to a feature vector, $Y \in \{0, 1\}$ is a true class and $S \in \{0, 1\}$ is an indicator, whether the observation is positive or unlabeled. In PU setting all labeled observations are positive. In this article, we consider single-case scenario, in which we assume that there is a common distribution of (X, Y, S) and the sample $(x_i, y_i, s_i)_{i=1}^n$ consists of independently drawn observations from that distribution. In standard classification the available data is $(x_i, y_i)_{i=1}^n$, whereas in PU learning we observe only $(x_i, s_i)_{i=1}^n$. Notice that some values of the vector $y = (y_1, y_2, \ldots, y_n)$ are known as when $s_i = 1$ then $y_i = 1$, but when $s_i = 0$ then y_i can be either 0 or 1.

A common assumption in PU learning is the *Selected Completely At Random* (SCAR) assumption, which states that the labeled examples are selected randomly from a set of positive examples independently of X, i.e.

$$P(S = 1|Y = 1, X = x) = P(S = 1|Y = 1). \tag{1}$$

Constant $c := P(S = 1|Y = 1)$ is called *label frequency*. Note that the condition (1) is equivalent to conditional independence of S and X given Y. A common task in PU learning under SCAR assumption is estimation of the parameter c and in this paper we also focus on that problem. We briefly describe some of the existing methods of estimation of c in Sect. 1.3.

1.2 Logistic Model Assumption for PU Data

In logistic model, in which we observe a class indicator Y, we assume that probability of the event $Y = 1$ is logit function in a linear combination of the variables X, namely

$$P(Y = 1|X = x) = \frac{e^{x'\beta}}{1 + e^{x'\beta}} =: \sigma(x'\beta), \tag{2}$$

where $\sigma(t) = e^t/(1 + e^t)$ is a standard logistic function and a symbol $'$ denotes transposition. In PU learning assuming SCAR we have

$$P(S = 1|X = x) = cP(Y = 1|X = x) \tag{3}$$

as LHS equals

$$P(S = 1|Y = 1, X = x)P(Y = 1|X = x) = P(S = 1, Y = 1|X = x)$$
$$= P(S = 1|X = x).$$

Hence, using (2) we obtain that

$$P(S = 1|X = x) = c \times \sigma(x'\beta), \tag{4}$$

where c is label frequency. The model for PU data has an additional parameter c in comparison to the standard logistic regression. The parameters (c, β) are identifiable in view of Theorem 1 in [12], which is not true for c in general setting for PU learning without some additional assumptions. In the proposed method we use an assumption that (Y, X) follow the logistic model as in (2). Other methods of estimation of parameters (c, β) are discussed in Sect. 1.3.

1.3   Methods of Label Frequency Estimation

In this section, we introduce methods of label frequency estimation, some of which will be used in Sect. 3.2. For a comprehensive survey, we refer to [6].

Elkan-Noto and TIcE Estimator. In a method proposed by Elkan and Noto [4] we divide the dataset into two subsets: a training set, on which the classifier $\hat{P}(S = 1|x)$ is trained and a validation set used to compute an estimator of c. The estimator of c is defined as

$$\hat{c}_{EN} = \frac{1}{|\mathcal{A}|} \sum_{i \in \mathcal{A}} \hat{P}(S = 1|X_i),$$

where $\mathcal{A}$ is a set of indices of observations in the validation set that are labeled. The method uses the fact, that

$$c = \frac{P(S = 1|X = x)}{P(Y = 1|X = x)}, \tag{5}$$

and thus if the classes are separable and we compute the denominator for a labeled example, then it equals 1. The method introduced in [1] is based on similar observation, namely that

$$c = P(S = 1|Y = 1) = P(S = 1|Y = 1, X \in \mathcal{A})$$
$$= \frac{P(S = 1, Y = 1, X \in \mathcal{A})}{P(Y = 1, X \in \mathcal{A})} = \frac{P(S = 1|X \in \mathcal{A})}{P(Y = 1|X \in \mathcal{A})}.$$

Next, we look for a so-called anchor set $\mathcal{A}$, for which $P(Y = 1|X \in \mathcal{A}) \approx 1$ using induction trees on a training set and on a test set we estimate $P(S = 1|X \in \mathcal{A})$.

KM Estimators. The estimators proposed in [10] are based on representing the distribution of unlabeled observations as a mixture of the distributions corresponding to $S = 0, Y = 1$ and $S = 0, Y = 0$. In [10] the authors estimate mixing proportion of the latter two distributions. Then, after the mixing proportion is estimated, the class frequency $P(Y = 1)$ can be easily computed, and as $P(Y = 1) = P(S = 1)/c$ we also obtain the estimator of c. Two ways of estimating mixing proportion are proposed, thus two estimators $\hat{c}_{KM1}$ and $\hat{c}_{KM2}$ are obtained.

JOINT and CD+MM Estimators. In view of (4), in order to obtain estimators of (c, β) the following log-likelihood function is maximised

$$l(c, b) = \sum_{i=1}^{n} (s_i \log(c\sigma(x_i'\beta) + (1 - s_i) \log(1 - c\sigma(x_i'\beta)))$$

with respect to c and β simultaneously. JOINT method [11] optimize $l(c, b)$ using simple gradient algorithm. CD+MM accounts for the fact that $l(c, b)$ is not a concave function and thus it may have multiple local minima. CD+MM algorithm [12] consists of two steps in each iteration i: first, using the fact that $l(c, b)$ is concave with respect to c, finds a maximizer $\hat{c}_i$ of $l(c, \hat{b}_{i-1})$. Next, using Minorization-Maximization algorithm (see [7]) maximizes $l(\hat{c}_i, b)$ with respect to b. The optimization algorithm is run until it converges to the local minimum.

MLR Estimator. [5] Note that from (5) it follows that $c \leq \max_x P(S = 1|X = x)$ and if $\max_x P(Y = 1|X = x) = 1$, then we obtain equality. In MLR the following model is fitted

$$g(x, b, \gamma) = \frac{1}{1 + b^2 + exp(\gamma'x)},$$

where $b > 0$ and $\gamma \in \mathbb{R}^p$. By noting that c can be estimated as $\max_x \hat{P}(S = 1|X = x)$ and $\max_x g(x, b, \gamma) = \frac{1}{1+b^2}$, we obtain $\hat{c} = \frac{1}{1+b^2}$.

2   Gibbs Sampler for Estimation of Label Frequency

First, we give a brief description of Gibbs sampler and Bayesian logistic regression introduced in [8], and then in Sect. 2.3 we present our adaptation to PU setting.

2.1   Gibbs Sampling

Gibbs sampling is a Markov chain Monte Carlo algorithm for obtaining a sequence of observations from a multivariate joint probability distribution. The algorithm is especially useful in the cases when direct sampling from the joint distribution of variables $(X_1, X_2, \ldots, X_p)$ is difficult, whereas sampling from conditional distributions $X_i|X_{-i} = x_{-i}$, where $X_{-i} = (X_1, \ldots, X_{i-1}, X_{i+1}, \ldots, X_p)$ is relatively simple. The output of the algorithm, among other applications, can be used to approximate marginal distribution of a chosen subset of variables or to compute their expected value. The variables $(X_1, X_2, \ldots, X_p)$ might represent latent variables of the model we want to sample from or parameters in Bayesian approach. Below we give a brief description of the algorithm.

Suppose we want to sample from the distribution $p(x_1, x_2, \ldots, x_p)$ and sampling from conditional distribution $p(x_j|x_{-j})$ for $j = 1, 2, \ldots, p$ is feasible. Then to obtain N observations from the distribution of $p(x_1, x_2, \ldots, x_p)$, one can proceed as follows:

(1) Set $x^{(0)} = (x_1^{(0)}, x_2^{(0)}, \ldots, x_p^{(0)})$ to a starting value.

(2) Sample $x_j^{(i)} \sim p\left(x_j | x_1^{(i)}, \ldots, x_{j-1}^{(i)}, x_{j+1}^{(i-1)}, \ldots, x_p^{(i-1)}\right)$ for $j = 1, 2, \ldots, p$.

Repeat (2) for $i = 1, 2, \ldots, N$, where N is a number of samples required.

Ideally, the initial value $x^{(0)}$ should be chosen from a region of high probability $p(x_1, x_2, \ldots, x_p)$, but as it is difficult, it is common to sample $N + B$ samples instead of N and discard B samples from the beginning.

Gibbs sampling is frequently used in Bayesian inference. In that approach, prior distribution $\pi(\theta)$ of the vector of parameters $\theta = (\theta_1, \theta_2, \ldots, \theta_p)$ is given and we assume that observations y come from the distribution $p(y|\theta)$, where p is known. In this case, the aim is to sample from the posterior distribution $p(\theta|y)$, as we are interested in the distribution of the parameters given the information about θ from the observed sample. In each step i of (2) of the Gibbs sampler we sample from the distribution $p(\theta_j | \theta_1^{(i)}, \ldots, \theta_{j-1}^{(i)}, \theta_{j+1}^{(i-1)}, \theta_p^{(i-1)}, y)$ for $j \in 1, 2, \ldots, p$.

2.2 Gibbs Sampler for Bayesian Logistic Regression

We describe now an algorithm introduced in [8] for sampling from the posterior distribution of the parameters β from the logistic model (cf. (2))

$$P(Y = y|\beta) = p(y|\beta) = \frac{(e^{x'\beta})^y}{1 + e^{x'\beta}}.$$

Gibbs sampler given in [8] uses latent variables following Pólya-Gamma distribution to enable efficient sampling from conditional distributions. The densities of distributions in Pólya-Gamma family $PG(1, a)$ with parameter $a > 0$ are defined as

$$f(x|a) = \cosh(a/2) e^{-\frac{a^2 x}{2}} g(x),$$

where g is a density of an infinite sum of properly scaled i.i.d. exponential variables (the definition of the density g is given in [8], p. 1340). We do not provide the formula for g, as in the following only the terms containing a will be used. For details see [2, 8].

To construct a Gibbs sampler for Bayesian logistic regression, latent variables ω are used, thus we estimate (β, ω). The step (2) of Gibbs algorithm has two sub-steps:

- Sample $\omega^{(i)} \sim p(\omega | \beta^{(i-1)}, y)$,
- Sample $\beta^{(i)} \sim p(\beta | \omega^{(i)}, y)$.

Using notation of the previous section we have $(\theta_1, \theta_2) = (\beta, \omega)$ (the first parameter is a p-dimensional vector, where p denotes the number of predictors and the second parameter is n-dimensional, where n denotes the number of observations) and y is observed. The dependence structure of variables (β, ω, Y) is represented by probabilistic graphical model shown in Fig. 1a, in which the vertices denote random variables and the orientation of the edges determines the direction of

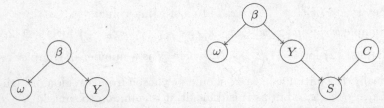

(a) Graphical model for Bayesian logistic sampler

(b) Graphical model for Bayesian logistic sampler for PU data

Fig. 1. Graphical models indicating dependence structure of the considered variables

dependence. The joint distribution corresponding to a graphical model is the product of the conditional probabilities for every node given its parents, thus the joint distribution of (β, ω, Y) factorizes in the following way

$$p(\beta, \omega, Y) = \pi(\beta)p(\omega|\beta)p(y|\beta). \tag{6}$$

Note that from (6) it follows that ω and Y are independent given β. We also assume that observations $(\omega_i, Y_i)_{i=1}^n$ are independent given β, hence we have $p(\omega_i|\beta, y) = p(\omega_i|\beta)$ and $p(\omega|\beta) = \prod_{i=1}^n p(\omega_i|\beta)$. Moreover for a given β the distribution of ω_i is $PG(1, |x_i'\beta|)$ and the prior for β is $\mathcal{N}(b_\beta, B_\beta)$, where b_β and B_β are fixed and we show that conditional distribution of β is also normal. In the following, we will use $\propto$ to denote equality up to multiplication by a constant. We have

$$p(\beta|\omega, y) \propto p(\beta, \omega, y) = \pi(\beta)p(\omega|\beta)p(y|\beta)$$

$$= \pi(\beta) \prod_{i=1}^n \left(\cosh\left(\frac{|x_i'\beta|}{2}\right) e^{-\frac{(x_i'\beta)^2 \omega_i}{2}} g(\omega_i) \right) \prod_{i=1}^n \left(\frac{(e^{x_i'\beta})^{y_i}}{1 + e^{x_i'\beta}} \right)$$

$$\propto 2^{-n} \pi(\beta) \prod_{i=1}^n \exp\left(y_i x_i'\beta - \frac{x_i'\beta}{2} - \frac{\omega_i(x_i'\beta)^2}{2} \right)$$

$$\propto \pi(\beta) \prod_{i=1}^n \exp\left(-\frac{\omega_i}{2} \left(x_i'\beta - \frac{y_i - 1/2}{\omega_i} \right)^2 \right)$$

where in the third expression we omitted the terms $g(\omega_i)$, as they do not depend on β and we used the fact that $\cosh(x) = \frac{e^x + e^{-x}}{2}$. Thus, after further transformations, we obtain that conditional distribution of β is $N(\mu(\omega), \Sigma(\omega))$, where $\Sigma(\omega) = (X'\Omega(\omega)X + B_\beta^{-1})^{-1}$, $\mu(\omega) = \Sigma(\omega)(X'(y - \frac{1}{2}\mathbb{1}_n) + B_\beta^{-1}b_\beta)$, $\Omega(\omega) = \text{diag}(\omega)$ and $\mathbb{1}_n$ is a n-dimensional vector of 1.

2.3 Gibbs Sampler for PU Data

In PU learning the true class Y is not always observed, thus the procedure needs to be modified. We use two additional variables in the model for PU data: observed vector of labels S and unobserved label frequency C treated as a random variable. We assume that the dependency structure is defined by Fig. 1b, thus the joint density of all considered in the model variables can be factorized in the following way (cf. (6))

$$p(\omega, \beta, y, s, c) = \pi(\beta)p(\omega|\beta)p(y|\beta)\pi(c)p(s|y, c). \qquad (7)$$

We now compute the conditional distributions of all the variables, which will be sampled, given the remaining ones. The conditional distributions for β and ω are described in Sect. 2. Below we compute conditional densities $p(y|\beta, \omega, c, s)$ and $p(c|\beta, \omega, y, s)$.

Note, that from (7) it easily follows that $p(y|\beta, \omega, c, s) = p(y|\beta, c, s)$. We also have

$$P(Y_i = y_i|S = s, \beta = b, C = c) \propto P(Y_i = y_i|\beta = b)P(S_i = s|Y = y, C = c). \quad (8)$$

We assume that variables (Y, X) satisfy (2). On the other hand, from SCAR assumption it follows that $P(S_i = 1|Y_i = 1, C = c) = 1 - P(S_i = 0|Y_i = 1, C = c) = c$ and if $Y_i = 0$, we have $P(S_i = 0|Y_i = 0, C = c) = P(S_i = 0|Y_i = 0) = 1$. Hence for $S_i = 1$ we obtain

$$\begin{aligned} P(Y_i = 1|S_i = 1, \beta, C) &\propto c \times \sigma(x_i'\beta), \\ P(Y_i = 0|S_i = 1, \beta, C) &= 0, \end{aligned} \qquad (9)$$

and for $S_i = 0$ we have

$$\begin{aligned} P(Y_i = 1|S_i = 0, \beta, C) &\propto (1 - c)\sigma(x_i'\beta), \\ P(Y_i = 0|S_i = 0, \beta, C) &\propto 1 - \sigma(x_i'\beta). \end{aligned} \qquad (10)$$

Equations (9) and (10) lead to

$$P(Y_i = 1|S_i = s, \beta = b, C = c) = \frac{(1 - c)\sigma(x_i'\beta)}{(1 - c)\sigma(x_i'\beta) + (1 - s)(1 - \sigma(x_i'\beta))}. \quad (11)$$

Now we derive the formula for $p(c|\beta, \omega, y, s)$. Prior density $\pi(c)$ of C is $Beta(\alpha_c, \beta_c)$. From (7) we obtain that C is independent of β and ω given S and Y. Thus we consider conditional distribution of C given only S and Y

$$p(c|S_i = s, Y_i = 1) \propto \pi(c)P(S_i = s|Y_i = 1, C = c).$$

Hence, assuming that the pairs $(S_i, Y_i)_{i=1}^n$ are independent given C, we obtain

$$p(c|S_i, Y_i = 1, i = 1, \ldots, n) \propto \pi(c)c^{\sum_{i=1}^n \mathbb{I}(S_i=1, Y_i=1)}(1 - c)^{\sum_{i=1}^n \mathbb{I}(S_i=0, Y_i=1)},$$

thus $C|S, Y \sim Beta(\alpha_c + \sum_{i=1}^n \mathbb{I}(S_i = 1, Y_i = 1), \beta_c + \sum_{i=1}^n \mathbb{I}(S_i = 0, Y_i = 1))$. Note that proposed prior distribution of C is conjugate for the likelihood which is Bernoulli distribution (for success being $S_i = 1, Y_i = 1$ and the failure $S_i = 0, Y_i = 1$). Thus the posterior is also Beta distribution with modified parameters according to the data.

Below we summarise the above derivations. We use the following prior distributions for β and C with hyperparameters (b_β, B_β) and (α_c, β_c)

$$\beta \sim \mathcal{N}(b_\beta, B_\beta), \quad C \sim Beta(\alpha_c, \beta_c).$$

Then in step (2) of the Gibbs sampler we sample from the following distributions (the definitions of $\mu(\omega)$ and $\Sigma(\omega)$ are given at the end of Sect. 2.2):

$$\omega_i | \beta \quad \sim PG(1, |x_i'\beta|) \text{ for } i = 1, 2, \ldots, n,$$

$$Y_i | \beta, S, C \sim Bern \left(\frac{(1 - C)\sigma(x_i'\beta)}{(1 - C)\sigma(x_i'\beta) + (1 - S_i)(1 - \sigma(x_i'\beta))} \right) \text{ for } i = 1, 2, \ldots, n,$$

$$\beta | \omega, Y \quad \sim \mathcal{N}(\mu(\omega), \Sigma(\omega)),$$

$$C | Y, S \quad \sim Beta \left(\alpha_c + \sum_{i=1}^{n} \mathbb{I}(S_i = 1, Y_i = 1), \beta_c + \sum_{i=1}^{n} \mathbb{I}(S_i = 0, Y_i = 1) \right).$$

Algorithm 1. One step of Gibbs sampler for PU data

Input: X, S, b_β, B_β, β_{old}, α_c, β_c, c_{old}
Output: β_{new}, c_{new}
1: **for** $i \in \{1, 2, \ldots, n\}$ **do**
2:     $\omega_{i,\text{new}} \leftarrow$ a sample from $PG(1, |X_i'.\beta_{\text{old}}|)$
3:     $\sigma_i \leftarrow \sigma(X_i'\beta_{old})$
4:     $p_{Y_i=1} \leftarrow (1 - c_{old})\sigma_i / [(1 - c_{old})\sigma_i + (1 - S_i)(1 - \sigma_i)]$
5:     $y_{i,\text{new}} \leftarrow$ a sample from $Bern(p_{Y_i=1})$
6: **end for**
7: $\Omega_{\text{new}} \leftarrow \text{diag}(\omega_{\text{new}})$
8: $\Sigma_\beta \leftarrow (X'\Omega_{\text{new}}X + B_\beta^{-1})^{-1}$
9: $\mu_\beta \leftarrow \Sigma_\beta(X'(y_{new} - \frac{1}{2}\mathbb{1}_n) + B_\beta^{-1}b_\beta)$
10: $\beta_{\text{new}} \leftarrow$ a sample from $\mathcal{N}_p(\mu_\beta, \Sigma_\beta)$
11: $n_{\text{pl}} \leftarrow \sum_{i=1}^{n} \mathbb{I}(S_i = 1, y_{i,\text{new}} = 1)$
12: $n_{\text{pu}} \leftarrow \sum_{i=1}^{n} \mathbb{I}(S_i = 0, y_{i,\text{new}} = 1)$
13: $c_{\text{new}} \leftarrow$ a sample from $Beta(\alpha_c + n_{\text{pl}}, \beta c + n_{\text{pu}})$

---

3   Numerical Experiments

In this section, we first present an illustrative example showing how the proposed method works. Next, we briefly describe methods of label frequency estimation existing in the literature and at the end we compare the accuracy of our method with other methods on real datasets. The R code is available on Github[1].

In Algorithm 1 we present one step of Gibbs sampler for PU learning. The input consists of a matrix of predictors X, a vector of labels S, hyperparameters

---

[1] github.com/lazeckam/PU_BayesLogistic.

of normal distribution b_β and B_β, hyperparameters of Beta distribution α_c and β_c and initial values or values from the previous step of β and c, namely β_{old} and c_{old}.

3.1 Example

Let $X_i = (X_{i1}, X_{i2}, \ldots, X_{ip})$ for $i \in \{1, 2, \ldots, n\}$. We sample observations $X_{i,j}$ independently from uniform $U([0,1])$ distribution for $i \in \{1, 2, \ldots, n\}$, $j \in \{1, 2, \ldots, p\}$ and let $n = 1000$, $p = 6$. For each row $X_{i,.} = x_i$ of the matrix X we sample Y_i according to the distribution $P(Y_i = 1 | \bar\beta, x_i) = \sigma(x_i'\bar\beta) =: \sigma_{0,i}$, where $\bar\beta = (7.5, 4.5, 1.5, -1.5, -4.5, -7.5)$ with intercept being 0. We fix $c = 0.8$ and sample S_i according to Bernoulli distribution with probability of success c for positive observations $(Y_i = 1)$ and for the remaining ones $S_i = 0$. To run the simulations we use the following hyperparameters and initial values: $b_\beta = 0_p$, $B_\beta = 10 \cdot I_p$, $\alpha_c = 1$, $\beta_c = 1$ and $\beta_{\text{start}} = 0_p$, $c_{\text{start}} = 0.5$, where 0_p denotes a vector of p zeros and I_p is a $p \times p$ identity matrix. Next, we repeat $B + N = 500$ times the step of the Gibbs sampler algorithm described in Algorithm 1.

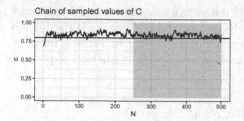 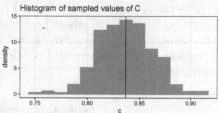

(a) The chain of sampled values of the variable C. The true value is marked with the horizontal line, the gray background shows which values are used to compute the estimator $\hat c$.

(b) The histogram of the values of C for iterations 251-500, which approximates marginal distribution of C and the point estimate $\hat c \approx 0.836$ marked with vertical line.

Fig. 2. Estimation of label frequency c.

The obtained chains of values of C and β are shown in Figs. 2a and 3a. We obtain a point estimate of c by discarding the first $B = 250$ values and averaging the remaining ones. In Fig. 2b the histogram of the estimator $\hat c$ is presented for the last 250 samples. Figure 3b shows scatterplot of estimated posterior values of probability of $Y = 1$, where posterior distribution of $Y_i | \beta, C, S$ follows $Bern\left(\frac{(1-C)\sigma(x_i'\beta)}{(1-C)\sigma(x_i'\beta)+(1-S_i)(1-\sigma(x_i'\beta))}\right)$, which corresponds to $p_{Y_i=1}$ from line 4 in Algorithm 1 (the values from the 500th iteration of Algorithm 1 are used) against $\sigma_{0,i} = \sigma(x_i'\bar\beta)$ values for $i \in \{1, 2, \ldots, n\}$. Both Fig. 3b and Fig. 3a indicating accurate estimation of β show, that the unlabeled observations with high probability of being positive can be detected based on the proposed method as they have also high values of $p_{Y_i=1}$.

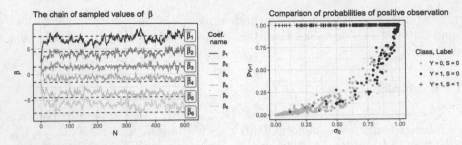

(a) The chains of sampled values for vector β compared with true values $\bar{\beta}$ marked with vertical lines.

(b) Comparison of true probabilities of $Y = 1$ and values of the posterior probabilities of $Y = 1$ for the last iteration of Algorithm 1.

Fig. 3. The chains of β parameters and posterior probabilities of positive class obtained by the proposed method.

3.2   Real Data Simulations

In this section, we artificially created PU datasets using the labeled benchmark 11 datasets from UCI Machine Learning Repository [3] and one from the IJCNN 2001 competition [9]. Detailed information about datasets is in Table 1, in which the number of observations and predictors is given as well as fraction of positive observations α.

Table 1. Information about datasets

Dataset	n	p	α	Dataset	n	p	α
BreastCancer	683	9	0.35	pop_failure	540	18	0.91
diabetes	768	8	0.35	SPECTF	79	44	0.49
heart-c	303	19	0.46	vote	435	32	0.39
ijcnn2001	35000	22	0.10	wdbc	569	31	0.37
mushroom	8124	21	0.48	Wholesale	440	7	0.32
parkinsons	195	22	0.75	wpbc	198	33	0.24

We run simulations to compare the proposed method (**PGPU**) with the existing ones listed in Sect. 1.3. Due to the lack of space, we present the results only for some of the methods. Extended results are available on Github. For each dataset, we select positive examples to be labeled with probability $c = 0.1, 0.2, \ldots, 0.9$ and for each c we repeat the experiment 100 times. All predictors are scaled to $[0, 1]$ suggested in [1]. Due to the computational costs of KM methods, for large dataset ijcnn2001 we subsampled the original dataset 5 times to obtain $n = 2000$ and we averaged results obtained on the subsamples. In our method, we use the same hyperparameters and initial values as in

Comparison of methods

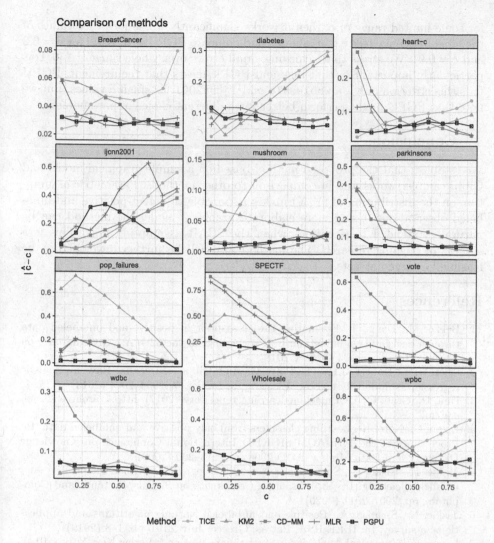

Fig. 4. Comparison of label frequency estimation methods.

the example from Sect. 3.1. For ijcnn2001 PGPU uses the same subsampling approach as for KM described above. PGPU is also computationally expensive for large datasets as in each iteration we generate n samples from Pólya-Gamma distribution and we take an inverse of $p \times p$ matrix to obtain Σ_β.

Figure 4 shows the results of the experiments. Each point on the plot is an average of 100 results of $|\hat{c} - c|$ for fixed method, dataset and label frequency c. The proposed method for all datasets except for ijcnn2001 and Wholesale outperforms or is as accurate as other methods for almost all c values in terms of the accuracy of c estimation. In the cases, when another method performs better for some limited range of c, then it works significantly worse for other values of the label frequency (see e.g. `diabetes` and compare PGPU with KM2 for $c = 0.2$ and $c = 0.9$). We stress that achieving small errors over whole range $c \in [0, 1]$ is particularly important in that task and PGPU meets that requirement. PGPU fails this criterion only on `Wholesale` and `ijcnn2001` for small c values, but we note that PGPU might perform better for a different choice of parameters.

4   Conclusions

We establish that the proposed method based on a simple graphical model and Gibbs sampler works well in comparison to other methods. Parametric assumption on the distribution of (Y, X) makes it possible to detect positive and unlabeled observations. Using more elaborate graphical model the method can be naturally extended to situations when the SCAR assumption fails. This is a subject of ongoing research. The method also will be further developed to be feasible for large datasets.

References

1. Bekker, J., Davis, J.: Estimating the class prior in positive and unlabeled data through decision tree induction. In: Proceedings of the 32th AAAI Conference on Artificial Intelligence, February 2018
2. Choi, H.M., Hobert, J.P.: The Pólya-Gamma Gibbs sampler for Bayesian logistic regression is uniformly ergodic. Electron. J. Statist. **7**, 2054–2064 (2013)
3. Dua, D., Graff, C.: UCI machine learning repository (2017). http://archive.ics.uci.edu/ml
4. Elkan, C., Noto, K.: Learning classifiers from only positive and unlabeled data. In: Proceedings of the 14th ACM SIGKDD International Conference on Knowledge Discovery and Data Mining. KDD 2008, pp. 213–220 (2008)
5. Jaskie, K., Elkan, C., Spanias, A.: A modified logistic regression for positive and unlabeled learning. In: 53rd Asilomar Conference on Signals, Systems, and Computers, pp. 2007–2011 (2020)
6. Jaskie, K., Spanias, A.: Positive and unlabeled learning algorithms and applications: a survey. In: IEEE IISA, Patras, Greece, July 2019, pp. 1–8 (2019)
7. Lange, K.: Numerical Analysis for Statisticians. Springer Verlag New-York (2010). https://doi.org/10.1007/978-1-4419-5945-4
8. Polson, N.G., Scott, J.G., Windle, J.: Bayesian inference for logistic models using Pólya-Gamma latent variables. J. Am. Stat. Assoc. **108**(504), 1339–1349 (2013)
9. Prokhorov, D.: IJCNN 2001 neural network competition. Slide presentation in IJCNN 2001, Ford Research Laboratory (2001)
10. Ramaswamy, H., Scott, C., Tewari, A.: Mixture proportion estimation via kernel embeddings of distributions. In: Proceedings of The 33rd International Conference on Machine Learning, vol. 48, pp. 2052–2060 (2016)
11. Teisseyre, P., Mielniczuk, J., Łazęcka, M.: Different strategies of fitting logistic regression for positive and unlabelled data. In: Proceedings of the International Conference on Computational Science. ICCS 2020 (2020)
12. Łazęcka, M., Mielniczuk, J., Teisseyre, P.: Estimating the class prior for positive and unlabelled data via logistic regression. Adv. Data Anal. Class. **15**(4), 1039–1068 (2021). https://doi.org/10.1007/s11634-021-00444-9

A Goal-Oriented Specification Language for Reinforcement Learning

Simon Schwan[1]($\boxtimes$), Verena Klös[2], and Sabine Glesner[1]

[1] Technische Universität Berlin, Berlin, Germany
{s.schwan,sabine.glesner}@tu-berlin.de
[2] Technische Universität Dresden, Dresden, Germany
verena.kloes@tu-dresden.de

Abstract. The design of reinforcement learning (RL) agents is difficult, especially in domains with complex and possibly conflicting objectives such as autonomous driving. In addition to the formal nature of RL with high technical barriers, the fragility of the reward signal results in the common trial-and-error practice in the design of RL agents. We propose a novel goal-oriented specification language that is tailored to reinforcement learning but abstracts from technical details. To overcome the problematic trial-and-error practice, our specification language provides the foundation for an easy and systematic design process in RL.

Keywords: goals · reinforcement learning · specification language

1 Introduction

Deep reinforcement learning (RL) is well suited for complex sequential tasks such as autonomous driving. Often, solutions to these tasks are nontrivial because of conflicting objectives, efficiency concerns and safety. In RL, objectives are encoded in the reward function and algorithms aim at the maximization of this reward. However, small adjustments to the reward yield significant impact on the behavior of the agent. This leads to the common trial-and-error in the design of RL agents that makes it very difficult to integrate multiple objectives. To overcome this problematic practice, a systematic design process is needed. In this paper, we propose our universal goal-based specification language that abstracts from technical details of RL and provides the basis for such a process. Our three main contributions are:

1. We define a *partitioning of a Markov decision process (MDP) into environment and requirements* to enable the separate definition of the requirements. Our formal definition of both parts allows to reconstruct a MDP that can be learned by existing RL algorithms.
2. We propose our universal language that enables *the specification of requirements in form of a goal tree* similar to goal-oriented requirements engineering (GORE) [13]. We represent goals as subsets of the state space since it is a

V. Torra and Y. Narukawa (Eds.): MDAI 2023, LNAI 13890, pp. 169–180, 2023.
https://doi.org/10.1007/978-3-031-33498-6_12

prevalent concept in GORE and in recent RL research. We enable goals to be hierarchically structured through definable operators. To support multi-faceted requirements, we enrich the plain goal tree with domain knowledge and annotations such as safety and efficiency constraints.

3. Finally, we demonstrate how our specification language *abstracts from technical details*. We show how to construct the MDP with flexible rules that integrate diverse RL techniques. If rules are well-defined, the construction can be automated to unfold a simple and structured design process.

Our goal-oriented approach provides an intuitive and visual means for requirements engineering for RL agents. The main purpose of GORE is to structure and analyze requirements in form of goals. By this, the designer can focus on specifying the objectives instead of getting lost in technical details of the solution. To maintain this purpose, our universal specification language constructs an abstraction layer between the specification of objectives and the underlying design techniques of RL. Based on our partitioning, we are able to define a MDP that integrates the goal-tree and the environment. This MDP can then be learned by existing state-of-the-art RL algorithms.

The paper is structured as follows. We present related work in Sect. 2, and give an introduction to reinforcement learning in Sect. 3. In Sect. 4, we describe our case study that is the lunar lander simulation environment. Following in Sect. 5, we define our partitioning of the MDP into the environment and requirements. Section 6 introduces our specification language in form of goals, operators and annotations. We demonstrate how our specification language abstracts from technical details in Sect. 7. Finally, we conclude in Sect. 8.

2   Related Work

Specification languages for reinforcement learning are rare and most of them are based on temporal logic. Truncated Linear Temporal Logic [8] enables the generation of a scalar reward function from temporal logic requirements. Another approach focuses on the specification based on reward machines [4]. Reward machines are mealy automata that are constructed from a reward specification in linear temporal logic. The approach focuses on a structure of reward that is powerful but non-markovian. This makes it difficult to apply to standard RL algorithms. A composable specification language based on a subset of temporal logic is presented in [6]. It allows the specification of (reachability and avoidance) objectives as elements of the state space that may be sequentially or disjunctively decomposed. In contrast to our language, all three approaches focus on the specification of reward rather than comprehensive requirements based on all components of the MDP. The formal specification of requirements is based on temporal logic. This has the advantage to guarantee behavior in safety-critical applications through the definition of optimal policies. However, these guarantees are weak if function approximation such as neural networks are used to learn. We integrate constraints into goals similar to Constrained MDPs [1] that, e.g., allows us to penalize. In contrast to our goal-oriented specification, requirements in temporal logic are not as intuitive and their design needs experts. Two of the approaches [4, 6] develop RL algorithms specific to their needs. Therefore, they cannot directly profit from the advancements in recent RL algorithms.

In [7], a goal model for self-adaptive systems is proposed that provides a distance metric to guide adaptation towards minimal goal violation. This approach inspired us to use a similar concept for goal- and reward specification in RL.

3   Reinforcement Learning

Reinforcement learning (RL) aims at solving problems of sequential decision making by maximizing a reward. The agent acts in an existing but often unknown environment (model-free). In discrete time steps, the agent chooses actions according to a learned policy based on its observations. It obtains a reward from the environment that transitions to its next state. Formally, RL is modeled as a Markov Decision Process (MDP) [12] with $MDP = (S, A, P, R)$ and

- State space S is the set of all states that satisfy the Markov property.
- Action space A is the set of all available actions.
- The transition probability P describes how the process moves to the next state s' from state s with action a:
  $P(s, a, s') = Pr[s_{t+1} = s' | s_t = s, a_t = a]$
- The reward signal $R : S \times A \times S \rightarrow \mathbb{R}$ is the immediate reward that is the target of the maximization.

The goal of RL is to find a policy $\pi : S \rightarrow A$ that maximizes the expected time-discounted sum of rewards. The optimal policy chooses the highest expected reward for all states. Deep RL allows to solve complex problems based on modern function approximation such as deep neural networks. Often, the input to this approximation (i.e. state $s \in S$) is a vector of features $S : S_1 \times ... \times S_n$ where each feature S_i describes a property of the environment. Sophisticated model-free RL algorithms such as TRPO [11] and TD3 [5] maximize a single scalar reward.

Sparse reward gives feedback to the agent at few but determined state transitions, e.g., if the agent solves the problem. This simplifies a correct reward specification but is especially difficult to learn in large state spaces. Dense reward continuously gives feedback to the agent to lead it into the right direction. However, it raises the probability of unexpected behavior if it is not carefully crafted. A popular technique to specify dense reward is potential-based reward shaping [9]. It is based on the idea to add a difference of potentials $F(s, a, s') = \Phi(s') - \Phi(s)$ to a reward. Thus, it preserves the original optimal policy.

4   Case Study - Lunar Lander

The *lunar lander* is a reinforcement learning environment from OpenAI Gym [3] which is a standardized collection of RL benchmark problems. The environment provides all parts of the MDP such as the state and action space, the transition probabilities and the reward described below in more detail. The objective of the lunar lander (Fig. 1) is to land a space ship at the landing zone (goal). The ship has three engines and the discrete action space contains four actions: $A_{lunar} = \{nothing, left, right, main\}$. The state space $S_{lunar} = \mathbb{R}^8$ contains eight features: x and y position and velocity (x, y, x_v, y_v), lander angle and angular velocity (α, α_v), leg 1 and 2 grounded (binary l_1, l_2). The landing zone is at $(x, y) = (0, 0)$. The reward function combines several rewards and penalties:

- A cumulative reward of about 100 - 140 is given as a dense reward over time to arrive at the landing zone with zero speed.
- A crash is penalized with -100 and the space ship at rest is rewarded with 100.
- Ground contact of each leg is rewarded by 10 and penalized with -10 if lost.
- Each time the main engine is fired, a penalty of -0.3 is given. For the side engines, the penalty is -0.03.

The environment terminates if the lunar lander crashes or rests. The problem is considered to be solved if the sum of rewards exceeds 200.

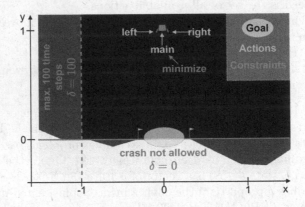

Fig. 1. The lunar lander simulation with landing zone (0,0) and constraints

5   Environment and Requirements

We aim at the goal-oriented specification of requirements for RL in an existing context. The formal concept behind RL are Markov decision processes. To be able to specify requirements, we present our partitioning of MDPs into two parts: the environment and the requirements. The environment contains the context such as states, physics and actions. Requirements comprise all aspects of MDPs that an engineer is able to define when designing an agent based on an existing context. Together, the environment and requirements form the MDP that can be learned by standard RL algorithms. Following, we formally describe the environment, our requirements and their integration into a MDP.

We define an environment through states (e.g. measured by sensors) and actions (e.g. available through actuators) that follow a specific transition model (e.g. physics). Formally, the environment $Env = (S^*, A^*, P^*)$ consists of:

1. The initial state space $S^* : S_1 \times ... \times S_n$ contains all possible states of the environment (e.g. physical and virtual sensors). It is composed of n features $x_i \in S_i$. We require states from S^* to satisfy the Markov property.
2. The initial action space A^* describes all available actions of the environment.
3. The initial transition probability P^* describes the state transition model of the environment similar to the transition probability P of MDPs from Sect. 3. Note: The transition probability does not need to be known since learning is based on samples from the environment in model-free RL.

Requirements comprise aspects of the MDP that are potentially definable by an RL engineer: The observation O_G and action space A_G are similar but not necessarily equal to the corresponding initial spaces S^* and A^* of Env. This enables a requirement to abstract from the original components and is further evaluated in Sect. 7. The transition probability P is specified in the environment. However, it may be possible to stop sampling. We represent this adaption of the transition probability through the termination set $P_{T,G}$. Finally, objectives of our requirement are specified in the reward R_G. Formally, we define the four components $(O_G, A_G, P_{T,G}, R_G)$ of a requirement as follows:

1. The observation space $O_G : O_1 \times ... \times O_m$ is the basic input for all decisions.
2. The action space A_G is the set of actions of the agent to reach the goal.
3. The termination set $P_{T,G} \subseteq A \times O$ defines pairs at which sampling in an episode terminates.
4. The reward $R_G : S \times A \times S \to \mathbb{R}$ is a single scalar signal.

Note: the indexed G in a requirement stands for *goal* that we introduce in our goal-oriented specification in the next section.

Given an environment (S^*, A^*, P^*) and a requirement $(O_G, A_G, P_{T,G}, R_G)$, we are able to construct a $MDP = (S, A, P, R)$ as follows:

1. The state space is defined by $S = O_G$. In order to transform a state $s^* \in S^*$ from the environment, we require a mapping $state : S^* \to O_G$ that preserves the Markov property from S^* in order to define a MDP.
2. The action space is defined by $A = A_G$. In order to execute an action from the agent in the environment, we require a mapping $execute : A_G \to A^*$.
3. The transition probability P is based on P^* that we overwrite with 0 iff. the action-state is in P_T:

$$P(s, a, s') = \begin{cases} 0 & \text{, for } (s, a) \in P_{T,G} \\ P^*(s^*, a^*, s'^*) & \text{, else with } execute(a) = a^*, \\ & state(s^*) = s, \ state(s'^*) = s' \end{cases}$$

4. The reward R is the reward R_G defined in our requirement:
$$R(s, a, s') = R_G(s^*, a^*, s'*) \quad \text{with } execute(a) = a^*,$$
$$state(s^*) = s, \ state(s'^*) = s'$$

The mappings *state* and *execute* enable a RL algorithm to learn the actions from the action space A based on states from the state space S of the MDP. However, state transitions are taken in the environment Env. The RL feedback loop at time step t starts at state $s_t^* \in S^*$ from Env that is converted to $s_t = execute(s_t^*) \in O_G$. This state s_t is handed to the RL algorithm that chooses an action $a_t \in A_G$. This action is converted into $a_t^* = execute(a_t) \in A^*$ that is executed in the environment. The environment transitions to the next state $s_{t+1}^* \in S^*$ with $s_{t+1} = state(s_{t+1}^*)$. The RL algorithm receives the reward $R(s_t, a_t, s_{t+1})$ and the next state s_{t+1}. Finally, the loop repeats.

At this point, we have introduced our partitioning of a MDP into an environment and requirements. We have shown that we are able to reconstruct a MDP from both these parts. Finally, we have demonstrated the application of the standard RL feedback loop. In the following section, we use our notation of requirements to create our novel goal-oriented specification language.

6   Goal-oriented Specification

Following, we introduce our graphical and formal notation of our novel goal-based specification language for reinforcement learning. We combine the well-known and intuitive concept from GORE [13] with our formal notation of requirements. The fundamental concept of our goal tree is that the requirements can be directly inferred from the structure of the goal tree (operators), additional information (annotations) and the related goal space G.

At first, we start with the definition of goals in Sect. 6.1. Then, we present the refinement of goals through operators (Sect. 6.2) and define annotations (Sect. 6.3) that allow the integration of constraints and domain knowledge. To illustrate our specification language, we use the lunar lander from Sect. 4.

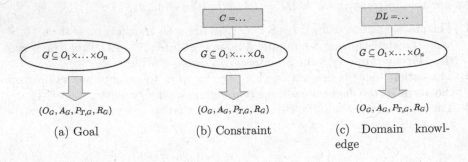

(a) Goal   (b) Constraint   (c) Domain knowledge

Fig. 2. Goals and annotations

6.1 Goals

Goals are objectives the agent has to satisfy in order to solve the given problem. Similar to GORE, each goal is a single node in our tree (Fig. 2a) that we overload with our formal notations of its goal space and requirements. We define goal spaces in relation to the observation space:

$$G \subseteq O_G$$

An agent satisfies a goal G iff. it reaches any state $o \in G$. The relation of goals to states is also used in popular work [2,10].

For example, the goal of the lunar lander is to reach the platform with zero velocity, zero angle, zero angular velocity and both legs on the ground. This can be represented by the goal space G_{lunar} (remember: $(x, y, x_v, y_v, \alpha, \alpha_v, l_1, l_2) \in O_{lunar}$) as follows :

$$G_{lunar} \subseteq O_{lunar} \text{ with } G_{lunar} = \{(0, 0, 0, 0, 0, 0, 1, 1)\}$$

6.2 Operators

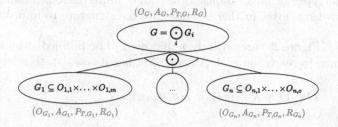

Fig. 3. Our generic operator of goals

Operators enable us to structure goals into subgoals. To allow the application of diverse techniques from RL, we define a generic operator. Figure 3 shows its graphical notation. The definition of an operator comprises a definition for each component of the requirements. Thus, the requirements of the parent goal are generated as a combination of the requirements of its n subgoals G_i:

$$(O_G, A_G, P_{T,G}, R_G) = \bigodot_i^n (O_i, A_i, P_{T,i}, R_i)$$

As an example, the and-operator $G = \bigcap_i G_i$ enables refinement of goals into subgoals similar to GORE [13]. According to the intersection, the goal G is satisfied iff. all subgoals G_i are satisfied. This refinement allows to structure goals into groups of features that belong together such as the dimensions of a position.

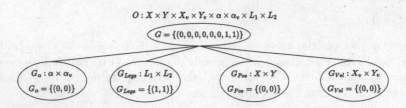

Fig. 4. The *and* refinement for the lunar lander

Figure 4 illustrates the and-operator for the lunar lander. We refine the root of our goal tree (introduced in Sect. 6.1) and obtain a separation of the features that belong thematically together. These are the angular properties ($\alpha \times \alpha_v$), the status of the legs ($L_1 \times L_2$), the position ($X \times Y$) and the velocity ($X_v \times Y_v$). Note: We use $G_{Pos} : X \times Y$ as abbreviation for $G = \{(x, y, x_v, y_v, ...)|x = 0, y = 0, x_v \in X_v, x_v \in Y_v, ...\}$ even though it is still of type $G_{Pos} : O$.

6.3   Annotations

We enable the annotation of goals by additional information that are mandatory or helpful to find a viable solution from the requirements. We differentiate between two types of annotations. Constraints limit the reachability of goals. Domain knowledge gives further insights into the structure to improve learning.

Constraints. (Figure 2b) are objectives that need to be fulfilled at all times while the agent aims to reach the goal. A constraint has its own state-action space C:

$$C \subseteq O \times A \quad \text{with} \quad cnt_C(o, a) = \begin{cases} 1 : (o, a) \in C \\ 0 : (o, a) \notin C \end{cases}$$

where $cnt_C(o, a) = 1$ specifies a constraint violation at a single time step. We define constraints over the time of an episode T and identify three types: soft safety, hard safety, efficiency. Soft safety constraints allow a specified number of violations δ over a single episode

$$\sum_{i=0}^{T} cnt_C(o_i, a_i) \leq \delta$$

with action a_i executed at observation o_i at time step i. Hard safety constraints are a special case of soft safety constraints which do not allow any violations through $\delta = 0$. Note: Our notion of safety constraints is similar to the definition used in Constrained MDPs [1]. More complex constraint objectives other than our linear sum may also be promising options. In contrast to safety, efficiency constraints minimize the occurrence of violations over an episode through

$$\text{minimize} \sum_{i=0}^{T} cnt_C(o_i, a_i) \tag{1}$$

with action a_i executed at observation o_i at time step i.

A soft constraint to the lunar lander restricts the x -deviation from a defined central region, e.g. $x < -1$ (cf. Fig. 1). With $\delta = 100$ and $C_{left} = \{(o, a) | a \in A, o = (x, ...) \in O, x < -1\}$ the agent is allowed to leave the central region on the left side for a maximum of 100 time steps. A hard constraint prohibits the action-state space of crashes (we assume crashes at $y < 0$ for simplicity) as follows: $C_{crash} = \{(o, a) | a \in A, o = (x, y, ...) \in O, y < 0\}$. The efficiency constraint with $C_{eff} = \{(o, a) | o \in O, a = main\}$ minimizes the choice of the actionmain .

Domain Knowledge. (Figure 2c) induces insights into the agent. Additional information about the environment may be available that is not integrated into the initial state space. Knowledge such as the distance to a goal, heuristics or a calculated path to a goal may exist. Often, this information is obvious to humans but not to algorithms. We determine two classes of domain knowledge. Static domain knowledge does not change over an episode. We define this as additional information about the environment DK^{env}. Dynamic domain knowledge can change over an episode. This can be e.g. the distance $DK^{dist}(o_t)$ (e.g. distance to a goal) or a heuristic $DK^{heur}(o_t)$ (e.g. calculated path to follow) that both depend on the current observation o_t at time step t.

For example, static domain knowledge for the lunar lander could be the position of the landing zone if it changes each episode. In contrast, dynamic domain knowledge may be the distance $DK_{G_{Pos}}^{dist}(x, y) = \sqrt{x^2 + y^2}$ that is dependent on the current position (x, y) of the lunar lander.

We have presented our goal-oriented specification language for reinforcement learning that allows to concentrate on objectives rather than technical details. In the following section, we evaluate how our goal tree is able to abstract from popular reinforcement learning techniques. For these techniques, we reveal similarities to the original reward of the lunar lander and finally discuss the possibility of an automatic generation of a MDP.

7   Abstraction of Technical Details

With our novel goal-oriented specification language, we aim at the abstraction of technical details to facilitate the design process for RL. Following, we discuss why this abstraction is possible and how we are able to construct a MDP based on common RL design techniques. Finally, we specify an example goal tree for the lunar lander and relate its reward specification to the goal tree.

The fundamental idea of our goal-oriented specification is to have a single requirements tuple $(O_G, A_G, T_{T,G}, R_G)$ at the root of a goal tree. According to Sect. 5, this single tuple combined with the environment defines the MDP. With our specification language, requirements engineers only specify the goal tree including goal spaces for each goal. To construct a combined requirements tuple at the root, we propose to traverse the tree structure and progressively generate and merge its goals. To achieve this, we require rules for the generation of each part of our tree (i.e. goal spaces, operators and annotations). As methods in RL advance and differ for specific domains, our approach is open to integrate multifaceted techniques. Following, we draft our vision for rules and demonstrate their flexible integration of diverse RL techniques.

The leafs of our goal tree define atomic objectives. Such objectives can be rewarded by a sparse signal iff. an agent reaches the specified goal state G:

$$R_G(o, a, o') = \begin{cases} 1 & \text{, for } o' \in G \\ 0 & \text{, else.} \end{cases}$$

Accordingly, $P_{T,G} = \{(a, o) | a \in A_G, o \in G\}$ defines a simultaneous termination. Other sparse rewards are also possible such as penalties when an agent leaves G.

Operators enable the refinement of goals from a top-down perspective. This allows rules to enforce the conformance to higher level requirements. To illustrate, all actions of the action space A_{leaf} need to relate to an action from A_{root} that we are able to execute in the environment. From a bottom-up perspective, goals grow in their complexity that peaks at the root of our tree. A rule for an operator constructs requirements to combine lower level objectives. For example, a popular technique for our and-operator is the weighted linear sum to combine the rewards R_i of all children in the reward R_G of the parent:

$$R_G = \sum_i \omega_i \cdot R_i$$

It introduces the challenge of fair weights and normalization. However, non-linear combinations are also possible.

To demonstrate the flexibility of operators, we shortly discuss a different use case. An operator for temporal abstractions [12] can decompose a task (parent goal) into sequential sub tasks (child goals). Each sub goal encodes its own objectives in the sub goal tree. The reward of the parent goal can then be defined by a combination of its children that also considers their sequential order.

Domain knowledge annotations enable rules for RL techniques that need more information. In large state spaces, sparse rewards are difficult to learn. Reward shaping techniques augment sparse rewards to obtain dense signals. A popular choice is potential-based reward shaping (PBRS) that e.g. can be realized by a distance metric annotated to a goal. However, with annotations it is possible to define other rules that are tailored to the needs of specific domains.

Safety and efficiency constraints specify restrictions to goals. Restrictive behavior is often realized through penalties in form of negative rewards. We are able to penalize based on hard, soft and efficiency constraints that are triggered by $C \subseteq O \times A$. In contrast to penalties, complex rules are possible to define the reward, e.g. max-min optimization based on Lagrange multipliers.

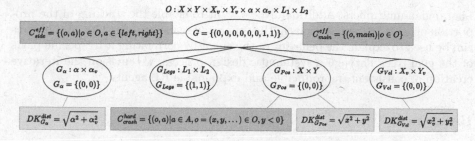

Fig. 5. Goal tree for Lunar Lander

Figure 5 illustrates an example goal tree for the lunar lander. The and-operator allows us to structure the observation space into features that semantically belong together. The original lunar lander reward is defined as the sum of rewards similar to our proposed rule for the reward of the and-operator. With our DK^{dist} annotations we enable the goals G_α , G_{Pos} and G_{Vel} to contain distance metrics. Similar metrics are used by the lunar lander to construct a potential-based reward shaping (i.e. the reward of 100 to 140 to arrive at the landing zone with zero speed). The goal spaces of our goal tree enable the construction of sparse rewards similar to the lunar lander (+10 for ground contact of each leg and +100 for the space ship at rest). Finally, we are able to penalize crashes through our safety constraint (i.e. −100 in the lunar lander) and the firing of engines through our efficiency constraints (i.e. −0.3 and −0.03 in the lunar lander).

We have shown how to construct the MDP from our goal tree based on rules. With well-defined rules, it is possible to automate the construction and unfold a simple and iterative design process for RL agents.

8   Conclusion

To overcome the problematic trial-and-error practice in the design of reinforcement agents, we have introduced our goal-oriented specification language and provide the foundation for a systematic design process. With our partitioning of Markov decision processes into environment and requirements, we have defined the formal basis for our specification language. Our goal tree enables the specification of complex and possibly conflicting requirements for RL. Operators allow to structure goals hierarchically and we annotate goals with domain knowledge, safety constraints and efficiency constraints. We have shown how our specification language abstracts from technical details and sketched the flexible rule-based construction of a MDP that can be learned by existing state-of-the-art RL algorithms. These rules can integrate popular RL design techniques and, if they are well defined, it is possible to automate the construction.

In future work, we plan to automatically construct the MDP from our goal trees and integrate popular RL techniques such as reward shaping and

Lagrangian multipliers. Additionally, we want to enable the tracking of the proportion of goals and annotations in the generated scalar reward. This proportions can be used to explain the behavior of the agent by correlating it to specific parts of the goal tree. Through a systematic design process, we envision the iterative creation of consistent, reproducible and explainable RL agents.

References

1. Altman, E.: Constrained Markov decision processes, vol. 7. CRC Press (1999)
2. Andrychowicz, M., et al.: Hindsight experience replay. In: Advances in Neural Information Processing Systems, pp. 5048–5058 (2017)
3. Brockman, G., et al.: OpenAI Gym (2016)
4. Camacho, A., Icarte, R.T., Klassen, T.Q., Valenzano, R.A., McIlraith, S.A.: LTL and beyond: formal languages for reward function specification in reinforcement learning. In: Proceedings of the International Joint Conference on Artificial Intelligence, pp. 6065–6073 (2019)
5. Fujimoto, S., Van Hoof, H., Meger, D.: Addressing function approximation error in actor-critic methods. In: 35th International Conference on Machine Learning (2018)
6. Jothimurugan, K., Alur, R., Bastani, O.: A composable specification language for reinforcement learning tasks. In: Advances in Neural Information Processing Systems, pp. 13021–13030 (2019)
7. Klös, V., Göthel, T., Glesner, S.: Runtime management and quantitative evaluation of changing system goals in complex autonomous systems. J. Syst. Softw. **144**, 314–327 (2018)
8. Li, X., Vasile, C.I., Belta, C.: Reinforcement learning with temporal logic rewards. In: IEEE International Conference on Intelligent Robots and Systems, pp. 3834–3839 (2017)
9. Ng, A.Y., Harada, D., Russell, S.J.: Policy invariance under reward transformations: theory and application to reward shaping. In: Proceedings of the Sixteenth International Conference on Machine Learning, pp. 278–287 (1999)
10. Schaul, T., Horgan, D., Gregor, K., Silver, D.: Universal value function approximators. In: Proceedings of the 32nd International Conference on Machine Learning, pp. 1312–1320 (2015)
11. Schulman, J., Levine, S., Abbeel, P., Jordan, M.I., Moritz, P.: Trust region policy optimization. In: Proceedings of the 32nd International Conference on Machine Learning, pp. 1889–1897 (2015)
12. Sutton, R.S., Barto, A.G.: Reinforcement learning: an introduction. MIT press, 2 edn. (2018)
13. Van Lamsweerde, A.: Goal-oriented requirements engineering: a guided tour. In: Proceedings of the IEEE International Conference on Requirements Engineering, pp. 249–261 (2001)

Improved Spectral Norm Regularization
for Neural Networks

Anton Johansson[1,3]([✉]), Niklas Engsner[1], Claes Strannegård[2],
and Petter Mostad[1]

[1] Chalmers University of Technology, Gothenburg, Sweden
erikantonjohansson@live.com
[2] Department of Applied Information Technology, University of Gothenburg,
Gothenburg, Sweden
[3] Volvo Group, Gothenburg, Sweden

Abstract. We improve on a line of research that seeks to regularize the spectral norm of the Jacobian of the input-output mapping for deep neural networks. While previous work rely on upper bounding techniques, we propose a scheme that targets the exact spectral norm. We evaluate this regularization method empirically with respect to its generalization performance and robustness.

Our results demonstrate that this improved spectral regularization scheme outperforms L2-regularization as well as the previously used upper bounding technique. Moreover, our results suggest that exact spectral norm regularization and exact Frobenius norm regularization have comparable performance. We analyze these empirical findings in the light of the mathematical relations that hold between the spectral and the Frobenius norms. Lastly, in light of our evaluation we revisit an argument concerning the strong adversarial protection that Jacobian regularization provides and show that it can be misleading.

In summary, we propose a new regularization method and contribute to the practical and theoretical understanding of when one regularization method should be preferred over another.

Keywords: Deep learning · Robustness · Jacobian regularization

1 Introduction

Ensuring that deep neural networks generalize can often be a question of applying the right regularization scheme. While long-established regularization schemes such as weight decay [17] can reduce the function complexity and prevent the network from overfitting, it can at times do so in a crude manner, reducing the complexity more than what is needed and inhibiting the overall performance of the network. Another important consideration for real-world generalizability that regularization schemes has to account for is robustness [26]. Robustness will aid in ensuring that the model behaves as expected even when the input is perturbed, e.g., by natural or adversarial noise specifically crafted to fool a

V. Torra and Y. Narukawa (Eds.): MDAI 2023, LNAI 13890, pp. 181–201, 2023.
https://doi.org/10.1007/978-3-031-33498-6_13

given model. With certain adversarial attack methods bridging the gap between theoretical concern and practical considerations by fooling commercial road signs detector with adversarial attacks [4,22], robustness is becoming a progressively more important aspect of model deployment.

Previous work has demonstrated that regularizing the l_p-norms of the Jacobian of the network mapping can meet these two goals concurrently and different techniques have thus been developed to target these quantities [28]. Although obtaining the Jacobian is theoretically straightforward, it is computationally expensive and thus most schemes only seek to approximate a given norm. For example, the Frobenius norm has been approximated through sampling schemes and layer-wise approximations [9,12] while the spectral norm has been targeted by upper-bounding the spectral norm of each weight matrix in the network [28,31].

In this work we extend on the schemes that target the spectral norm. While penalizing an upper-bound of the spectral norm does improve generalization and robustness, it is also crude in the sense that it does not directly target the quantity of interest and might thus inhibit the performance more than necessary. We instead provide an efficient algorithm that targets the *exact* spectral norm of the Jacobian. Using this algorithm we demonstrate that targeting the exact spectral norm yields an improved generalization performance while preserving a healthy defence against natural and adversarial perturbations.

2   Background

We follow [31] and represent an L-layer neural network $f : \mathbb{R}^{n_{in}} \to \mathbb{R}^{n_{out}}$ recursively as $x^l = f^l(G^l(x^{l-1}) + b^l)$, $l = 1, 2, ..., L$ where G^l is either a linear operator (e.g., convolution) or a piecewise linear operator (e.g., max-pool), f^l the corresponding activation function, $b_l \in \mathbb{R}^{n_l}$ is the associated bias for layer l and we set the input $x = x^0$. Denoting the collection of all parameters of the network as θ, and making the dependence of the network on the parameters explicit as f_θ, the full network function will be given as $f_\theta(x) = x^L$.

Momentarily restricting ourselves to the classification setting, the task that we are interested in is then the supervised learning problem of finding parameters θ such that f_θ can associate feature-values $x \in \mathbb{R}^{n_{in}}$ with one-hot encoded labels $y \in \mathbb{R}^{n_{out}}$ obtained from an unknown distribution P. This is achieved by collecting a training set $\mathcal{D}_t := \{(x_i, y_i)\}_{i=1}^N$ where $(x_i, y_i) \sim P$ and employing an appropriate loss function $l : \mathbb{R}^{n_{out}} \times \mathbb{R}^{n_{out}} \to \mathbb{R}$ which encourages f_θ to model a probability distribution for the possible labels for a given feature-value. Minimizing the full loss $l_{\mathrm{bare}}(\theta, \mathcal{D}_t) := 1/|\mathcal{D}_t| \sum_{(x_i, y_i) \in \mathcal{D}_t} l(f_\theta(x_i), y_i)$ will thus align the distribution of $f_\theta(x_i)$ with that of the ground-truth label y_i. The minimization is done through some variant of stochastic gradient descent (SGD) where we split $\mathcal{D}_t$ into smaller disjoint random batches $\bigcup_i \mathcal{B}_i = \mathcal{D}_t$ and subsequently minimize $l_{\mathrm{bare}}(\theta, \mathcal{D}_t)$ by reducing the partial loss $l_{\mathrm{bare}}(\theta, \mathcal{B}_i)$ for every batch $\mathcal{B}_i$, whereupon the training set is split into new batches and the process repeated. We additionally utilize a validation set $\mathcal{D}_v := \{(x_i, y_i)\}_{i=1}^M$ with $(x_i, y_i) \sim P$ and $\mathcal{D}_t \cap \mathcal{D}_v = \emptyset$ to measure the performance of the model.

2.1   Regularization

Although the sole minimization of $l_{\mathrm{bare}}(\theta, \mathcal{D}_t)$ can yield networks that perform adequately, the networks are often lacking in different regards such as generalization and robustness. While there exists a wide variety of methods that attempt to mitigate these deficiencies, for example by controlling the magnitude of the weights as in weight decay, by utilizing knowledge distillation techniques [3,24] or by augmenting the training data with adversarially perturbed examples [20], here we focus on the regularization techniques obtained by penalizing with some function $h : \mathbb{R} \to \mathbb{R}$ the norm of the Jacobian. This means that we seek to minimize

$$l_{\mathrm{jac}}(\theta, \mathcal{D}_t, \lambda) := l_{\mathrm{bare}}(\theta, \mathcal{D}_t) + \frac{\lambda}{|\mathcal{D}_t|} \sum_{(x_i, y_i) \in \mathcal{D}_t} h\left(\left\|\frac{df_\theta(x_i)}{dx}\right\|\right), \tag{1}$$

where λ is a hyper-parameter that controls the trade-off between the two terms and with typical choices for h being either $h(x) = x$ or $h(x) = x^2$.

For most norms the regularized loss (1) does not yield itself to any effective optimization schemes, requiring time-consuming operations to obtain the Jacobian for each x_i in every batch $\mathcal{B}_i$. An exception to this is the Frobenius norm where one can estimate the exact Frobenius norm either through a double-backpropagation scheme [8] or by using a more efficient sampling scheme [12] where one samples n_{proj} vectors v^j from the $n_{out} - 1$ dimensional unit sphere $S^{n_{out}-1}$ to approximate the squared Frobenius norm as

$$\left\|\frac{df_\theta(x)}{dx}\right\|_F^2 = n_{out} \mathbb{E}_{v \sim S^{n_{out}-1}}\left[\left\|v\frac{df_\theta(x)}{dx}\right\|^2\right] \approx \frac{n_{out}}{n_{proj}} \sum_{j=1}^{n_{proj}} \left[\frac{d(v^j \cdot x^L)}{dx}\right]^2, \tag{2}$$

and thus minimizes the expression

$$l_{\mathrm{frob}}(\theta, \mathcal{D}_t, \lambda) := l_{\mathrm{bare}}(\theta, \mathcal{D}_t) + \frac{\lambda n_{out}}{|\mathcal{D}_t| n_{proj}} \sum_{(x_i, y_i) \in \mathcal{D}_t} \sum_{j=1}^{n_{proj}} \left[\frac{d(v^j \cdot x_i^L)}{dx}\right]^2. \tag{3}$$

We on the other hand are interested in penalizing the spectral norm of the Jacobian at a point x, defined as

$$\left\|\frac{df_\theta(x)}{dx}\right\|_2 = \max_{\substack{v \in \mathbb{R}^{n_{in}} \\ \|v\|=1}} \left\|\frac{df_\theta(x)}{dx}v\right\|_2 = \sigma_{max}, \tag{4}$$

where σ_{max} denotes the largest singular value of $df_\theta(x)/dx$. A constraint on (4) implies that we restrict the maximum rate at which f_θ can change as the input x is perturbed, thus promoting robustness of our model. While the spectral norm does not immediately give itself to any viable method, [31] managed to develop an efficient scheme by restricting themselves to the setting where all activation functions are piecewise linear. Networks with piecewise linear activation functions are themselves piecewise linear functions and the input space can thus be decomposed into a partition $\mathcal{R}$ where for each $R \in \mathcal{R}$ there exists $W_R \in \mathbb{R}^{n_{in} \times n_{out}}$, $b_R \in \mathbb{R}^{n_{out}}$ such that $f_\theta(x) = W_R x + b_R$, $\forall x \in R$ [10]. For these piecewise linear networks, the Jacobian df_θ/dx is constant in each region $R \in \mathcal{R}$ and given by W_R. Calculating the spectral norm of the Jacobian at some input x is thus reduced to calculating the spectral norm of W_R associated with $R \ni x$.

Although the regularization scheme is valid for all piecewise linear activation functions, it is easiest to present for networks with only ReLU [23] activation functions and we thus momentarily restrict ourselves to this setting. By restricting ourselves to these networks and by using the fact that all linear and piecewise linear operators G^l can locally be represented as a matrix W^l, one can obtain the identity

$$W_R = W^L Z_R^{L-1} W^{L-1} \cdots W^2 Z_R^1 W^1 \qquad (5)$$

where Z_R^i is a diagonal boolean matrix indicating which neurons in layer i that have an output > 0 when passing $x \in R$ through the network. Using this identity, an upper bound for $||W_R||_2$ can be obtained as $||W_R||_2 \leq \prod_l ||W^l||_2$ and subsequently [31] regularize the spectral norm by bounding the spectral norm of each weight matrix. They thus minimize the expression

$$l_{\text{specUB}}(\theta, \mathcal{D}_t, \lambda) := l_{\text{bare}}(\theta, \mathcal{D}_t) + \lambda \sum_{l=1}^{L} ||W^l||_2^2, \qquad (6)$$

and additionally suggest to further effectivize the scheme by using power iteration on the matrices W^l as $v \sim S^{n_l - 1}$, $u \leftarrow W^l v$, $v \leftarrow (W^l)^T u$ to approximate the spectral norm as $||W^l||_2 \approx ||u||_2/||v||_2$. While this scheme will penalize the spectral norm of the Jacobian, it only does so through an upper bound, thus potentially inhibiting the performance of the network more than necessary.

While previous work has mainly investigated the Spectral and Frobenius norm penalization schemes in isolation from each other, one can argue that they are strongly connected through the equivalence of all finite-dimensional norms [14], with the specific relation given as

$$||W||_2 \leq ||W||_F \leq \sqrt{r}||W||_2, \qquad (7)$$

where r is the rank of the matrix W.

While Eq. (7) allows for a large discrepancy between the norms of matrices of large rank r, their distinction might not be that significant in practice, with the consequence that the penalization schemes yield effectively equivalent models. We are thus also interested in the empirical difference between networks trained with regularization schemes targeting these two norms.

3   Method

Here we introduce our method which penalizes the spectral norm of the Jacobian directly. Our scheme relies on power iteration as previous methods but targets

$||W_R||_2$ directly. We will follow prior research and momentarily restrict ourselves to piecewise linear networks without skip-connections since this provides a scheme that is easy to present and implement, but keep in mind that the ensuing methodology is valid for networks with skip-connection and non-linear activation functions as well at the cost of a more complex implementation scheme.

3.1   Exact Spectral Norm Regularization

To perform power iteration on W_R we need a way to efficiently perform the steps $v \sim S^{n_{in}-1}$, $u \leftarrow W_R v$, $v \leftarrow W_R^T u$ to subsequently approximate the norm as $||W_R||_2 \approx ||u||_2/||v||_2$. Given that the main obstacle for an efficient scheme is the construction of W_R, our scheme circumvents the construction by directly focusing on the matrix-vector products $W_R v$ and $W_R^T u$. Returning to the identity (5), we can see that, given the constituent weight matrices W^l and boolean matrices Z_R^l, one can obtain the desired matrix-vector products as

$$W_R v = W^L Z_R^{L-1} W^{L-1} \cdots W^2 Z_R^1 W^1 v, \tag{8}$$

$$W_R^T u = (W^1)^T Z_R^1 (W^2)^T \cdots (W^{L-1})^T Z_R^{L-1} (W^L)^T u. \tag{9}$$

While the matrices Z_R^l can easily be obtained by recording which neurons that have an output > 0 when passing $x \in R$ through the network, the construction of the matrices W^l is inefficient for most network layers except for the very simplest ones, making the direct application of (8)–(9) impractical.

While the direct application is impractical, we can obtain a practical scheme by interpreting Eq. (8)–(9) in a particular manner. Equation (8) is nothing other than the forward-pass of v through the network *with all bias vectors set to 0* and *the activation functions replaced with multiplication with boolean matrices Z_R^l*, hereby referred to as the *forward mode* of the network. Similarly, Eq. (9) is the output obtained by passing u *backwards* through the network, meaning that we start at the final layer and transform u layer by layer with analogous modifications to the bias vectors and activation functions as in the forward mode until we reach the input layer. We will hereby refer to this reverse pass as the *backward mode*[1] of the network. This interpretation circumvents the formation of the matrices W^l and instead relies on forward and backward operators F^l and $(F^L)^T$ that make use of the linear and piecewise linear operators G^l and their corresponding transposed version $(G^l)^T$ that implicitly define W^l and $(W^l)^T$, e.g., through convolution and transposed convolution operators. While for many layers we have that the layer transformations G^l and the resulting forward operators F^l coincide, meaning $F^l = G^l$, there do exist some exceptions to this rule where a little bit of extra care is needed to ensure that the forward and backward modes correctly map to $W_R v$ and $W_R^T u$ respectively, e.g., max-pooling layers where the max-indices of the forward-pass has to be utilized. The reader

---

[1] Note that the backward mode can be obtained by a standard backward pass to evaluate $d(x^L \cdot u)/dx$. We refer to it here as backward mode to highlight the symmetry with the forward mode which does not have a standard equivalent counterpart.

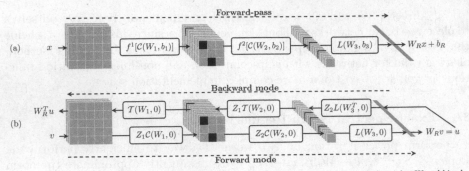

Fig. 1. The difference between a regular forward-pass and the forward and backward modes for a two hidden layer network. (a) A regular forward-pass of x through the network. Each box showcases the operation that maps the input between the layers. The black squares indicate the neurons mapped to zero by the ReLU activation functions f^i. (b) The forward and backward modes used to estimate $||W_R||_2$. An input v is sent through the network to yield u whereupon u is sent backwards through the network. Note how each operation is now bias-free with the same weights as during the forward-pass. The activation functions are replaced by multiplication with the Boolean matrices designed to keep the activation pattern fixed, see Eq. (8)–(9). The backward mode is achieved through transposed convolutions and linear transformations.

is referred to Appendix B to see the conversion between the operators G^l, F^l and $(F^l)^T$ for some commonly used layers.

Thus we can target the exact spectral norm of W_R by performing power iteration with $v \sim S^{n_{in}-1}$ and obtain the matrix-vector products $W_R v$ and $(W_R)^T u$ through the forward and backward mode respectively, thereupon estimating the spectral norm as $||W_R||_2 \approx ||u||_2 / ||v||_2$.[2] For a visualization of the difference between a regular forward-pass, the forward and backward mode of the network and the involved operators, see Fig. 1 where all of this is visualized for a simple three layer convolutional network. The network only utilizes ReLU activation functions so that $f^1 = f^2 =$ ReLU and G^1, G^2 are given by convolutional layers while G^3 is a linear layer.

Making the association between R and an input $x, x \in R$, explicit as R_x, we can formulate our exact spectral loss as

$$l_{\text{spec}}(\theta, \mathcal{D}_t, \lambda) := l_{\text{bare}}(\theta, \mathcal{D}_t) + \frac{\lambda}{|\mathcal{D}_t|} \sum_{(x_i, y_i) \in \mathcal{D}_t} ||W_{R_{x_i}}||_2. \tag{10}$$

Further, converting the matrix multiplication with the Boolean matrices Z_R^i to component-wise Hadamard products $\odot$ with vectors z^i, we can formulate the entire scheme on a batch level which can be seen in Algorithm 1 below.

---

[2] It is possible to perform power iteration multiple times to get a better estimate but we found that performing it once gave sufficiently accurate estimates.

Algorithm 1. Forward-backward algorithm for a ReLU network.

1: **Input:** Mini-batch $\mathcal{B}_i$ of feature-value pairs (x, y), weight factor λ, number of power iterations N
2: **Output:** Approximate gradient $\nabla_\theta l_{spec}(\theta, \mathcal{B}_i, \lambda)$
3: $x^0 = x$ ▷ Forward-pass start
4: **for** $l = 1$ **to** L **do**
5:     $x^l = f^l(G^l(x^{l-1}) + b^l)$
6:     **if** $l < L$ **then**
7:         $z^l = \mathbb{I}\{x^l > 0\}$
8: $u \sim \mathcal{N}(0, I)$ ▷ u is of shape $(|\mathcal{B}_i|, n_{in})$
9: **for** $n = 1$ **to** N **do**   ▷ Forward-mode start
10:     $v = u/\|u\|_2$
11:     **for** $l = 1$ **to** L **do**
12:         $v = F^l(v)$
13:         **if** $l < L$ **then**
14:             $v = v \odot z^l$
15:     $u = v, \ u = u/\|u\|_2$
16:     **for** $l = L$ **to** 1 **do**   ▷ Backward-mode start
17:         $u = (F^l)^T(u)$
18:         **if** $l > 1$ **then**
19:             $u = u \odot z^{l-1}$
20: $R_{spec}(\theta) = \sum_{(x_i, y_i) \in \mathcal{B}_i} \|W_{R_{x_i}}\|_2$ ▷ $\sum_{(x_i, y_i) \in \mathcal{B}_i} \|W_{R_{x_i}}\|_2 = \text{sum}(\|u\|_2/\|v\|_2)$
21: $\nabla_\theta l_{spec}(\theta, \mathcal{B}_i, \lambda) = \nabla_\theta l_{\text{bare}}(\theta, \mathcal{B}_i) + \nabla_\theta \frac{\lambda}{|\mathcal{B}_i|} R_{spec}(\theta)$

3.2   Extension to Non-piecewise Linear Transforms

While the scheme detailed in Algorithm 1 is capable of regularizing the spectral norm of the Jacobian, it is easiest to implement and most efficient in the piecewise linear setting where all layer-wise transformations are given by piecewise linear functions. Although this is a restriction, many well performing networks rely solely on non-linearities given by piecewise linear activation functions with the addition of batch-normalization layers, see for example VGG [27] and ResNet [11] among others. Creating an easily implementable regularization scheme for this well-performing setting thus only requires us to additionally ensure the validity of the scheme when using batch-normalization.

Batch-normalization poses two issues which complicates the extension of the regularization scheme.

1. Division by the variance of the input makes batch-normalization a non-piecewise linear transformation during training.
2. Since the mean and variance are calculated per batch, batch-normalization induces a relation between input x_j and output $f_\theta(x_i)$ where $x_i, x_j \in \mathcal{B}, i \neq j$. This induced relation adds multiple components $df_\theta(x_i)/dx_j$ to the Jacobian which represents how an input x_j affects an output $f_\theta(x_i)$. We believe these components are not relevant in practice and effort should thus not be spent controlling them.

Since both of these issues are only present during training, we circumvent them by penalizing the spectral norm of the Jacobian obtained by momentarily engaging a pseudo-inference mode where we set the running mean and variance of the batch-normalization layers to be fixed and given by the variance and mean obtained from the batch.

Additionally, Algorithm 1 can be efficiently extended to networks employing non-piecewise linear transformations as well at the cost of a more complicated implementation scheme. While not explicitly stated, Algorithm 1 can be used for non-piecewise linear transformations, replacing the Boolean matrices Z^l with matrices given by df^l/dx^{l-1}. However, the calculations and storage of these matrices is likely to be cumbersome and memory intensive for most naive implementations and networks and we thus recommend that one instead utilizes the internal computational graph present in most deep learning libraries. Calculating Eq. (9) is equivalent to calculating $(df/dx)^T u$ and can thus be obtained by simply applying back-propagation to $d(x^L \cdot u)/dx$ which is a valid scheme for all networks, not only piecewise linear ones. Similarly we can obtain the matrix-vector product $(df/dx)v$ by utilizing the same computational graph used to obtain $d(x^L \cdot u)/dx$, but reverse the direction of all relevant constituent edges and adding a fictitious node to represent the inner product with v, see Fig. 2 for a demonstration of this fact for a simple computational graph. We present a proof of the validity of this extension scheme this in Appendix D.

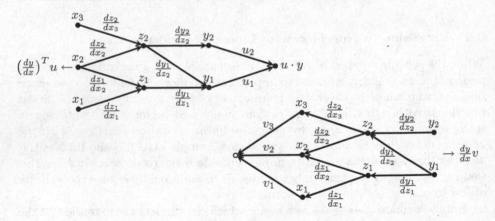

Fig. 2. Illustration of the extension scheme. (Top-left) The computational graph associated with the forward-pass. Each node can perform any non-linear transformation of the associated input. To obtain the i:th component of $(dy/dx)^T u$ we sum the product of the edge elements along every path from the right-most node to x_i. (Bottom-right) The modified computational graph to obtain $(dy/dx)v$. The direction of all edges are flipped, we remove the right-most node and we add a fictitious node to the computational graph (marked as a empty circle) with connecting edge elements being given by components of v. All other relevant edge elements are preserved from the top graph. The i:th component of $(dy/dx)v$ can then be obtained by starting at the fictitious node and summing the product of the edge elements along every path to y_i

For this work we choose not to focus on this possible implementation further though since the piecewise linear setting already encompasses a large amount of models and we believe that most will find the scheme in Algorithm 1 more straightforward to implement than delving deep into the mechanics of computational graphs. Further adding on to this fact is that the internals of the computational graphs of popular deep learning frameworks (such as PyTorch [25] and TensorFlow [1]) are written in C++ and having to perform modifications of the graph would thus potentially impede the Python-based workflow which many practitioners operate with. However, if one wishes to utilize spectral regularization for networks that employ non-piecewise linear activation functions, for example sigmoids which can be of relevance for attention mechanisms [29], then the extension scheme provides a well-principled and efficient approach that one can follow. In that case one would replace the Forward-mode and Backward-mode in Algorithm 1 with the computational graph manipulation techniques to obtain $(df/dx)v$ and $(df/dx)^T u$ respectively.

4   Experiments

In this section we evaluate how targeting the exact spectral norm, hereby referred to as the Spectral method, compares to other regularization methods, namely the Frobenius method given by Eq. (3), the Spectral-Bound method given by Eq. (6) and weight decay [17] (also referred to as L2-regularization). We compare the generalization performance across different data sets and investigate the robustness of the obtained networks.

4.1   Generalization

In-domain Generalization. The considered data sets where the generalization performance is measured are MNIST [19], KMNIST [5], FashionMNIST (which at times we will abbreviate as FMNIST) [30] and CIFAR10 [16]. The generalization performance is measured by measuring the accuracy on the corresponding validation set $\mathcal{D}_v$ for each data set. A variant of the LeNet architecture [18] is used for the MNIST, KMNIST and FMNIST dataset while the VGG16 [27] architecture is used for CIFAR10. All four data sets are preprocessed so that they have channelwise mean of 0 and a standard deviation of 1. We perform a grid-search to find the optimal hyperparameters for each network and regularization scheme, see Appendix A for more details regarding the training setup. Each experiment is repeated five times and the model that has the lowest mean loss over all hyperparameters over these five runs is chosen as the representative of a given method. The results of this experiment can be seen in Table 1.

From these results we can see that penalizing the exact spectral norm yields models with a higher mean accuracy than the Spectral-Bound method, demonstrating that targeting the exact spectral norm yields an improved generalization performance compared to working with an upper bound. Further, we can see that the differences in accuracy between the Frobenius and the Spectral methods are

Table 1. Mean test accuracy ± one standard deviation for the different regularization methods on four data sets computed over 5 runs. Bold indicates best mean accuracy.

Method	CIFAR10	KMNIST	FMNIST	MNIST
Spectral	90.04 ± 0.57	96.49 ± 0.15	**90.94 ± 0.33**	99.34 ± 0.03
Frobenius	**90.15 ± 0.63**	**96.52 ± 0.11**	90.92 ± 0.18	**99.39 ± 0.04**
Spectral-Bound	89.41 ± 0.66	95.86 ± 0.19	90.73 ± 0.10	99.26 ± 0.05
L2	89.92 ± 0.71	95.90 ± 0.19	90.66 ± 0.10	99.21 ± 0.02
None	88.62 ± 0.69	94.69 ± 0.52	90.51 ± 0.21	99.09 ± 0.09

slim, showcasing the small practical difference between training neural networks with one of these methods over the other.

Out-of-Domain Generalization. To get a full picture of how well the models trained with the different regularization schemes generalize we additionally measure their performance on a cross-domain generalization task, a situation which practitioners can often encounter. To measure this generalization ability we use our best performing models on the MNIST data set, and measure their performance on the combined train and test data of the USPS data set [13]. These results can be seen in Table 2 below. As can be seen from Table 2, we obtain similar conclusions as in the in-domain generalization experiment. The Spectral method obtains a higher mean accuracy than the Spectral-Bound method, while the Frobenius and Spectral method give rise to virtually equally well performing models.

Table 2. Mean test accuracy ± one standard deviation and loss for the different regularization methods on the USPS data set for the best performing models on MNIST. Bold indicates best accuracy and loss.

Method	Accuracy	Loss
Spectral	**83.76 ± 1.15**	**0.59 ± 0.06**
Frobenius	**83.76 ± 0.68**	0.63 ± 0.05
Spectral-Bound	82.16 ± 1.80	0.66 ± 0.07
L2	83.02 ± 1.95	0.62 ± 0.07
None	83.56 ± 0.39	0.78 ± 0.10

4.2 Robustness

While generalization on a validation or test set gives an indication of model performance in practice, data encountered in reality is often not as exemplary as a curated benchmark data set and ensuring robustness against both natural and adversarial noise can often be a precondition for model deployment.

As previously mentioned, earlier research has indicated that controlling the norm of the Jacobian is beneficial for robustness of our networks and we thus follow the path of [12] and investigate how the robustness of the different schemes compare.

Robustness Against White Noise. We measure the robustness against white noise by creating a noisy validation set $\mathcal{D}_{v,\sigma^2}$ for FashionMNIST and KMNIST, consisting of data points $\tilde{x}$ obtained by adding independent Gaussian distributed noise to each individual pixel of validation points $x \in \mathcal{D}_v$ as

$$\tilde{x}_{ij} = x_{ij} + \epsilon, \quad \epsilon \sim \mathcal{N}(0, \sigma^2) \tag{11}$$

whereupon we clip the value of all pixels into the range [0,1] and perform the aforementioned pre-processing. Further, to enable a fair comparison between the different methods and to not have the result obscured by the initial baseline accuracies, we measure the difference between the baseline accuracy on $\mathcal{D}_v$ and the accuracy on $\mathcal{D}_{v,\sigma^2}$. These results can be seen to the left in Fig. 3 where we see that there is not a large difference in robustness between either of the training schemes.

Robustness Against Adversarial Noise. The last decade has seen an increased growth in the amount of research into adversarial noise, noise that may be imperceptible to the human eye but which has a considerable impact on the prediction of a deep learning model. Here we will work with the adversarial noise technique known as projected gradient descent (PGD) method [20] and related variants. PGD obtains the perturbation $\tilde{x}$ through a constrained gradient ascent, moving in a direction which increases the loss $l_{bare}(\theta, \{(x, y)\})$ while simultaneously restricting the ascent to the ball $B_\delta = \{z \in \mathbb{R}^{n_o} : ||x - z||_\infty \le \delta\}$ which ensures that the perturbation $\tilde{x}$ is visually similar to x. Formally, PGD obtains $\tilde{x}$ as

$$\tilde{x} = \text{Proj}_{B_\delta}\left[x + \eta\text{sign}\left(\frac{dl_{bare}(\theta, \{(x, y)\})}{dx}\right)\right], \tag{12}$$

where Proj denotes the projection operator and η the step-size for the gradient ascent. The gradient ascent process can be repeated over several iterations to yield perturbations $\tilde{x}$ indistinguishable from x but for which the network predicts an incorrect label. After the ascent procedure we clip the pixel values into the range [0,1] and perform the pre-processing as before. We will additionally consider the adversarial attack methods TPGD [32] that performs PGD on a Kullback-Leibler divergence of the softmax-scores, and the gradient-free attack Square [2]. All attacks are implemented through the torchattacks library [15] with default parameters except for the parameters δ, η which we set to be 32/255 and 2/255 respectively.

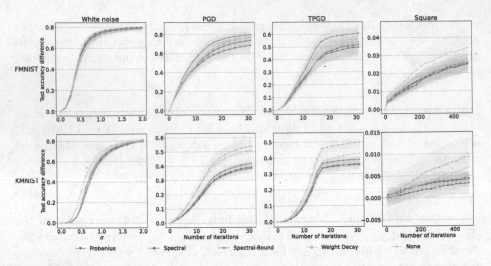

Fig. 3. Robustness against perturbations. Each plot displays how the test accuracy drops as the perturbations gets stronger. Each column corresponds to a perturbation method and each row is associated with a given data set. The curves and intervals are obtained as the mean and standard deviation over 5 different networks.

To control the strength of the adversarial noise we vary the number of iterations for each attack. As before, to enable a fair comparison we compute the difference between the baseline accuracy on FashionMNIST and KMNIST with the adversarially perturbed validation sets. These results can be seen in Fig. 3 where we see that the Spectral regularization scheme is able to consistently ensure stronger robustness for the PGD and TPGD attacks on KMNIST and FMNIST compared to Spectral-Bound. Additionally, we can see that the differences between the Frobenius and Spectral methods are small and superior to the other techniques, further showcasing the small practical difference between these methods and that exact penalization of the Jacobian improves the safeguard against adversarial noise.

Distance to Decision Boundary. One way to attempt to understand how penalizing the Jacobian strengthens the robustness is to analyze the distance to the closest decision boundary. Previous research demonstrated that controlling the Frobenius norm enlarged the decision cells and thus argued that this made the network more robust to perturbations [12]. We extend their experiments and perform an extensive investigation to measure the robustness where we measure the distance to the decision boundary for all validation points in FashionMNIST and KMNIST. To measure the distance to the decision boundary for a given point we sample points uniformly on concentric spheres of different radii and perform a binary search to find the smallest radii such that a sampled point obtains a predicted class different from the validation point at the center of the sphere. These results are summarized in Fig. 4.

From these results we see that penalizing the Jacobian on KMNIST gives rise to larger regions in general, as showcased by the large regions obtained by the Spectral, Frobenius and Spectral-Bound method. On FashionMNIST we can instead see that the Frobenius and Spectral-Bound method gives rise to the largest regions on average. That the Spectral-Bound method achieves large regions on average for FashionMNIST yet provides one of the weaker safeguards against adversarial noise in Fig. 3 implies that the enlargening of the regions cannot fully capture the nuances of robustness against adversarial attacks. Choosing a model based on this intuition that larger regions provide a stronger safeguard can even yield a subpar model in this case.

We hypothesize that one aspect of robustness that this intuition fails to take into account is the structure of the loss landscape. Since a smooth loss landscape with large gradients will facilitate the creation of adversarial examples through gradient ascent we must also consider this aspect to get a holistic view of a regularization methods robustness.

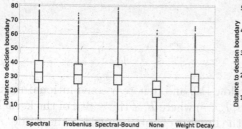 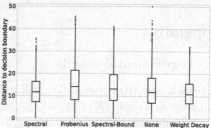

Fig. 4. Distance to the decision boundary. (Left) Distance to the nearest boundary for validation points in KMNIST. (Right) Distance to the nearest boundary for validation points in FashionMNIST.

5   Conclusion

We have demonstrated a method to improve spectral norm regularization for neural networks. While previous methods relied on inexact upper bounding techniques, our technique targets the exact spectral norm. In the piecewise linear setting our method is easily implemented by performing power iteration through a forward-backward scheme.

This scheme obtained an improved generalization performance as compared to regularizing the spectral norm through the minimization of an upper bound and we could additionally see an indication that our scheme and a scheme targeting the exact Frobenius norm of the Jacobian gives rise to virtually equivalent results in terms of robustness and accuracy. Further, we investigated the intuition that Jacobian regularization provides a strong defence against adversarial attacks by the enlargening of the decision cells and found that the size of the regions is not necessarily indicative of the robustness of the network.

Our work has built on and further solidified the body of research that demonstrates the usefulness of Jacobian regularization. Future work should further investigate both the practical and theoretical difference between the developed schemes for penalizing the exact Jacobian on a larger variety of models and data sets. Additionally, by implementing the extension scheme to enable the algorithm for networks with general activation functions these differences can be investigated in more generality and provide further insight into the exact relation between these regularization schemes. Future practical applications also involve investigating the potentially gain in robustness that our scheme can provide in situations practitioners can often encounter, such as fine-tuning pre-trained models [7] and working with data of varying quality [21].

Acknowledgement. This work was supported by the Wallenberg Artificial Intelligence, Autonomous Systems and Software Program (WASP), funded by the Knut and Alice Wallenberg Foundation. The computations were enabled by resources provided by the Swedish National Infrastructure for Computing (SNIC) at Kebnekaise partially funded by the Swedish Research Council through grant agreement no. 2018-05973.

Appendix

A   Experimental details

Network Architectures. We will follow [12] and denote a convolutional-maxpool layer as a tuple $(K, C_{in} \to C_{out}, S, P, M)$ where K is the width of the kernel, C_{in} is the number of in-channels, C_{out} the number of out-channels, S the stride, P the padding of the layer and M the size of the kernel of the max-pool following the convolutional layer. The case $M = 1$ can be seen as a convolutional layer followed by an identity function. Linear layers we will denote as the tuple (N_{in}, N_{out}) where N_{in} is the dimension of the input and N_{out} the size of the output. For KMNIST and FashionMNIST we used the LeNet network which consist of a convolutional-maxpool layer $(5, 1 \to 6, 1, 2, 2)$, convolutional-maxpool layer $(5, 6 \to 16, 1, 0, 2)$, linear layer $(400, 120)$, linear layer $(120, 84)$ and linear layer $(84, 10)$.

We use the VGG16 network as is available from the torchvision package. For this network we use batch-norm layers directly after every convolutional layers. This network consist of the layers $(3, 3 \to 64, 1, 1, 1)$, $(3, 64 \to 64, 1, 1, 2)$, $(3, 64 \to 128, 1, 1, 1)$, $(3, 128 \to 128, 1, 1, 1)$, $(3, 128 \to 256, 1, 1, 2)$, $(3, 256 \to 256, 1, 1, 1)$, $(3, 256 \to 256, 1, 1, 1)$, $(3, 256 \to 512, 1, 1, 2)$, $(3, 512 \to 512, 1, 1, 1)$, $(3, 512 \to 512, 1, 1, 1)$, $(3, 512 \to 512, 1, 1, 2)$, $(512, 10)$.

Training Details. We train the LeNet networks for 50 epochs with SGD (with momentum=0.8). For every regularization method we perform a hyperparameter search over these three following parameters and values.

- Learning rate: [0.01, 0.001]
- Batch size: [16, 32]
- Weight factor λ: [0.0001, 0.001, 0.01, 0.1]

For the VGG16 network we trained the network for 100 epochs with a batch size of 128, SGD with momentum of 0.8 and performed a hyperparameter search over these parameters and values

- Weight factor λ: [0.00001, 0.0001, 0.001, 0.01, 0.1]

For VGG16 we additionally used a cosine annealing learning rate scheduler with an initial learning rate of 0.1 and the data augmentation techniques of random cropping and horizontal flipping.

For each hyperparameter setting we repeat the training procedure 5 times to be able to obtain mean and standard deviation. We pick the final representative model for each regularization method as the one that achieves the lowest mean validation loss over these 5 training runs.

For the Frobenius regularization we set $n_{proj} = 1$ and for the Spectral-Bound we estimate the spectral norm of the weight matrices through one power iteration.

Details for Figures. Figure 4: The model for each regularization method was chosen randomly among the 5 models from the hyperparameter setting that obtained the best results in Table 1. The distance is only calculated for the points in the validation set that all models predict correctly. In total the distance is predicted for between 8000–9000 validation points on FashionMNIST and KMNIST.

Figure 5 (**left**): The time for a batch was measured on a computer with NVIDIA K80 GPU as available through Google Colab[3]. The analytical method works by sequentially calculating $d(x^L \cdot e_i)/dx$ where e_i is a basis-vector for $\mathbb{R}^{n_{out}}$ for $i = 1, 2, ..., n_{out}$. This yields the full Jacobian matrix which we then calculate the singular values of by using inbuilt functions in PyTorch.

Figure 5 (**right**): The upper bound was evaluated on a network trained with the Spectral-Bound regularization scheme for all data points in the training set. The curve for the spectral method was evaluated on a network trained with the spectral method for all data points in the training set. For the spectral method there was no significant difference in the shape of the curve when using a different network or by working with data points in the validation set.

B   Conversion Between Operators

In this section we detail how to convert between the forward F, backward F^T and regular operators G. These can be seen in Table 3 - 5. Other non-linearities such as Dropout can be incorporated identically to ReLU by simply storing the active neurons in a boolean matrix Z.

---

[3] colab.research.google.com.

Skip-Connections. Utilizing networks with skip-connections does not change the forward and backward modes. Simple turn off the bias of all layer transformations and replace the activation functions with the matrices Z_R^i instead. That this is true follows from the definition of a network with skip-connections. For simplicity of presentation, we will assume that the skip-connections only skip one layer. Assume that we have a network with L layers and additionally have skip-connections between layers with indices in the set $\mathcal{S} := \{s_1, s_2, ..., s_m\}$, $1 \leq s_i \leq L$. Then the network f_θ is given recursively as before with

$$x^l = \begin{cases} f^l(G^l(x^{l-1}) + b^l) & \text{if } l \in \mathcal{S}^C, \\ x^{l-1} + f^l(G^l(x^{l-1}) + b^l) & \text{if } l \in \mathcal{S}. \end{cases}$$

Assuming that we are only working with piecewise linear or linear operators G^l, then for $x \in R$ we know that each operator can be represented as a matrix and we can write the derivative of the two cases as

$$\frac{dx^l}{dx^{l-1}} = \begin{cases} Z^l W^l & \text{if } l \in \mathcal{S}^C, \\ I + Z^l W^l & \text{if } l \in \mathcal{S}, \end{cases}$$

where I denotes a unit-matrix. The Jacobian-vector product $W_R v$ can thus be obtained as

$$W_R v = \left(\prod_{l=1}^{L} (I - \mathbb{I}\{l \in \mathcal{S}^C\} + Z^l W^l) \right) v \tag{13}$$

where $\mathbb{I}\{l \in \mathcal{S}^C\}$ is an indicator for the unit-matrix so that we can concisely write the two cases. Thus we see that we can interpret this equation in the same manner as we did for the networks without skip-connections. We simply pass the input v through the network and turn off all the biases and replace the activation functions with Z^l. The same is true for the backward mode (Table 4).

Table 3. Conversion table for the linear operator.

Forward-pass (G)	Forward-mode (F)	Backward-mode (F^T)
Input: x, W, b	**Input:** x, W	**Input:** x, W
$y = \text{Linear}(x, W, b)$	$y = \text{Linear}(x, W, 0)$	$y = \text{Linear}(x, W^T, 0)$
return: y	**return:** y	**return:** y

Table 4. Conversion table for the convolutional operator.

Forward-pass (G)	Forward-mode (F)	Backward-mode (F^T)
Input: x, W, b	**Input:** x, W	**Input:** x, W
$y = \text{Conv}(x, W, b)$	$y = \text{Conv}(x, W, 0)$	$y = \text{ConvTranspose}(x, W, 0)$
return: y	**return:** y	**return:** y

Table 5. Conversion table for the max-pool operator.

Forward-pass (G)	Forward-mode (F)	Backward-mode (F^T)
Input: x	**Input:** x, I	**Input:** x, I, S
y, indices = maxpool(x)	$y = $ x[I]	y = maxunpool(x,
I = indices	**return:** y	indices=I, shape = S)
S = x.shape		**return:** y
return: y, I, S		

C Time Efficiency and Relative Error

In this section we investigate the difference between targeting the exact spectral norm of the Jacobian compared to working with an upper bound. From Table 1 we saw that this yields an improved generalization performance and from Fig. 3 we observed that the two methods provide a similar protection against noise, with different strengths against different attacks on the two considered data sets.

While an improved generalization performance is beneficial, it cannot come at a too large of a computational cost. Additionally, with approximate methods it is also important to measure the trade-off between computational speed and accuracy of the approximated quantity. We thus analyze the computational overhead that they add to the training routine and the relative error with the analytical spectral norm.

In Fig. 5 (left) we can thus see the average time taken to optimize over a batch for the Spectral method, the Spectral-Bound method, an analytical method that calculates $\|W_R\|_2$ exactly and a regular forward-pass. In Fig. 5 (right) the relative error for the power iteration scheme is visible.

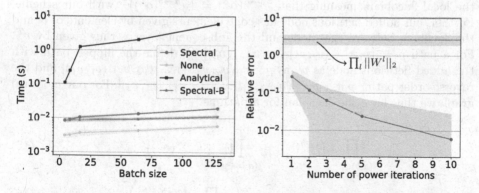

Fig. 5. Time and error comparison between the Spectral and Spectral-Bound method for the LeNet network. (Left) Time taken to pass over one batch of data points. The Spectral method is slower than the Spectral-Bound method for larger batch sizes but still around two orders of magnitude faster than calculating the exact spectral norm analytically. (Right) The relative error as the number of power iterations is increased. The relative error decreases quickly and is significantly closer to the exact quantity compared to the upper bound $\prod_l \|W^l\|_2$.

From these plots we can see there is a small extra incurred cost of working with our method compared to regularizing with Spectral-Bound, but that our method has a significantly lower relative error while still being orders of magnitude faster than calculating the analytical spectral norm.

D   Proof for Extension Scheme

We will denote the directed acyclic graph which when summing the product of every edge element along every path from output to input yields $(df/dx)^T$ as G.

Theorem: *Consider the graph F obtained by flipping the direction of all edges of G and adding a node at the end of F with edge elements given by components of v. Summing the product of every edge element along every path from output to input of F yields $(df/dx)v$.*

Proof: We will follow the notation of [6], Theorem 1 and denote the Jacobian between variables $y = f_\theta(x)$ and x as the sum of the product of all intermediate Jacobians, meaning

$$\frac{dy}{dx} = \sum_{p \in \mathcal{P}(x,y)} \prod_{(a,b) \in p} J^{a \to b}(\alpha^b) \tag{14}$$

where $\mathcal{P}(x,y)$ is the set of all directed paths between x and y and (a,b) is two successive edges on a given path.

In our scheme we flip the direction of all relevant edges and add a fictitious node at the end of the path the flipped paths. Since we preserve the edge elements, we can realize that flipping the direction of the edges simply transposes the local Jacobian, meaning that $J^{b \to a}(\alpha^b) = \left(J^{a \to b}(\alpha^b)\right)^T$ with our scheme. Further, our added fictitious node has edge elements given by elements of v, and the Jacobian between that node and the subsequent layer is thus given by v^T. For a path $p = [(v_1, v_2), (v_2, v_3), ..., (v_{n-1}, v_n)]$ we define the flipped path with the added fictitious node as p^T as $p^T = [(v_n, v_{n-1}), ..., (v_2, v_1), (v_1, v_f)]$ and the reverse-order path $\neg p$ as $\neg p = [(v_{n-1}, v_n), ..., (v_2, v_3), (v_1, v_2)]$. For our modified graph we thus have the Jacobian for a path as

$$\prod_{(a,b) \in p^T} J^{a \to b}(\alpha^b) = \prod_{(a,b) \in p^T} \left(J^{b \to a}(\alpha^b)\right)^T \tag{15}$$

$$= v^T \left(\prod_{(a,b) \in p} J^{a \to b}(\alpha^b) \right)^T \tag{16}$$

$$= v^T \left(\prod_{(a,b) \in \neg p} J^{a \to b}(\alpha^b)^T \right) \tag{17}$$

Denoting the fictitious node as n_f and summing over all paths we thus get

$$\sum_{p^T \in \mathcal{P}(y, n_f)} \prod_{(a,b) \in p^t} J^{a \to b}(\alpha^b) \tag{18}$$

$$= \sum_{p^T \in \mathcal{P}(y, n_f)} v^T \left(\prod_{(a,b) \in \neg p} J^{a \to b}(\alpha^b)^T \right) \tag{19}$$

$$= v^T \sum_{p^T \in \mathcal{P}(y, n_f)} \left(\prod_{(a,b) \in \neg p} J^{a \to b}(\alpha^b)^T \right) \tag{20}$$

$$= v^T \left(\frac{dy}{dx} \right)^T = \left(\frac{dy}{dx} v \right)^T \tag{21}$$

which proves that working with the modified graph will yield the desired matrix-vector product $\frac{dy}{dx} v$ $\square$.

References

1. Abadi, M., et al.: TensorFlow: large-scale machine learning on heterogeneous systems (2015). Software available from tensorflow.org
2. Andriushchenko, M., Croce, F., Flammarion, N., Hein, M.: Square attack: a query-efficient black-box adversarial attack via random search. In: Vedaldi, A., Bischof, H., Brox, T., Frahm, J.-M. (eds.) ECCV 2020. LNCS, vol. 12368, pp. 484–501. Springer, Cham (2020). https://doi.org/10.1007/978-3-030-58592-1_29
3. Arani, E., Sarfraz, F., Zonooz, B.: Noise as a resource for learning in knowledge distillation. In: IEEE Winter Conference on Applications of Computer Vision, WACV 2021, Waikoloa, HI, USA, 3–8 January 2021, pp. 3128–3137. IEEE (2021)
4. Chen, S.-T., Cornelius, C., Martin, J., (Polo) Chau, D.H.: Shapeshifter: robust physical adversarial attack on faster R-CNN object detector. **11051**, 52–68 (2018)
5. Clanuwat, T., Bober-Irizar, M., Kitamoto, A., Lamb, A., Yamamoto, K., Ha, D.: Deep learning for classical japanese literature. CoRR, abs/1812.01718 (2018)
6. Collins, M.: Lecture notes on computational graphs, and backpropagation. Colombia University (2018). http://www.cs.columbia.edu/~mcollins/ff2.pdf. Accessed 19 Mar 2023
7. Dong, X., Luu, A.T., Lin, M., Yan, S., Zhang, H.: How should pre-trained language models be fine-tuned towards adversarial robustness? In: Ranzato, M., Beygelzimer, A., Dauphin, Y.N., Liang, P., Vaughan, J.W. (eds.), Advances in Neural Information Processing Systems 34: Annual Conference on Neural Information Processing Systems 2021, NeurIPS 2021, 6–14 December 2021, virtual, pp. 4356–4369 (2021)
8. Drucker, H., LeCun, Y.: Improving generalization performance using double backpropagation. IEEE Trans. Neural Networks **3**(6), 991–997 (1992)
9. Gu, S., Rigazio, L.: Towards deep neural network architectures robust to adversarial examples. In: Bengio, Y., LeCun, Y. (eds.) 3rd International Conference on Learning Representations, ICLR 2015, San Diego, CA, USA, May 7–9, 2015, Workshop Track Proceedings (2015)

10. Hanin, B., Rolnick, D.: Deep relu networks have surprisingly few activation patterns. In: Wallach, H.M., Larochelle, H., Beygelzimer, A., d'Alché-Buc, F., Fox, E.B., Garnett, R. (eds.), Advances in Neural Information Processing Systems 32: Annual Conference on Neural Information Processing Systems 2019, NeurIPS 2019, 8–14 December 2019, Vancouver, BC, Canada, pp. 359–368 (2019)

11. He, K., Zhang, X., Ren, S., Sun, J.: Deep residual learning for image recognition. In 2016 IEEE Conference on Computer Vision and Pattern Recognition, CVPR 2016, Las Vegas, NV, USA, 27–30 June, 2016, pp. 770–778. IEEE Computer Society (2016)

12. Hoffman, J., Roberts, D.A., Yaida, S.: Robust learning with Jacobian regularization. CoRR, abs/1908.02729 (2019)

13. Hull, J.J.: A database for handwritten text recognition research. IEEE Trans. Pattern Anal. Mach. Intell. **16**(5), 550–554 (1994)

14. Johnson, S.G.: Notes on the equivalence of norms

15. Kim, H.: Torchattacks: a pytorch repository for adversarial attacks. arXiv preprint arXiv:2010.01950 (2020)

16. Krizhevsky, A.: Learning multiple layers of features from tiny images. Technical report (2009)

17. Krogh, A., Hertz, J.A.: A simple weight decay can improve generalization. In: Moody, J.E., Hanson, S.J., Lippmann, R. (eds.) Advances in Neural Information Processing Systems 4, NIPS Conference, Denver, Colorado, USA, December 2–5, 1991, pp. 950–957. Morgan Kaufmann (1991)

18. Lecun, Y., Bottou, L., Bengio, Y., Haffner, P.: Gradient-based learning applied to document recognition. Proc. IEEE **86**(11), 2278–2324 (1998)

19. LeCun, Y., Cortes, C.: MNIST handwritten digit database (2010)

20. Madry, A., Makelov, A., Schmidt, L., Tsipras, D., Vladu, A.: Towards deep learning models resistant to adversarial attacks. In: 6th International Conference on Learning Representations, ICLR 2018, Vancouver, BC, Canada, April 30 - May 3, 2018, Conference Track Proceedings. OpenReview.net (2018)

21. Mathov, Y., Levy, E., Katzir, Z., Shabtai, A., Elovici, Y.: Not all datasets are born equal: on heterogeneous tabular data and adversarial examples. Knowl. Based Syst. **242**, 108377 (2022)

22. Morgulis, N., Kreines, A., Mendelowitz, S., Weisglass, Y.: Fooling a real car with adversarial traffic signs. CoRR, abs/1907.00374 (2019)

23. Nair, V., Hinton, G.E.: Rectified linear units improve restricted boltzmann machines. In: Fürnkranz, J., Joachims, T. (eds.) Proceedings of the 27th International Conference on Machine Learning (ICML-10), June 21–24, 2010, Haifa, Israel, pp. 807–814. Omnipress (2010)

24. Papernot, N., McDaniel, P.D., Wu, X., Jha, S., Swami, A.: Distillation as a defense to adversarial perturbations against deep neural networks. In: IEEE Symposium on Security and Privacy, SP 2016, San Jose, CA, USA, May 22–26, 2016, pp. 582–597. IEEE Computer Society (2016)

25. Paszke, A., et al.: Pytorch: an imperative style, high-performance deep learning library. In: Wallach, H.M., Larochelle, H., Beygelzimer, A., d'Alché-Buc, F., Fox, E.B., Garnett, R. (eds.) Advances in Neural Information Processing Systems 32: Annual Conference on Neural Information Processing Systems 2019, NeurIPS 2019, 8–14 December 2019, Vancouver, BC, Canada, pp. 8024–8035 (2019)

26. Silva, S.H., Najafirad, P.: Opportunities and challenges in deep learning adversarial robustness: a survey. CoRR, abs/2007.00753 (2020)

27. Simonyan, K., Zisserman, A.: Very deep convolutional networks for large-scale image recognition. In: Bengio, Y., LeCun, Y. (eds.) 3rd International Conference on Learning Representations, ICLR 2015, San Diego, CA, USA, May 7–9, 2015, Conference Track Proceedings (2015)
28. Sokolic, J., Giryes, R., Sapiro, G., Rodrigues, M.R.D.: Robust large margin deep neural networks. IEEE Trans. Signal Process. **65**(16), 4265–4280 (2017)
29. Vaswani, A., et al.: Attention is all you need. In: Guyon, I., et al. (eds.) Advances in Neural Information Processing Systems 30: Annual Conference on Neural Information Processing Systems 2017, December 4–9, 2017, Long Beach, CA, USA, pp. 5998–6008 (2017)
30. Xiao, H., Rasul, K., Vollgraf, R.: Fashion-mnist: a novel image dataset for benchmarking machine learning algorithms. CoRR, abs/1708.07747 (2017)
31. Yoshida, Y., Miyato, T.: Spectral norm regularization for improving the generalizability of deep learning. CoRR, abs/1705.10941 (2017)
32. Zhang, H., Yu, Y., Jiao, J., Xing, E.P., El Ghaoui, L., Jordan, M.I.: Theoretically principled trade-off between robustness and accuracy. In: Chaudhuri, K., Salakhutdinov, R. (eds.) Proceedings of the 36th International Conference on Machine Learning, ICML 2019, 9–15 June 2019, Long Beach, California, USA, volume 97 of Proceedings of Machine Learning Research, pp. 7472–7482. PMLR (2019)

Preprocessing Matters: Automated Pipeline Selection for Fair Classification

Vladimiro González-Zelaya[1], Julián Salas[2(✉)], Dennis Prangle[3],
and Paolo Missier[4]

[1] Universidad Panamericana, Facultad de Ciencias Económicas y Empresariales,
Mexico City, Mexico
`cvgonzalez@up.edu.mx`
[2] Internet Interdisciplinary Institute, Universitat Oberta de Catalunya,
Barcelona, Spain
`jsalaspi@uoc.edu`
[3] University of Bristol, Institute for Statistical Science, Bristol, UK
`dennis.prangle@bristol.ac.uk`
[4] Newcastle University, School of Computing, Newcastle upon Tyne, UK
`paolo.missier@ncl.ac.uk`

Abstract. Improving fairness by manipulating the preprocessing stages of classification pipelines is an active area of research, closely related to AutoML. We propose a genetic optimisation algorithm, FAIRPIPES, which optimises for user-defined combinations of fairness and accuracy and for multiple definitions of fairness, providing flexibility in the fairness-accuracy trade-off. FAIRPIPES heuristically searches through a large space of pipeline configurations, achieving near-optimality efficiently, presenting the user with an estimate of the solutions' Pareto front. We also observe that the optimal pipelines differ for different datasets, suggesting that no "universal best" pipeline exists and confirming that FAIRPIPES fills a niche in the *fairness-aware AutoML* space.

Keywords: Algorithmic Fairness · AutoML · Data Preprocessing · Ethical AI · Genetic Algorithms · Preprocessing Pipelines

1 Introduction

The prevalence of decision-making mechanisms in life-impacting decisions, ranging from bank loans to probation decisions, makes understanding and controlling the *fairness* of automated decisions indispensable, pushing *fairness-aware* Machine Learning to the forefront of ML research. Many definitions of fairness have been proposed [19] with no definitive agreement [12]. Regardless of the specific metric adopted to measure fairness, it is broadly accepted that the origins of *unfairness* can be traced back to training data [9]; in this regard, the database community ideally positioned to help fix this problem [29,30]. The focus of this paper is on the data preprocessing steps that are deployed to transform the raw input data into its final form as a training set, and on their effect on the fairness of

V. Torra and Y. Narukawa (Eds.): MDAI 2023, LNAI 13890, pp. 202–213, 2023.
https://doi.org/10.1007/978-3-031-33498-6_14

the resulting model. Several catalogues and classifications have been proposed for data preprocessing operators, e.g., by ML Bazaar [28], Orange [10] and others [13].

A summary of the most common preprocessing steps is given in Table 1, where the operators are grouped into five categories: encoders, imputers, scalers, samplers, and feature selectors; the top row lists the strategies considered in this paper. Some of these steps are required by the classification framework, e.g., encoding categorical variables and imputing missing data, while others may optionally be deployed to improve model performance, e.g., class balancing, scaling and feature selection. These steps are generally selected and combined into pipelines based on best practice considerations, with model performance as the main objective [25]. While the effect of preprocessing on classification performance has been analysed for individual operators [8,14,32], we study the effect of such preprocessing on the fairness of the resulting classifier.

Table 1. Preprocessors offered by FAIRPIPES and other AutoML packages.

Package	Encoders	Imputers	Scalers	Samplers	Feature Selectors
FAIRPIPES	One-Hot, LOO, Target, Count, WoE, Ordinal	Mean, Median, Most Frequent	Quantile, Normalizer, MinMax, MaxAbs, None	Over, Under, None	K-Best, None
TPOT	One-Hot	Median	Robust, Standard, MinMax, MaxAbs, None	None	Polynomial, None
ML Bazaar	Categorical, Label	Mean	MinMax, MaxAbs, Robust, None	None	SelectFromModel, None
auto-sklearn	One-Hot	Mean	Normalizer, None	None	PCA, Polynomial, Extra Trees, None
H2O	Target	Mean, Median, Most Frequent	None	Over, Under, None	None

1.1 Related Work

Fairness-aware preprocessing is usually attained by applying fairness-specific methods, e.g., [4,7,15,18,26]. However, these are not always readily available, and they may cause undesired side-effects such as loss of accuracy, since they involve the introduction of synthetic data into the original dataset, e.g., by synthetic oversampling [6] or by feature engineering [20]. It is important to note that

FairPipes *does not* directly compete with these methods. Instead, FairPipes can easily be adapted to incorporate them to its pipeline search-space.

Evolutionary optimisation algorithms have shown to work well in many real-world applications, particularly on two-objective problems [17,22]. Specifically, they have been used to optimise specific data preprocessing tasks, e.g., for feature selection [31] and data correction [1], as well as to build full preprocessing pipelines, e.g., TPOT [24].

1.2   Fairness

In this work we focus on binary classification tasks with positive class 1 and negative class 0, and a single binary protected attribute (PA). This is a user-selected attribute that is considered sensitive and with respect to which fairness is defined. The two values of the PA determine a two-way partition of the training set. For each of the two groups, their positive rate (PR) is the proportion of positive instances found in the corresponding training subset. The group with higher PR is denoted as *favoured* (F), while the other is the *unfavoured* group (U). If necessary, the single binary PA requirement may be relaxed to support multiple multi-class PAs by considering a "combined" binary PA, which may be obtained through a linear combination of each instance's subgroup PRs, as explained in [15]. While our approach is agnostic to several group-fairness metrics, in our experiments we focus on one of the most commonly seen in the literature, demographic parity (DP), defined in [19] as:

$$\text{DP}(\hat{Y}) := |P(\hat{Y} = 1 \mid \text{PA} = F) - P(\hat{Y} = 1 \mid \text{PA} = U)|,$$

where small DP values indicate a "fairer" model.

1.3   Problem Formulation

It has been shown that preprocessing choices have an impact over the fairness of a classifier, as they can cause side-effects such as an increase in the under-representation of minority groups [35]. Our goal is to automatically generate "fairness-aware" pipelines, where the data scientist has control over the well-known trade-off between the fairness and the performance of a classifier [23]. We formulate FairPipes as a multi-objective optimisation problem, working over pre-processing pipelines, as follows.

Given a universe of configurable data processing operators (as in Table 1) and a target performance–fairness objective (for some choice of fairness definition), we want to find a sequence of configured operators that forms an optimal pipeline with respect to the target.

For any decision problem involving two or more optimisation objectives, a point in the solution space (i.e., a specific configured pipeline) is said to be *Pareto-efficient* (or Pareto-optimal) if none of the individual objectives can be improved without worsening at least one of the other objectives.

The set of all Pareto-efficient solutions is called the *Pareto front* [36]. In our setting, the Pareto front consists of all the pipelines such that fairness *and* performance cannot improve *at the same time*.

A naive approach to addressing the problem is to consider each possible pipeline as an ordered combination of operators, learn a classifier for each of those, and calculate both its accuracy and its fairness (note that this is a vector of values, one for each of the fairness metrics). This is a combinatorial problem, however. For example, there are 3,240 such pipelines in our test bed, resulting from five operator families with varying number of options: six encoders, three imputers, five scalers, three re-samplers, two feature selectors and six possible orderings. To address this complexity we take a heuristic approach.

1.4   Contributions and Overview of Results

We introduce FAIRPIPES, a genetic algorithm producing fairness-aware prepro-cessing pipelines that are optimised for any combination of fairness and accu-racy, for three different exemplar definitions of fairness. FAIRPIPES presents the data scientist with an estimate of the pipeline space's Pareto front, providing them with performance–fairness trade-offs. We present an extensive experimen-tal evaluation of the approach using four benchmark datasets: *Adult Income (Income)* [11], *COMPAS* [21], *German Credit (German)* [11] and *Titanic* [5], and a universe of 3,240 pipeline configurations. Using this test bed, we show that pipelines that are measurably close to the Pareto front for the chosen multi-objectives are discovered by exploring about 6% of the search space.

Our experimental results, presented in Sect. 3, show that (i) fairness and per-formance stand in contrast with each other, as expected [18], and (ii) FAIRPIPES converges on pipelines that optimise for different objectives. In our setting, eval-uating the performance of 200 out of 3,240 possible pipelines—roughly 6% of them—lead to estimated Pareto fronts with the average instance in the estimate less than 0.04 DP/ACC units away from a true Pareto instance.

2   FAIRPIPES

FAIRPIPES performs a genetic-algorithm search [34] over the space of all pre-processing pipelines[1]. In our experimental setting, pipelines are characterised by six *genes*, the first five representing a choice for each of the preprocessor options presented in the FAIRPIPES row of Table 1, with the sixth one representing the order in which the operators are applied over the data; this preprocessor set was selected as a representative sample of they typical data preprocessing pipeline, but by no means is FAIRPIPES restricted to these, as it may easily be extended with any preprocessor that adheres to `scikit-learn`'s *fit-transform* paradigm.

FAIRPIPES optimises a linear combination of fairness and performance met-rics to turn fairness and accuracy into a single objective. Single-objective metrics

---

[1] FAIRPIPES is available at https://github.com/vladoxNCL/fairPipes.

are a particular case, e.g., DP = 1 × DP + 0 × ACC. It has four tunable parameters: n_gen: the number of generations, n: the number of pipelines per generation, c: the proportion of crossed-over pipelines in the next generation and m: the probability of a *gene* mutation.

2.1 The FAIRPIPES Algorithm

The FAIRPIPES algorithm is now presented using the example in Fig. 1, with reference to the corresponding methods in Algorithms 1, 2 and 3.

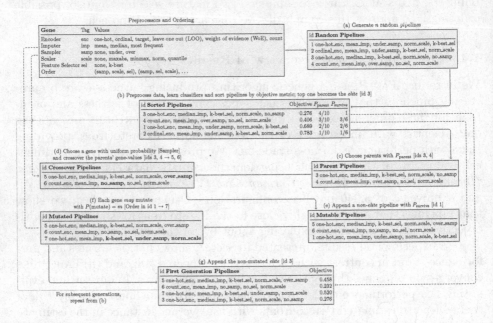

Fig. 1. A FAIRPIPES run over *Income*, with population size $n = 4$, crossover rate $c = 0.5$, mutation rate $m = 0.4$ and objective DP + (1 − ACC).

Step (a) — Initialisation: FAIRPIPES generates n random pipelines by choosing one option per gene for each pipeline (`GenPipes` in Algorithm 1).

Step (b) consists of two parts:

Evaluation: n copies of the raw dataset are separately processed through each of these pipelines, with the resulting processed datasets train/test split. Binary classifiers, e.g., logistic regression (LR), are learnt from each of the training sets and the objective metrics are evaluated on the corresponding test sets (`GetMetrics` in Algorithm 2).

Selection: Pipelines are ranked and sorted with respect to the objective. The best-ranking pipeline becomes the *elite*, i.e., it will move onto the next generation unmodified. The *elite* is kept in order to guarantee that the next generation will be at least as good as the current one with respect to its *best* individual.

Rank in Algorithm 1 then assigns the i-th pipeline a probability of becoming "parent" of a pair of next generation "children" pipelines

$$P_{\text{parent}}(i) = \frac{n+1-i}{\sum\limits_{k=1}^{n} k} \quad \text{for } i \in \{1, \ldots n\},$$

and a probability for the *non-elites* of "surviving" for the next generation of

$$P_{\text{survive}}(i) = \frac{n+1-i}{\sum\limits_{k=1}^{n-1} k} \quad \text{for } i \in \{2, \ldots n\}.$$

Algorithm 3 consists of steps (c), (d), (e), (f) and (g).

Steps (c) and (d) — Crossover: are repeated $\lfloor c \cdot n \rfloor / 2$ times. Each time two parents are chosen without replacement with probability $P_{\text{parent}}()$. One of the six genes, randomly selected, is swapped between the two parents, and the resulting pipelines are appended to the *next_gen* list. The main reason for swapping over just one gene is to reduce the variability between parents and children, given that there are only six genes to modify. In standard genetic-algorithm terminology, this is a *two-point crossover* with consecutive crossover points.

Step (e) — Selection: $n - \lfloor c \cdot n \rfloor - 1$ different *non-elite* pipelines are chosen with probability $P_{\text{survive}}()$ and appended to *next_gen*. This second part of the *selection* process again makes use of probabilities to allow for a small chance of additional exploration, at the expense of exploitation [3].

Step (f) — Mutation: Each *gene* of every *next_gen* pipeline may *mutate* once with probability m into a different random option of the same kind, e.g., an encoder may mutate into another encoder, but not into an imputer.

Step (g) — Selection: The *elite* pipeline is appended to *next_gen* unmodified, completing the next generation. The *elite* is added at the end to prevent it from mutating.

This process is repeated from step (b) *n_gen* times, using the previous generation's *next_gen* instead of a random pipeline list to continue after the first generation.

3   Experimental Evaluation

As a baseline for the computational cost of using FAIRPIPES, an exhaustive search over *Income*, evaluating all 3,240 pipelines, takes an average of 25 min on a *Microsoft Azure d64as_v4* VM with 64 vCPUs and 256 GB of RAM. An average FAIRPIPES run evaluates 200 pipelines—roughly 6% of the search space—in less than 1.5 min under the same configuration. A comparison of the average FAIRPIPES run time using a single Azure vCPU with 220 replicates per dataset over the four analysed datasets is presented in Table 2.

Algorithm 1: The FAIRPIPES algorithm.

input : D: dataset to process, with binary PA-and-label, pp_options: dict of preprocessors and task order,
        n_gens: number of generations to run,
        pop_size: number of pipelines per generation,
        clf: classifier,
        policy: optimisation strategy to follow,
        co_rate: crossover rate,
        mut_rate: mutation rate
output: pareto_front: Estimated front for the pp_options space

/* Generate pipe_pop, a pipeline list of size pop_size. The pipelines are built by randomly choosing an element of each of
    pp_options: *encoder, imputer, feat_selector, sampler, scaler* and *permutation* */

pipe_pop ← GenPipes(pp_options, pop_size);
all_metrics ← empty_df;   // Empty data frame to store pipeline metrics
for i ← 1 to n_gens **do**
    processed_dsets ← {pipeline(D) | pipeline ∈ pipe_pop};
    metrics_df ← GetMetrics(processed_dsets, clf);   // Algorithm 2
    ranked ← Rank(pipe_pop, metrics_df, policy);
    pipe_pop ← GetNextGen(ranked, co_rate, mut_rate);   // Algorithm 3
    all_metrics ← Append(all_metrics, metrics_df);

pareto_front ← GetPareto(all_metrics);   // Locate non-dominated pipelines.

Algorithm 2: GetMetrics method.

input : processed_dsets: list of preprocessed datasets,
        clf: classifier,
        k: number of cross-validation folds
output: metrics_df: data frame of fairness and accuracy (ACC) metrics

metrics_df ← empty_df;
foreach D in processed_dsets **do**
    trains, tests ← KFoldSplit(D, k);
    metrics_list ← empty_list;
    for i ← 1 to k **do**
        clf ← Fit(clf, trains[i]);
        preds ← Predict(clf, tests[i]);
        metrics_fold ← GetFairnessPerformance(preds);
        metrics_list ← Append(metrics_list, metrics_fold);

    metrics_average ← Average(metrics_list);
    metrics_df ← Append(metrics_df, metrics_average);

Algorithm 3: GetNextGen method.

input : ranked: ordered list of pipelines,
        co_rate: proportion of crossovers in next_gen,
        mut_rate: probability of a gene mutation
output: next_gen: pipeline list of length |ranked|

elite ← ranked[1];   // the best-ranked pipeline
next_gen ← empty_list;   // stores next generation
n_child ← Round_to_Integer(co_rate * |ranked|);   // round to nearest integer
while |next_gen| < n_child **do**
    {p_1, p_2} ← Parents(ranked);   // select p_1, p_2 with rank-dependant probability
    {c_1, c_2} ← Crossover(p_1, p_2);   // select gene and swap values for p_1, p_2 */
    /* prevents duplicate pipelines
    if c_1 and c_2 not in next_gen **then**
        next_gen ← Append(next_gen, c_1);
        next_gen ← Append(next_gen, c_2);

/* −1 kept for elite space   */
while |next_gen| < |ranked| − 1 **do**
    s ← Survive(ranked \ {elite});   // select s with rank-dependant probability */
    /* prevents duplicate pipelines
    if s not in next_gen **then**
        next_gen ← Append(next_gen, s);

foreach pipe in next_gen **do**
    foreach gene in pipe **do**
        gene ← Mutate(gene, mut_rate);   // modify gene with probability mut_rate

next_gen ← Append(next_gen, elite);   // elite is kept for next generation

Table 2. Size and average FAIRPIPES run time for the analysed datasets.

Dataset	Attributes	Instances	Avg FAIRPIPES Run (s)	Per 100 Datum (s)
Income	14	32561	2472.12 ± 2462.97	0.5424
COMPAS	27	11038	539.93 ± 246.94	0.1812
German	22	1000	93.07 ± 23.43	0.4230
Titanic	10	891	44.48 ± 12.29	0.4992

As may be seen, when normalised per 100 datum, the run times are similar across datasets. All experiments were conducted over the space of pipelines obtained from all possible combinations of the preprocessors listed in the FAIRPIPES row of Table 1, consisting of 3,240 data points. Although the most typically used preprocessors have been included, FAIRPIPES can be further extended to include additional tasks, as long as they comply with the fit/transform interface used by *sci-kit learn*.

3.1 Baseline Mapping of the Search Space

ACC and fairness values for *all* of the pipelines in the search space were computed. LR was used throughout, owing to its fast training and ease of interpretability. Each training instance included 4-fold cross-validation with a fixed random seed. The crossover and mutation rates were based on the literature [16] and further fine-tuned by running FAIRPIPES 128 replicates, optimising for DP + ACC. Fairness and ACC metrics were collected for each pipeline and dataset, replicating each training session 64 times using different random seeds for robustness. The default parameters for FAIRPIPES were used in all the experiments: 0.6 crossover rate, 0.4 mutation rate, populations of 10 individuals, 20 generations per run, and 1-elitism.

DP/ACC Evolution. Figure 2 shows how the solutions approach optimality (bottom left corner in the DP/ACC space) for different linear combinations of the objective. Interestingly, for all datasets except *Titanic*, the initial random pipelines lie on the top right of the space, indicating poor fairness as well as poor ACC. FAIRPIPES achieves a combination of both, when the objectives are not initially in contrast with one another. *Titanic* shows that, under certain circumstances, DP and ACC can become mutually exclusive: the "fairer" a model gets (both sexes receive a similar predicted death-rate), the less accurate it will become, as in reality most men died and most women lived.

4 Performance Evaluation

To the best of the authors' knowledge, there are no other existing pipeline-optimisation solutions that include fairness as a single or multi-goal objective.

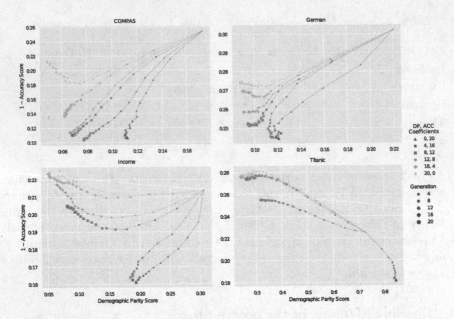

Fig. 2. Average DP and ACC per generation for different objective coefficients.

As a baseline to compare FAIRPIPES's performance, two performance metrics were used:

Averaged Hausdorff Distance (AHD). A *global* metric defined in [2,27] as

$$\text{AHD}(X,Y) := \frac{1}{2}\left(\frac{1}{|X|}\sum_{x \in X}\min_{y \in Y}d(x,y) + \frac{1}{|Y|}\sum_{y \in Y}\min_{x \in X}d(x,y)\right),$$

which measures the similarity of the *estimated* and *true* Pareto fronts.
Best to Best Distance (B2B). A *local* similarity metric, defined as

$$\text{B2B}(X,Y) := \min_{x \in X}\left[k_{\text{DP}}\text{DP}(x) + k_{\text{ACC}}\text{ACC}(x)\right]$$
$$- \min_{y \in Y}\left[k_{\text{DP}}\text{DP}(y) + k_{\text{ACC}}\text{ACC}(y)\right],$$

comparing the best pipeline found by FAIRPIPES against the overall best.

The similarity metrics were measured on random pipeline selections with a size equivalent to 20 FAIRPIPES generations, i.e., 210 pipelines. Eleven representative DP/ACC linear combinations were used as objective values, and the resulting metrics were averaged out for averaged Hausdorff distance (AHD) and best to best distance (B2B). These measurements were replicated and averaged 128 times for every benchmark dataset, and a two-sample t-test was performed using *SciPy* [33]. Table 3, shows that FAIRPIPES outperforms random sampling for AHD, albeit not significantly.

In the case of B2B, the difference is significant for every dataset, as the average B2B for FAIRPIPES is 34–55% smaller than for random sampling. This indicates that FAIRPIPES did not only estimate the Pareto front adequately, but estimated the optimal pipeline much better than random search. The computing-time difference between running FAIRPIPES and performing the equivalent random search is negligible, as FAIRPIPES' genetic selection mechanism takes virtually no time to be computed.

Table 3. Performance comparison between FAIRPIPES after 20 generations and a random pipeline sample without replacement of the same size (210 pipelines). For both metrics, lower values are better.

		FAIRPIPES		Random Sample		Two-Sample t-Test	
Metric	Dataset	Mean	SD	Mean	SD	t-value	p-value
AHD	COMPAS	**0.0049**	0.0050	0.0050	0.0048	−0.1666	.867
	German	**0.0053**	0.0032	0.0059	0.0019	−2.3357	**.019**
	Income	**0.0030**	0.0019	0.0032	0.0015	−0.8856	.376
	Titanic	0.0048	0.0038	**0.0042**	0.0023	1.8093	.071
B2B	COMPAS	**0.0021**	0.0132	0.0032	0.0154	−1.9686	**.049**
	German	**0.0699**	0.1319	0.1070	0.1513	−6.9388	**< .001**
	Income	**0.0063**	0.0204	0.0099	0.0210	−4.6448	**< .001**
	Titanic	**0.0121**	0.0596	0.0270	0.0977	−4.8908	**< .001**

5   Conclusions

This work presents FAIRPIPES, a genetic-algorithm approach for the discovery of data preprocessing pipelines that are near-Pareto-optimal with respect to both the fairness and performance of binary classifiers learnt from the data. FAIRPIPES can optimise user-defined objective metrics defined through both linear combinations of fairness and accuracy, presenting its users with estimates of the pipeline space's Pareto front, allowing them to select an adequate fairness/performance trade-off. Besides an adequate estimation of the Pareto front, FAIRPIPES significantly improves the estimation of the best pipeline for a given objective metric over an equivalent random pipeline search with an insignificant increase in computing time. In further work, additional preprocessing operators may be introduced, as well as other types of classifiers, and higher-dimensional Pareto fronts may be explored, e.g., optimising for several fairness and performance metrics at once.

References

1. Andersson, F.O., Kaiser, R., Jacobsson, S.P.: Data preprocessing by wavelets and genetic algorithms for enhanced multivariate analysis of LC peptide mapping. J. Pharm. Biomed. Anal. **34**(3), 531–541 (2004)

2. Aydin, O.U., et al.: On the usage of average Hausdorff distance for segmentation performance assessment: hidden error when used for ranking. Europ. Radiol. Exp. **5**(1), 1–7 (2021)
3. Berger-Tal, O., Nathan, J., Meron, E., Saltz, D.: The exploration-exploitation dilemma: a multidisciplinary framework. PLoS ONE **9**(4), e95693 (2014)
4. Calmon, F., Wei, D., Vinzamuri, B., Natesan Ramamurthy, K., Varshney, K.R.: Optimized pre-processing for discrimination prevention. Adv. Neural. Inf. Process. Syst. **30**, 3992–4001 (2017)
5. Cason, T.E.: Titanic Dataset. http://biostat.app.vumc.org/wiki/Main/DataSets (1999). Accessed 25 May 2021
6. Chawla, N.V., Lazarevic, A., Hall, L.O., Bowyer, K.W.: SMOTEBoost: improving prediction of the minority class in boosting. In: Lavrač, N., Gamberger, D., Todorovski, L., Blockeel, H. (eds.) PKDD 2003. LNCS (LNAI), vol. 2838, pp. 107–119. Springer, Heidelberg (2003). https://doi.org/10.1007/978-3-540-39804-2_12
7. Chiappa, S., Gillam, T.P.: Path-specific counterfactual fairness. arXiv preprint arXiv:1802.08139 (2018)
8. Crone, S.F., Lessmann, S., Stahlbock, R.: The impact of preprocessing on data mining: an evaluation of classifier sensitivity in direct marketing. Eur. J. Oper. Res. **173**(3), 781–800 (2006)
9. Danks, D., London, A.J.: Algorithmic bias in autonomous systems. In: IJCAI, vol. 17, pp. 4691–4697 (2017)
10. Demšar, J., et al.: Orange: data mining toolbox in python. J. Mach. Learn. **14**(1), 2349–2353 (2013)
11. Dua, D., Graff, C.: UCI machine learning repository (2017). http://archive.ics.uci.edu/ml/
12. Friedler, S.A., Scheidegger, C., Venkatasubramanian, S.: The (im) possibility of fairness: different value systems require different mechanisms for fair decision making. Commun. ACM **64**(4), 136–143 (2021)
13. García, S., Ramírez-Gallego, S., Luengo, J., Benítez, J.M., Herrera, F.: Big data preprocessing: methods and prospects. Big Data Anal. **1**(1), 9 (2016). https://doi.org/10.1186/s41044-016-0014-0
14. González-Zelaya, V.: Towards explaining the effects of data preprocessing on machine learning. In: 2019 IEEE 35th International Conference on Data Engineering (ICDE), pp. 2086–2090. IEEE (2019)
15. González-Zelaya, V., Salas, J., Prangle, D., Missier, P.: Optimising fairness through parametrised data sampling. In: Proceedings of the 2021 EDBT Conference (2021)
16. Hassanat, A., Almohammadi, K., Alkafaween, E., Abunawas, E., Hammouri, A., Prasath, V.: Choosing mutation and crossover ratios for genetic algorithms-a review with a new dynamic approach. Information **10**(12), 390 (2019)
17. Ishibuchi, H., Tsukamoto, N., Nojima, Y.: Evolutionary many-objective optimization: A short review. In: 2008 IEEE congress on evolutionary computation (IEEE world congress on computational intelligence), pp. 2419–2426. IEEE (2008)
18. Kamiran, F., Calders, T.: Data preprocessing techniques for classification without discrimination. Knowl. Inf. Syst. **33**(1), 1–33 (2012)
19. Kusner, M., Loftus, J., Russell, C., Silva, R.: Counterfactual fairness. In: Proceedings of the 31st International Conference on Neural Information Processing Systems, pp. 4069–4079 (2017)
20. La Cava, W., Moore, J.H.: Genetic programming approaches to learning fair classifiers. In: Proceedings of the 2020 Genetic and Evolutionary Computation Conference, pp. 967–975 (2020)

21. Larson, J., Mattu, S., Kirchner, L., Angwin, J.: How we analyzed the compas recidivism algorithm. ProPublica **5**, 9 (2016)
22. Li, M., Yang, S., Liu, X.: Bi-goal evolution for many-objective optimization problems. Artif. Intell. **228**, 45–65 (2015)
23. Menon, A.K., Williamson, R.C.: The cost of fairness in binary classification. In: Conference on Fairness, Accountability and Transparency, pp. 107–118. PMLR (2018)
24. Olson, R.S., Moore, J.H.: TPOT: a tree-based pipeline optimization tool for automating machine learning. In: Workshop on Automatic Machine Learning, pp. 66–74. PMLR (2016)
25. Pyle, D.: Data preparation for data mining. Morgan Kaufmann (1999)
26. Salas, J., González-Zelaya, V.: Fair-MDAV: an algorithm for fair privacy by microaggregation. In: Torra, V., Narukawa, Y., Nin, J., Agell, N. (eds.) MDAI 2020. LNCS (LNAI), vol. 12256, pp. 286–297. Springer, Cham (2020). https://doi.org/10.1007/978-3-030-57524-3_24
27. Schutze, O., Esquivel, X., Lara, A., Coello, C.A.C.: Using the averaged Hausdorff distance as a performance measure in evolutionary multiobjective optimization. IEEE Trans. Evol. Comput. **16**(4), 504–522 (2012)
28. Smith, M.J., Sala, C., Kanter, J.M., Veeramachaneni, K.: The machine learning bazaar: Harnessing the ml ecosystem for effective system development. In: Proceedings of the 2020 ACM SIGMOD International Conference on Management of Data, pp. 785–800 (2020)
29. Stoyanovich, J., Howe, B., Jagadish, H.: Responsible data management. Proceed. VLDB Endow. **13**(12), 3474–3488 (2020)
30. Stoyanovich, J., Howe, B., Jagadish, H., Miklau, G.: Panel: a debate on data and algorithmic ethics. Proceed. VLDB Endow. **11**(12), 2165–2167 (2018)
31. Tan, F., Fu, X., Zhang, Y., Bourgeois, A.G.: A genetic algorithm-based method for feature subset selection. Soft. Comput. **12**(2), 111–120 (2008)
32. Uysal, A.K., Gunal, S.: The impact of preprocessing on text classification. Inf. Process. Manage. **50**(1), 104–112 (2014)
33. Virtanen, P., et al.: SciPy 1.0: fundamental algorithms for scientific computing in python. Nat. Methods **17**(3), 261–272 (2020)
34. Whitley, D.: A genetic algorithm tutorial. Stat. Comput. **4**(2), 65–85 (1994)
35. Yang, K., Huang, B., Stoyanovich, J., Schelter, S.: Fairness-aware instrumentation of preprocessing pipelines for machine learning. In: Workshop on Human-In-the-Loop Data Analytics (HILDA2020) (2020)
36. Yoo, S., Harman, M.: Pareto efficient multi-objective test case selection. In: Proceedings of the 2007 International Symposium on Software Testing and Analysis, pp. 140–150 (2007)

Predicting Next Whereabouts Using Deep Learning

Ana-Paula Galarreta[1] , Hugo Alatrista-Salas[1(✉)] ,
and Miguel Nunez-del-Prado[1,2,3]

[1] Pontificia Universidad Católica del Perú, San Miguel 15088, Peru
{a.galarreta,halatrista}@pucp.edu.pe
[2] Peru Research, Development and Innovation Center (Peru IDI), Lima, Peru
[3] Instituto de investigación de la Universidad de Andina del Cusco, Cusco, Peru
miguel.nunezdelprado@vrin.uandina.edu.pe

Abstract. Trajectory prediction is a key task in the study of human mobility. This task can be done by considering a sequence of GPS locations and using different mechanisms to predict the following point that will be visited. The trajectory prediction is usually performed using methods like Markov Chains or architectures that rely on Recurrent Neural Networks (RNN). However, the use of Transformers neural networks has lately been adopted for sequential prediction tasks because of the increased efficiency achieved in training. In this paper, we propose AP-Traj (Attention and Possible directions for TRAJectory), which predicts a user's next location based on the self-attention mechanism of the transformers encoding and a directed graph representing the road segments of the area visited. Our method achieves results comparable to the state-of-the-art model for this task but is up to 10 times faster.

Keywords: Trajectory prediction · Transformers · Node prediction ·
Self-attention · Neural Network

1 Introduction

Spatiotemporal data allow us to understand complex phenomena simultaneously involving spatial and temporal dynamics. Specifically, several moving objects equipped with GPS sensors broadcast accurate information about their movements. The analysis of moving objects has gained much relevance in recent years, and it has been successfully applied in tasks of predicting the following positions of various moving objects, such as ships, animals and humans [2,8,10,12,13]. As many applications were developed, techniques for exploring moving objects' trajectories are growing. Markov chain [5], RNN and LSTM models were usually applied when the sequence of positions represented trajectories. Other techniques were used to improve the quality of next-position predictions. Nevertheless, few papers tackled the time consumption problem when generating the model for predicting a moving object's next position. Indeed, due to the nature of the phenomena described by the study of moving objects, prediction tasks must be fast, for example, to avoid possible vehicle collisions. This paper proposes a new model called Attention and Possible directions for TRAJectory prediction - AP-Traj. This method predicts future trajectories based on the past street intersections (nodes) visited by the user and a graph of the travelled area. This is achieved using a node self-attention module, a possible directions module, and embedding the input sequence's last node. The first module takes the self-attention mechanism in the transformer's encoding to capture the dependencies between nodes. The second uses a graph to determine the possible directions that can be taken from an original node so the user can get to the adjacent one. Our results show that our proposal has results comparable to the state-of-the-art model for this task (superior for 3 out of 4 tested datasets) but is considerably faster (up to 10 times faster).

The remainder of this study is organised as follows. First, Sect. 2 shows scientific studies about trajectory prediction. Section 3 detailed the methodology used in this contribution. Then, Sect. 4 detailed the heart of our contribution. Section 5 presents the experiments and results. This contribution ends with the conclusions and future research directions detailed in Sect. 6.

2   State of the Art

Several studies for trajectory prediction were proposed in the literature. Transformers were first used in the Natural Language Processing field. Vaswani *et al.* [14] propose the Transformer, an attention mechanism to perform sequence prediction for a machine-translation task. The authors use an encoder-decoder structure that, instead of using recurrence and convolutions, is based only on attention mechanisms. In order to preserve information regarding the order of the sequence, positional encodings are added to the input embeddings. The authors used the BLEU (bilingual evaluation understudy) metric to evaluate the performance of Transformers in two datasets, an English-german one (4.5M sentence pairs) and an English-french one (36M sentences). For the first dataset, a score of 28.4 was obtained, outperforming previous models. For the second dataset, a score of 41.0 was achieved. In addition, the model training step was four times faster than architectures based on recurrent or convolutional layers.

Other papers concentrate on time series forecasting through the use of Transformers. For instance, Grigsby, Wang, and Qi [6] propose Spacetimeformer, a method that uses transformers for multivariate time series forecasting. Given a sequence of multivariate vectors, the proposed model relies heavily on using embeddings to pre-process the different variables (such as power produced in a solar plant, weather, latitude, longitude and time) and produce a sequence that can be fed into a transformers module. The Spacetimeformer was evaluated on the weather dataset (6 variables, 569K timesteps), a solar energy production dataset (137 variables, 52K timesteps) and two traffic forecasting datasets (207 and 325 variables, 34K and 52K timesteps). The baselines were methods based on regression, LSTM and GNN. An MSE of 21.35 was obtained for the weather dataset using Spacetimeformer, against an MSE of 22.11 when using LSTM.

In the same spirit, [9] proposes NetTraj, a method that predicts the trajectory of a vehicle based on its past trajectory, a graph of the city and context information characterised by the week's hour, vehicle or driver identifier and weather conditions. For the prediction task, each trajectory is represented as a sequence of nodes (street intersections) and associated movement directions (eight possible directions to take from a node). Both inputs are encoded using an embedding layer. Then, a spatial attention mechanism uses the city graph to compute the importance score of each adjacent node. This information is fed into a Long-Short Term Memory (LSTM) encoder-decoder module with a temporal attention mechanism. Finally, the embeddings of the context features are concatenated with the output of the LSTM, followed by a linear layer to predict the sequence of directions to obtain the output nodes. The proposal was evaluated on the Beijing Taxi and the Shanghai Trajectories Data containing 15M and 4M records, respectively. The authors compared their results with Markov Chains, LSTM, Convolutional Sequence Embedding Recommendation Model (Caser), Attentional LSTM Encoder-Decoder, Attentional Spatiotemporal LSTM, Self-Attention Based Sequential Model and Geography-Aware Self-Attention Network.

Feng *et al.* [4] proposes a multi-step methodology. First, trajectories were split into the current and past trajectories. Later, the one-hot vectors of these features are fed into a multimodal embedding module. In parallel, a context adapter module uses the embeddings of the POI label, user text and dwell time to model the semantic effects of the current location. The former trajectory's information is fed into a recurrent LSTM module. Finally, all these inputs are combined into three independent linear layers that predict the next location, time and activity of the user. The proposal was evaluated on four datasets: Foursquare check-in data of NYC with 82K records, 10K locations) and Tokyo (537K records, 21K locations), Mobile application location data (15M records, 31K locations), and Call detail records (491K records, 17K locations). Finally, the proposal was compared with five baseline algorithms: Markov, Periodic Mobility Model (PMM), Factorizing personalized Markov chains (FPMC), Geo-teaser and SimpleRNN.

Similarly, in [3], the authors tackle problems such as the sequential transition regularities and the heterogeneity and sparsity of data in the POI recommendation task. So, the authors propose a 3-step algorithm called DeNavi (Deep Navigator). Also, the authors integrated the Exponential Weight Moving Average EWMA model into the model learning process to capture the spatiotemporal context in the prediction process. Two public LBSN datasets were used to test the proposal: Gowalla and BrightKite, with 6.4 million and 4.5 million trajectories, respectively. DeNavi was compared with nine state-of-the-art algorithms through accuracy, precision, recall and F-measure.

Also, [15] describes the PreCLN (Pretrained-based Contrastive Learning Network) transformer-based algorithm that embeds the input trajectory sequences into fixed-length representations. The authors used three metrics to compare it with five state-of-the-art algorithms. The proposal was tested on the Porto taxi trajectory with 1.7 million complete trajectories and the T-drive trajectory dataset containing about 17 million trajectories. The authors conclude that Pre-CLN tackled the problem of unlabeled trajectory data with contrastive learning and pre-training techniques.

In the same vein, Ye, Martin and Raubal [7] predict the next location a user will visit based on its past locations, time of visit and travel mode. First, the embeddings of the location, time of the day (grouped into 15-minute bins), day of the week, travel mode and user were calculated. Then, all the embeddings are added along a positional encoding. The resulting vector is fed into the transformer decoder. Later, the output vector is concatenated with the user embedding and fed into a fully-connected residual block. Finally, using two linear layers, the aggregated vector is used to predict the next location and the next travel mode. The model was tested against Markov models, Deepmove, LSTM, MobTcast and LSTM with self-attention using the Green Class (GC) study and the Yumuv study datasets. Both datasets contain the GPS trajectories of 139 and 498 participants, respectively, who also reported the activity labels in each stay point (home, work, errand, leisure, etc.) and the travel mode.

As illustrated in the related-works section, several efforts were performed in order to improve the performance of the trajectory prediction task. In this work, we intend to improve the training time, maintaining the accuracy of the predictions.

3 Methodology

In this section, we will describe the steps followed to obtain trajectories from raw data, transform them into sequences of nodes based on graph information, obtain the relative direction between nodes and use the obtained sequences to predict the next nodes. In summary, the main objective of the current effort is to predict a user's next whereabouts based on previous locations. The following paragraphs detail our methodology.

The first step is the **point selection** that are located within a specific bounding box are selected. Each point has a latitude and longitude. With the remaining points, sequences of coordinates $S_c = \{(lat_1, lon_1), (lat_2, lon_2), ..., (lat_n, lon_n)\}$ are built for each user.

The next step is the **trajectory identification** using the *Infostop* algorithm [1]. It takes as parameters the maximum roaming distance allowed for two points within the same stay (r_1), the typical distance between two stays in the same destination (r_2). Also, Infostop takes the minimum time difference between two consecutive records for them to be considered within the same stay (t_{min}) and the maximum time difference between two consecutive records to be considered within the same stay (t_{max}). Infostop aims to tag the sequence of points representing movement and stops, as shown in Eq. 1.

$$traj_{initial} = \{traj_1, stop_1, traj_2, stop_2, ...\} \tag{1}$$

Then, the stops are removed using the information obtained, and the initial trajectories are split based on the inter-point distance. Thus, the distances of consecutive points within each trajectory are calculated using Euclidean distance. Then, the maximum inter-point distance in each trajectory is calculated. A smaller distance between points means a better point-node match. Finally, trajectories are discarded based on a maximum inter-point distance threshold $d_{threshold}$.

Next, in the **edge matching** step, each sequence of coordinates S_c is transformed into a sequence of road segments $S_e = \{e_1, e_2, ..., e_n\}$, using Fast Map Matching (FMM) [16] or ST-Matching [11] for small, middle and large scale graphs, respectively. It is important to note that the directed graph representing the road segments is obtained from *OpenStreetMap* (OSM).

Once the edges are matched, the **direction calculation** is performed. In this step, the possible direction to follow from a node i to an adjacent node $i + 1$ is discretised in k directions. Thus, inspired from [9], for each edge e_i in the directed graph, the node $node_i$ and the direction taken to get to the next node dir_i is obtained. Hence, for each node, a sequence of neighbors is built $node_i = \{neighbor_1 : dir_1, neighbor_2 : dir_2, ..., neighbor_M : dir_M\}$. Where $dir_i \in [0, K]$. For example, if $K = 8$, there are 8 possible directions, where 0 represents a direction between the north and the north-east.

All the information of a node's neighbors and associated directions are represented as the sequence of nodes $S_n = \{n_1, n_2, ..., n_n\}$ and directions $S_d = \{d_1, d_2, ..., d_n\}$.

Finally, the **model training** is performed. Using both S_n and S_d sequences as input and use d_{n+1} to calculate the loss in the training process. In the next section, we detail the proposed prediction model.

4   Attention and Possible Directions for TRAJectory

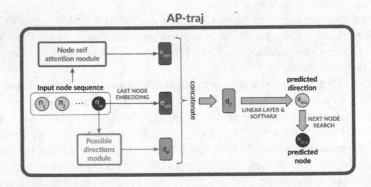

Fig. 1. Attention and Possible directions for TRAJectory schema.

The Attention and Possible directions for TRAJectory (AP-TRAJ) model is depicted in Fig. 1. It consists of a Node self-attention and Possible directions modules, whose outputs are combined with the Embedding of the last node to produce a single vector fed into a linear layer to predict the next direction a user is going to take. Then, this direction is used to determine the specific node that is going to be visited. The *Node self-attention* takes as input a sequence of nodes to transform them into a vector capturing the relations between them (Subsect. 4.1). And the *Possible directions* takes the last node of the input sequence and uses the graph related to it to find the possible directions that can be taken in order to get to another node (Subsect. 4.2). The output of these modules is concatenated to the **last node embedding** and passed through a linear layer in order to predict the next direction to be taken from the last input node, which is then used to predict the next node (Subsect. 4.3). In the following paragraphs, we detail the different modules.

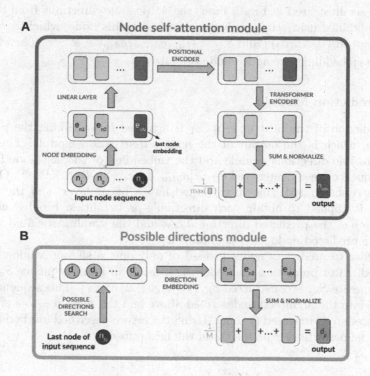

Fig. 2. Node self-attention and Possible directions modules

4.1   Node Self-attention Module

This module takes a sequence of nodes $S_n = \{n_1, n_2, ..., n_n\}, n \in N$ and produces an output vector $n_{attn} \in \mathbb{R}^{1 \times d}$. First, the input sequence is transformed into a sequence of embeddings $S_{e_n} = \{e_{n1}, e_{n2}, ..., e_{nN}\} \in \mathbb{R}^{N \times d}$ as shown in Fig. 2A. Then, a linear layer is applied to S_{e_n} in order to adjust the magnitude of each vector e_{ni}. Thus, they are not strongly affected by positional encoding. This produces the vector sequence $S_{l_n} = \{l_{n1}, l_{n2}, ..., l_{nN}\} \in \mathbb{R}^{N \times d}$.

Following the method proposed by Vaswani et al. [14], a positional encoder is used to preserve the information on the order of the input sequence. This consists of adding a vector that represents its position to each l_{ni}, producing the sequence $S_{p_n} = \{p_{n1}, p_{n2}, ..., p_{nN}\} \in \mathbb{R}^{N \times d}$. It is then fed into the transformer encoder that transforms it into a different representation $S_{t_n} = \{t_{n_1}, t_{n_2}, ..., t_{n_N}\} \in \mathbb{R}^{N \times d}$. Finally, the output of the transformer encoder is added and normalized $n'_{attn} = \frac{1}{max(t_{ni})} \sum_{i=1}^{N} t_{ni}, \quad n_{attn} \in \mathbb{R}^{1 \times d}$.

4.2 Possible Directions Module

The present module takes the last node of the input sequence n_N and produces a vector with information on all possible directions that can be taken from the node n_N as illustrated in Fig. 2. First, the M possible directions from the node n_N are obtained using the graph associated with this node, which is retrieved from $S_{pd} = \{d_1, d_2, ..., d_M\}$ and $S_{e_d} = \{e_{d_1}, e_{d_2}, ..., e_{d_M}\} \in \mathbb{R}^{M \times d}$. Therefore, the direction embeddings are added and normalized $d_P = \frac{1}{M} \sum_{i=1}^{M} e_{d_i}, \quad d_P \in \mathbb{R}^{1 \times d}$

4.3 Prediction Module

The prediction of the next node n_{N+1} is achieved by obtaining the predicted direction, which is the output of the node self-attention module. The output of the possible directions module and the embedding of the last node from the input sequence are concatenated $d_C = [n_{attn}; d_P; e_{nN}] \quad d_C \in \mathbb{R}^{1 \times (3d)}$. Once this vector is concatenated, this vector is fed into a linear layer, and the softmax function is applied to obtain each direction's probabilities. Finally, using the last node n_N, the predicted direction d_{n+1}, and the graph associated with the node, the predicted node n_{n+1} is obtained.

In order to predict O nodes instead of only one, a sliding window method is applied. After predicting the node n_{N+1}, using an input sequence S_{n_1} a new input sequence S_{n_2} is constructed $S_{n_2} = \{n_2, n_3, ..., n_{N+1}\}$. This sequence S_{n_2} is then fed into the architecture described above and the node n_{N+2} is predicted. This procedure is repeated O times. Using the before described methodology, we present the performed experiments in the next subsection.

5 Experiments and Results

In this section, we will describe how AP-Traj was evaluated against the NetTraj algorithm by using two different datasets. The first one is **The Beijing Taxi Trajectory Dataset** [17,18], which contains the GPS trajectories of 10,357 taxis during the period of Feb. 2 to Feb. 8, 2008 within Beijing. It has a total of 15 million points. The second is **The Geolife Dataset** [19–21], which contains the GPS trajectories of 182 users from April 2007 to August 2012. The majority of the data was created in Beijing, China. It contains 17,621 trajectories.

Table 1. Number of train, test and validation trajectories, as well as number of edges per subset

name	train	test	test	num edges	area (km^2)
taxis-small	5314	295	295	206	2×2
taxis-large	322 164	17 898	17 898	3 803	10×10
geolife-small	2 170	121	121	7 989	15×15
geolife-large	60 998	3 389	3 389	41 765	50×50

The first step for obtaining the sequences of nodes and directions was the **point selection**. For both datasets, the same bounding box used by [9] was selected: [39.74, 40.05, 116.14, 116.60].

Then, the **trajectory identification** was performed using the *Infostop* [1] tool. This was done for both datasets, sice the trajectories for each taxi had no *occupied* tag, and the movement of each user in the Geolife dataset had no information regarding whether the user was stopping at a POI or not.

For the Geolife dataset, the vast majority of trajectories (82.8%) generated using the default Infostop configuration ($r_1 = 10$, $r_2 = 10$, $min_{time} = 300$, $max_{time} = 86400$) had a small maximum inter-point distance ($< 100\,m$). Hence, the values of the parameters were not changed and no further filtering was done in this dataset. However, since taxis tend to hover around the same area while waiting for passengers and the stops tend to be smaller, the radius was increased ($r_1 = 100$, $r_2 = 100$), and the minimum stay time decreased ($min_{time} = 60$) for this dataset. Given the nature of the taxi's movement, the trajectories produced had a much larger maximum inter-point distance (61, 3% larger than 1 km). This meant that the FMM could have problems when identifying the sequence of edges, so all trajectories with a maximum inter-point distance larger than 10 km were discarded. This value was chosen in order to keep as many trajectories as possible after filtering (87, 6% were kept).

Next, **Edge matching** was performed. The routable network was downloaded using the bounding box [39.74, 40.05, 116.14, 116.60]. Then, the default configuration for ST-Matching was used, except for the search radius (10 km) and the gps error (1 km) for both datasets.

After that, the **Direction calculation** was executed using $K = 8$, which means that there are 8 possible directions. Then, the trajectories were split into sequences of length 15 ($N = 10$ for the input and $O = 5$ for the output).

Finally, the **Train-test-validation split** was done. Four smaller datasets were produced by taking different subsets of the original ones. To generate *taxis-small* the bounding box [39.886, 39.904, 116.361, 116.379] was used, which had an area of $2 \times 2\,km^2$. The other generated datasets are *taxis-large* ([39.850, 39.940, 116.325, 116.415]), *geolife-small* ([39.827, 39.963, 116.302, 116.438]) and *geolife-large* ([39.670, 40.120, 116.145, 116.595]).

The resulting train-test-val number of trajectories, as well as the number of edges contained in each are shown in Table 1. Finally, all four datasets were trained using both the *NetTraj* and *AP-Traj*.

5.1   Hyperparameter Tuning

For **NetTraj**, we used the same hyperparameter values reported by the authors (*dim embedding = 256, hidden size = 512, num hidden layers = 2, dropout = 0.1, learning rate initial = 0.5, learning rate decay = 0.8*). However, the type of learning rate (LR) decay was not specified, so we experimented with both linear and exponential decay. Also, the authors mentioned that scheduled sampling was used. This consists of feeding the model with either the ground truth observation with probability α (alpha) or the predicted result with probability $1 - \alpha$ during training, where α decreases gradually as the iteration increases. Since the scheduled sampling configuration is not known, we tested different combinations for initial alpha values (0, 0.25, 0.5, 0.9, 1.0), decay types (linear, sigmoid, exponential) and decay rates (0.01 and 0.05 for linear; 10.0, 15.0, 20.0 for sigmoid; and 0.01, 0.95 for exponential). For taxis-small, the best configuration was a linear LR with an initial alpha value of 0.9 and linear decay with a rate of 0.01. For geolife-small, the best results were obtained with linear LR, alpha initial value of 0.9 and exponential decay with a rate of 0.95.

On the other hand, six hyperparameters of **AP-Traj** needed tuning. The first one is the embedding dimensions of nodes and directions (*dim embedding = [64,128,256]*), which coincides with the number of expected features in the input of the transformer encoder (d). Also, the hyperparameters related to the transformers encoder were the dimension of the feedforward dimension (*dim feedforward = [256,512,1024]*), the number of heads of the multi-head attention model used (*num heads = [2,4]*), the number of sub-encoder-layers in the encoder (*num layers = [2,4]*) and the dropout rate used to prevent overtraining (*dropout = [0.1, 0.2]*). Finally, to initialize the weights of the different layers, a uniform distribution was used, where the highest possible value is *init range*, and the lowest is *-init range* (tested values [0.1, 0.2]). For taxis-small, the best results were obtained with *dim embedding = 256, dim feedforward = 512, num heads = 2, num layers = 4, dropout = 0.1* and *init range = 0.2*. And for geolife-small, the best configuration was *dim embedding = 256, dim feedforward = 512, num heads = 4, num layers = 2, dropout = 0.2* and *init range = 0.2*.

The training was done using an NVIDIA GeForce RTX 2080 Ti graphics card (taxis-small, taxis-large, geolife-large) and NVIDIA GeForce RTX 2060 (geolife-small). We use a stochastic gradient descent optimizer with a *batch size = 20, maximum number of iterations = 100* and early stopping with *patience = 2*, which means that the training stops the second time the validation loss increases. The Cross-Entropy Loss was calculated by comparing the predicted direction and the ground truth.

5.2   Preliminary Results

In order to measure the effectiveness of AP-Traj, the time per epoch and Average Match Ratio (AMR) for the first 5 predicted nodes was measured. The second is defined in Eq. 2:

Table 2. Performance comparison of *NetTraj* and *AP-Traj*

dataset	method	AMR	MR(1)	time(s/iter)	num iters
taxis-small	transformers	0.624	0.825	**28**	12
	netTraj	**0.657**	0.879	153	13
taxis-large	transformers	**0.680**	0.855	**3105**	8
	netTraj	0.627	0.840	9155	11
geolife-small	transformers	**0.418**	0.692	**10**	55
	netTraj	0.417	0.725	82	17
geolife-large	transformers	**0.527**	0.749	**324**	20
	netTraj	0.394	0.683	7001	8

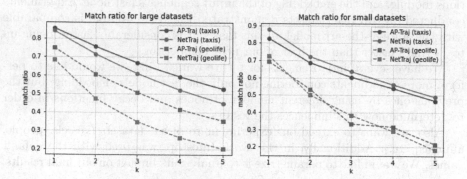

Fig. 3. Match ratio for both large and small datasets.

$$AMR = \frac{1}{O} \sum_{k=1}^{O} MR(k) \qquad MR(k) = \frac{1}{k} \sum_{i=1}^{k} match(y, \hat{y}), \qquad (2)$$

where $match(y, \hat{y})$ is 1 if the predicted value matches the ground truth and 0 otherwise.

The AMR, MR(1) and time per epoch obtained for both datasets are shown in Table 2, and the MR(k) is shown in Fig. 3. We can observe that the AMR is higher for three of the four datasets but is considerably faster than the baseline.

Finally, an ablation study was done to determine whether all the proposed modules for AP-Traj were necessary or not. Table 3 shows the average match ratio depending on whether the last node embedding (LN), the node self-attention module (NA) or the possible directions module (PD) were used. We can observe that the best results are obtained when the three elements are used and that the last node greatly influences the prediction quality.

In sum, AP-Traj shows an improvement in training time compared to Net-Traj, and the results obtained are better for three of the four datasets generated. Also, the ablation study shows that the three components used for generating the prediction are necessary.

Table 3. Ablation study results on taxis-large dataset

	LN	NA	PD	LN+NA	LN+PD	NA+PD	LN+NA+PD
AMR	0.523	0.305	0.200	0.633	0.528	0.198	**0.680**

6   Conclusions and Future Works

This paper proposes a new model for the prediction of future trajectories based on the past street intersections (nodes) visited by the user and a graph of the travelled area. Our proposal, called Attention and Possible directions for TRAJectory prediction (AP-Traj), uses a node self-attention module, a possible directions module, and the embedding of the input sequence's last node. Experiments conducted on two real datasets demonstrated that our proposal is comparable with the state-of-the-art model for this task but is considerably faster, being up to 10 times faster than the best of our near competitor.

We have several improvements for future works. First, we would like to perform more experiments considering not only the last node's embedding, but the previous ones by using different number of nodes and decay functions in order to determine how this influences the results.

Also, we want to extend our experiment to other datasets (vessels, people, animals, etc.). Additionally, in this work Infostop, was used with the default values. We would like to parametrize it to analyze its impact on our final results.

References

1. Aslak, U., Alessandretti, L.: Infostop: Scalable stop-location detection in multi-user mobility data. arXiv preprint arXiv:2003.14370 (2020)
2. Bray, J., Feldblum, J.T., Gilby, I.C.: Social bonds predict dominance trajectories in adult male chimpanzees. Anim. Behav. **179**, 339–354 (2021)
3. Chen, Y.C., Thaipisutikul, T., Shih, T.K.: A learning-based poi recommendation with spatiotemporal context awareness. IEEE Trans. Cybern. **52**(4), 2453–2466 (2022). https://doi.org/10.1109/TCYB.2020.3000733
4. Feng, J., Li, Y., Yang, Z., Qiu, Q., Jin, D.: Predicting human mobility with semantic motivation via multi-task attentional recurrent networks. IEEE Transactions on Knowledge and Data Engineering (2020)
5. Gambs, S., Killijian, M.O., del Prado Cortez, M.N.: Next place prediction using mobility Markov chains. In: Proceedings of the First Workshop on Measurement, Privacy, and Mobility, pp. 1–6 (2012)
6. Grigsby, J., Wang, Z., Qi, Y.: Long-range transformers for dynamic spatiotemporal forecasting. arXiv preprint arXiv:2109.12218 (2021)
7. Hong, Y., Martin, H., Raubal, M.: How do you go where? improving next location prediction by learning travel mode information using transformers. arXiv preprint arXiv:2210.04095 (2022)
8. Huang, L., Zhuang, J., Cheng, X., Xu, R., Ma, H.: STI-GAN: multimodal pedestrian trajectory prediction using spatiotemporal interactions and a generative adversarial network. IEEE Access **9**, 50846–50856 (2021)

9. Liang, Y., Zhao, Z.: NetTraj: a network-based vehicle trajectory prediction model with directional representation and spatiotemporal attention mechanisms. IEEE Transactions on Intelligent Transportation Systems (2021)
10. Liu, R.W., et al.: STMGCN: mobile edge computing-empowered vessel trajectory prediction using spatio-temporal multi-graph convolutional network. IEEE Transactions on Industrial Informatics (2022)
11. Lou, Y., Zhang, C., Zheng, Y., Xie, X., Wang, W., Huang, Y.: Map-matching for low-sampling-rate GPS trajectories. In: Proceedings of the 17th ACM SIGSPATIAL International Conference on Advances in Geographic Information Systems, pp. 352–361 (2009)
12. Pang, Y., Zhao, X., Hu, J., Yan, H., Liu, Y.: Bayesian spatio-temporal graph transformer network (b-star) for multi-aircraft trajectory prediction. Knowledge-Based Systems, p. 108998 (2022)
13. Shao, K., Wang, Y., Zhou, Z., Xie, X., Wang, G.: TrajForesee: how limited detailed trajectories enhance large-scale sparse information to predict vehicle trajectories? In: 2021 IEEE 37th International Conference on Data Engineering (ICDE), pp. 2189–2194. IEEE (2021)
14. Vaswani, A., et al.: Attention is all you need. In: Advances in Neural Information Processing Systems 30 (2017)
15. Yan, B., Zhao, G., Song, L., Yu, Y., Dong, J.: PreCLN: pretrained-based contrastive learning network for vehicle trajectory prediction. World Wide Web, pp. 1–23 (2022)
16. Yang, C., Gidofalvi, G.: Fast map matching, an algorithm integrating hidden Markov model with precomputation. Int. J. Geogr. Inf. Sci. 32(3), 547–570 (2018). https://doi.org/10.1080/13658816.2017.1400548
17. Yuan, J., Zheng, Y., Xie, X., Sun, G.: Driving with knowledge from the physical world. In: Proceedings of the 17th ACM SIGKDD International Conference on Knowledge Discovery and Data Mining, pp. 316–324 (2011)
18. Yuan, J., et al. : T-drive: driving directions based on taxi trajectories. In: Proceedings of the 18th SIGSPATIAL International Conference on Advances in Geographic Information Systems, pp. 99–108 (2010)
19. Zheng, Y., Li, Q., Chen, Y., Xie, X., Ma, W.Y.: Understanding mobility based on GPS data. In: Proceedings of the 10th International Conference on Ubiquitous Computing, pp. 312–321 (2008)
20. Zheng, Y., Xie, X., Ma, W.Y., et al.: GeoLife: a collaborative social networking service among user, location and trajectory. IEEE Data Eng. Bull. 33(2), 32–39 (2010)
21. Zheng, Y., Zhang, L., Xie, X., Ma, W.Y.: Mining interesting locations and travel sequences from GPS trajectories. In: Proceedings of the 18th International Conference on World Wide Web, pp. 791–800 (2009)

A Generalization of Fuzzy c-Means with Variables Controlling Cluster Size

Yuchi Kanzawa[✉]

Shibaura Institute of Technology, Tokyo, Japan
kanzawa@shibaura-it.ac.jp

Abstract. This study constructs two general fuzzy clustering algorithms with a cluster size controller. The first algorithm includes the standard fuzzy c-means (SFCM), modified SFCM, and generalized fuzzy c-means, and the second one includes the entropy-regularized fuzzy c-means (EFCM), modified EFCM (mEFCM), and regularized fuzzy c-means (RFCM). Furthermore, the results of this study demonstrate that the behavior of the fuzzy classification functions of the first proposed algorithm at points far from clusters are similar to that for mSFCM, and those of the second one are similar to those for EFCM, mEFCM, and RFCM. some conventional clustering algorithms.

Keywords: fuzzy c-means clustering · cluster size controller · fuzzy classification function

1 Introduction

Fuzzy clustering algorithms yield object membership shared among all clusters, rather than ones constrained to individual clusters. Fuzzy c-means (FCM), proposed by Bezdek [2], is the most representative fuzzy clustering algorithm, while Entropy-regularized FCM (EFCM), proposed by Miyamoto [3], is another variant. The former is referred to as standard FCM (SFCM) to distinguish it from EFCM. Besides the development of algorithms that yield correct clustering results, investigation of their properties is also an important research topic. SFCM and EFCM exhibit different properties. Miyamoto [4] reported that the features of fuzzy clustering methods can be clarified, at least theoretically, in terms of the fuzzy classification function (FCF) of SFCM and EFCM. This yields an allocation rule that classifies new objects into Voronoi cells, with Voronoi seeds as the cluster centers. The FCF of SFCM approaches the reciprocal of the given cluster number as the object approaches infinity, whereas that of EFCM approaches one or zero as the object approaches infinity. While SFCM fuzzifies the clustering by replacing the membership in the HCM objective function with nonlinear expressions, EFCM does so by introducing a regularizer of entropy. Thus, novel fuzzy clustering algorithms may be developed by adopting various nonlinear functions that are different from those in SFCM or by adopting regularizers different from those in EFCM. However, the features of these algorithms

V. Torra and Y. Narukawa (Eds.): MDAI 2023, LNAI 13890, pp. 226–237, 2023.
https://doi.org/10.1007/978-3-031-33498-6_16

require clarification. Kanzawa and Miyamoto [5] generalized SFCM to yield generalized FCM (GFCM), and proved theoretically that the FCF of GFCM approaches the reciprocal of the given cluster number as the object approaches infinity, as in the case of the FCF of SFCM. Further, Kanzawa and Miyamoto [6] generalized EFCM to yield regularized FCM (RFCM), and theoretically proved that the FCF of RFCM approaches one or zero as the object approaches infinity, as in the case of the FCF of EFCM.

One disadvantage of the aforementioned algorithms is that they tend to produce clusters of equal size. Consequently, if the cluster sizes are unbalanced, objects that ought to be assigned to a large cluster may be misclassified into smaller clusters. To overcome this issue, some approaches have introduced the cluster size controller [7,8] — the method derived from SFCM is referred to as the modified SFCM (mSFCM) and that derived from EFCM is referred to as the modified EFCM (mEFCM). Further, Komazaki and Miyamoto [9] theoretically proved that the FCF of mSFCM approaches the value of cluster size controller as the object approaches infinity, unlike those of SFCM and GFCM. They further proved that the FCF of mEFCM approaches one or zero as the object approaches infinity, as in the case of the FCFs of EFCM and RFCM. The current state of research on fuzzy clustering algorithms engenders two questions: (1) Can fuzzy clustering algorithms be constructed by generalizing mSFCM or mEFCM? In other words, can a cluster size controller be introduced into GFCM or RFCM using mSFCM or mEFCM? (2) If so, what are the properties of such algorithms?

In this study, we provide partial positive answers to these questions. In the first part of the paper, mSFCM is generalized in three steps. First, an optimization problem from modified GFCM clustering (mGFCM) is considered, where the power of the membership and the cluster size controllers in the mSFCM objective function are replaced with a general nonlinear function. This optimization problem is reduced to both mSFCM and GFCM. Second, an mGFCM algorithm and its associated FCF are constructed by solving this optimization problem. Third, it is experimentally demonstrated that the FCF of mGFCM approaches the value of the cluster size controller as the object approaches infinity, as in the case of mSFCM. Subsequently, mEFCM is generalized in three steps. First, an optimization problem for modified RFCM (mRFCM) is considered by replacing the Kullback-Leibler divergence of membership and cluster size controller in the mEFCM objective function with a general nonlinear function. This optimization problem is reduced to both mEFCM and RFCM. Second, an mRFCM algorithm and its associated FCF are constructed by solving this optimization problem. Third, it is experimentally demonstrated that the FCF of mRFCM approaches one or zero as the object approaches infinity, as in the case of mEFCM.

The remainder of this paper is organized as follows. The notations used in this study are introduced in Section 2 and the conventional methods are also described. In Sect. 3, mGFCM and mRFCM are conceptually introduced and their algorithms are derived. Finally, several numerical experiments are described in Sect. 4, and the concluding remarks are presented in Sect. 5.

2 Preliminaries

Let $X = \{x_k \in \mathbb{R}^M \mid k \in \{1, \cdots, N\}\}$ be a dataset of containing M-dimensional points. We assume $x_k \neq x_{k'}$ for $k \neq k'$. Consider the problem of classifying the objects in X into C separated subsets $\{G_i\}_{i=1}^{C}$, which are termed 'clusters'. The membership degree of x_k with respect to the i-th cluster is denoted by $u_{i,k}$ ($i \in \{1, \cdots, C\}, k \in \{1, \cdots, N\}$), and the set of all $u_{i,k}$ is denoted by U, which is known as the partition matrix. The set of cluster centers is denoted by $V = \{v_i \mid v_i \in \mathbb{R}^M, i \in \{1, \cdots, C\}\}$. The squared Euclidean distance between the k-th object and the i-th cluster center is given by

$$d_{i,k} = \|x_k - v_i\|_2^2. \tag{1}$$

The HCM algorithm iterates the following steps: (i) Calculate the memberships, $u_{i,k}$, and (ii) Calculate the cluster centers, v_i [1]. These steps are obtained by solving the following optimization problem:

$$\underset{U,V}{\text{minimize}} \sum_{i=1}^{C} \sum_{k=1}^{N} u_{i,k} d_{i,k}, \tag{2}$$

$$\text{subject to} \sum_{i=1}^{C} u_{i,k} = 1. \tag{3}$$

SFCM [2] and EFCM [4] representations are obtained by solving the optimization problems

$$\underset{U,V}{\text{minimize}} \sum_{i=1}^{C} \sum_{k=1}^{N} (u_{i,k})^m d_{i,k}, \tag{4}$$

$$\underset{U,V}{\text{minimize}} \sum_{i=1}^{C} \sum_{k=1}^{N} u_{i,k} d_{i,k} + \lambda^{-1} \sum_{i=1}^{C} \sum_{k=1}^{N} u_{i,k} \ln (u_{i,k}), \tag{5}$$

respectively, subject to Eq. (3), where $m > 1$ and $\lambda > 0$ denote fuzzification parameters. Further, we introduce a cluster size controller, denoted by $A = \{\alpha_i \in (0,1)\}_{i=1}^{C}$, satisfying the constraint

$$\sum_{i=1}^{C} \alpha_i = 1. \tag{6}$$

The mSFCM and mEFCM representations are obtained by solving the optimization problems

$$\underset{U,V,A}{\text{minimize}} \sum_{i=1}^{C} \sum_{k=1}^{N} (u_{i,k})^m d_{i,k}, \tag{7}$$

$$\underset{U,V,A}{\text{minimize}} \sum_{i=1}^{C} \sum_{k=1}^{N} u_{i,k} d_{i,k} + \lambda^{-1} \sum_{i=1}^{C} \sum_{k=1}^{N} u_{i,k} \ln \left(\frac{u_{i,k}}{\alpha_i}\right), \tag{8}$$

respectively, which are based on Eqs. (3) and (6).

FCFs [4] describe the degree to which any point in object space is quintessen-tially attached to a cluster by broadening the membership, $u_{i,k}$, over the entire space. The FCF, $u_i(x)$, with respect to a new object, $x \in \mathbb{R}^M$, is defined to be the solution to the following optimization problems for SFCM, EFCM, mSFCM, and mEFCM, respectively:

$$\underset{U}{\text{minimize}} \sum_{i=1}^{C} (u_i(x))^m d_i(x), \tag{9}$$

$$\underset{U}{\text{minimize}} \sum_{i=1}^{C} u_i(x)d_i(x) + \lambda^{-1} \sum_{i=1}^{C} u_i(x)\ln(u_i(x)), \tag{10}$$

$$\underset{U}{\text{minimize}} \sum_{i=1}^{C} (\alpha_i)^{1-m}(u_i(x))^m d_i(x), \tag{11}$$

$$\underset{U}{\text{minimize}} \sum_{i=1}^{C} u_i(x)d_i(x) + \lambda^{-1} \sum_{i=1}^{C} u_i(x)\ln\left(\frac{u_i(x)}{\alpha_i}\right), \tag{12}$$

subject to

$$\sum_{i=1}^{C} u_i(x) = 1, \tag{13}$$

where

$$d_i(x) = \|x - v_i\|_2^2, \tag{14}$$

and $\{v_i\}_{i=1}^{C}$ denote the cluster centers obtained using the corresponding fuzzy clustering algorithms. We define the crisp allocation rule [4] to classify $\mathbb{R}^M$ based on the following:

$$x \in G_i \overset{\text{def}}{\equiv} u_i(x) > u_j(x) \text{ for } j \neq i. \tag{15}$$

It has been theoretically proved [4,9] that the subsets, $\{G_i\}_{i=1}^{C}$ obtained from SFCM and EFCM yield Voronoi sets, whereas those obtained from mSFCM yield multiplicatively weighted Voronoi sets and those obtained from mEFCM yield locally additively weighted Voronoi sets. Furthermore, [4,9] proved that $u_i(x)$ of SFCM, EFCM, mSFCM, and mEFCM approach $1/C$, "0 or 1", α_i, and "0 or 1", respectively.

For a strictly convex, increasing, non-negative, and smooth function, f_{GFCM}, defined over $[0,1)$, the optimization problems for the GFCM and its FCF are described below.

$$\underset{U,V}{\text{minimize}} \sum_{i=1}^{C} \sum_{k=1}^{N} f_{\text{GFCM}}(u_{i,k})d_{i,k}, \tag{16}$$

$$\underset{U}{\text{minimize}} \sum_{i=1}^{C} f_{\text{GFCM}}(u_i(x))d_i(x) \tag{17}$$

subject to Eqs. (3) and (13), respectively. Theoretically, it has been shown [5] that the subsets, $\{G_i\}_{i=1}^{C}$, obtained from GFCM yield Voronoi sets and $u_i(x)$ of GFCM approaches $1/C$. For a convex smooth function, f_{RFCM}, defined over $[0, 1]$, the optimization problems for the RFCM and its FCF are described as follows:

$$\underset{U,V}{\text{minimize}} \sum_{i=1}^{C} \sum_{k=1}^{N} u_{i,k} d_{i,k} + \lambda^{-1} \sum_{i=1}^{C} \sum_{k=1}^{N} f_{\mathrm{RFCM}}(u_{i,k}) \tag{18}$$

$$\underset{u}{\text{minimize}} \sum_{i=1}^{C} u_i(x) d_i(x) + \lambda^{-1} \sum_{i=1}^{C} f_{\mathrm{RFCM}}(u_i(x)), \tag{19}$$

subject to Eqs. (3) and (13), respectively. Finally, it has been shown [6] that the subsets, $\{G_i\}_{i=1}^{C}$, produced from RFCM yield Voronoi sets, and $u_i(x)$ of RFCM approaches zero or one.

3   mGFCM: A Generalization of mSFCM and GFCM, and mRFCM: A Generalization of mEFCM and RFCM

For $f_{\mathrm{mGFCM}} : \mathbb{R}_+ \rightarrow \mathbb{R}$, let us assume that $a f_{\mathrm{mGFCM}}(a/b)$ is non-negative, smooth, and strictly convex for $a \in (0,1)$ and $b \in (0,1)$. Further, let us assume that it is increasing with respect to $a \in (0,1)$. For an example, when $f_{\mathrm{mGFCM}}(a/b) = (a/b)^{m-1}$ ($m > 1$), $a f_{\mathrm{mGFCM}}(a/b) = a^m b^{1-m}$ is non-negative, smooth, and strictly convex for $a \in (0,1)$ and $b \in (0,1)$. For $f_{\mathrm{mRFCM}} : \mathbb{R}_+ \rightarrow \mathbb{R}$, we assume that $a f_{\mathrm{mRFCM}}(a/b)$ is strictly convex and smooth both for $a \in (0,1)$ and $b \in (0,1)$. For example, when $f_{\mathrm{mRFCM}}(a/b) = \ln(a/b)$, $a f_{\mathrm{mRFCM}}(a/b) = a \ln(a/b)$ is strictly convex with respect to both $a \in (0,1)$ and $b \in (0,1)$.

The mGFCM and mRFCM algorithms are obtained by solving the following optimization problems

$$\underset{U,V,A}{\text{minimize}} \sum_{i=1}^{C} \sum_{k=1}^{N} u_{i,k} f_{\mathrm{mGFCM}} \left(\frac{u_{i,k}}{\alpha_i} \right) d_{i,k}, \tag{20}$$

$$\underset{U,V,A}{\text{minimize}} \sum_{i=1}^{C} \sum_{k=1}^{N} u_{i,k} d_{i,k} + \sum_{i=1}^{C} \sum_{k=1}^{N} u_{i,k} f_{\mathrm{mRFCM}} \left(\frac{u_{i,k}}{\alpha_i} \right), \tag{21}$$

respectively, subject to Eqs. (3) and (6). The mGFCM optimization problem is a generalizations of that of mSFCM because it reduces to Eq. (4), with $f_{\mathrm{mGFCM}}(u_{i,k}/\alpha_i) = (u_{i,k}/\alpha_i)^{m-1}$. Additionally, it is a generalization of that of GFCM because it reduces to Eq. (16), with $f_{\mathrm{mGFCM}}(u_{i,k}/\alpha_i) = f_{\mathrm{GFCM}}(u_{i,k}/(1/C))/u_{i,k}$. This optimization problem is a generalization of that for mEFCM because it reduces to Eq. (8), with $f_{\mathrm{mRFCM}}(u_{i,k}/\alpha_i) = \lambda^{-1} \ln(u_{i,k}/\alpha_i)$. It is also a generalization of that for RFCM because it reduces to Eq. (18), with $f_{\mathrm{mRFCM}}(u_{i,k}/\alpha_i) = f_{\mathrm{RFCM}}(u_{i,k}/(1/C))/u_{i,k}$.

We describe the Lagrangians, $L_{\mathrm{mGFCM}}(U, A, \gamma, \eta)$ and $L_{\mathrm{mRFCM}}(U, A, \gamma, \eta)$, as follows:

$$L_{\mathrm{mGFCM}}(U, A, \gamma, \eta) = \sum_{i=1}^{C} \sum_{k=1}^{N} f_{\mathrm{mGFCM}} \left(\frac{u_{i,k}}{\alpha_i} \right) d_{i,k} + \sum_{k=1}^{N} \gamma_k \left(1 - \sum_{i=1}^{C} u_{i,k} \right)$$

$$= \eta \left(1 - \sum_{i=1}^{C} \alpha_i \right), \tag{22}$$

$$L_{\mathrm{mRFCM}}(U, A, \gamma, \eta) = \sum_{i=1}^{C} \sum_{k=1}^{N} u_{i,k} d_{i,k} + \sum_{i=1}^{C} \sum_{k=1}^{N} u_{i,k} f_{\mathrm{mGFCM}} \left(\frac{u_{i,k}}{\alpha_i} \right)$$

$$+ \sum_{k=1}^{N} \gamma_k \left(1 - \sum_{i=1}^{C} u_{i,k} \right) + \eta \left(1 - \sum_{i=1}^{C} \alpha_i \right), \tag{23}$$

with Lagrange multipliers, $\gamma = (\gamma_1, \ldots, \gamma_N)$ and η.

The membership value are obtained using the following algorithm if the optimal value of γ is given (the derivation is omitted):

Algorithm 1.

STEP 1. Set the lower and higher bounds for $u_{i,k}$ as $(\underline{u_{i,k}}, \overline{u_{i,k}}) = (0, 1)$. Set the threshold value $\delta > 0$.

STEP 2. Set $\widehat{u_{i,k}} = (\underline{u_{i,k}} + \overline{u_{i,k}})/2$.

STEP 3. If $|\underline{u_{i,k}} - \overline{u_{i,k}}| < \delta$, then terminate the algorithm and set the optimal value of $u_{i,k}$ as $\widehat{u_{i,k}}$.

STEP 4. If

$$\left(f_{\mathrm{mGFCM}} \left(\frac{\widehat{u_{i,k}}}{\alpha_i} \right) + \frac{\widehat{u_{i,k}}}{\alpha_i} f'_{\mathrm{mGFCM}} \left(\frac{\widehat{u_{i,k}}}{\alpha_i} \right) \right) d_{i,k} > \gamma_k. \tag{24}$$

for mGFCM, and

$$d_{i,k} + f_{\mathrm{mRFCM}} \left(\frac{\widehat{u_{i,k}}}{\alpha_i} \right) + \frac{\widehat{u_{i,k}}}{\alpha_i} f'_{\mathrm{mRFCM}} \left(\frac{\widehat{u_{i,k}}}{\alpha_i} \right) > \gamma_k, \tag{25}$$

for mRFCM, $\widehat{u_{i,k}}$ is higher than the optimal $u_{i,k}$. In this case, set $\overline{u_{i,k}} \leftarrow \widehat{u_{i,k}}$. Otherwise, $\widehat{u_{i,k}}$ is lower than the optimal $u_{i,k}$. In this case, set $\underline{u_{i,k}} \leftarrow \widehat{u_{i,k}}$. Return to Step. 1.

The optimal value of γ is obtained using the following algorithm (the derivation is omitted):

Algorithm 2.

STEP 1. Set $(\underline{\gamma_k}, \overline{\gamma_k})$ to be

$$\underline{\gamma_k} = \min_{1 \leq i' \leq C} \left\{ \left(f_{\mathrm{mGFCM}} \left(\frac{1/C}{\alpha'_i} \right) + \frac{1/C}{\alpha'_i} f'_{\mathrm{mGFCM}} \left(\frac{1/C}{\alpha'_i} \right) \right) d_{i',k} \right\}, \tag{26}$$

$$\overline{\gamma_k} = \max_{1 \leq i' \leq C} \left\{ \left(f_{\mathrm{mGFCM}} \left(\frac{1/C}{\alpha'_i} \right) + \frac{1/C}{\alpha'_i} f'_{\mathrm{mGFCM}} \left(\frac{1/C}{\alpha'_i} \right) \right) d_{i',k} \right\}, \tag{27}$$

232   Y. Kanzawa

for mGFCM, and

$$\underline{\gamma_k} = \min_{1 \le i' \le C} \left\{ d_{i',k} + f_{\mathrm{mRFCM}}\left(\frac{1/C}{\alpha_{i'}}\right) + \frac{1/C}{\alpha_{i'}} f'_{\mathrm{mRFCM}}\left(\frac{1/C}{\alpha_{i'}}\right) \right\}, \quad (28)$$

$$\overline{\gamma_k} = \max_{1 \le i' \le C} \left\{ d_{i',k} + f_{\mathrm{mRFCM}}\left(\frac{1/C}{\alpha_{i'}}\right) + \frac{1/C}{\alpha_{i'}} f'_{\mathrm{mRFCM}}\left(\frac{1/C}{\alpha_{i'}}\right) \right\}. \quad (29)$$

for mRFCM. We set the threshold value $\delta > 0$.

STEP 2. Set $\widehat{\gamma_k} = (\underline{\gamma_k} + \overline{\gamma_k})/2$.

STEP 3. If we have $|\underline{\gamma_k} - \overline{\gamma_k}| < \delta$, then terminate the algorithm and set the optimal value of γ_k to be $\widehat{\gamma_k}$.

STEP 4. Obtain $\{u_{i,k}\}_{i=1}^{C}$ using Algorithm 1 for $\widehat{\gamma_k}$.

STEP 5. If $\sum_{i=1}^{C} u_{i,k} < 1$, $\widehat{\gamma_k}$ is lower than the optimal γ_k. In this case, set $\underline{\gamma_k} \leftarrow \widehat{\gamma_k}$. Otherwise, $\widehat{\gamma_k}$ is higher than the optimal γ_k. in this case, set $\overline{\gamma_k} \leftarrow \widehat{\gamma_k}$. Return to STEP. 2.

The optimal cluster size controller is obtained using the following algorithm if the optimal value of η is given (the derivation is omitted):

Algorithm 3.

STEP 1. Set the lower and higher bounds for α_i to be $(\underline{\alpha_i}, \overline{\alpha_i}) = (0, 1)$. Set the threshold value $\delta > 0$.

STEP 2. Set $\widehat{\alpha_i} = (\underline{\alpha_i} + \overline{\alpha_i})/2$.

STEP 3. If $|\underline{\alpha_i} - \overline{\alpha_i}| < \delta$, then terminate this algorithm, and set the optimal value of α_i to be $\widehat{\alpha_i}$.

STEP 4. If

$$\sum_{k=1}^{N} \left(\frac{u_{i,k}}{\widehat{\alpha_i}}\right)^2 f'_{\mathrm{mGFCM}}(\frac{u_{i,k}}{\widehat{\alpha_i}}) d_{i,k} > \eta \quad (30)$$

for mGFCM, and

$$-\sum_{k=1}^{N} \left(\frac{u_{i,k}}{\widehat{\alpha_i}}\right)^2 f'_{\mathrm{mRFCM}}\left(\frac{u_{i,k}}{\widehat{\alpha_i}}\right) > \eta, \quad (31)$$

for mRFCM, the value of $\widehat{\alpha_i}$ is higher than the optimal α_i. In this case, set $\overline{\alpha_i} \leftarrow \widehat{\alpha_i}$. Otherwise, the value of $\widehat{\alpha_i}$ is lower than the optimal α_i. in this case, set $\underline{\alpha_i} \leftarrow \widehat{\alpha_i}$. Return to STEP. 3.

The optimal value of η is obtained using the following algorithm (the derivation is omitted):

Algorithm 4.

STEP 1. Set $(\underline{\eta}, \overline{\eta})$ to be

$$\underline{\eta} = \min_{1 \leq i \leq C} \left\{ \sum_{k=1}^{N} \left(\frac{u_{i',k}}{1/C} \right)^2 f'_{\text{mGFCM}} \left(\frac{u_{i',k}}{1/C} \right) d_{i',k} \right\} \overset{\text{def}}{=} \eta_{\min}, \qquad (32)$$

$$\overline{\eta} = \max_{1 \leq i \leq C} \left\{ \sum_{k=1}^{N} \left(\frac{u_{i',k}}{1/C} \right)^2 f'_{\text{mGFCM}} \left(\frac{u_{i',k}}{1/C} \right) d_{i',k} \right\} \overset{\text{def}}{=} \eta_{\max}. \qquad (33)$$

for mGFCM, and

$$\underline{\eta} = \min_{1 \leq i' \leq C} \left\{ -\sum_{k=1}^{N} \left(\frac{u_{i',k}}{1/C} \right)^2 f'_{\text{mRFCM}} \left(\frac{u_{i',k}}{1/C} \right) \right\}, \qquad (34)$$

$$\overline{\eta} = \max_{1 \leq i' \leq C} \left\{ -\sum_{k=1}^{N} \left(\frac{u_{i',k}}{1/C} \right)^2 f'_{\text{mRFCM}} \left(\frac{u_{i',k}}{1/C} \right) \right\}. \qquad (35)$$

for mRFCM. Set the threshold $\delta > 0$.

STEP 2. Set $\widehat{\eta} = (\underline{\eta} + \overline{\eta})/2$.

STEP 3. If $|\underline{\eta} - \overline{\eta}| < \delta$, then terminate this algorithm, and set the optimal value of α_i to be $\widehat{\eta}$.

STEP 4. Obtain the values of $\{\alpha_i\}_{i=1}^{C}$ using Algorithm 3 with $\widehat{\eta_k}$.

STEP 5. If $\sum_{i=1}^{C} \alpha_i < 1$, the value of $\widehat{\eta}$ is lower than the optimal η. In this case, set $\underline{\eta} \leftarrow \widehat{\eta}$. Otherwise, the value of $\widehat{\eta}$ is higher than the optimal η. In this case, set $\overline{\eta} \leftarrow \widehat{\eta}$.

Then, we propose the mGFCM and mRFCM algorithms as follows:

Algorithm 5 (mGFCM and mRFCM).

STEP 1. Specify the number of clusters, C. Set the initial membership, U, and cluster size controller, A.

STEP 2. Calculate V using

$$v_i = \frac{\sum_{k=1}^{N} u_{i,k} f_{\text{mGFCM}}(u_{i,k}/\alpha_i) x_k}{\sum_{k=1}^{N} u_{i,k} f_{\text{mGFCM}}(u_{i,k}/\alpha_i)} \quad (\text{for mGFCM}), \qquad (36)$$

$$v_i = \frac{\sum_{k=1}^{N} u_{i,k} x_k}{\sum_{k=1}^{N} u_{i,k}} \quad (\text{for mRFCM}). \qquad (37)$$

STEP 3. Obtain η using Algorithms 4 and the cluster size controller A using Algorithm 3.

STEP 4. Obtain γ using Algorithms 2 and the membership U using Algorithm 1.

STEP 5. Check the termination criterion for (U, V, A). If the criterion is not satisfied, return to STEP 5.

The FCFs of mGFCM and mRFCM are obtained by solving the optimization problem

$$\underset{U}{\text{minimize}} \sum_{i=1}^{C} u_i(x) f_{\text{mGFCM}} \left(\frac{u_i(x)}{\alpha_i} \right) d_i(x), \tag{38}$$

$$\underset{U}{\text{minimize}} \sum_{i=1}^{C} u_i(x) d_i(x), + \sum_{i=1}^{C} u_i(x) f_{\text{mGFCM}} \left(\frac{u_i(x)}{\alpha_i} \right), \tag{39}$$

respectively, with $\sum_{i=1}^{C} u_i(x) = 1$, where $d_i(x) = \|x - v_i\|_2^2$. These are achieved using the following algorithm:

Algorithm 6 (FCFs of mGFCM and mRFCM).

STEP 1. Obtain V, and A from Algorithm 5, and set $x \in \mathbb{R}^p$.
STEP 2. Obtain $\gamma(x)$ using Algorithm 2 along with $\{u_i(x)\}_{i=1}^{C}$ using Algorithm 1, where $\widehat{\gamma_k}$, $\overline{\gamma_k}$, $\underline{\gamma_k}$, and $d_{i,k}$ are replaced with $\widehat{\gamma(x)}$, $\overline{\gamma(x)}$, $\underline{\gamma(x)}$, and $d_i(x)$, respectively.

4   Numerical Experiment

This section describes numerical experiments performed to observe the properties of the mGFCM and mRFCM (Algorithms 5 and 6) proposed in the previous sections. We consider the pairs of actual functions corresponding to mGFCM and mRFCM for an artificial dataset.

The two functions for mGFCM are defined as follows:

$$f_1 \left(\frac{u_{i,k}}{\alpha_i} \right) = \left(\frac{u_{i,k}}{\alpha_i} \right) + \left(\frac{u_{i,k}}{\alpha_i} \right)^{0.6}, \tag{40}$$

$$f_2 \left(\frac{u_{i,k}}{\alpha_i} \right) = 1.5^{u_{i,k}/\alpha_i} - 1 \tag{41}$$

for all $i \in |1, \ldots, C$, $k \in \{1, \ldots, N\}$. Clearly, $u_{i,k} f_1(u_{i,k}/\alpha_i)$ and $u_{i,k} f_2(u_{i,k}/\alpha_i)$ are defined over $u_{i,k} \in [0, 1]$ and $\alpha_i \in (0, 1)$ and are strictly convex, increasing, non-negative, and smooth. The two functions for mRFCM are defined as follows:

$$f_3 \left(\frac{u_{i,k}}{\alpha_i} \right) = 4 \left(\left(\frac{u_{i,k}}{\alpha_i} \right)^2 + \left(\frac{u_{i,k}}{\alpha_i} \right) \right), \tag{42}$$

$$f_4 \left(\frac{u_{i,k}}{\alpha_i} \right) = 3 \times 2^{(u_{i,k}/\alpha_i)} \tag{43}$$

for all $i \in \{1, \ldots, C\}$, $k \in \{1, \ldots, N\}$. Obviously, $u_{i,k} f_3(u_{i,k}/\alpha_i)$ and $u_{i,k} f_4(u_{i,k}/\alpha_i)$ are defined in $u_{i,k} \in [0, 1]$ and $\alpha_i \in (0, 1)$ and are strictly convex and smooth.

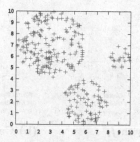

Fig. 1. Artificial dataset.

The dataset, comprising three clusters, is depicted in Fig. 1. One comprises 180 objects distributed randomly in a circle of radius three. Another comprises 80 objects distributed randomly in a circle of radius two. The final cluster comprises 20 objects distributed randomly in a circle of radius one. This dataset is partitioned into three clusters via mGFCM based on f_1 and f_2 and mRFCM based on f_3 and f_4. The characteristics of the classification rule are elicited. The top-left cluster is denoted by cluster #1, the bottom-left cluster is denoted by cluster #2, and the right cluster is denoted by cluster #3. The derived FCFs are illustrated in Fig. 2, where the red points represent the objects in cluster #1, the purple points represent the objects in cluster #2, the blue points represent the objects in cluster #3, the purple surface represent the FCF for cluster #1, the blue surface represent the FCF for cluster #2, and the yellow surface represent the FCF for cluster #3. It is evident from Fig. 2c and d that the values of FCFs derived from mRFCM are one or zero at the points far away from the clusters. This property is identical to those of RFCM and mEFCM. Thus, we hypothesize that mRFCM satisfies the same properties as RFCM and mEFCM. On the other hand, Fig. 2a and b do not yield any conclusions. The FCFs derived from mGFCM over a wider range are depicted in Fig. 3. Figure 3a and b correspond to Fig. 2a and b. It is evident from Figs. 3 that the values of FCFs corresponding to cluster #1 are greater than 0.6, those of FCFs corresponding to cluster #2 are nearly 0.3, and those of FCFs corresponding to cluster #3 are less than 0.1. These values, $(0.6, 0.3, 0.1)$, are similar to the ratios of the cluster sizes, $(180/(180+80+20), 80/(180+80+20), 20/(180+80+20) \simeq (0.642, 0.286, 0.071)$, mSFCM also exhibits this property. Thus, we hypothesize that mGFCM inherits the properties of mSFCM. The results obtained from these experiments are expected to serve as a useful basis for theoretically investigating the properties of mGFCM and mRFCM based on actual functions of f_{mGFCM} and f_{mRFCM} in future research.

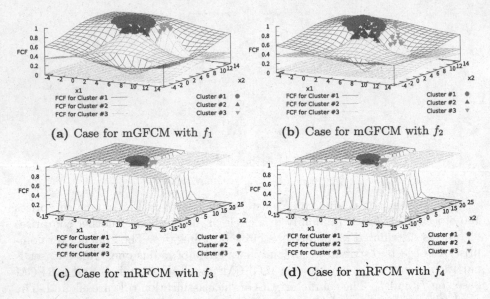

(a) Case for mGFCM with f_1 **(b)** Case for mGFCM with f_2

(c) Case for mRFCM with f_3 **(d)** Case for mRFCM with f_4

Fig. 2. FCFs

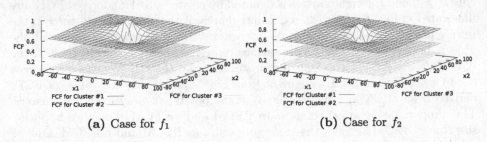

(a) Case for f_1 **(b)** Case for f_2

Fig. 3. FCFs for mGFCM: a wider view

5   Conclusion

In this study, we generalize both mSFCM and mEFCM into mGFCM and mRFCM, respectively, construct corresponding algorithms, and experimentally demonstrate that the FCFs of mGFCM and mRFCM inherit the properties of mSFCM and mEFCM, respectively.

In future work, we intend to prove that the FCF of mGFCM approaches the value of the cluster size controller values as the object approaches infinity, and that the FCF of mRFCM approaches one or zero as the object approaches infinity. Further, we intend to consider further generalization of mGFCM and mRFCM while preserving their properties.

References

1. MacQueen, J.B.: Some methods of classification and analysis of multivariate observations. In: Proceedings of the 5th Berkeley Symposium on Mathematical Statistics and Probability, pp. 281–297 (1967)
2. Bezdek, J.: Pattern recognition with fuzzy objective function algorithms. Plenum Press, New York (1981)
3. Miyamoto, S., Mukaidono, M.: Fuzzy c-means as a regularization and maximum entropy approach. In: Proceedings of the 7th International Fuzzy Systems Association World Congress (IFSA1997), Vol. 2, pp. 86–92 (1997)
4. Miyamoto, S., Ichihashi, H., Honda, K.: Algorithms for Fuzzy Clustering, Springer, Heidelberg (2008). https://doi.org/10.1007/978-3-540-78737-2
5. Kanzawa, Y., Miyamoto, S.: Generalized fuzzy c-means clustering and its property of fuzzy classification function. JACIII **25**(1), 73–82 (2021)
6. Kanzawa, Y., Miyamoto, S.: Regularized fuzzy c-means clustering and its behavior at point of infinity. JACIII **23**(3), 485–492 (2019)
7. Miyamoto, S., Kurosawa, N.: Controlling cluster volume sizes in fuzzy c-means clustering. In: Proceedings SCIS&ISIS2004, pp 1–4 (2004)
8. Ichihashi, H., Honda, K., Tani, N.: Gaussian mixture pdf approximation and fuzzy c-means clustering with entropy regularization. In: Proceedings of the 4th Asian Fuzzy System Symposium, pp. 217–221 (2000)
9. Komazaki, Y., Miyamoto, S.: Variables for controlling cluster sizes on fuzzy c-means. In: Torra, V., Narukawa, Y., Navarro-Arribas, G., Megías, D. (eds.) MDAI 2013. LNCS (LNAI), vol. 8234, pp. 192–203. Springer, Heidelberg (2013). https://doi.org/10.1007/978-3-642-41550-0_17

Data Privacy

Local Differential Privacy Protocol for Making Key–Value Data Robust Against Poisoning Attacks

Hikaru Horigome[1], Hiroaki Kikuchi[1]([✉])(iD), and Chia-Mu Yu[2]

[1] Graduate School of Advanced Mathematical Science, Meiji University,
4-21-1 Nakano, Tokyo 164-8525, Japan
{cs212030,kikn}@meiji.ac.jp
[2] Department of Information Management and Finance,
National Yang Ming Chiao Tung University, Hsinchu, Taiwan

Abstract. Local differential privacy is a technique for concealing a user's information from collectors by randomizing the information within the user's own device before sending it to unreliable collectors. Ye et al. proposed PrivKV, a local differential privacy protocol for securely collecting key–value data, which comprises two-dimensional data with discrete and continuous values. However, such data is vulnerable to a "poisoning attack," whereby a fake user sends data to manipulate the key-value dataset. To address this issue, we propose an Expectation-Maximization (EM) based algorithm, in conjunction with a cryptographical protocol for ensuring secure random sampling. Our local differential privacy protocol, called emPrivKV, offers two main advantages. First, it is able to estimate statistical information more accurately from randomized data. Second, it is robust against manipulation attacks such as poisoning attacks, whereby malicious users manipulate a set of analysis results by sending altered information to the aggregator without being detected. In this paper, we report on the improvement in the accuracy of statistical value estimation and the strength of the robustness against poisoning attacks achieved by applying the proposed method to open datasets.

Keywords: local differential privacy · key–value data · expectation maximization

1 Introduction

Our personal data are being used by many services such as item recommendation for online shops, personalized medical assistance, and fake user detection. For example, in a smartphone survey, users indicate their favorite apps such as $\langle \texttt{YouTube}, 0.5 \rangle$, and $\langle \texttt{Instagram}, 0.2 \rangle$, by stating the total time they used each of the apps. These data were stored in a key–value database, whereby each "key" is an app title and its associated "value" is the rating of that app by a particular user. However, collecting this data poses a significant challenges.

© The Author(s), under exclusive license to Springer Nature Switzerland AG 2023
V. Torra and Y. Narukawa (Eds.): MDAI 2023, LNAI 13890, pp. 241–252, 2023.
https://doi.org/10.1007/978-3-031-33498-6_17

Local Differential Privacy (LDP) is one approach to addressing the challenge. Here, each user locally perturbs their personal data before sending it to an (untrusted) server. Many LDP protocols have been proposed for different types of data, including Erlingsson et al. [7] proposed an LDP. Ye et al. [1] proposed PrivKV, an LDP scheme that securely collects key–value data, two-dimensional data with discrete and continuous values. Other LDP protocols [2] [3] for key–value data have also been proposed.

However, because the perturbation is being performed locally, LDP protocols are vulnerable to "poisoning attacks," whereby an attacker injects fake users who send fake data for a target key, aiming to manipulate the server's analytical results such as the frequency of particular keys or their mean reputation scores. If a fake user sends fake key and value data without following the predetermined LDP protocol, the server would not be able to detect these data because of the privacy guarantee of LDP. Cao et al. [4] studied poisoning attacks on LDP schemes. Wu et al. [5] identified three types of poisoning attacks for PrivKV and demonstrated that PrivKV is vulnerable to these types of attacks. They also proposed defense methods against poisoning attacks. However, these methods require long-term observation of the collection of the data.

In this paper, we address the issues of poisoning attacks on the LDP protocol for key–value data. First, we use a cryptographical protocol called oblivious transfer (OT) [6] to prevent fake users from choosing keys intentionally. Instead of performing random sampling locally, our protocol ensures that the server is involved jointly in the secure sampling process. Second, we claim that the estimation algorithm used in PrivKV is the source of its vulnerability to poisoning. Because it is computed using a single frequency for a key, it is easily to manipulated when the number of targeted keys is small. Instead, we address this limitation by using an Expectation Maximization (EM) algorithm [8]. Because EM estimates posterior probabilities iteratively, so that the estimated probabilities are more consistent across all observed values, it can improve the accuracy when the number of users is large and much observed data are available.

To investigate whether our proposed protocol is robust against various types of poisoning attacks, we conducted experiments using both synthetic data and open datasets. The results enable us to compare our proposed scheme with the conventional schemes such as PrivKV and PrivKVM.

Our contributions are as follows.

- We propose a new LDP algorithm that is robust against some types of poisoning attacks. Our proposed algorithm improves the accuracy of estimates based on the iterative process of Bayesian posterior probabilities and preserves the statistics against poisoning data.
- We show the experimental results that show the robustness of the proposed protocol using both synthetic data and open data. The results show that the proposed method performs better than the PrivKV protocol in estimation accuracy and in robustness against poisoning attacks.

2   Local Differential Privacy

2.1   Fundamental Definition

Suppose that users periodically submit their location data to a service provider. Differential privacy guarantees that the randomized data do not reveal any privacy disclosure from these data. By contrast, LDP needs no trusted party in providing the guarantee. LDP is defined as follows.

Definition 1. *A randomized algorithm Q satisfies ϵ-local differential privacy if for all pairs of values v and v' of domain V and for all subset S of range Z $(S \subset Z)$, and for $\epsilon \geq 0$, $Pr[Q(v) \in S] \leq e^{\epsilon} Pr[Q(v') \in S]$.*

2.2   PrivKV

PrivKV takes input data in the key–value from, a two-dimensional data structure of discrete ("key") and continuous ("value") variables, and estimates each key's frequency and its mean values. PrivKV's approach idea combines two LDP protocols, randomized response (RR) [13] for randomizing keys and value perturbation protocol (VPP) [12] for perturbing values. The dimension is restricted to two, but the key–value is known as a primitive data structure commonly used for several applications.

Sampling. Let S_i be a set of key–value tuples $\langle k, v \rangle$ owned by the i-th user. In PrivKV, the set of tuples is encoded as a d-dimensional vector, where d is the cardinality of the domain of keys K and a missing key is represented as $\langle k, v \rangle = \langle 0, 0 \rangle$. For instance, a set of key–values $S_i = \{\langle k_1, v_1 \rangle, \langle k_4, v_4 \rangle, \langle k_5, v_5 \rangle\}$ is encoded as a $d = 5$ dimensional vector $\boldsymbol{S}_i = (\langle 1, v_1 \rangle, \langle 0, 0 \rangle, \langle 0, 0 \rangle, \langle 1, v_4 \rangle, \langle 1, v_5 \rangle)$ where keys k_1, k_4 and k_5 are specified implicitly with 1 at the corresponding location. PrivKV performs 1-out-of-d random sampling to choose one element $\langle k_a, v_a \rangle$ from the d-dimensional vector $\boldsymbol{S}_i$ of key–value data.

Perturbing. The process has two steps: perturbing values and perturbing keys. It uses the VPP used in Harmony [12] for the chosen tuple. A value v_a in the key–value pair is discretized as $v'_a = \begin{cases} 1 & \text{with probability } (1 + v_a)/2, \\ -1 & \text{with probability } (1 - v_a)/2. \end{cases}$ The discretized value v' of the tuple $\langle 1, v_a \rangle$ is perturbed to give $v^+{}_a = VPP(v_a, \epsilon_2)$, defined as $v_a^+ = \begin{cases} v'_a & \text{w/p. } p_2 = e^{\epsilon_2}/(1 + e^{\epsilon_2}), \\ -v'_a & \text{w/p.} q_2 = 1/(1 + e^{\epsilon_2}), \end{cases}$ where ϵ_2 is the privacy budget for values. The value of the "missing" tuple $\langle 0, 0 \rangle$ is replaced by $v^+{}_a = VPP(v'_a, \epsilon_2)$, where v'_a is chosen uniformly from $[-1, 1]$.

A key is perturbed by the RR scheme [13] as

$$\langle k_a^*, v_a^+ \rangle = \begin{cases} \langle 1, v_a^+ \rangle & \text{w/p. } p_1 = \frac{e^{\epsilon_1}}{1 + e^{\epsilon_1}}, \\ \langle 0, 0 \rangle & \text{w/p. } q_1 = \frac{1}{1 + e^{\epsilon_1}}, \end{cases}$$

where v_a^+ is perturbed as described above. A "missing" tuple $\langle 0, 0 \rangle$ is randomized as

$$\langle k_a^*, v_a^+ \rangle = \begin{cases} \langle 0, 0 \rangle & w/p. \ p_1 = \frac{e^{\epsilon_1}}{1+e^{\epsilon_1}}, \\ \langle 1, v_a^+ \rangle & w/p. \ q_1 = \frac{1}{1+e^{\epsilon_1}}. \end{cases}$$

Each user submits the perturbed tuple $\langle k_a^*, v_a^+ \rangle$ together with the index a of the tuple.

Estimating. Let f_i be a true frequency of key k_i and let f_i' be the observed key frequencies among the perturbed vectors, for which $k_i = 1$. We can have the maximum likelihood estimation (MLE) of the frequency as $\hat{f_i} = \frac{n(p-1)+f_i'}{2p_1-1}$, where $p_1 = \frac{e^{\epsilon_1}}{1+e^{\epsilon_1}}$.

From the compositional theorem of differential privacy [9], the sequential composition of randomized algorithms with privacy budgets ϵ_1 (for keys) and ϵ_2 (for values) is $(\epsilon_1 + \epsilon_2, 0)$-differential private.

2.3 Poisoning Attack

We assume that an attacker is able to inject m fake users into a system. The attacker has access to open information about the target LDP scheme, such as its privacy budget ϵ and perturbation procedure. With n genuine users, the server estimates the frequencies and the mean values for r target keys among the $n + m$ users. The attacker aims to intentionally manipulate the estimated frequency and mean value for the set of targeted keys. We assume that the attacker targets r keys out of d, aiming maximize the manipulation in terms of frequencies and mean values.

Wu et al. [5] proposed the following three types of poisoning attacks;

1. Maximal Gain Attack (M2GA). All fake users craft the optimal fake output of perturbed message so that both the frequency and mean gains are maximized, i.e., they choose a target key k (a random key out of r targeted keys) and send $\langle 1, 1 \rangle$ to the server.
2. Random Message Attack (RMA). Each fake user picks a message uniformly at random from the domain and sends $\langle 0, 0 \rangle$, $\langle 1, -1 \rangle$, $\langle 1, 1 \rangle$, with probabilities $1/2$, $1/4$, and $1/4$, respectively.
3. Random Key–Value Pair Attack (RKVA). Each fake user picks a random key k from a given set of target keys, with a designated value of 1, and perturbs $\langle 1, 1 \rangle$ according to the protocol.

Wu et al. [5] proposed two methods to detect fake users, (1) one-class classifier-based detection, where observations of multiple rounds for each user gives the feature vector used for outlier detection, which can distinguish between genuine and fake groups. (2) anomaly score based detection, where the anomalous behavior of sending the same key in multiple rounds is detected from the frequencies of keys in multiple rounds for each user. They reported that these defense methods are effective when the number of targeted keys is small. However, their methods assume that each user sends data in multiple rounds, implying that realtime detection would not be feasible.

3 Proposed Algorithm

3.1 Idea

To prevent attacker from poisoning fake key–value data, we propose two defense methods, a perturbation with OT (see Sect. 3.2) and an EM estimation for frequency and mean values (see Sect. 3.3).

First, we note that a poisoning attempt to increase the frequencies of target keys is performed by the intentional choice of keys without random sampling. Therefore, if the server performs the random sampling on the behavior of fake users, the poisoning attempt would fail. Even if the server chooses a random key, no information of the key–value data is compromised. Note that privacy budgets (ϵ_1 and ϵ_2) are spent only for perturbing keys and values. In this way, we ensure a secure sampling using a cryptographical protocol (OT).

Second, we consider the reasons why the estimation might have been subject to a poisoning attack. We claim that the MLE used in PrivKV has low estimate accuracy for a biased distribution because it is computed on the single frequency for a key. It is therefore vulnerable when the number of targeted keys is small. Instead, we attempt to address this limitation by using the EM algorithm. Because EM estimates posterior probabilities iteratively, giving estimated probabilities that are more consistent with all observed values, it can improve the accuracy when the number of users n is large and much observed data are available.

Table 1 summarizes our approach for each of the steps in PrivKV, that involve sampling, perturbing, and estimating.

Table 1. Comparison of defenses approaches

step	PrivKV [1]	Our work
1 Pre-sampling	1-out-of-d sampling	–
2 Perturbing	Value $VPP(v, \epsilon_2)$	
	Key $RR(k, \epsilon_1)$	
3 Post-sampling	–	**1-out-of-d OT**
4 Estimating	MLE	**EM**

3.2 Oblivious Transfer

An OT is a two-party cryptographical protocol whereby a sender transfers one of many pieces of information to a receiver, but remains oblivious as to which of the pieces has been sent.

Naor and Pinkas [6] proposed an 1-out-of-N OT protocol using the 1-out-of-2 OT as a building blocks, as follows.

1-out-of-N OT [6] Suppose A has N messages $m_0, \ldots, m_N \in \{0,1\}^n$, where $N = 2^\ell - 1$.

1. A generates 2ℓ secret key pairs $(K_1^0, K_1^1), \ldots, (K_\ell^0, K_\ell^1)$.
2. A sends to B the ciphertexts $C_0, \ldots, C_N$, where $C_I = m_I \oplus F_{K_1^{I_1}}(I) \oplus \cdots \oplus F_{K_\ell^{I_\ell}}(I)$ and I is the ℓ-bit string $I_1 \ldots I_\ell \in \{0,1\}^2$ and F_K is a pseudo-random function.
3. A and B perform ℓ 1-out-of-2 OT (K_i^0, K_i^1) so that B learns $K_1^{t_1}, \ldots, K_\ell^{t_\ell}$ where t is the index that B chooses from N messages such that $t = 1_1 \ldots t_i \in \{0,1\}^\ell$.
4. B decrypts C_t using $K_1^{t_1}, \ldots, K_\ell^{t_\ell}$ to obtain m_t.

We aim to prevent an M2GA attack where fake users intentionally choose a target key (or set of keys) with aim of increasing the frequency and the mean value of the particular targeted keys. Simply, we replace the 1-out-of-d random sampling of PrivKV by an 1-out-of-d OT protocol performed between the user (A in OT) with d key–value pairs and the server (B), which chooses one element $\langle k_a, v_a \rangle$. However, the server cannot perform the subsequent perturbing steps because it must learn neither whether the user has key k_a nor the private value $v_a \in [0,1]$. Therefore, we change the order of steps so that users perturb the keys and values before the server chooses randomly a key–value pair via OT.

Algorithm 1 describes the proposed perturbation process using OT protocol for sampling. The perturbed key–value pairs will be used for estimating the frequency and the mean for the keys. With the reordering of steps, users have to perturb key–value pairs for all d keys, which will increase the computational cost on the user side by a factor of d. We regard this increase in computation cost as negligibly small because perturbation is a lightweight process in comparison with the cryptographical cost of the 1-out-of-d OT. The algorithm is robust against poisoning attacks.

Proposition 1. *An M2GA poisoning attack against the PrivKV scheme with 1-out-of-d OT for sampling key–value pairs has the frequency and the mean gains as large as an RMA poisoning attack has.*

Proof. Using an OT protocol, the fake users in the M2GA attack are not able to intentionally select the targeted keys. They may craft an arbitrary value but the server can detect invalid pairs other than the valid perturbed pairs $\langle 0, 0 \rangle$, $\langle 1, -1 \rangle$ and $\langle 1, 1 \rangle$. Therefore, they can prepare the valid perturbed pairs with arbitrary fractions, which is equivalent to an RMA attack. Therefore, the frequency and the mean gains will be less than or equal to those of an RMA attack.

3.3   EM Estimation for Key–Value Data

The EM algorithm performs an iterative process whereby posterior probabilities are updated through Bayes' theorem [8]. We propose using the EM algorithm

---

Algorithm 1. Perturbation of key–value pairs with OT

$S_1, \ldots, S_n \leftarrow$ key–value data for n users.
for all $u \in \{1, \ldots, n\}$ **do** perturbs all $\langle k_a, v_a \rangle \in S_u$
$\quad v_a^+ \leftarrow VPP(v_a', \epsilon_2)$ and $k_a^* \leftarrow RR(k_a', \epsilon_1)$
$\quad u$ with $\langle v_1^+, k_1^* \rangle, \ldots, \langle v_d^+, k_d^* \rangle$ performs 1-out-of-d OT with a server.
end for return The server has n perturbed key–value pairs.

Algorithm 2. EM algorithm for PrivKV

$\langle v^+, k^* \rangle \ldots \leftarrow$ the perturbed key–value pair for n users.
$\Theta^{(0)} \leftarrow$ a uniform probability for $X = \{\langle 1, 1 \rangle, \langle 1, -1 \rangle, \langle 0, 1 \rangle, \langle 0, -1 \rangle\}$.
repeat(E-step)
$\quad t \leftarrow 1$
$\quad$ Estimate posterior probability $\hat{\theta}_{u,i}^{(t)} \leftarrow Pr[x_i | z_u] = \frac{Pr[z_u | x_i] \theta_i{}^{(t-1)}}{\sum_{s=1}^{|X|} Pr[z_u | x_s] \theta_s{}^{(t-1)}}$,
$\quad$ (M-step) Update marginal probability $\theta^{(t)} \leftarrow \frac{1}{n} \sum_{u=1}^{n} \hat{\theta}_u^{(t-1)}$.
until $|\theta_i^{(t+1)} - \theta_i^{(t)}| \leq \eta$
for all $a \in K$ **do** estimate
$\quad \hat{f}_a \leftarrow n(\theta_{\langle 1,1 \rangle}^{(t)} + \theta_{\langle 1,-1 \rangle}^{(t)})$ and $\hat{m}_a \leftarrow \frac{\theta_{\langle 1,1 \rangle}^{(t)} - \theta_{\langle 1,-1 \rangle}^{(t)}}{\theta_{\langle 1,1 \rangle}^{(t)} + \theta_{\langle 1,-1 \rangle}^{(t)}}$
end for return $\hat{f}_1, \hat{m}_1, \ldots, \hat{f}_d, \hat{m}_d$

---

for estimating the frequency and mean values from key–value data perturbed in PrivKV.

Algorithm 2 shows the overall process for the proposed EM algorithm for estimating the frequency and means of key–value data. Given n perturbed values $z_1, \ldots, z_n$, we iterate the estimation of posterior probabilities for $x_1, \ldots, x_d$ as $\Theta^{(t)} = (\theta_1{}^{(t)}, \theta_2{}^{(t)}, \ldots, \theta_d{}^{(t)})$ until convergence.

4 Evaluation

4.1 Data

Our synthetic data comprises a Key–value data for each of three distributions: Gaussian ($\mu = 0, \sigma = 10$), Power-law ($F(x) = (1 + 0.1x)^{-\frac{11}{10}}$), and Linear ($F(x) = x$). Table 2 gives the means and variances of the synthetic data, where $d = 50$ distinct keys are evaluated for $n = 10^5$ users. Table 3 shows the statistics for the two open datasets used in our experiments.

4.2 Methodology

Accuracy Metrics. Given a set of key–value data provided by n users, we use emPrivKV, PrivKV, and PrivKVM(c=3) to estimate the frequency of key k, $\hat{f}_k$, and the mean value for k, $\hat{m}_k$. The Mean Square Error (MSE) for these estimates are defined as $MSE_f = \frac{1}{|K|} \sum_{i=1}^{|K|} (\hat{f}_i - f_i)^2$, $MSE_m = \frac{1}{|K|} \sum_{i=1}^{|K|} (\hat{m}_i - m_i)^2$, where f_k and m_k are the real frequency and mean for key k. After repeating each estimation 10 times, we evaluate the estimation accuracy.

Table 2. Synthetic Data ($n = 10^5$, $d = 50$)

distribution	$E(f_k/n)$	$Var(f_k/n)$	$E(m_k)$	$Var(m_k)$
Gaussian	0.49506	0.10926	−0.00987	0.43702
Power-law	0.20660	0.06290	−0.58681	0.25160
Linear	0.51	0.08330	0	0.34694

Table 3. Open datasets

item	MoveiLens [10]	Clothing [11]
# ratings	10,000,054	192,544
# users (n)	69,877	9,657
# items (d)	10,677	3,183
value range	0.5 − 5	1 − 10

Robustness Metrics. The estimation algorithm is *robust* against poisoning attacks if a poisoning attack fails to alter the estimation results. We quantify the robustness via *frequency gain* as the sum of the distance between the estimated and the poisoned frequency for the key, i.e., the frequency gain is $G_f(Y) = \sum_{k \in T} E[\Delta \hat{f}_k]$, where $\Delta \hat{f}_k = \tilde{f}_k - \hat{f}_k$ is the distance and $\tilde{f}_k$ is the estimated frequency when key k is targeted by a poisoning attack. Similarly, the *mean gain* is the sum of the distance between the estimated and the poisoned value, defined as $G_m(Y) = \sum_{k \in T} E[\Delta \hat{m}_k]$ where $\Delta \hat{m}_k = \tilde{m}_k - \hat{m}_k$, and $\tilde{m}_k$ is the estimated mean value when key k is targeted by a poisoning attack.

4.3   Experimental Results

Accuracy with respect to ϵ. Figs. 1a, 1b, 2a and 2b show the MSE distributions of frequencies and mean values for the open datasets, MovieLens and Clothing, respectively. Note that the MSE for emPrivKV are the minimum for both datasets and all ϵ. The accuracies with respect to the conventional PrivKV and PrivKVM are better by a factor of 100–1000 for small $\epsilon = 0.1$.

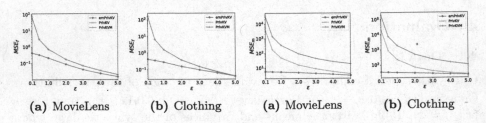

| (a) MovieLens | (b) Clothing | (a) MovieLens | (b) Clothing |

Fig. 1. MSE_f with respect to privacy budget ϵ

Fig. 2. MSE_m with respect to privacy budget ϵ

Frequency Gain. Figures 3a, 3b, 3c show the distributions of frequency gain with respect to the fraction of malicious users b, the privacy budget ϵ and the number of target key r, respectively, for the three types of poisoning attacks (M2GA, RMA and RKVA), when using the synthetic data (Gaussian distribution).

Note that an M2GA (see Figs. 3a, and 3b) causes the greatest gains for the three poisoning schemes. This is to be expected because it makes the strongest assumption (i.e., that malicious users are able to control the output arbitrarily) and therefore represents the greatest risk to LDP schemes.

The emPrivKV results show almost always the least gain for all types of poisoning attack and all parameters b, ϵ and r. As the fraction of malicious users b increases, the gains for PrivKV increase accordingly (see Fig. 3a). By contrast, the gain of emPrivKV is stable at 0.5. The gain of emPrivKV for $b = 0.2$ is 70.3% of PrivKV. Therefore, it is more robust against the worst type of poisoning attack (M2GA).

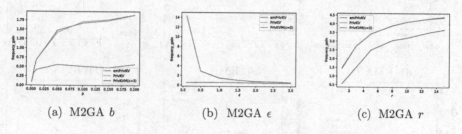

(a) M2GA b (b) M2GA ϵ (c) M2GA r

Fig. 3. Frequency gain for poisoning attacks(Gaussian)

Figure 4 shows the frequency gains for the MovieLens dataset. The gains distributions are similar to those using the Gaussian synthetic data, except for the effect the fraction-of-malicious-users parameter b (see Figs. 4a and 4g). The gain does not depend on b for M2GA (Fig. 4a), and is unstable for RKVA (Fig. 4g). The MovieLens data shows greater gains than the synthetic data (by a factor of 2–5) because the keys are not distributed as for the Gaussian distribution and there are many low-frequency keys (such as minor movie titles with very small audiences). These low-frequency keys are more vulnerable to low-resource poisoning attacks. With the same number of malicious users, the manipulated keys were already saturated in the MovieLens dataset. Therefore, the gains are greater in this case than for the synthetic-data case.

Mean Gain. The emPrivKV had always smaller gain than the PrivKV and PrivKVM had. For example, the gain for emPrivKV at $b = 0.2$ is stable around 1.0, which is 1/3 of that for PrivKV and 1/10 of that for PrivKVM. We observe similar results for the three LDP schemes with the MovieLens dataset (see Fig. 5a). Here, PrivKVM is seen as the most vulnerable against poisoning attacks.

The emPrivKV has the smallest gain with respect to privacy budget ϵ, as shown in Figs. 5b. The mean gains increase for PrivKV and PrivKVM as ϵ decreases. By contrast, the gain for the emPrivKV stays low, i.e., showing only minimal effects from poisoning attacks. This demonstrates the robustness of

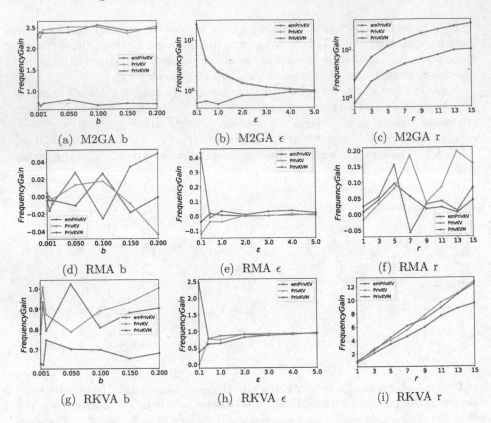

Fig. 4. Frequency gains for poisoning attacks (MovieLens)

emPrivKV. The gain increases linearly with number of targeted keys r. Figures 5c and 5i show the linear increase of the mean gains. Note that emPrivKV has the least coefficient for all the LDP schemes.

The LDP schemes did not show the significant differences with respect to RMA poisoning. Figure 5d shows that the differences in gain increase as the fraction of malicious users b increases.

4.4   Discussion

The experimental results demonstrate that the emPrivKV scheme is more robust than other LDP schemes. There are three possible reasons for this.

First, the PrivKV is based on the MLE, where the single-highest frequency is regarded as the expected value of the perturbation. Therefore, the scheme is likely to be affected by manipulating the highest frequency. By contrast, the EM algorithm iteratively adjusts the probabilities based on all the observed frequencies. Therefore, even if the highest frequency has been manipulated, the other elements help to mitigate against the manipulation of frequency.

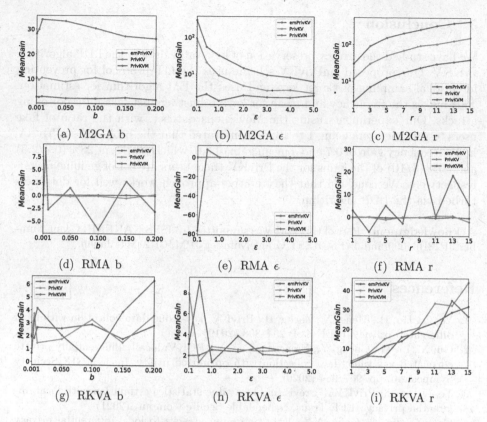

Fig. 5. Mean gain of poisoning attacks (MovieLens)

Second, we estimate the mean value based not only on the positive statistics ($v'_k = 1$) but also on both positive and negative statistics ($v'_k = 1$ and 0). This makes the estimation more robust against poisoning attacks and is the reason why the emPrivKV had a smaller mean gain.

Finally, based on our experimental results for gains, we can estimate the overall robustness of the proposed protocol. Following Proposition 1, M2GA is not relevant if perturbation with the OT protocol is used. Therefore, the gains from poisoning attacks on the proposed protocol can be estimated as the maximum of the gains for RMA and RKVA attacks (see Figs 4 and 5), as summarized in Table 4.

Table 4. Robustness against poisoning attacks (MovieLens, $b = 0.1$)

Attack	PrivKV [1]	Our work
Frequency gain	2.5 (M2GA)	0.7 (RKVA)
Mean gain	10 (M2GA)	3 (RKVA)

5   Conclusion

We have studied the privacy preservation of key–value data in the LDP algorithm PrivKV. Our proposed emPrivKV scheme uses the OT protocol for preventing intentional sampling of target keys and uses the EM algorithm for estimation. This makes the frequency and mean for keys robust against fake-data poisoning attacks. Our experiments using the MovieLens dataset, with the ratio of fake users to genuine users being 1 to 10, demonstrated that the proposed emPrivKV had a frequency gain of 0.7 and a mean gain of 3.0, which represent 28% (0.7/2.5) and 30% (3/10) of the gains for the PrivKV (fake users are 0.1 of genuine users), respectively. We conclude that the iterative approach works well for data perturbed via the LDP algorithm.

Acknowledgment. Part of this work was supported by JSPS KAKENHI Grant Number JP18H04099 and JST, CREST Grant Number JPMJCR21M1, Japan.

References

1. Ye, Q., Hu, H., Meng, X., Zheng, H.: PrivKV: key-value data collection with local differential privacy. IEEE S&P 294–308 (2019)
2. Gu, X., Li, M., Cheng, Y., Xiong, L., Cao, Y.: PCKV: locally differentially private correlated key-value data collection with optimized utility. In: USENIX Security Symposium, pp. 967–984 (2020)
3. Ye, Q., et al.: PrivKVM*: revisiting key-value statistics estimation with local differential privacy. IEEE Trans. Dependable Secure Comput. (2021)
4. Cao, X., Jia, J., Gong, N.Z.: Data poisoning attacks to local differential privacy protocols. In: USENIX Security Symposium, pp. 947–964 (2021)
5. Wu, Y., Cao, X., Jia, J., Gong, N.Z.: Poisoning attacks to local differential privacy protocols for key-value data. In: USENIX Security Symposium, pp. 519–536 (2022)
6. Naor, M., Pinkas, B.: Computationally secure oblivious transfer. J. Cryptol. **18**(1), 1–35 (2005)
7. Erlingsson, Ú., Pihur, V., Korolova, A.: RAPPOR: randomized aggregatable privacy-preserving ordinal response. In: ACM Conference on Computer and Communications Security, pp. 1054–1067 (2014)
8. Miyagawa, M.: EM algorithm and marginal applications. Adv. Stat. 16(1), 1–19. (in Japanese)
9. Dwork, C., Roth, A.: The algorithmic foundations of differential privacy. Found. Trends Theor. Comput. Sci. **9**(3–4), 211–407 (2014)
10. MovieLense 10M Dataset. https://grouplens.org/datasets/movielens/. Accessed 2022
11. Clothing Fit Dataset for Size Recommendation. https://www.kaggle.com/datasets/rmisra/clothing-fit-dataset-for-size-recommendation. Accessed 2022
12. Nguyên, T.T., Xiao, X., Yang, Y., Hui, S.C., Shin, H., Shin, J.: Collecting and analyzing data from smart device users with local differential privacy. arXiv:1606.05053 (2016)
13. Warner, S.L.: Randomized response: a survey technique for eliminating evasive answer bias. J. Am. Stat. Assoc. 63–69 (1965)

Differentially Private Graph Publishing Through Noise-Graph Addition

Julián Salas[1]($\boxtimes$), Vladimiro González-Zelaya[2], Vicenç Torra[3],
and David Megías[1]

[1] Internet Interdisciplinary Institute,
Universitat Oberta de Catalunya, Barcelona, Spain
{jsalaspi,dmegias}@uoc.edu
[2] Facultad de Ciencias Económicas y Empresariales,
Universidad Panamericana, Mexico, Mexico
cvgonzalez@up.edu.mx
[3] Department of Computing Science, Umeå Universitet, Umea, Sweden
vicenc.torra@umu.se

Abstract. Differential privacy is commonly used for graph analysis in the interactive setting, were a query of some graph statistic is answered with additional noise to avoid leaking private information. In such setting, only a statistic can be studied. However, in the non-interactive setting, the data may be protected with differential privacy and then published, allowing for all kinds of privacy preserving analyses. We present a noise-graph addition method to publish graphs with differential privacy guarantees. We show its relation to the probabilities in the randomized response matrix and prove that such probabilities can be chosen in such a way to preserve the sparseness of the original graph in the protected graph. Thus, better preserving the utility for different tasks, such as link prediction. Additionally, we show that the previous models of random perturbation and random sparsification are differentially private, and calculate the ϵ guarantees that they provide depending on their specifications.

Keywords: Local Differential Privacy · Noise Graph Addition ·
Randomized Response · Random Perturbation · Random Sparsification

1 Introduction and Related Work

For achieving Local Differential Privacy (LDP) on different graph statistics, the randomized response mechanism (RR) is commonly used, e.g. in [9] for counting the number of triangles or stars, in [11] for calculating graph modularity, clustering and assortativity coefficient, in [10] it is used for graph clustering, in [15] for data collection, while in [12] for data publication.

Most commonly, RR is defined as a flipping coin mechanism, e.g., in [5] define RR as follows:

1. Flip a coin
2. If tails, then respond truthfully.

© The Author(s), under exclusive license to Springer Nature Switzerland AG 2023
V. Torra and Y. Narukawa (Eds.): MDAI 2023, LNAI 13890, pp. 253–264, 2023.
https://doi.org/10.1007/978-3-031-33498-6_18

3. If heads, then flip a second coin and respond YES if heads and NO if tails.

This is known as Warner's RR mechanism and was generally defined in [16], here the probability of randomization is the same regardless of the input value. It must equal $\frac{1}{e^\epsilon+1}$ to provide ϵ-LDP, and it was shown in [8] that such probability minimizes the estimation error when randomized response is applied to privately estimate the proportion of individuals having a sensitive attribute.

However, when applied to graphs or to their adjacency matrices it yields dense graphs (or matrices). Thus, it may return matrices with huge amounts of edges (equivalently, adjacency matrices with lots of 1's). This implies a large information loss and noise, that most of the times makes the protection algorithm unsustainable since graph datasets that in most cases are sparse become dense after protection.

Recently, [13] showed that different probabilities in the randomization matrix can be chosen that provide LDP for the same value of ϵ, and thus they can be tuned to improve the properties of the randomized data, e.g., fairness of privacy guarantees.

In this paper, following the results in [13,14], we apply RR through the Noise-Graph addition method and show that it provides ϵ-LDP. Further, we show that the probabilities in the RR matrix can be defined in such a way to preserve the sparseness of the original graph in the protected graph. Thus, better preserving the utility and making the LDP algorithms through RR more sustainable. Additionally, we show that the models of random perturbation and random sparsification can be defined such that they are LDP, and calculate the ϵ depending on their specifications.

2   Basic Definitions

In this section, we provide the main definitions of local differential privacy, randomized response and noise-graph that are used through the following sections.

Definition 1 (Local Differential Privacy). *A randomized algorithm* $\mathcal{A}$ *satisfies* ε-*local differential privacy if for all inputs* i, j *and all outputs* $k \in Range(\mathcal{A})$:

$$Pr[\mathcal{A}(i) = k] \le e^\varepsilon Pr[\mathcal{A}(j) = k], \tag{1}$$

we say that $\mathcal{A}$ *is* ε-*locally differentially private* (ε-LDP).

Any LDP algorithm obtained through randomized response is uniquely determined by its design matrix.

Definition 2 (Design Matrix for Randomized Response). *The design matrix* R *for a binary randomized response mechanism is defined as follows:*

$$R = \begin{pmatrix} p_{00} & p_{01} \\ p_{10} & p_{11} \end{pmatrix}$$

where the entry $p_{jk} = Pr[X_i = k|x_i = j]$, *and* X_i *is the random output for original random variable* $x_i \in \{0, 1\}$.

Therefore, p_{00} denotes the probability that the randomized value is 0 and the original value is 0; p_{01} denotes the probability that the published value is 1 and the original value 0; and so on.

Remark 1. For the probability mass functions of each X_i to sum to 1, it is necessary that $p_{00} + p_{01} = 1$ and $p_{10} + p_{11} = 1$. The design matrix simplifies to:

$$P = \begin{pmatrix} p_{00} & 1 - p_{00} \\ 1 - p_{11} & p_{11} \end{pmatrix} \tag{2}$$

where $p_{00}, p_{11} \in [0,1]$. Hence, it is enough to define p_{00} and p_{11} to define P.

Remark 2. Warner's randomized response mechanism may be represented by the following design matrix:

$$P_w = \begin{pmatrix} p_w & 1 - p_w \\ 1 - p_w & p_w \end{pmatrix} \tag{3}$$

In [10] follow the same logic of the flipping coin mechanism for RR in [5] but consider the privacy parameter $s \in (0,1]$ and proceed as follows:

For each entry in the adjacency matrix, it is determined if preservation or randomization should be performed. Preservation is chosen with probability $(1-s)$, whereas randomization is chosen with probability s, after randomization is chosen, then 0 or 1 are chosen with probability $\frac{1}{2}$. Which is the same as the parameter used for bit randomization in RAPPOR [6].

All these three RR mechanisms are represented by choosing $p_w = 1 - \frac{s}{2}$ in (3), and are represented by the following randomization matrix:

$$P_s = \begin{pmatrix} 1 - \frac{s}{2} & \frac{s}{2} \\ \frac{s}{2} & 1 - \frac{s}{2} \end{pmatrix} \tag{4}$$

It was shown in [8] that P_w (and thus P_s) should equal the following randomization matrix P_{rr} to provide ϵ-LDP and minimize the estimation error. This result is used throughout all the LDP literature that uses RR.

$$P_{rr} = \begin{pmatrix} \frac{e^\varepsilon}{e^\varepsilon+1} & \frac{1}{e^\varepsilon+1} \\ \frac{1}{e^\varepsilon+1} & \frac{e^\varepsilon}{e^\varepsilon+1} \end{pmatrix} \tag{5}$$

2.1 Noise-Graph Addition

We consider the same definition of noise-graph addition as in [12], that is, a simplification from the original definition in [14], assuming that the original graph and the noise-graph have the same sets of nodes.

We denote by $G(V, E)$ the graph with the set of nodes V and set of edges E.

We denote the *symmetric difference* $E_1 \triangle E_2 := \{e | e \in E_1 \text{ and } e \notin E_2\} \cup \{e | e \notin E_1 \text{ and } e \in E_2\}$.

Definition 3. *Let $G_1(V, E_1)$ and $G_2(V, E_2)$ be two graphs with the same nodes V; then the addition of G_1 and G_2 is the graph $G = (V, E)$ where:*

$$E = E_1 \triangle E_2$$

We denote G as

$$G = G_1 \oplus G_2.$$

So, to add noise to a graph G, we will draw a random graph g from the Gilbert model (i.e., $g \in \mathcal{G}(n, p)$) and add it to G, to obtain $\tilde{G} = G \oplus g$.

In the *Gilbert model*, which is denoted by $\mathcal{G}(n, p)$, there are n nodes and each edge is chosen with probability p. The Gilbert and the Erdös-Rényi random graph models, are the most common and general in the literature. It has been proved that they are asymptotically equivalent in [3].

Now, we can define the general noise-graph mechanism that we will use.

Definition 4 (Noise-Graph Mechanism). *For any graph G with n nodes, and two probabilities p_0 and p_1 We define the following noise-graph mechanism:*

$$\mathcal{A}_{p_0,p_1}(G) = G \oplus g_0 \oplus g_1. \tag{6}$$

Such that:

$$g_0 \in \mathcal{G}(n, 1 - p_0) \cap \bar{G},$$
$$g_1 \in \mathcal{G}(n, 1 - p_1) \cap G.$$

3 Differential Privacy, Sparseness, Random Perturbation and Sparsification

In this section we show that the noise-graph mechanism is differentially private, we show that there are different possible randomizations that preserve the exact density of the graph G, depending on the parameters p_0, p_1. Then, based on the noise-graph mecanism we define differentially private versions of random perturbation [7] and random sparsification [4] methods.

Lemma 1. *The noise-graph mechanism $\mathcal{A}_{p_0,p_1}$ is equivalent to applying the matrix from (2) to the adjacency matrix of G. Hence, it is an edge-LDP mechanism, and the values of ϵ for which it is ϵ-LDP (obtained from [13]) are:*

$$\epsilon = \ln \max \left\{ \frac{p_0}{1 - p_1}, \frac{p_1}{1 - p_0}, \frac{1 - p_1}{p_0}, \frac{1 - p_0}{p_1} \right\} \tag{7}$$

On the other hand, for any given ϵ we obtain the values of p_0 and p_1 for which $\mathcal{A}_{p_0,p_1}$ is ϵ-tight from the following equations, cf. [13]:

$$(p_0(z), p_1(z)) = \begin{cases} (e^\epsilon z, 1 - z); \text{ or} \\ (1 - z, e^\epsilon z); \text{ or} \\ (1 - e^\epsilon z, z); \text{ or} \\ (z, 1 - e^\epsilon z) \end{cases} \text{ for } 0 < z \leq \frac{1}{1 + e^\epsilon} \tag{8}$$

3.1 Sparseness of Randomized Graphs

We recall the results from [10], that use $\frac{s}{2}$ as the parameter for randomization and consider that it provides DP for $\epsilon = \log(2/s - 1)$. Then they calculate the expected number of edges in the randomized graph that we denote as $\tilde{G}$. Which in our notation are:

$$E_{\tilde{G}} = (1 - \frac{1}{2})sq + \frac{s}{2}q_{\bar{G}} = (1 - s)q + \frac{s}{2}q_{\bar{G}} \text{ where } q_{\bar{G}} = \binom{n}{2} - q$$

Then the expected density $d\tilde{G}$ of $\tilde{G}$ equals [10]:

$$d_{\tilde{G}} = \frac{E_{\tilde{G}}}{\binom{n}{2}} = (1 - s)d_G + \frac{s}{2}$$

Combining both observations, we calculate the expected density for an ϵ-LDP algorithm from [10], which equals:

$$\left(1 - \frac{2}{e^\epsilon + 1}\right) \frac{q}{\binom{n}{2}} + \frac{1}{e^\epsilon + 1} \tag{9}$$

This yields dense randomized graphs for small ϵ values. For example, for $\epsilon = 0.1$ it is more than 0.47. In general, the density of the randomized graphs through RR is determined by the probabilities of randomization.

Remark 3. The density of a randomized graph can be calculated by considering the probabilities, p_{00}, p_{11} as follows:

$$d_{\tilde{G}} = \frac{(1 - p_{00})q_{\bar{G}} + p_{11}q}{\binom{n}{2}} \tag{10}$$

In fact, there are several possible randomizations that preserve the exact density of the graph G.

Remark 4. The randomizations that preserve the density (i.e., $d_{\tilde{G}} = d_G$) are expressed by the formula:

$$p_{00} = 1 - \frac{q}{q_{\bar{G}}}(1 - p_{11}) \tag{11}$$

Hence, we will show that by parameterizing $\mathcal{A}_{p_0, p_1}$ with (8) we may obtain ϵ-LDP graphs, which are sparser.

Remark 5. The density of the randomized graphs $\tilde{G}$ for a given ϵ can be calculated by the following formulas obtained by replacing the probabilities $p_0(z), p_1(z)$ from (8) in (10).

$$d_{\tilde{G}}(z) = \frac{1}{\binom{n}{2}} \begin{cases} \binom{n}{2} - z(e^\epsilon q_{\bar{G}} + q) \\ z(q_{\bar{G}} + e^\epsilon q) \\ z(e^\epsilon q_{\bar{G}} + q) \\ \binom{n}{2} - z(q_{\bar{G}} + e^\epsilon q) \end{cases} \text{ for } 0 < z \leq \frac{1}{1 + e^\epsilon} \tag{12}$$

3.2   Random Perturbation and Random Sparsification

In [7] suggested a random perturbation method that consisted on adding m edges and removing m edges from a graph. This method was later studied from an information theoretic perspective in [4], were the random sparsification method was proposed. In [14] it was shown that they can be defined through Noise-graph addition. In this section we present two mechanisms that generalize each of these methods to show that they are ϵ-LDP.

Definition 5 (m-Random Perturbation Mechanism). *For given parameters n, q and m we define the m-random perturbation mechanism $\mathcal{A}(m,n,q)$ as follows:*

$$\mathcal{A}_{m,n,q} = \mathcal{A}_{p_0,p_1} \tag{13}$$

Such that:

$$p_0 = 1 - \frac{m}{\binom{n}{2} - q}$$
$$p_1 = 1 - \frac{m}{q}$$

Theorem 1. *The m-random perturbation mechanism $\mathcal{A}_{m,n,q}$ applied to a graph G with n nodes and q edges is equivalent to adding and removing m random edges from G. And, it is ϵ-LDP. For:*

$$\epsilon = \ln \max \left\{ \frac{q}{m} \frac{q_{\bar{G}} - m}{q_{\bar{G}}}, \frac{q - m}{qm} q_{\bar{G}}, \frac{m}{q} \frac{q_{\bar{G}}}{q_{\bar{G}} - m}, \frac{m}{q - m} \frac{1}{q_{\bar{G}}}, \right\} \tag{14}$$

Proof. Note that p_0 is such that $q_{\bar{G}}(1 - p_0) = m$ and p_1 such that $q(1 - p_1) = m$. This implies that, the mechanism $\mathcal{A}_{p_0,p_1}$ in expectation adds m edges and removes m edges from G. Recall that in the m-random perturbation mechanism, $p_0 = 1 - \frac{2m}{(n^2-n)-2q}$ and $p_1 = 1 - \frac{m}{q}$, replacing them in the first two elements in (7), we obtain:

$$\epsilon = \ln \max \left\{ \frac{q}{m} - \frac{2q}{(n^2 - n) - 2q}, \frac{(q - m)}{m} \frac{(n^2 - n) - 2q}{2q}, \right\}$$

Observe that the last two elements in (7) are the reciprocal of the first two. Finally, replacing $2q_{\bar{G}} = (n^2 - n) - 2q$ we obtain (14). ∎

For random sparsification, we recall that such method consists in performing an independent Bernoulli trial with a given probability parameter p for each edge in the graph, remove the edge in case of success and keep it otherwise. This is equivalent to applying $\mathcal{A}_{p_0,p_1}$, with $p_0 = 1$, and $p_1 = p$. It is not ϵ-LDP for any $\epsilon > 0$, since replacing $1 - p_0 = 0$ in (7) gives ∞.

However, we may choose p_0 close to 1 and such that we allow the mechanism to add t-new edges (in expectation). This implies that $(1 - p_0)q_{\bar{G}} = t$.

Definition 6 (Threshold-Random Sparsification). *Let G be a graph with n nodes and q edges. For parameters p, t we define the* threshold-random sparsification $\mathcal{A}_{p,t}$ *as follows:*

$$\mathcal{A}_{p,t} = \mathcal{A}_{p_0,p_1} \tag{15}$$

Such that:

$$p_0 = 1 - \frac{t}{q_{\bar{G}}}$$

$$p_1 = p$$

Theorem 2. *For threshold-random sparsification to be ϵ-LDP, for given p fixed. Then t is as follows:*

$$t = \max\left\{ q_{\bar{G}}(1 + pe^\epsilon - e^\epsilon), \frac{pq_{\bar{G}}}{e^\epsilon}, \frac{1}{q_{\bar{G}}(1 + pe^\epsilon - e^\epsilon)}, \frac{e^\epsilon}{pq_{\bar{G}}} \right\} \tag{16}$$

Proof. We use the first two elements in (7) to obtain that:

$$\epsilon = \ln \max\left\{ \frac{1 - \frac{t}{q_{\bar{G}}}}{1 - p}, \frac{p}{t/q_{\bar{G}}} \right\}$$

From this equation we can calculate the value for t.

4   Experimental Evaluation

For the experimental evaluation we use the following three datasets obtained from SNAP https://snap.stanford.edu/data/. We only use the largest connected component from the original graph. The statistics and dataset description are as follows:

- *soc-facebook*: In the Facebook network, nodes represent users, and edges represent a friendship relation between any two users. The network has $n = 4,039$ nodes, $q = 88,234$ edges, and density $d = 0.0054$.
- *ca-HepTh*: High Energy Physics - Theory collaboration network, with $n = 8,638$, $q = 24,827$ and $d = 0.0003$. Each edge represents co-authorship between two author nodes.
- *ca-AstroPh*: Astro Physics collaboration network, with $n = 17,903$, $q = 197,031$ and $d = 0.0006$. Each edge represents co-authorship between two author nodes.

In Fig. 1 we show the densities obtained from (10) after protecting the *soc-facebook* graph by tuning the p_{11} parameter while keeping the ϵ fixed. We note that in the case of all previous RR mechanisms (e.g., [5,6,8,10,12,15]), the Density obtained is the highest of all the values for each line, and corresponds to $p_{11} = \frac{e^\epsilon}{e^\epsilon + 1}$.

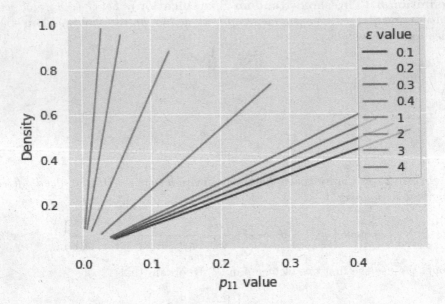

Fig. 1. Densities obtained after protecting the *soc-facebook* graph by tuning the p_{11} parameter while keeping the ϵ fixed.

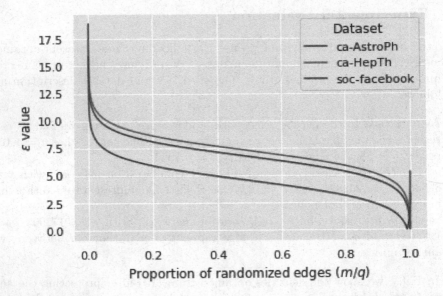

Fig. 2. ϵ values obtained for each dataset as a function of m randomized edges considered as a proportion of the total edges q.

In Fig. 2 we show the ϵ values obtained as a function of m randomized edges considered as a proportion of the total edges q. This figure shows that the privacy provided by the m-random perturbation mechanism is more related to the proportion m/q than to the exact value m, the values of m that provide more privacy are closer to q but do not reach it.

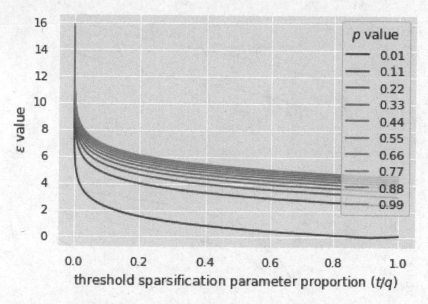

Fig. 3. ϵ values obtained for *soc-facebook* graph as a function of the threshold parameter t considered as a proportion of the total edges q, when varying the sparsification parameter p.

In Fig. 3, we show for the *soc-facebook* graph, that allowing for adding t edges provides more privacy to the sparsification mechanism than only removing edges according to p. Also, that the sparsification parameter has a more direct effect on the privacy provided.

Finally, to test the utility of the protected graphs we consider the task of link prediction, for this we calculate the Singular Value Decomposition (SVD) of its adjacency matrix. For this calculations we use the algorithms from [1], which use the train-test splits from [2]. We consider the AUC to measure the quality of the prediction, based on the SVD obtained from the adjacency matrix of the protected graphs.

In Fig. 4 we show the ϵ and AUC values obtained as a function of each probability p_{11}, while preserving the density of the original graph, as in (11). We note the trade-off between privacy and utility, and show that the probability of keeping the original edges is closely related to the privacy and utility of the noise-graph mechanism.

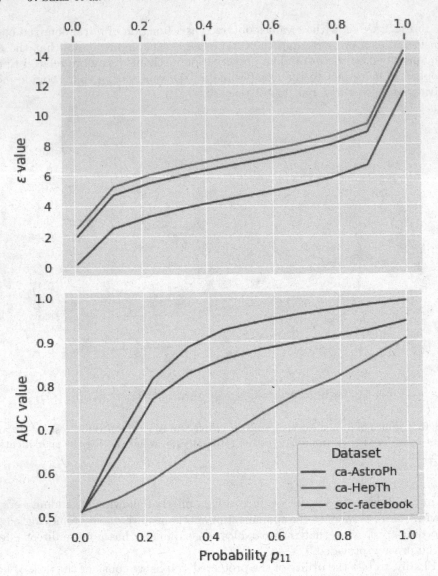

Fig. 4. ϵ and AUC values obtained as a function of each probability p_{11}, while preserving the density of the original graph.

5   Conclusions

In this paper we defined the Noise-graph mechanism with different probabilities of randomization for the edges and for the non-edges in the graph. We showed that there are several ways of choosing the probabilities for the randomization matrix that provide the same ϵ values for differential privacy. Thus, such probabilities can be tuned to return a sparser graph than those obtained through the most common randomized response mechanisms (e.g., Warner's mechanisms).

We define differentially private versions of random perturbation [7] and random sparsification [4] methods. We also showed that it is possible to choose different probabilities of randomization that preserve the same density as the protected graph, we study the relationship between such probabilities, the ϵ values obtained and the utility measured in a link prediction task.

Acknowledgements. This research was partly supported by the Spanish Ministry of Science and Innovation under project PID2021- 125962OB-C31 "SECURING".

References

1. Abu-El-Haija, S., Mostafa, H., Nassar, M., Crespi, V., Ver Steeg, G., Galstyan, A.: Implicit SVD for graph representation learning. Adv. Neural Inf. Process. Syst. **34**, 8419–8431 (2021)
2. Abu-El-Haija, S., Perozzi, B., Al-Rfou, R., Alemi, A.A.: Watch your step: learning node embeddings via graph attention. In: Advances in Neural Information Processing Systems. vol. 31 (2018)
3. Aiello, W., Chung, F., Lu, L.: A random graph model for power law graphs. Exp. Math. **10**(1), 53–66 (2001)
4. Bonchi, F., Gionis, A., Tassa, T.: Identity obfuscation in graphs through the information theoretic lens. Inf. Sci. **275**, 232–256 (2014)
5. Dwork, C., Roth, A.: The algorithmic foundations of differential privacy. Found. Trends Theor. Comput. Sci. **9**(3–4), 211–407 (2014)
6. Erlingsson, U., Pihur, V., Korolova, A.: RAPPOR: randomized aggregatable privacy-preserving ordinal response. In: Proceedings of the 2014 ACM SIGSAC Conference on Computer and Communications Security, pp. 1054–1067. CCS 2014, Association for Computing Machinery, New York, USA (2014)
7. Hay, M., Miklau, G., Jensen, D., Towsley, D., Weis, P.: Resisting structural re-identification in anonymized social networks. Proc. VLDB Endowment **1**(1), 102–114 (2008)
8. Holohan, N., Leith, D.J., Mason, O.: Optimal differentially private mechanisms for randomised response. Trans. Info. For. Sec. **12**(11), 2726–2735 (2017)
9. Imola, J., Murakami, T., Chaudhuri, K.: Locally differentially private analysis of graph statistics. In: 30th USENIX Security Symposium (USENIX Security 21), pp. 983–1000 (2021)
10. Mülle, Y., Clifton, C., Böhm, K.: Privacy-integrated graph clustering through differential privacy. In: EDBT/ICDT Workshops. vol. 157 (2015)
11. Qin, Z., Yu, T., Yang, Y., Khalil, I., Xiao, X., Ren, K.: Generating synthetic decentralized social graphs with local differential privacy. In: Proceedings of the 2017 ACM SIGSAC Conference on Computer and Communications Security, pp. 425–438 (2017)
12. Salas, J., Torra, V.: Differentially private graph publishing and randomized response for collaborative filtering. In: Proceedings of the 17th International Joint Conference on e-Business and Telecommunications, ICETE 2020 - Vol. 2: SECRYPT, Lieusaint, Paris, France, 8–10 July 2020, pp. 415–422. ScitePress (2020)

13. Salas, J., Torra, V., Megías, D.: Towards measuring fairness for local differential privacy. In: Data Privacy Management, Cryptocurrencies and Blockchain Technology: ESORICS 2022 International Workshops, DPM 2022 and CBT 2022, Copenhagen, Denmark, 26–30 Sep 2022, Revised Selected Papers. pp. 19–34. Springer (2023). https://doi.org/10.1007/978-3-031-25734-6_2

14. Torra, V., Salas, J.: Graph perturbation as noise graph addition: a new perspective for graph anonymization. In: Pérez-Solà, C., Navarro-Arribas, G., Biryukov, A., Garcia-Alfaro, J. (eds.) DPM/CBT -2019. LNCS, vol. 11737, pp. 121–137. Springer, Cham (2019). https://doi.org/10.1007/978-3-030-31500-9_8

15. Wang, Y., Wu, X., Hu, D.: Using randomized response for differential privacy preserving data collection. In: EDBT/ICDT2016WS (2016)

16. Warner, S.L.: Randomized response: A survey technique for eliminating evasive answer bias. J. Am. Stat. Assoc. **60**(309), 63–69 (1965)

Author Index

A
Alatrista-Salas, Hugo 214
Armengol, Eva 146
Augustin, Thomas 45

B
Boczek, Michał 83

D
Doria, Serena 70
Dujmović, Jozo 3

E
Engsner, Niklas 181

F
Fukuda, Ryoji 58

G
Galarreta, Ana-Paula 214
Glesner, Sabine 169
González-Zelaya, Vladimiro 202, 253

H
Honda, Aoi 58
Horigome, Hikaru 241
Hutník, Ondrej 83

J
Jansen, Christoph 45
Johansson, Anton 181
Johansson, Ulf 133

K
Kalina, Martin 106
Kanzawa, Yuchi 226
Kikuchi, Hiroaki 241
Kleinová, Miriam 83

Klonecki, Tomasz 121
Klös, Verena 169

L
Łazęcka, Małgorzata 157
Lee, Jaesung 121
Löfström, Helena 133
Löfström, Tuwe 133

M
Megías, David 253
Missier, Paolo 202
Mostad, Petter 181

N
Nunez-del-Prado, Miguel 214

O
Okazaki, Yoshiaki 58

P
Prangle, Dennis 202

S
Salas, Julián 202, 253
Schollmeyer, Georg 45
Schwan, Simon 169
Šeliga, Adam 96
Selmi, Bilel 70
Sönströd, Cecilia 133
Strannegård, Claes 181

T
Teisseyre, Paweł 121
Torra, Vicenç 3, 253

Y
Yu, Chia-Mu 241

Printed in the United States
by Baker & Taylor Publisher Services

Printed in the United States
by Baker & Taylor Publisher Services